Formal Approaches to Computing and
Information Technology

Also in this series:

Proof in VDM: a Practitioner's Guide
J.C. Bicarregui, J.S. Fitzgerald, P.A. Lindsay, R. Moore
and B. Ritchie
ISBN 3-540-19813-X

On the Refinement Calculus
C. Morgan and T. Vickers (eds.)
ISBN 3-540-19809-1

Systems, Models and Measures
A. Kaposi and M. Myers
ISBN 3-540-19753-2

Notations for Software Design

by Loe M.G. Feijs, Hans B.M. Jonkers and
Cornelis A. Middelburg

Springer-Verlag
London   Berlin   Heidelberg   New York
Paris   Tokyo   Hong Kong
Barcelona   Budapest

Loe M.G. Feijs and Hans B.M. Jonkers
Philips Research Laboratories, Building WL1
Prof. Holstlaan 4, 5656 AA Eindhoven
The Netherlands

Cornelis A. Middelburg
Department of Philosophy, Utrecht University
PO Box 80.126, 3508 TC Utrecht, The Netherlands and
PTT Research
PO Box 421, 2260 AK Leidschendam, The Netherlands

Series Editor

Steve A. Schuman, BSc, DEA, CEng
Department of Mathematical and Computing Sciences
University of Surrey, Guildford, Surrey GU2 5XH, UK

ISBN-13: 978-3-540-19902-1   e-ISBN-13: 978-1-4471-2107-7
DOI: 10.1007/978-1-4471-2107-7

British Library Cataloguing in Publication Data
Feijs, L.M.G.
    Notations for Software Design. – (Formal Approaches to Computing &
    Information Technology Series)
    I. Title II. Series
    005.12

Library of Congress Cataloging-in-Publication Data
Feijs, L.M.G. (Loe M.G.)
    Notations for software design / Loe M.G. Feijs, Hans B.M. Jonkers, and Cornelis A.
Middelburg.
        p.   cm. – (Formal approaches to computing and information technology)
    Includes bibliographical references and index.

    1.   Computer software–Development.   I.   Jonkers, H.B.M.
II.   Middelburg, Cornelis A.   III.   Title.   IV.   Series.
QA76.76.D47F47 1994   94-29179
005.1'2'028–dc20   CIP

Typesetting: Camera ready by authors

34/3830-543210 Printed on acid-free paper

Preface

This book is about particular ingredients of a sound software design process. It explains formal notations, meant to be helpful in designing software systems, to practitioners in software development. Various links are established with familiar pictorial notations. The aim of the book is to bring practitioners in software development currently using informal approaches to the point where they make a step towards a more formal approach, which in some places is already being put into practice for the construction of dependable software. The following notations are used in this book:

1. the formal, textual notations combined in COLD-1, a specification language in the tradition of VDM and Z;

2. a variety of well-known pictorial notations which are frequently used in the current practice of software development.

COLD-1 is a wide-spectrum specification language with a syntax and semantics which describes the form and meaning of its constructs in a mathematically precise way. It is a common language for describing a software system in any stage of its design, ranging from specification to implementation. The language combines a wide variety of notations for property-oriented and model-oriented specification, including state-based specification, in a unifying semantic framework. Many existing styles of specification are supported: specification in equational style, specification in pre- and post-condition style, inductive definitions, algorithmic definitions in functional as well as imperative style, etc. More than that, it offers facilities for the modular structuring of specifications. COLD stands for "Common Object-oriented Language for Design".

The pictorial notations used in this book provide strong links with the present state of the practice. Many methods, which are currently in use, are based on one or more of these notations. The book uses only existing kinds of pictorial notations. It puts them together in a coherent framework, based on COLD-1, and explains practical ways of exploiting them in conjunction with this language. Commonly, a COLD-1 text provides many details whereas each picture presents a particular view which could be obtained from the text by leaving out a lot. The pictures are used to enrich the formal text, but they miss the mathematical precision of the formal text, which guarantees that the design can be rigorously analysed. The pictorial notations addressed include Venn diagrams, state charts, HOOD diagrams, state transition diagrams, data flow diagrams, flow charts, Petri nets, SDL-like diagrams and sequence charts.

The accent of the book is on explaining formal notations for software design. COLD-1 is used because it is a wide-spectrum language: software systems can be described at many levels of detail, in any well-suited combination of styles and according to various paradigms. An additional virtue is the apposite support of modularity, which is important to cope with the size and complexity of many systems. Its permissive mechanisms for naming are also very convenient in practice. The book treats the language in a practical and user-oriented way: the examples, explanations and pictures convey a working knowledge of the meaning of the language constructs. The links established between formal notations and pictorial notations are helpful in two ways: they impart an intuition about the formal notations and they deepen the understanding of the pictorial notations.

COLD-1 was developed at the Philips Research Laboratories in Eindhoven. It is the result of insights gained during about a decade of work in cooperation with industrial divisions of Philips, academic research groups and partners in the ESPRIT projects METEOR and ATMOSPHERE. It has been put into use for real product design within Philips.

This book is intended to be used in software engineering courses. It is also suited for self-study. Some familiarity with logic and elementary set theory is assumed. The book provides material which is suitable for practitioners in software development who are interested in formal notations for software design. The material will also be valuable for students of computer science. Most of it has been used in industrial training courses as well as in academic courses at undergraduate level.

The book is organized as follows. The first part, consisting of Chapters 1 and 2, gives an introduction and a first case study. This part is meant to excite interest in the later chapters and to make them more comprehensible. After reading Chapter 2, which is a case study concerning a vending machine, the reader will be familiar with important COLD-1 notations and pictorial notations. The second part, consisting of Chapters 3, 4 and 5, gives a systematic treatment of all COLD-1 notations. Chapter 3 is concerned with definitions, axioms and theorems, Chapter 4 with modularization, and Chapter 5 with issues related to names, such as overloading and strong typing. The third part, consisting of Chapters 6 to 9, contains a large case study, material on pictorial notations and advanced topics. This part shows the notations in action. Chapter 6, which is a large case study concerning a computer-controlled railway system, shows how the COLD-1 notations presented in the second part can be put to work and used effectively. Chapters 7 and 8 give a systematic treatment of many important pictorial notations and their connections with COLD-1.

Finally, Chapter 9 connects several well-established principles, guidelines and techniques of specification and design with COLD-1.

The concrete syntax of COLD-1 is presented in Appendix A.
Specifications of the common data types used in this book – extracted
from IGLOO, the "standard library" associated with COLD-1 - are
given in Appendix B. A glossary of the terms connected with formal
approaches to software development, so far as they are used in this
book, is given in Appendix C.

Acknowledgements

We wish to express our gratitude to A. de Bunje, R.J. Bril, F.J. van der
Linden, C.P.J. Koymans and R.C. van Ommering for their interest in
the work presented in this book and in particular for their detailed and
valuable comments on preliminary versions of parts of it. Special
thanks go to Jan Bergstra for providing inspiration and encouragement.

Contents

1 Introduction 1
  1.1 Software Design 1
  1.2 Software Specification 4
  1.3 Notations for Software Design 6

2 The Vending Machine Case 9
  2.1 Objectives 9
  2.2 Analysing the Application 9
  2.3 Analysing the Building Blocks 22
  2.4 Design 29
  2.5 Realization 34
  2.6 Concluding Remarks 38

3 Patterns for Definitions 39
  3.1 Introduction and Motivation 39
  3.2 States and State Transformers 40
  3.3 Patterns for Function Definitions 41
  3.4 Patterns for Predicate Definitions 47
  3.5 Patterns for Sort Definitions 51
  3.6 Patterns for Procedure Definitions 52
  3.7 Axioms and Theorems 56
  3.8 Assertions 58
  3.9 Expressions 61
  3.10 Concluding Remarks 70

4 Patterns for Components 71
  4.1 Introduction and Motivation 71
  4.2 Basic Pattern 71
  4.3 Using Components 76
  4.4 Signatures 80
  4.5 Renamings 85
  4.6 More on Component Definitions 87
  4.7 Structure of Complete Descriptions 92
  4.8 More on Instantiating Components 95
  4.9 Concluding Remarks. 100

5   Mechanisms for Naming 103
  5.1   Introduction and Motivation 103
  5.2   Structure of Names 104
  5.3   Names in Definitions and Axioms 106
  5.4   Names in Signatures and Renamings 109
  5.5   Names in Instantiations 111
  5.6   Object Names 114
  5.7   Name Clashes 117
  5.8   Names and Notational Conventions 122
  5.9   Concluding Remarks 124

6   The Automatic Railway Case 125
  6.1   Objectives 125
  6.2   Vocabulary of the Application Domain 128
  6.3   Analysis of the Application Domain 139
  6.4   System Requirements 149
  6.5   The Architecture of Safety 150
  6.6   Components for Safety and Reachability 153
  6.7   Putting the Components Together 164
  6.8   Refinements of the Safety Requirement 176
  6.9   Data Structures 178
  6.10 Invariant Assertions 181
  6.11 Algorithms 186
  6.12 Proof Aspects 191
  6.13 Real-time Aspects 195
  6.14 Realization Aspects 196
  6.15 Concluding Remarks 198

7   Pictorial Representations 201
  7.1   Survey 201
  7.2   Area Diagrams: General 203
  7.3   Venn diagrams 203
  7.4   Statecharts 221
  7.5   Nassi-Shneidermann Diagrams 226
  7.6   HOOD diagrams 229
  7.7   Graph Diagrams: General 243
  7.8   Function Graphs 243
  7.9   State Transition Diagrams 244
  7.10 Call Graphs 255
  7.11 Import Graphs 256
  7.12 Concluding Remarks 258

8   More Pictorial Representations 259
  8.1   Network Diagrams: General 259
  8.2   Data Flow Diagrams 260
  8.3   Data Flow Diagrams with Stores 264

8.4 Flow Charts 266
8.5 Abstract Hardware Diagrams 273
8.6 State-based Abstract Hardware Diagrams 280
8.7 Petri Nets 291
8.8 SDL-like Diagrams 298
8.9 Sequence Charts: General 316
8.10 Asynchronous Sequence Charts 317
8.11 Synchronous Sequence Charts 319
8.12 Concluding Remarks 322

9 Advanced Topics 325
9.1 Introduction and Motivation 325
9.2 Review of Modular Structuring 325
9.3 How to Set up Basic Components 329
9.4 Sharing a State Space 333
9.5 Principles of Modular Structuring 336
9.6 Guidelines and Techniques 339
9.7 Mirroring 341
9.8 Object-orientedness 345
9.9 Conservativity and Visibility Consistency 349
9.10 Black Box Correctness 353
9.11 Component Invariants 358
9.12 Loop Invariants 365
9.13 Memoization 370
9.14 Concluding Remarks 376

Bibliography 377

A Syntax of COLD-1 383
A.1 Introduction 383
A.2 Lexical Units 383
A.3 Grammar 385
A.4 Operator Priorities and Associativities 389

B Standard Library 393
B.1 Items 393
B.2 Ordered Items 393
B.3 Booleans 394
B.4 Natural Numbers 396
B.5 Integer Numbers 398
B.6 Enumerations 402
B.7 Characters 403
B.8 Tuples 405
B.9 Unions 406
B.10 Finite Sets 408
B.11 Finite Bags 410

B.12 Finite Sequences 412
B.13 Finite Maps 414

C Glossary of Terms 417

Index 421

Chapter 1
Introduction

Language is the light of the mind. (John Stuart Mill)

1.1 Software Design

This book is about notations for software design. Many facts, choices and assumptions play a rôle in the design process of a software system. They are concerned with the available software, the computing machinery and peripherals, as well as the intended use of the system. Designing means making decisions about the artifacts being designed: terminology, components, system structure, user interface, data structures and algorithms.

For complex systems it is important that many of these facts, choices, assumptions and decisions are made explicit. They must be written down. If they are not, valuable information will get lost; this may cause software errors, confused or dissatisfied users, unmanageable development projects and maintenance problems.

The notations presented in this book are meant to be helpful in *software engineering*, defined as the application of science and mathematics to the problem of making computers useful for people via software [1].[1]

Designing amounts to defining the structure of artifacts with due regard for user requirements and resource constraints. A design is a structure which includes a listing of the components of the system, specifications of their interfaces and the way in which the components must be assembled. A good design can be verified and analysed with respect to its user requirements and resource constraints; yet, a good design allows implementation freedom in the choice of the details of the components and the sub-components. Its structure should be easily adaptable to deal with certain kinds of future changes in requirements and constraints. Design is only one of the issues in software engineering and other issues like requirements analysis, process metrics, coding, event reporting, cost control, testing, etc. are of great interest too. But the "design" of a

---

[1]Throughout this book numbers between square brackets refer to numbered references in the bibliography (see page 377).

system is the most important amongst these issues, because it determines the *structure* of the system and because of that it will sooner or later affect all other aspects of the system's development. Moreover, defects in a component or subcomponent can often be repaired, but if the overall structure is poorly chosen it will take a lot of requirements analysis, process metrics, coding, event reporting, cost control and testing effort to compensate for the bad design.

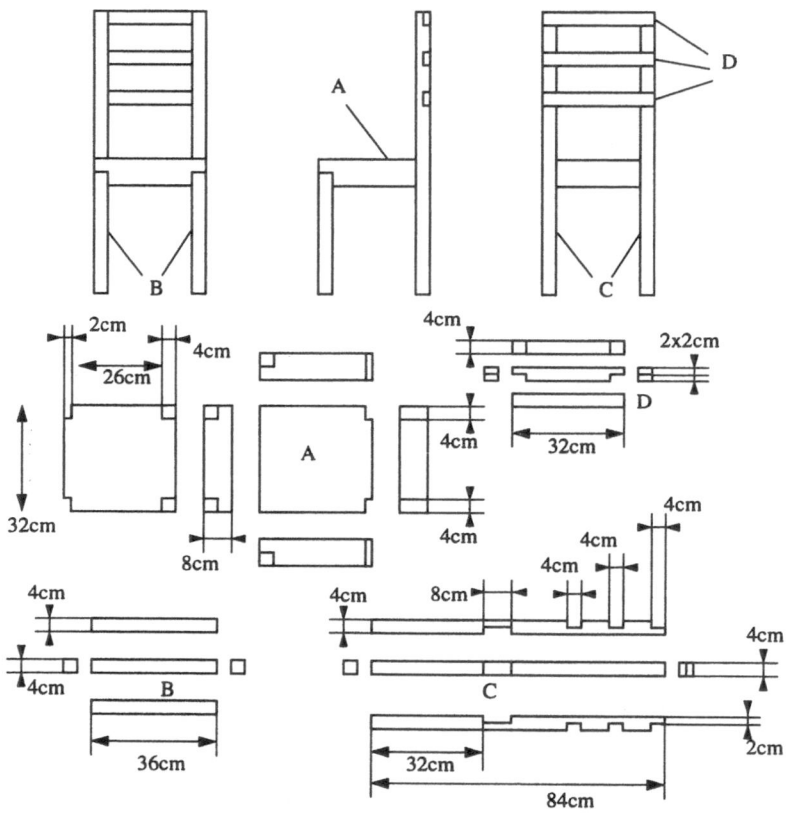

Figure 1.1: Elementary design of a chair.

The notion of design (a structure including a component listing, interface specifications and the way in which the components are to be put together) is important. This is illustrated in Figure 1.1. This can be viewed as a design of a chair and one easily recognizes the main components A (seat), B (front leg), C (back post) and D (bars of the back). The top drawings in Figure 1.1 show how A, two instances of B and C each, and three instances of D are put together. Additional design information not indicated in the diagram concerns the type of wood and the glue to be used. Of course, a chair is outside the scope of software engineering. But the question is whether the concepts of decomposition and component specification which are so obvious in designing chairs, and which are well established in many engineering disciplines, should apply to software engineering too. They should. Actually, it is hard to justify that many software engineering projects still work with ill-defined interfaces and with unspecified constraints.

Good notations for software design are amongst the most important communication mechanisms available to the people assigned to software engineering tasks – other communication mechanisms are natural language and experimental validation of the system under development. The choice of good notations is far from trivial; it is tempting to say that syntax is not important, but a simple example already shows that this is not true: consider the manipulation of Roman numbers when doing a multiplication, such as XCII × XIV, which is MCCLXXXVIII. Compare this with the corresponding manipulation when calculating 92 ×14. We refer to Figure 1.2

```
        XCII
  92    XIV
  14   ————
 ——    +LDVV  =  D      -L +X
 368   -XCII  =     -C  +X      -II
  92   +CMXX  = M  -C   +XX
————                 ———————————————————————————————
1288          MD -CC -L +XXXX -II = MCCC - XII = MCCLXXXVIII
```

Figure 1.2: Arabic and Roman notations for numbers.

The field of software engineering is far from mature and there are still many questions and problems to be addressed. Partial answers and partial solutions to the problems of software engineering are available thanks to several decades of fruitful research and development in applied logic, theoretical computer science, tool construction, and last but not least, computer hardware construction. But one can not expect the best of the present answers to be the final answers: research goes on, and technologies change. Yet it is worthwhile to package certain results into a coherent 'software engineering module'. This is the way in which the notations presented in this book are to be understood: they reflect insights and results gathered during almost 10 years of research, development and application at Philips Research together with Industrial Divisions, University researchers in applied logic and partners of several ESPRIT projects. The COLD-1 language which has resulted from this research combines a wide variety of notations in a unified semantic framework. Moreover, this book explains the most widespread graphical notations, their syntax, their meaning, options for symbolic manipulation, translation and execution, and practical ways of exploiting them.

Some disclaimers are in order: this book does not address all aspects of software engineering and it does not indicate how to organize software projects, it does not define a design process model, it does not discuss configuration management, nor does it describe automated tools for supporting the software engineering tasks. Instead, the book offers one "module" with ingredients of a sound design process: notations for software design and the elementary manipulations to be performed upon them.

1.2   Software Specification

Specification is nothing but "setting up theories". A specification of a software system S is a theory about the behaviour and the properties of S. The advantages of setting up theories are manifold: first of all it helps in making facts and assumptions explicit, and then in avoiding the mistakes caused by forgetting implicit assumptions. Secondly, it makes it possible eliminate many details, problems and uncertainties through abstraction and at the same time keep some of the most important system properties. Thirdly, the availability of explicit specifications enables the use of many sophisticated tools: analysis, logical reasoning, calculation and simulation – which are not only mental tools, but also offer many options of automated support.

It is important to have the right expectations regarding the gains of specification. One can not expect all concerns of reality to be completely covered by specifications and models. Some of the common misunderstandings are: specifications must be complete, specifications must always be ready before system construction starts and specifications must be simpler than the computer programs they are about. Another misunderstanding is that there is always a unique and obvious way of mapping the notions in the theory to things in the real world. Sometimes one should not even expect that all specifications are true, in the sense of corresponding to facts of the computer-based system and its environment.

The relevance of formulating theories and subjecting them to experiment and criticism has been put forward by K. Popper in the context of the methodology of science [2]. As he puts it, objective knowledge is produced by a process of formulating theories and trying to falsify them. There is no such thing as absolute truth, but a theory which turns out false must be rejected. If no experiments can be conceived that could be done to test a certain theory, then it is a worthless theory.

In the present book we will not be dealing with theories of physics, which are about fundamental properties of matter, but mostly with much simpler theories about the properties, the structure and the implementation of artifacts in computer-based systems. Not every software engineer is A. Einstein, but if someone constructs a component, then it could be asked what exactly the component is supposed to do. Falsifying such a theory (with respect to a given realization) boils down to finding a bug in the realized component. But since the component is an artifact, the facts can be adjusted to fit the theory instead of the other way around, as suggested by Popper.

Let us look at a very simple example. Software engineer A. Quittenstein is working on a division algorithm as a part of an "arithmetic-component" in an embedded robot-control system. At first sight, there is no need for specification or for setting up a theory. He just creates a header file `qarithmetic.h` to make sure his colleagues can proceed to compile their programs:

```
#define Nat int
Nat z,y,x;
void qdivide();
```

Quittenstein has a clear mental image of the operation of the division software, but his colleague programmers will find some "minor" details that still have to be filled in. They start making their own implicit theories about `qdivide`. As it happens, Quittenstein quits for a holiday and in the meantime his colleagues devise other software components using `qdivide`. One of the colleagues proceeds from the assumption that the first two variables, z and y, are the program inputs. Moreover he assumes that `qdivide` does should not affect the inputs, so he does not save the old input values. He does not know that Quittenstein intends to use the input variables for holding intermediate results. Another colleague feels that the x, y and z denote "first input","second input" and "result", respectively. He interprets `Nat` as the set containing 0,1,2, etc. and so, in his view, `qdivide` should work for *all* natural numbers and even when y is 0, the result should be defined. In his opinion, z should become 0 too in that case. It is not hard to imagine that this robot-control software project runs into trouble.

In an approach based on specifications, Quittenstein would have set up a simple theory about `qdivide`. In the notation of COLD-1, which is independent of the language C, he could have written a specification which mentions the standardized component `NAT`, introducing the set of natural numbers `Nat` and well-defined operations like +, -, *, and /. It could contain a pre- and post-condition style specification of `qdivide`:

```
PROC qdivide : ->
PRE   y /= 0
SAT   MOD x,y,z
POST z = x' / y'
```

The `SAT MOD` clause states that `qdivide` can modify the variables x, y and z, but no other variables. The quote notation is used in the post-condition to state that z equals the *old* value of x divided by the *old* value of y. The specification can be annotated with one or more diagrams.

Figure 1.3 contains a data flow diagram, which shows the interaction of the procedure with its variables, and a state transition diagram, which shows two of the many possible states and one of the possible transitions between them. The specification can be used as a basis for reasoning. For example, the equation `z = x' / y'` shows that x and y are the inputs and that z is the

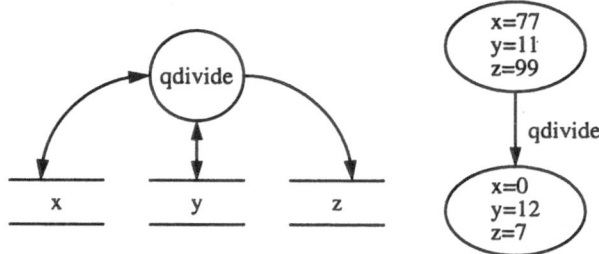

Figure 1.3: Data flow and state transition of `qdivide`.

result. Also, it follows that `qdivide` fails when y equals zero.

The specification serves as the basis for a kind of "theory" about `qdivide`. It is a simple theory, not like the deep theories of physics (cf. relativity theory). Nor is there some kind of universality in it; the theory is about certain artifacts with a scope of one person, one team or one organization at most. Yet, experience shows that a software system can consist of many pieces of software like `qdivide`, each introducing simple assumptions. If many such assumptions remain implicit, and if no systematic communication and reasoning takes place, projects end up in chaos.

1.3 Notations for Software Design

Notations supporting efficient communication are needed to make things explicit. Good notations are compact and precise, they appeal to the mind and are easy to learn. Both textual representations and pictures are needed. The use of textual representations relies on man's talents for using natural language, on the achievements of mathematical logic and on experiences with programming languages. The use of pictures is vital because images play an important rôle in the thought process of most people – including most software designers.

Software systems are often very complex. Automated tools exist to assist software designers in managing this complexity (and more such tools are on their way). This adds another aspect to the notations to be used: some notations serve as inputs for tools whereas other notations are generated by tools. In this book the following notations are used:

1. COLD-1 as a textual and machine-readable notation;

2. a variety of well-established pictorial representations.

This combines the advantages of both kinds of notations and makes it possible to exploit the attractiveness and intuitiveness of the pictures and at the same time retain the mathematical precision of the textual notation. The advantages are explained in more detail below. First of all, COLD-1 is a wide-spectrum language with a precise syntax and precise semantics, based on widely accepted concepts like algebraic data types, pre- and post-conditions and modular structuring.

Secondly, the variety of well-established pictorial representations provides a strong link with current practice in which many methods based on particular pictorial representations are in use. The book will not propose new types of pictorial representations but will rather reuse existing ideas, which it will combine in a unifying framework – both syntactically and semantically.

The textual representation plays a rôle in the semantic integration. Typically, a COLD-1 text contains a lot of detailed information while each picture is a particular view whose essential information could be derived from the text. Picture layout and interactive tools for picture drawing are interesting subjects too, but they are outside the scope of this book.

Many useful pictures can be invented. But most of them are based on a limited number of basic principles, which reoccur over and over again in various combinations and are embedded in various software development methods. In this book these basic principles will be made explicit.

The focus of this book is on explaining the language constructs of COLD-1 in a practical and use-oriented way, and not on mathematical semantics, proof theory or model theory. The COLD-1 language is based on the concepts of the kernel language COLD-K, whose mathematical semantics problem has been addressed elsewhere [3, 4].

The added value of COLD-1, when compared with COLD-K, is the former's user-oriented syntax. The main advantages are:

- specifications are organized according to helpful patterns with appealing keywords; the notation is based on widely accepted concepts (algebraic data types, pre- and post-conditions and modular structuring);

- several mechanisms are available to manage the name-space of the user-defined identifiers.

This book serves to present the main research results and experiences associated with COLD-1 in a user-oriented way. No knowledge of other versions of the language is needed. The book is self-contained and instead of going into the formal semantics of the language, it will convey a working knowledge of the meaning of the language constructs via the examples, the explanations and the pictures.

The notations presented are intended for sequential software systems. Even when some notations and pictures have a generalized interpretation as parallel processes they will be approached as denoting sequential systems. Most of the work on SPRINT (a COLD-1 based design method dealing with parallellism and code generation) is outside the scope of this book.

The proposed textual representations are in the tradition of "formal methods", or "rigorous methods" as they are sometimes called. COLD-1 is a language in the tradition of VDM and Z. The most obvious advantage of the language is that it helps to describe the details of a system in an unambiguous and precise way. But COLD-1 offers more than that: it also offers support in *structuring* the system, which is even more important. As Hagelstein [5], discussing requirements engineering, puts it: *The remarkable point is that formality in itself only addresses ambiguity, which is the least problem. If formal languages are to be accepted in industry, they must first bring an answer to the problem of unstructuredness. To this end, the proposed language must include appropriate structuring mechanisms, which clarify the interfaces between loosely coupled parts.*

Chapter 2
The Vending Machine Case

A problem well stated is a problem half solved. (C. Kettering)

2.1 Objectives

The objective of the present chapter is to show a number of notations with the aid of a concrete example. The example is simple enough to serve as an easy introduction. After reading the example, the reader will be familiar with several important COLD-1 notations as well as several important picture types. This will pave the way for a systematic treatment of these notations and of the various pictorial representations in other chapters.

The example concerns a simple vending machine which accepts coins and selections, validates the coins and selections and provides the products requested. Vending machines have been used as examples by many authors in many settings; see for example [6] or [7].

A model of the vending machine, the relevant data types and a number of distinct views on the machine will be developed in an approach of stepwise refinement. A simple model called VENDING1 is made first, and to this further details are added to obtain VENDING2, VENDING3, etc. After that, in Sections 2.3, 2.4 and 2.5, a vending machine prototype will be designed and realized. In this way a complete COLD-1 description of the vending machine model and its design will be constructed. At the same time, various pictorial representations will be used to illustrate the model and the design.

2.2 Analysing the Application

We will start with a short description concerning the input and output of a function called **vend**. It represents the functional behaviour of a vending machine as experienced by its user. The user can introduce a coin, enter a selection and obtain some product. The machine operator manages the coins, the coin acceptor mechanism and the product supplies. To keep the example simple, the procedures to be performed by the machine operator will be omitted from the model.

```
COMPONENT VENDING1 SPECIFICATION
CLASS
  SORT Coin
  SORT Selection
  SORT Product

  FUNC vend : Coin # Selection -> Product FREE
END
```

The above reads as follows: there are three sorts called Coin, Selection and Product, respectively, whose object structure is at present not considered relevant. The word *sort* comes from algebraic specification theory and it means "value set" or just "data type". The function **vend** maps pairs consisting of a coin and a selection to products. The keyword FREE indicates that this is a preliminary definition or, in other words a forward declaration. The actual definition will come later when the specification is refined. These four definitions have been packaged into a component (a module) called VENDING1, which is the first and simplest of a series of views on the vending machine.

The sort Coin could model the nickels, dollars, units of plastic money or software money that are to be introduced into the machine, depending on the payment medium used. For this case study we have decided do define a peculiar kind of software money for the payment medium: large numbers. Consider for example a user who has acquired the knowledge that 187632 has the value of 1 ECU (European Currency Unit) and that 567456 has the value of 2 ECUs, etc. This knowledge is also kept in the administration of the vending machine. The user should not share his knowledge with others, for that would be like giving his money away. To enter the the value of 1 ECU into the vending machine, the user types "187632" on the machine's keyboard. The machine can verify 187632 and remove it from the administration after product delivery (the user can not spend the same money twice). Of course a fraudulent user can try to enter a random number, but if values are represented by *large* numbers, and if most numbers are worthless, then the probability of this user getting a product just by luck can be made sufficiently small.

The sort Selection models the numbers, or labels, that refer to products. The sort Product models the products that are to be yielded by the machine, typically something with a certain entertainment value, to be detailed later.

The data flow diagram of Figure 2.1 shows the function **vend** in graphical notation.

In order to see more details of the internals of **vend** we need the concept of *values*, which are modelled as natural numbers. NAT is a standardized COLD-1 description, which is not included here. It has constants 0, 1, etc. and many of the usual functions.

```
COMPONENT VALUE SPECIFICATION
IMPORT
```

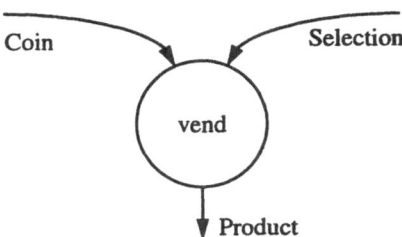

Figure 2.1: Data flow diagram of **vend**.

```
NAT' RENAMING SORT Nat TO Value END
END
```

The definition of the sort **Value** has again been packaged into a module, called **VALUE**. VALUE has no CLASS section. It only has an import list. The quote after NAT indicates that VALUE is treated as a *copy* of NAT (not an alias). We distinguish explicitly between natural numbers, values, selections, coins, etc. (although in an implementation they could be the same again). Distinguishing them here makes the model more clear; also, it gives more options for tracing mistakes by means of typechecking.

The function graph of Figure 2.2 shows the set of values as well as the arrows of the functions 0, 1, 2, etc. (constants are viewed as functions of zero arguments). The relation **<=**, which denotes "less or equal", is shown by the vertical lines, as in a Hasse diagram (proposed by H. Hasse in [8]). If a value a is shown below another value b and is connected to it by means of a line labelled with "$\leq$", then this indicates that a is less than or equal to b.

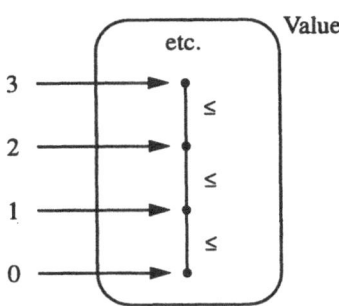

Figure 2.2: Sort **Value** with function graph.

More details of the **vend** function will be filled in in the description below. Three kinds of tables are introduced, named **ValueTable**, **PriceTable** and **ProdTable**. The internal structure of these tables will be given later.

Three functions are also introduced: **validate**, **price** and **yield**. The function **validate** determines the value of a coin for a given value table. The function **price** serves to look up the price of a selected product for a given price table. The function `yield` produces a selected product from a given product table.

There are three tables, modelled as functions of no arguments: `value_table` is a value table, `price_table` is a price table and `product_table` is a product table. The value table contains the values of all valid coins. The price table contains the values that are necessary to obtain products indicated by selections. The product table is used as a storage of products for certain selections.

```
COMPONENT VENDING2 SPECIFICATION
IMPORT
  VENDING1,
  VALUE
CLASS
  SORT ValueTable FREE
  SORT PriceTable FREE
  SORT ProdTable  FREE

  FUNC validate : ValueTable # Coin      -> Value   FREE
  FUNC price    : PriceTable # Selection -> Value   FREE
  FUNC yield    : ProdTable # Selection  -> Product FREE

  FUNC value_table   : -> ValueTable FREE
  FUNC price_table   : -> PriceTable FREE
  FUNC product_table : -> ProdTable  FREE

  FUNC vend : Coin # Selection -> Product
  IN   c,s
  DEF  ( price(price_table,s) <= validate(value_table,c) ?
       ; yield(product_table,s)
       )
  END
```

The definitions of the three sorts, `ValueTable`, `PriceTable` and `ProdTable`, the six functions, `validate`, `price`, `yield`, `value_table`, `price_table` and `product_table`, and the refined definition of **vend** have been packaged into a module, called `VENDING2`. It has an import list and a CLASS section. Although COLD-1 offers the option of having an export list, this is not used because there is not much sense in hiding certain sorts or operations here. The above component is part of a system specification. It is not an implementation module whose internal details must be shielded.

The functions `value_table`, `price_table` and `product_table` will turn out to be variables, with the typical property that their value may change in time due to state transitions. But the actual definition of the variables, requiring the keyword VAR, is postponed because variables are defined in the same module as the procedures modifying them. Instead of that, the keyword FREE is used, stating that the definitions of `value_table`, `price_table` and `product_table` are like "forward declarations" (as they are called in Pascal) or

"external declarations" (as they are called in C, C++ or Estelle). The product
vend(c,s) is defined by the composition of a guard, which is an inequality
followed by the "?" operator, and the expression yield(product_table,s).
This means that vend(c,s) is undefined if the inequality does not hold. If it
holds, however, vend(c,s) returns yield(product_table,s).

The data flow diagram of Figure 2.3 shows the input and output of the
function **vend** again, only now its functional decomposition is shown too.
More precisely, the figure shows the input and output types for the functions **vend**, **validate**, **price**, and **yield**, where it is assumed that each of
their FREE definitions can be interpreted as a normal function (not a variable).
For **value_table**, **price_table** and **product_table** the output type is also
shown, but here it is assumed that their FREE definitions can be interpreted
as a variable. When drawing data flow diagrams a choice (normal function
or variable) has to be made, but in COLD-1 the choice can be postponed.
Therefore the picture can only be drawn if certain assumptions are made. Of
course, the diagram as a whole shows the functional decomposition of **vend**.
All this is still only about the functional behaviour of the vending machine,
and does not yet include dynamic behaviour.

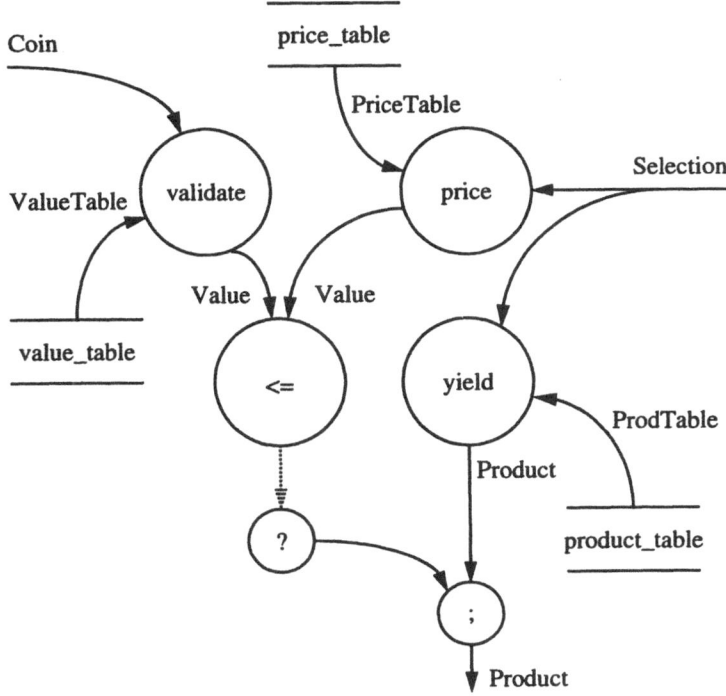

Figure 2.3: Data flow diagram of **vend**.

The dynamic behaviour of the vending machine will be modelled by means of four procedures named **insert**, **check**, **select**, and **produce**, which operate on certain variables, as will be explained below. In the COLD-1 notation, dynamic behaviour is described by means of procedures (keyword PROC). They are similar to functions in the sense that they can have inputs and outputs, but in addition to that they have modification rights with respect to certain variables (clause starting with SAT MOD).

The first procedure is named **insert** and its task is to put the machine in a certain control state and to transfer coins from the user into a variable called **coin**.

The procedure **check** operates on **value** and **control_state**. Furthermore it has access to the **coin** variable, because the coins must be checked against the table and once they have been used, the value table must be updated to make them invalid (a coin is called invalid if **validate(value_table,c) = 0**). This is necessary if we want to use large numbers as software money. Among other things, the procedure **check** applies the function **validate**. Actually **check** is still not fully specified; more requirements will be added in VENDING6.

The procedure **select** puts the user's selections in a local variable called **selection** and of course adapts the control state.

Finally **produce** uses the price table, the selection table as well as the product table. Its main task is to apply the function **price** to make the appropriate comparison of values and to apply the function **yield** in order to output the product.

To keep the case study simple, we have not included the operator interface of the machine (defining new coins, replacing products, etc.). The tables **price_table** and **product_table** are variables, but no procedures are given to modify them.

```
COMPONENT VENDING3 SPECIFICATION
IMPORT
  VENDING2,
  ENUM4' RENAMING Enum4 TO ControlState,
                  x0    TO idle,
                  x1    TO coin_inserted,
                  x2    TO coin_checked,
                  x3    TO product_selected
          END
CLASS
  FUNC control_state : -> ControlState VAR
  FUNC coin          : -> Coin         VAR
  FUNC value         : -> Value        VAR
  FUNC selection     : -> Selection    VAR

  FUNC value_table   : -> ValueTable VAR
  FUNC price_table   : -> PriceTable VAR
  FUNC product_table : -> ProdTable  VAR
```

```
PROC insert : Coin ->
IN   c
PRE  control_state = idle
SAT  MOD coin,control_state
POST coin = c AND control_state = coin_inserted

PROC check : ->
PRE  control_state = coin_inserted
SAT  MOD value,value_table,control_state
POST value = validate(value_table',coin) AND
     ( value = 0 => control_state = idle
     ; value > 0 => control_state = coin_checked
     )

PROC select : Selection ->
IN   s
PRE  control_state = coin_checked
SAT  MOD selection,control_state
POST selection = s AND control_state = product_selected

PROC produce : -> Product
OUT  p
PRE  control_state = product_selected
SAT  MOD control_state; p
POST ( price(price_table,selection)^
       => control_state = coin_checked
     ; price(price_table,selection) > value
       => control_state = coin_checked
     ; price(price_table,selection) <= value
       => p = yield(product_table,selection)
          AND control_state = idle
     )

AXIOM INIT => ( control_state = idle )

PRED machine_inv :
DEF ( ( control_state = coin_inserted
        OR control_state = coin_checked
        OR control_state = product_selected
        ) => coin!
      ; ( control_state = coin_checked
          OR control_state = product_selected
        ) => value!
      ; ( control_state = product_selected
        ) => selection!
      )
```

END

The definitions of the variables `control_state`, `coin`, `value` and `selection` and the refined definitions of `value_table`, `price_table` and `product_table` and the procedures `insert`, `check`, `select`, `produce`, as well as the axiom about the initial state and an invariant assertion `machine_inv` have been packaged into a module, called `VENDING3`. It has a `CLASS` section and an import list containing `VENDING2` and a module providing an enumerated data type `ControlState` that contains four distinct values. The latter module is obtained as a renamed version of `ENUM4`, which comes from the standard library. In its standard form, `ENUM4` provides the sort `Enum4` which has four values, denoted as `x0`, `x1`, `x2`, and `x3`. Here the sort is named `ControlState` and its four values are denoted by `idle`, `coin_inserted`, `coin_checked`, and `product_selected`, respectively.

In `VENDING3` there are procedures, described in a pattern delimited by the keywords `PROC`, `IN`, `OUT`, `PRE`, `SAT MOD`, and `POST`. `PROC` stands for "procedure", which is an operation with a side-effect, performing state transformations. `IN` of course concerns input parameters, `OUT` output parameters and `PRE` the "pre-condition" of the procedure. The two keywords `SAT` and `MOD` precede a list of variables to which the procedure has "modification rights". `POST` indicates the "post-condition" of the procedure. Note the operators "!" and "^", which denote definedness and undefinedness, respectively (roughly speaking, `coin!` guarantees that the variable `coin` has been properly initialised).

Also note the predicate `machine_inv` introduced by `PRED`. The word *predicate* comes from mathematical logic where it means "formula which is either true or false".

The state transition diagram of Figure 2.4 shows the dynamic behaviour of the vending machine in terms of the procedures `insert`, `check`, `select` and `produce`.

The data flow diagram of Figure 2.5 shows the input and output as well as the modification rights of a number of procedures with respect to the variables `coin`, `value`, `selection`, `control_state` and the three tables. Of these tables only `value_table` is modified. The others only provide inputs. The arrow from `insert` to `control_state` indicates that `insert` modifies the `control_state`. The pre-condition of `insert` involves `control_state`, which explains why there is a double arrow here (we have adopted the convention that dependencies due to procedure pre-conditions are also indicated by arrows).

The four procedures named `insert`, `check`, `select` and `produce` can be classified into two groups of two procedures each. `insert` and `select` are actions to be prompted by the user; `check` and `produce` are autonomous actions of the machine.

```
COMPONENT VENDING4 SPECIFICATION
IMPORT
  VENDING3
CLASS
```

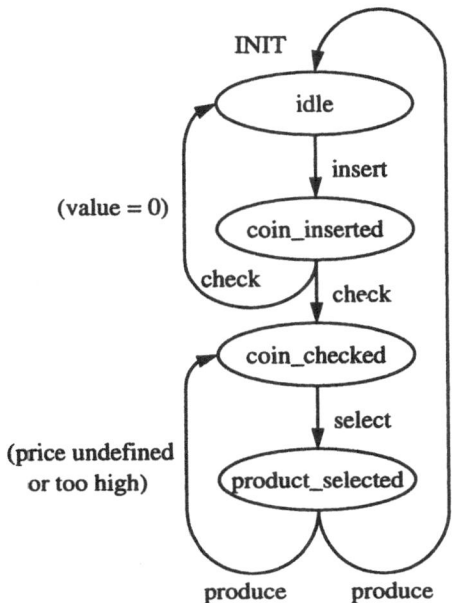

Figure 2.4: State transition diagram of vending machine.

```
PROC user : ->
DEF  ( insert($)
     | select($)
     )

PROC machine : ->
DEF  ( check
     | FLUSH produce
     )
END
```

The procedure **user** is defined (keyword DEF) as a choice (operator "|") be-
tween **insert($)** and **select($)**. The dollar-sign is a kind of wild-card, denoting arbitrary arguments of **insert**. The keyword FLUSH indicates that the
result of **produce** plays no rôle here; in this way the types of the sub-expressions
of the "|" construct are made equal.

It is useful to consider a few traces, or, more generally, *sequence charts*, of
interleaved user actions and machine actions. Figure 2.6 is a sequence chart
which corresponds to a straightforward user behaviour and the corresponding actions of the machine. In the diagram an arrow from left to right denotes a state transition after which `control_state` becomes `coin_inserted`
or `product_selected`. Note that such a transition enables the machine to
perform the next action. An arrow from right to left denotes a state transition
after which the `control_state` becomes `idle` or `coin_checked`. Note that

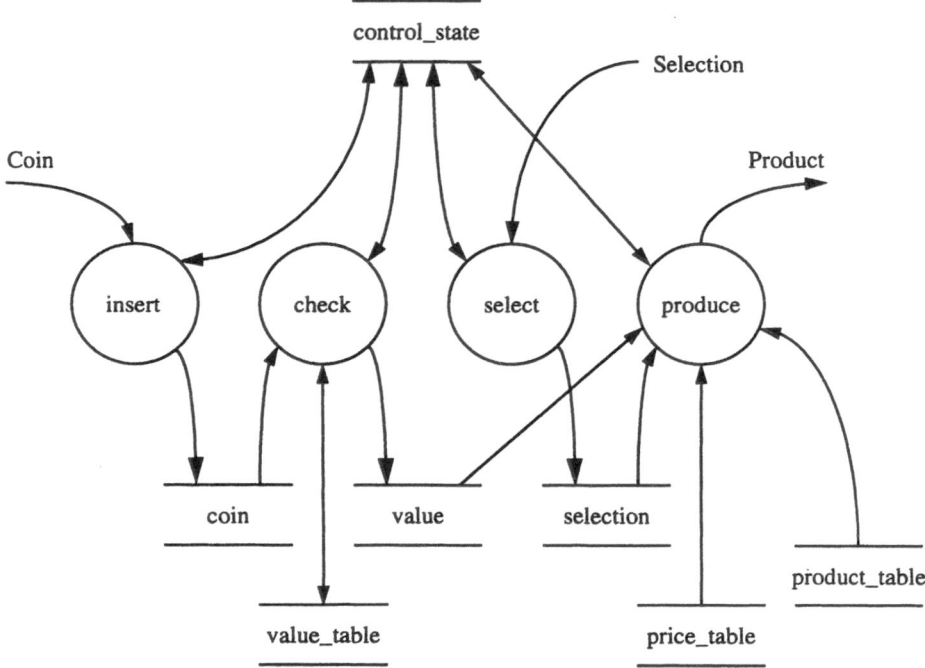

Figure 2.5: Data flow diagram of vending machine procedures.

such a transition enables the user to perform the next action.

In a sequence chart there are two or more "time lines", drawn as vertical lines, and labelled by a procedure name. The sequence of actions performed by such a procedure can be viewed as a process. The arrows are used to indicate communication, either by means of buffers, communication channels or synchronization mechanisms. In this example the control_state serves as a synchronization mechanism between the user and the machine. These diagrams have been proposed and named "message sequence charts" (MSCs) in the context of SDL and CCITT study group X, [9], [10], [11] or [12].

Figure 2.7 shows another sequence chart, which corresponds to a scenario of a user persistently inserting worthless coins.

The module VENDING5 below serves to establish an explicit link between the functional behaviour, modelled by the function vend, and the dynamic behaviour, modelled by the four procedures insert, check, select and produce.

```
COMPONENT VENDING5 SPECIFICATION
IMPORT
  VENDING3
CLASS
  DECL c:Coin, s:Selection, v:Value
```

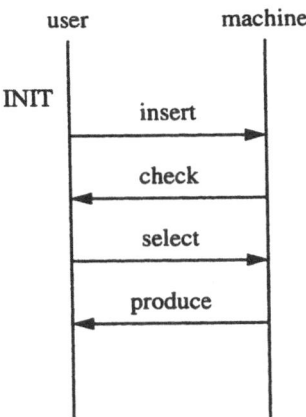

Figure 2.6: Sequence chart of vending machine.

```
THEOREM ( control_state = idle
        ; v = validate(value_table,c)
        ; v > 0
        ; price(price_table,s) <= v
        ) => AFTER
              ( LET p:Product
              ; insert(c)
              ; check
              ; select(s)
              ; p := produce
              ) THEN p = vend(c,s)
END
```

Next we shall discuss more details of the sorts `ValueTable`, `ProdTable` and `PriceTable`. Recall that coins are large numbers, defined by the machine operator (possibly in cooperation with a bank), who updates the value table. Values are non-negative integer numbers of ECUs and selections are non-negative integer numbers. Finally let us fill in the details concerning the nature of the product (previously said to be something with a certain entertainment value). Here the "products" are rock and roll song lyrics – their entertainment value is a matter of taste. See Figure 2.9.

A value table is a mapping from coins to values. A product table is a mapping from selections to products. A price table is a mapping from selections to values. To model this we will use the standard data type `Map` of finite maps (provided by `MAP` in Section B.13 of the standard library) extended to `XMAP` through the addition of an infix application operator `@`. The following clause can be used to describe the priorities, associativities and "fixities" of the operators used:

OPERATORS

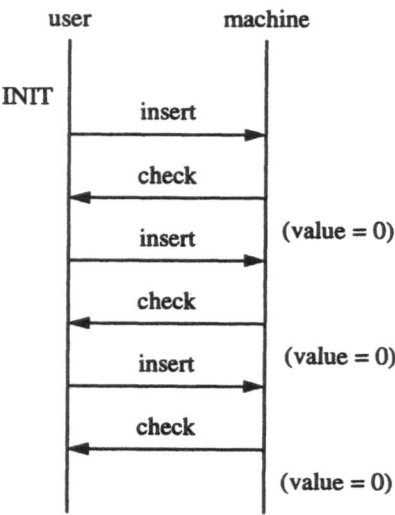

Figure 2.7: User inserting invalid coins.

```
PREFIX          -,    '
INFIX LEFT      *,   /, @
INFIX LEFT      +,    -
INFIX           <,   >,   <=,   >=
```

The definition of XMAP is given below. The details of add, rem, etc. can be found in Section B.13.

```
COMPONENT XMAP[Item1,Item2] SPECIFICATION
ABSTRACT
  ITEM1, ITEM2
EXPORT
  SORT Map
  FUNC empty :                      -> Map,
       add   : Map # Item1 # Item2 -> Map,
       rem   : Map # Item1          -> Map,
       @     : Map # Item1          -> Item2,
       dom   : Map                  -> Set[Item1],
       ran   : Map                  -> Set[Item2]
IMPORT
  MAP[Item1,Item2]
CLASS
  FUNC @ : Map # Item1 -> Item2
  IN    m,i
  DEF   app(m,i)
END
```

It is a generic description which can be instantiated in many different ways. In particular, XMAP[Coin,Value] introduces the sort Map of finite mappings from coins to values. The name "Map" is renamed to ValueTable in order to avoid confusion with other maps. Similarly the sort of finite mappings from selections to products is renamed from Map to ProdTable and the sort of finite mappings from selections to values is named PriceTable.

Now m @ x is the value of map m applied to argument x. This is used to define the functions validate, price and yield. The missing details, which indicate how the procedure check affects the variable value_table, are also added.

```
COMPONENT VENDING6 SPECIFICATION
IMPORT
 VENDING3,
 XMAP[Coin,Value] RENAMING Map TO ValueTable END,
 XMAP[Selection,Value] RENAMING Map TO PriceTable, @ TO price END,
 XMAP[Selection,Product] RENAMING Map TO ProdTable, @ TO yield END
CLASS
 FUNC validate : ValueTable # Coin -> Value
 IN   t,c
 DEF  ( (t @ c)! ? ; (t @ c)
      | (t @ c)^ ? ; 0
      )

 AXIOM dom(price_table) = dom(product_table)

 AXIOM control_state = coin_inserted =>
       AFTER check
       THEN  value > 0 => value_table = rem(value_table',coin)
 END
```

Note the second axiom, explaining exactly how the procedure check changes value_table. When the outcome of the check is that value > 0, then the new value table is obtained by removing the coin from the old value table (the notation value_table' refers to the previous contents of value_table). So each valid number can be used as a valid coin just once. After a coin has been checked, subsequent calls of validate will yield 0, as follows from the clause (t @ c)^ ? ; 0 in its definition.

Figure 2.8 shows examples of a value table and a price table. Figure 2.9 shows an example of a product table.

Now that various views on the vending machine have been developed so far, it is useful to show their import structure in a diagram. This is done in Figure 2.10. Let us briefly summarize the rôle of each module. NAT introduces the natural numbers with their properties and operations. VALUE introduces values with their properties and operations. XMAP introduces finite mappings with their properties and operations. ENUM4 introduces an enumerated data type. VENDING1 introduces the function type of vend. VENDING2 describes a

coin	value
111	1
222	1
187632	1
333	5

selection	value
1	1
2	1
3	3

Figure 2.8: Examples of value table and price table.

selection	product
1	Summertime Blues: I'm a gonna raise a fuss..
2	Bye bye Johnny, Goodbye Johnny B. Goode..
3	Hee, hee, hee, kom van dat dak af..

Figure 2.9: Example of product table.

decomposition of the functional behaviour. VENDING3 concerns the dynamic behaviour of the vending machine. VENDING4 enables grouping of the various actions into user actions and machine actions. VENDING5 is an explicit statement on the relation between the functional behaviour and the dynamic behaviour. VENDING6 is a detailing of the various tables involved and also a further detailing of the functional and dynamic properties. Figure 2.10 has been simplified in the sense that it does not precisely show how the three instances of XMAP are made; instead just one XMAP is shown. Also the imports of XMAP itself have been omitted.

It may seem strange that VENDING4, VENDING5 and VENDING6 do not occur in a linear sequence in Figure 2.10. This is because they describe distinct aspects of the vending machine and its behaviour in an independent manner. Of course, when necessary, one could introduce another module, say VENDING_ALL, importing VENDING4, VENDING5 and VENDING6, to close the diagram.

At this point the specification is considered sufficiently refined. All loose ends introduced by free definitions have been resolved.

2.3   Analysing the Building Blocks

Before any design issues of the vending machine are addressed, the available building blocks will be presented. After that, the functionality of the vending machine can be mapped onto the available building blocks. By explicitly separating the vending machine from its building blocks, the design can be made explicit. In general there may be a structure clash between a specification and an implementation, that is: although they correctly describe the same system, the structures of the specification and the implementation need not be the same.

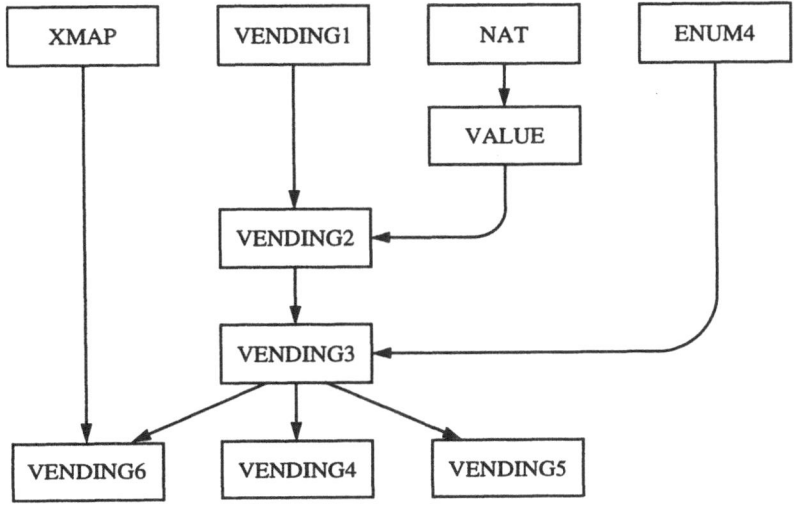

Figure 2.10: Imports of vending machine.

The component SVAR will be presented, which is useful for representing storage variables like coin, value, etc. This is the subject of Section 2.3.1.

In the specification of the vending machine the sort Product occurs, which formally has not yet been refined. It is assumed that every product is a string (a sequence of characters). For this purpose the component STRING will be introduced in Section 2.3.2 below. It is assumed that an efficient implementation of this component is available.

In the specification of the vending machine there are three tables, which are modelled as maps (sort Map). These are value_table, price_table and product_table. Their representation is an important design issue. Their similarity can be exploited by employing a reusable implementation component which can serve for all three tables. Although a first idea could be to use arrays for representing maps, the example of coin 187632 shows that some care is needed to avoid gross inefficiencies. The well-known technique of hashing can be used. Therefore a generic component called HASHMAP will be specified in Section 2.3.3. It serves to encapsulate some of the implementation details of the map representation, such as the question whether open or closed hashing is used.

2.3.1 Storage Variables

The component SVAR concerns simple programming variables, which serve to store values. The specification of SVAR is as follows.

```
COMPONENT SVAR[Item] SPECIFICATION
ABSTRACT
```

```
  ITEM
EXPORT
  FUNC var : -> Item
  PROC set : Item ->
CLASS
  FUNC var : -> Item  VAR

  PROC set : Item ->
  IN    i
  PRE   TRUE
  SAT   MOD var
  POST  var = i
END
```

The state transition diagram of Figure 2.11 shows the dynamic behaviour of
SVAR[Bool], which is a variable obtained by instantiating SVAR with the two-
valued sort Bool. Here Bool just serves as a simple example to avoid too many
states in the diagram. Note that there are three states instead of two, because
var may be undefined. The state in which var is undefined is characterized
by the assertion var^.

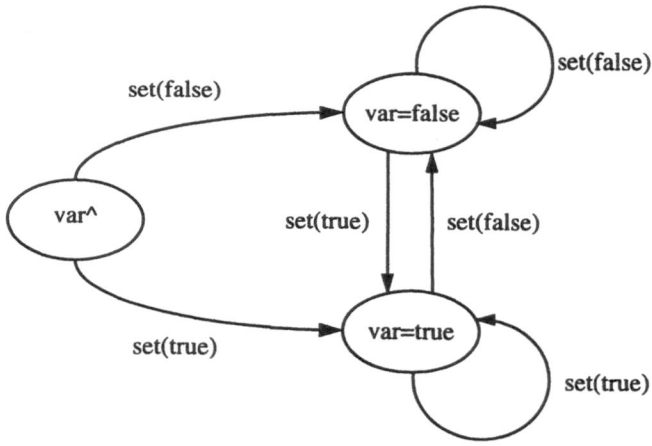

Figure 2.11: State transition diagram of SVAR[Bool].

The data flow diagram of Figure 2.12 shows the procedure set with its
input of type Item. The diagram also shows that set has modification rights
with respect to the variable var.

2.3.2   Strings

Let us assume that we have implementations of NAT and STRING. The definition
of STRING uses SEQ and CHAR. These are standard data types, described in
Sections B.12 and B.7, respectively.

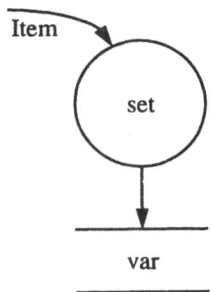

Figure 2.12: Data flow diagram of SVAR[Item].

The following operations are specified: **empty** is the empty string. **len**(s) denotes the length of string s, **sel**(s,i) is the character at position i in string s, and **cat**(s,t) denotes concatenation of the strings s and t. Finally **seq**(c) is the sequence of length one that contains the character c.

```
COMPONENT STRING SPECIFICATION
EXPORT
  SORT String
  FUNC empty :                    -> String,
       len   : String             -> Nat,
       sel   : String # Nat       -> Char,
       cat   : String # String    -> String,
       seq   : Char               -> String
IMPORT
  CHAR,
  SEQ'[Char] RENAMING Seq TO String END
END
```

2.3.3   Hash Maps

A useful implementation technique for tables is *hashing*. The COLD-1 description below gives a generic component called HASHMAP. It has parameters, which are the sorts Item1 and Item2, a constant **max**, and the **hash** function that maps Item1 values to natural numbers. The precise specification of these parameters is postponed and it is assumed that they will be specified later in components called ITEM1, ITEM2 and HASHPARAMETERS.

HASHMAP provides one hidden variable, **the_map** of type Map. There are also a number of operations using or modifying this map. The procedure **clear** makes the map empty, **add**(i,j) modifies the map by adding the value j for the entry i and **rem**(i) removes the entry i and the value stored for that entry. Finally **lookup** i yields the value that was stored for entry i, if present, and is undefined otherwise. The predicate **exists** serves to check whether there is an entry for a given Item1 value.

Implementation-related details such as **max** and **hash** are visible at the specification level because HASHMAP is the specification of an (efficient) implementation module. The specification given here anticipates the fact that these details must be filled in when *using* the implementation.

```
COMPONENT HASHMAP[Item1,Item2,max,hash] SPECIFICATION
ABSTRACT
  ITEM1,
  ITEM2,
  HASHPARAMETERS[Item1]
EXPORT
  PROC clear  : ->,
       add    : Item1 # Item2 ->,
       rem    : Item1         ->
  FUNC lookup : Item1         -> Item2
  PRED exists : Item1
IMPORT
  NAT,
  SET[Item1],
  XMAP[Item1,Item2]
CLASS
  FUNC the_map : -> Map VAR

  PROC clear : ->
  PRE   TRUE
  SAT   MOD the_map
  POST the_map = empty

  PROC add : Item1 # Item2 ->
  IN    i,j
  PRE   is_in(i,dom(the_map)) OR card(dom(the_map)) < max
  SAT   MOD the_map
  POST the_map = add(the_map',i,j)

  PROC rem : Item1 ->
  IN    i
  PRE   TRUE
  SAT   MOD the_map
  POST the_map = rem(the_map',i)

  FUNC lookup : Item1 -> Item2
  IN    i
  OUT   j
  PRE   is_in(i,dom(the_map))
  POST j = the_map @ i

  PRED exists : Item1
  IN    i
  DEF   is_in(i,dom(the_map))
```

END

The above specification uses **XMAP** and the standard description **SET**, describing the mathematical data types of finite maps and finite sets, respectively. Recall that, among other things, **XMAP** provides the constant **empty**, the function **@**, which is used in infix notation, and operations **rem** (remove) and **dom** (domain). For example, **the_map @** i is the value of map **the_map** applied to argument i. Similarly, **SET** provides the constant **empty** and an operation **is_in** for set membership test.

The above definition of the operation **add** will be explained in detail. Note that the name **add** is *overloaded* in the sense that there are two distinct operations called **add**. First, there is the **add** operation on mathematical maps. Secondly, there is the **add** operation defined here, which operates on the hidden variable **the_map**. Their applied occurrences are easily distinguished because the former operation has three arguments and the latter operation only two. The definition of **add** given here is written in pre- and post-condition style. The clause **IN** i,j introduces the formal parameters. Its pre-condition states that a call of **add**(i,j) will succeed only if i is in the domain of **the_map** or there are fewer than **max** elements in the domain. The pre-condition models implementation restrictions due to limited storage capacity. If i is already in the domain of **the_map**, no new storage is required. If there are fewer than **max** elements in the domain, this means that space is still available. But when card(dom(the_map)) = **max**, the available space is exhausted. The SAT clause gives a restriction that must be *sat*isfied by all state transitions caused by **add**(i,j). The restriction is that the only variable modified is **the_map**. All other variables may not be changed. Finally the post-condition states that in the result state the new value of **the_map** is equal to **add(the_map'**,i,j), where **the_map'** denotes the previous value of **the_map**. This notion of "previous value" refers to the state just before the call of **add**(i,j), which is the state in which the pre-condition is to be considered.

Now it is time to fill in the missing details concerning the parameters **Item1**, **Item2**, **max** and **hash**. The sorts **Item1** and **Item2** have no special requirements; their specifications are the simple descriptions **ITEM1** and **ITEM2**.

```
LET ITEM1 :=
CLASS
  SORT Item1
END

LET ITEM2 :=
CLASS
  SORT Item2
END
```

The diagram of Figure 2.13 shows a typical example of a value set of **Item1**. The specification component **ITEM1** does not require the existence of any functions or predicates, so the diagram does not have any function arrows or lines as in a Hasse diagram.

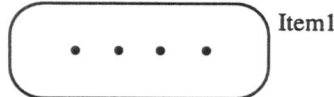

Figure 2.13: Example value set of sort Item1.

The constant **max** indicates the maximum number of entries a map can have. The function **hash** maps **Item1** objects to numbers and it plays a rôle in the technique of mapping the **Item1** objects to entries in an array. It can be noted that the function **hash** does not occur in the specification of **HASHMAP**, so it must be explained why it is a parameter. It is because a hash function must be defined every time **HASHMAP** is instantiated. One might assume that the function defined by **hash**(n) = **mod**(n,**max**) satisfies all needs, but this is not the case because when **Item1** objects are tuples, or strings, there is no unique modulo function. Of course one can easily define a hash function on strings, but that can not be done *in* the hashmap implementation (after all, the implementation is generic). This approach supports a component-oriented way of working, where a component has both an implementation and a specification associated with it. The specification must contain all assumptions and facts that are relevant in instantiating and using the implementation.

```
LET HASHPARAMETERS[Item1] :=
ABSTRACT
  ITEM1
EXPORT
  FUNC max  : -> Nat,
       hash : Item1 -> Nat
IMPORT
  NAT
CLASS
  FUNC max : -> Nat
  PRE  TRUE
  POST max > 0

  FUNC hash : Item1 -> Nat
  IN   i
  PRE  TRUE
  POST hash(i) < max

  AXIOM FORALL n:Nat (n < max => EXISTS j:Item1 (n = hash(j)))
END
```

The function graph of Figure 2.14 shows an example of the set of values as well as the arrows of the functions **max** and **hash**. **max** is shown by just one arrow, whereas there are a number of arrows for **hash**.

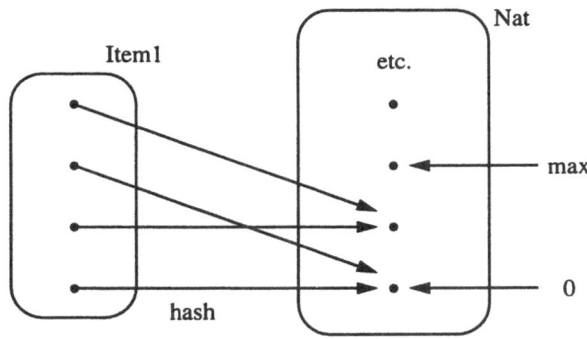

Figure 2.14: Function graph of max and hash.

2.4   Design

Let us assume that the design task to be performed is to provide operations **insert**, **check**, **select** and **produce** with a behaviour as prescribed
by VENDING6. The first design decision is to use the components NAT, STRING,
SVAR, and HASHMAP, as described in Sections B.4, 2.3.2, 2.3.1 and 2.3.3, respectively.

The sort Coin is refined by modeling coins as natural numbers. An instance
of SVAR is used to implement the storage function of the variable function coin.

```
COMPONENT COIN SPECIFICATION
EXPORT
  SORT Coin
  FUNC coin     :       -> Coin,
       nat      : Coin -> Nat
  PROC set_coin : Coin ->
IMPORT
  NAT,
  NAT' RENAMING Nat TO Coin END,
  SVAR'[Coin] RENAMING var TO coin, set TO set_coin END
CLASS
  DECL c : Coin

  FUNC nat : Coin -> Nat
  IND  nat(0) = 0;
       nat(c + 1) = nat(c) + 1
END
```

The above COIN not only provides the sort Coin and a storage facility, but
also contains a function for conversion from coins to natural numbers. The
point is that the strong typing system of COLD-1 excludes expressions like
mod(c,max), which will arise naturally in attempts to instantiate the hash

maps. With the conversion function the correct expression is `mod(nat(c),max)`. The keyword IND indicates that this is an *inductive* definition. In the coding phase such conversions can be omitted, so they do not give rise to inefficiencies.

The sort `Selection` is refined by modeling selections as natural numbers. An instance of SVAR is used to implement the storage function of `selection`.

```
COMPONENT SELECTION SPECIFICATION
EXPORT
  SORT Selection
  FUNC selection      :              -> Selection,
       nat            : Selection -> Nat
  PROC set_selection : Selection ->
IMPORT
   NAT,
   NAT' RENAMING Nat TO Selection END,
   SVAR'[Selection] RENAMING var TO selection,
                             set TO set_selection
                  END
CLASS
  DECL s : Selection

  FUNC nat : Selection -> Nat
  IND  nat(0) = 0;
       nat(s + 1) = nat(s) + 1
END
```

Just like COIN, the above SELECTION contains a function for conversion from selections to natural numbers.

The sort `Product` is refined by modeling products as strings.

```
COMPONENT PRODUCT SPECIFICATION
IMPORT
  STRING' RENAMING String TO Product END
END
```

Another instance of SVAR is used to implement the storage function of `value`.

```
COMPONENT SVALUE SPECIFICATION
EXPORT
  FUNC value : -> Value
  PROC set_value : Value ->
IMPORT
   VALUE,
   SVAR'[Value] RENAMING var TO value, set TO set_value END
END
```

The sort `ControlState` is described by ENUM4. An instance of SVAR is used to implement the storage function of the variable function `control_state`.

```
COMPONENT CONTROL_STATE SPECIFICATION
IMPORT
```

```
ENUM4' RENAMING Enum4 TO ControlState,
               x0    TO idle,
               x1    TO coin_inserted,
               x2    TO coin_checked,
               x3    TO product_selected
       END,
    SVAR'[ControlState] RENAMING var TO control_state,
                                 set TO set_control_state
                        END
END
```

An instance of HASHMAP is used to implement the storage function of the variable function value_table.

To perform the instantiation it is necessary to define a constant for max and a function for hash. They will be denoted as max1 and hash1. The operator "mod" is used in the definition of hash1 below. It refers to the modulo operator on natural numbers, defined in NAT. Instances of HASHMAP are also used to implement the storage functions of price_table and product_table. The latter two instances may have the same actual parameters for max and hash. They will be denoted as max2 and hash2.

After these preparations, the vending machine can be constructed. Its specification is obtained by exporting only the four main procedures from VENDING6. The implementation is based on COIN, VALUE, SELECTION, PRODUCT, SVALUE, and CONTROL_STATE.

```
COMPONENT MACHINE

SPECIFICATION
EXPORT
  PROC insert  : Coin      ->,
       check   :           ->,
       select  : Selection ->,
       produce :           -> Product
IMPORT
  VENDING6
END

IMPLEMENTATION
IMPORT
   COIN,
   VALUE,
   SELECTION,
   PRODUCT,
   SVALUE,
   CONTROL_STATE,
   HASHMAP'[Selection,Product,max2,hash2]
           RENAMING lookup TO yield,
```

```
                    exists TO exists_product
           END,
    HASHMAP'[Selection,Value,max2,hash2]
           RENAMING lookup TO price,
                    exists TO exists_price
           END,
    HASHMAP'[Coin,Value,max1,hash1]
           RENAMING rem    TO rem_value,
                    add    TO add_value,
                    exists TO exists_value
           END
CLASS
  FUNC max1 : -> Nat
  DEF   100

  FUNC hash1 : Coin -> Nat
  IN    c
  DEF   mod(nat(c),max1)

  FUNC max2 : -> Nat
  DEF   50

  FUNC hash2 : Selection -> Nat
  IN    s
  DEF   mod(nat(s),max2)

  PROC insert : Coin ->
  IN    c
  PRE   control_state = idle
  DEF   set_coin(c);
        set_control_state(coin_inserted)

  FUNC validate : Coin -> Value
  IN    c
  DEF   ( exists_value(c)     ? ; lookup(c)
        | NOT exists_value(c) ? ; 0
        )

  PROC check : ->
  PRE   control_state = coin_inserted
  DEF   set_value(validate(coin));
        ( value = 0 ? ; set_control_state(idle)
        | value > 0 ? ; set_control_state(coin_checked);
                        rem_value(coin)
        )

  PROC select : Selection ->
```

```
IN   s
PRE  control_state = coin_checked
DEF  set_selection(s);
     set_control_state(product_selected)

PROC produce : -> Product
PRE  control_state = product_selected
DEF  LET v:Value;
     ( NOT exists_price(selection) ?;
          set_control_state(coin_checked);
          empty
     | exists_price(selection) ?;
          v := price(selection);
          ( v > value ?;
               set_control_state(coin_checked);
               empty
          | v <= value ?;
               set_control_state(idle);
               yield(selection)
     )    )
END
```

In the CLASS clause of the above implementation the four procedures insert, check, select and produce have been redefined by means of algorithmic definitions. An algorithmic definition is indicated by a DEF clause. In the specification phase they were already described by means of pre- and post-conditions. The algorithmic definitions make the post-conditions hold (the pre-conditions are still the same). Consider the expression select(s). Recall its post-condition, which consists of the two equations selection = s and control_state = product_selected. By using the post-condition of set_selection as given by the (renamed) instance of SVAR, it is easily verified that set_selection(s) makes the equation selection = s hold. In the same way the other equation is verified.

At this stage in the development of the design of the vending machine it is useful to show its structure in diagrams. We will employ two diagrams. Figure 2.15 is a HOOD-like component diagram, which serves to explicitly separate the specification and the implementation view of the component. Figure 2.16 is the import diagram of the implementation part of MACHINE.

In this diagram the three (anonymous) instantiations of HASHMAP are explicitly shown. For SVAR, the presentation has been simplified. Also, not all the import arrows of NAT are shown. This concludes the design phase of the example.

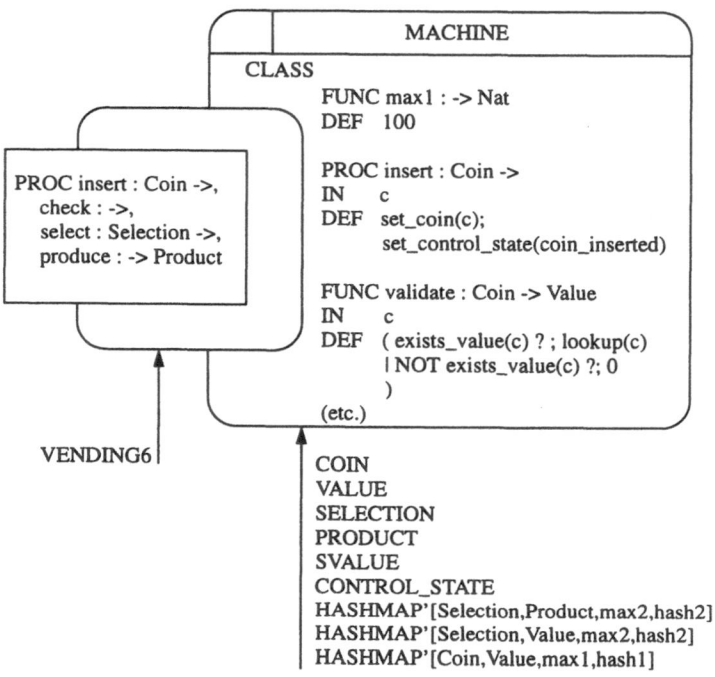

Figure 2.15: HOOD-like component diagram of vending machine.

2.5 Realization

A working prototype has been realized on the basis of the analysis and design of the previous sections. To that end the design was coded in the programming language C. Other languages instead of C could have been used as well. There are many distinct technical options for this coding process which depend on the programming language chosen and the availability of tools. For this example the coding was done manually.

The implementation of HASHMAP can be taken from any standard text book on data structures and algorithms. The important point to note is that we have encapsulated it into a component with a COLD-1 specification and with its four parameters made explicit.

The renamings of HASHMAP can be realized using the macro-preprocessor of the C compiler. No attempt has been made to achieve code-sharing for HASHMAP, so three copies have been used. The pre-condition checks have been removed from the procedures. They reappear as conditions in the case construct of the main loop.

The macro definitions corresponding to the three distinct instantiations of HASHMAP are given in Figure 2.17. In fact there are a few more definitions, but as they just resolve name clashes they are not shown in the table. It is obvious

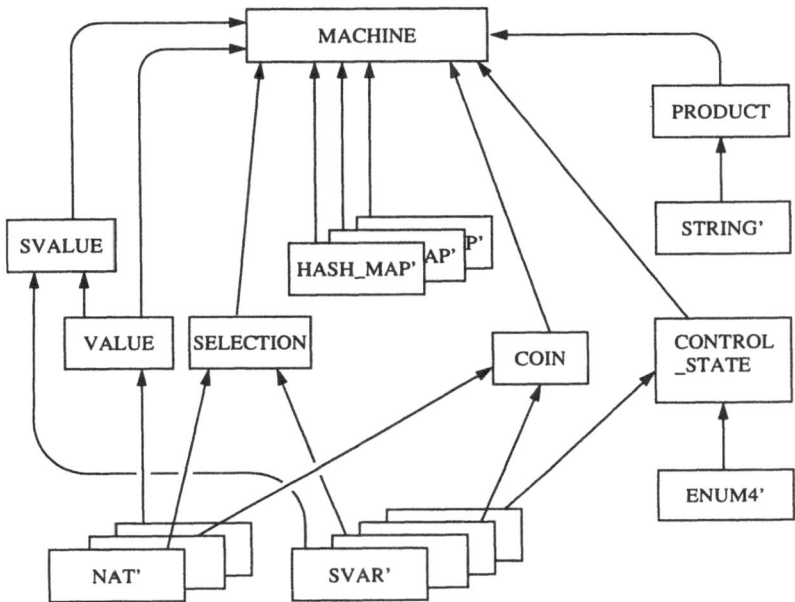

Figure 2.16: Import structure of vending machine implementation.

that if a programming language had been used that supports generic modules or polymorphism, other solutions may have been obtained.

The main program provides the initialization and an infinite loop scheduling the four main procedures of the machine. Admittedly this initialization is not completely formally specified, and has been added to the realization in an ad-hoc way. It puts the machine in a state where the various tables have a non-empty contents which is interesting enough to perform test runs.

The C program below was preceded by a few macro definitions to give "COLD-1 look" to some of the C functions: PROC is defined as void, DEF is {, NOT is !, and empty is "". Getting rid of the closing } is a bit harder, for this requires true compilation (not done here). The instances of the C implementation of HASHMAP are not shown here.

```
#include <stdio.h>
#define Selection int
#define Product   char *
#define Value     int
#define Coin      int

static Coin      coin;
static Selection selection;
static Value     value;
static int       control_state;
```

	product table	*price table*	*value table*
#define Item1	Selection	Selection	Coin
#define Item2	Product	Value	Value
#define max	50	50	100
#define hash(i)	((int)i)%50	((int)i)%50	((int)i)%100
#define the_map	product_table	price_table	value_table
#define clear	clear_product_table	clear_price_table	clear_value_table
#define lookup	yield	price	lookup
#define add	add_product	add_price	add_value
#define rem	rem_product	rem_price	rem_value
#define exists	exists_product	exists_price	exists_value

Figure 2.17: Instantiations of hash map.

```
#define  idle              0
#define  coin_inserted      1
#define  coin_checked       2
#define  product_selected 3

PROC insert(c)
Coin c;
DEF  coin=(c);
     control_state=(coin_inserted);}

Value validate(c)
Coin  c;
DEF   if (exists_value(c))
         return(lookup(c));
         else return(0);}

PROC check()
DEF  value=(validate(coin));
     if (value==0)
        control_state=(idle);
        else { control_state=(coin_checked);
                rem_value(coin);}}

PROC select(s)
Selection s;
DEF  selection=(s);
     control_state=(product_selected);}

Product produce()
DEF  Value v;
        if (NOT exists_price(selection))
```

```
                {control_state=(coin_checked);
                return(empty);}
                else  {v = price(selection);
                        if (v > value)
                            {control_state=(coin_checked);
                            return(empty);}
                        else {control_state=(idle);
                                return(yield(selection));}}}

main()
{ clear_product_table();
add_product(1,"Summertime Blues: \n I'm a gonna raise a fuss...
add_product(2,"Bye bye Johnny:\n She drew out all her money at...
add_product(3,"Kom van dat dak af:\n Hee, hee, hee, kom van ...

clear_price_table();
add_price(1,1);
add_price(2,1);
add_price(3,3);

clear_value_table();
add_value(111,1);
add_value(222,1);
add_value(333,5);
add_value(187632,1)

while (1)
{ Coin c;
  Selection s;
  switch(control_state) {
    case idle               : printf("insert coin\n");
                              scanf("%d",&c);
                              insert(c);
                              break;
    case coin_inserted      : check();
                              break;
    case coin_checked       : printf("make selection\n");
                              scanf("%d",&s);
                              select(s);
                              break;
    case product_selected : printf(produce());
                              break; }}}
```

Recall Figure 2.6 which shows a straightforward user behaviour and the corresponding machine actions. After implementation, the scenario of Figure 2.6 can be used to perform a test run. If the user performs insert and select actions, the machine should perform the corresponding check and produce actions. As the C program shows, the implementation embodies specific choices for the user interface and hints to the user, such as "insert coin" and "make selection". One test session has been recorded and is shown in Figure 2.18.

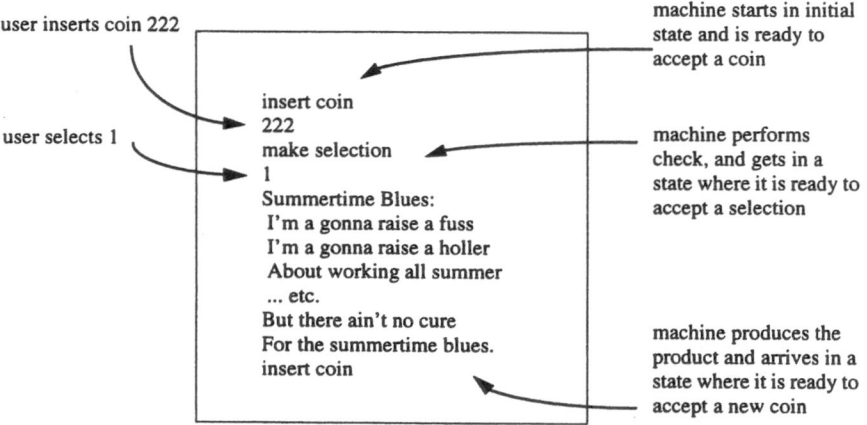

Figure 2.18: Use case of the vending machine.

This concludes the example. In other chapters the precise format of the COLD-1 notations and of the pictorial representations will have to be dealt with. It is not claimed that the method used for the vending machine case is the "right" or "preferred" method. It is just one of the many options that arise when using the notations presented in this book.

2.6 Concluding Remarks

The example indicates that well-known pictorial representations, such as dataflow diagrams, sequence charts, HOOD-like diagrams, hierarchy graphs and state transition graphs, can be used to enrich the formal notation of COLD-1. The formal semantics of COLD-1 guarantee that the design can be rigorously analysed.

Chapter 3
Patterns for Definitions

3.1   Introduction and Motivation

In COLD-1, systems and system components are described by definitions of sorts and operations as well as axioms and theorems. This chapter treats all relevant language constructs with the accent on the form, the intended use and typical examples. Some examples will be taken from the vending machine case in the previous chapter.

Sorts are collections of objects; data types can be viewed as sorts together with operations defined on them. The following kinds of operations are distinguished:

1. functions
2. predicates
3. procedures

Functions are mappings from one data type to another. Also mathematical operators and even tables and arrays can be viewed as functions. Predicates include properties of objects of a data type and relations between objects of several data types. Tests which either succeed or fail and even bitmaps can be viewed as predicates. Procedures are operations which are affected by and affect a state. Procedures have side-effects: they may modify mutable entities (such as programming variables) or dynamically create new objects. Procedures are "state-transformers".

For each kind of operations, there is a standard pattern for defining an operation. The pattern is helpful for organizing all facts and assumptions about the operation being defined, such as its name, types and names of its arguments and its results, its pre-condition, further restrictions it satisfies and finally an algorithm or a post-condition. There is also a standard pattern for defining sorts. Often, not all basic properties of sorts and operations can be expressed in this way. Axioms are available to characterize defined sorts and/or operations further by stating additional properties. Theorems can be added to indicate that certain properties should follow from the definitions and axioms. This chapter presents the above-mentioned patterns for defining sorts and operations as well as the axioms and theorems for postulating and conjecturing additional properties.

The provisions of COLD-1 for describing systems and system components are based on a particular view of states and state transformations. This view will be explained first. Many properties of sorts and operations are formulated using assertions and expressions. They will be explained in the last two sections of this chapter.

3.2   States and State Transformers

COLD-1 is based on the view that a software *system* has a collection of *states*, one *initial state*, and a number of state transformers which are called *procedures*. There is nothing special about this view. However, in COLD-1 the states of a system have a structure associated with them. The states have a number of components which are identified by a fixed collection of names, called the *state signature*. There are three kinds of state components:

1. *sorts*, which are collections of *objects*;
2. *functions*, which are partial mappings from a number of (domain) sorts to a number of (range) sorts;
3. *predicates*, which are relations on a number of (domain) sorts.

In mathematical terms this means that the states are modelled as many-sorted algebras. The kind and, in so far as appropriate, the domain sorts and the range sorts of the state component with a certain name are the same in all states of the system. The components of a state can be regarded as the observable entities in the state.

A distinction can be made between state components that are *variable*, i.e. that may vary from state to state, and others that are *constant*, i.e. that are the same in all states. The components that are constant are generally immutable entities such as the collection of natural numbers, the addition of natural numbers, etc. Procedures transform states to states by modifying state components that are variable, leaving state components that are constant unchanged. This allows a uniform treatment of the mutable entities which are usually extant in a computer-based system – such as the programming variables of classical programming languages – and the immutable, static entities. Figure 3.1 pictures a system with four states and three state transformers. Its states have two constant sorts and one variable function as state components.

Obviously, in COLD-1 we are concerned with systems which are abstractions of real-life systems. Modification of a sort amounts to the creation of new objects and modification of a function or predicate amounts to modifying its value for certain or all arguments. This is sufficiently flexible to model almost any part of the states of a system. For example, the concept of variable functions generalizes concepts like arrays and pointers from classical imperative programming – found in, for example, Pascal [13] and C [14]. This is

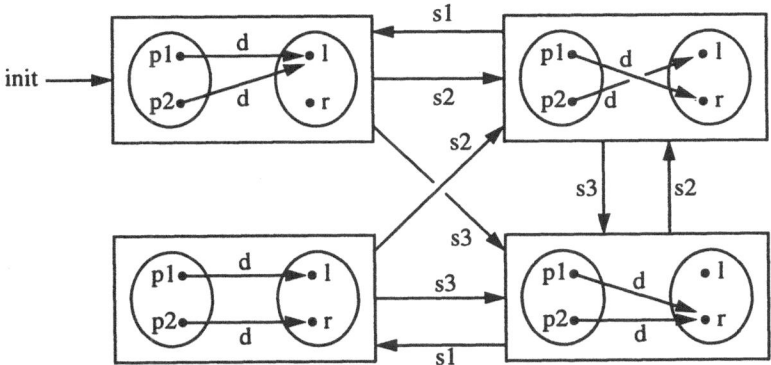

Figure 3.1: A system with four states.

illustrated below. Objects in the sense of object-oriented programming, which have attributes and can be dynamically created, can be modelled as well.

A simple programming variable can be viewed as a variable nullary function. For example, a simple programming variable i of type Int corresponds to the function defined in COLD-1 by:

```
FUNC i : -> Int   VAR
```

In COLD-1, pointers are just objects and dereferencing can be viewed as a variable unary function. Consider a pointer p of the type IntPtr consisting of pointers to values of type Int (^Int in Pascal). Dereferencing p (p^ in Pascal) yields a value of type Int. This pointer type and the dereferencing operation associated with it correspond to the sort and the function defined in COLD-1 by:

```
SORT IntPtr
FUNC deref : IntPtr -> Int   VAR
```

For dereferencing an object p of sort IntPtr, we write deref(p).

An n-dimensional array can be viewed as a variable n-ary function. For example, a two-dimensional array a with indices of type Index and elements of type Int corresponds to the function defined in COLD-1 by:

```
FUNC a : Index # Index -> Int   VAR
```

assuming that the sort Index has been appropriately defined.

The notation used here for introducing variable functions is treated in the next section. An example of the use of variable functions which is not so directly related to concepts from programming languages will also be given.

3.3   Patterns for Function Definitions

A function definition in COLD-1 has the following general form:

```
FUNC f : T₁ # ... # Tₘ -> V₁ # ... # Vₙ
IN     x₁, ... , xₘ
OUT    y₁, ... , yₙ
PRE    pre
fbody
POST   post
```

Here FUNC $f : T_1 \# \ldots \# T_m \to V_1 \# \ldots \# V_n$ $(m \geq 0, n > 0)$ introduces a name for the function being defined. The T_is and V_is are sort names introduced elsewhere. The keyword FUNC is a qualifier indicating that f is the name of a function. The domain type $T_1 \# \ldots \# T_m$ together with the range type V_1 $\# \ldots \# V_n$ indicates that it is a function from $T_1 \times \ldots \times T_m$ to $V_1 \times \ldots \times V_n$. So a function can take a tuple of arguments and can yield a tuple of results. Dependent on the context where the function name occurs, the qualifier and/or the domain and range type may or should be omitted. This is explained in Chapter 5.

The object names $x_1, \ldots, x_m$ listed in the IN section are names for the arguments of the function being defined and the object names $y_1, \ldots, y_n$ listed in the OUT section are names for the results. The PRE and POST sections contain assertions *pre* and *post*, respectively, in which these names are generally used to refer to the arguments and the results. They can also be used for that purpose in the function body *fbody*, if it is present. The IN and OUT sections are both optional. If these sections are not present, the objects concerned can not be denoted by a name in the remainder of the definition.

Functions defined in COLD-1 are in general partial. A partial function does not always yield a result. The PRE section is used to bound the circumstances under which the function f must yield a result: the argument tuples x_1, $\ldots, x_m$ for which the pre-condition *pre* holds are exactly those for which it must be the case that $f(x_1, \ldots, x_m)$ yields a result. The POST section is used to delimit the possible results: if $f(x_1, \ldots, x_m)$ yields $y_1, \ldots, y_n$, then the post-condition *post* must hold between the argument tuple $x_1, \ldots, x_m$ and the result tuple $y_1, \ldots, y_n$. The PRE and POST sections are optional as well. If these sections are not present, no restrictions of the kind concerned have to be met. So the absence of the PRE section should not be confused with the presence of PRE TRUE. The latter expresses a rather strong restriction: it permits only total functions, i.e. functions that yield results for all argument tuples. The absence of a POST section actually has the same effect as the presence of POST TRUE, because the latter also expresses that the possible results are not at all restricted.

The function body *fbody*, if present, has one of the following forms:

1. VAR

2. DEP $e_1, \ldots, e_l$

3. IND A

4. DEF X

5. FREE

So there are actually six alternatives which correspond to six kinds of definition. There is one kind for "preliminary" definitions (form 5) and five kinds for actual definitions. The latter ones can be further subdivided into two kinds that uniquely characterize the function being defined (forms 3 and 4) and the remaining three kinds that do not.

If no function body is present, then the definition introduces a function that is *constant*, i.e. the same in all states. The function concerned can be further characterized, in a not necessarily unique way, by the pre- and post-condition of the definition or by axioms.

This kind of definition is usually found in specifications of primitive data types such as natural numbers, ordered pairs, etc. In that case, the objects concerned and the basic operations on them are not characterized by pre- and post-conditions but by axioms. In general, (conditional) equations are used as the basic constituents of the axioms concerned. For example, in a specification of ordered pairs (i.e. 2-tuples) one finds function definitions such as:

```
FUNC tup   : Item1 # Item2 -> Tup2
FUNC proj1 : Tup2         -> Item1
FUNC proj2 : Tup2         -> Item2
```

The axioms characterizing the functions tup, proj1 and proj2 could include:

```
AXIOM FORALL i1 : Item1, i2 : Item2
      ( proj1(tup(i1,i2)) = i1
      ; proj2(tup(i1,i2)) = i2
      )
```

However, the use of function definitions without a function body is not restricted to the specification of data types in an axiomatic, equational style. They also occur, for example, in definitions of functions in pre- and post-condition style.

In the specification of HASHPARAMETERS, given in Section 2.3, there are two function definitions without a body:

```
FUNC max  : -> Nat
PRE   TRUE
POST  max > 0

FUNC hash : Item1 -> Nat
IN    i
PRE   TRUE
POST  hash(i) < max
```

Both max and hash are constant. Although they are thus fixed functions, they are far from uniquely characterized. Of all natural numbers, the post-condition for max only excludes 0 as a possible value of max. For all arguments of **hash**, the post-condition for **hash** only excludes results not less than **max**. Note that the pre-condition **TRUE** excludes all functions that are not total. In both definitions, an **OUT** section is missing. The terms **max** and **hash(i)** are used to refer to the results of the functions instead of names.

If *fbody* is of the form **VAR**, then the definition introduces a function that is *variable* and can vary independently of other variable state components. Such a state component is called an *independent* variable state component. The function concerned can be further characterized by the pre- and post-condition of the definition or by axioms.

In the specification of **VENDING3**, given in Section 2.2, there are various function definitions with a body of the form **VAR** including:

```
FUNC control_state :  -> ControlState   VAR
FUNC coin          :  -> Coin           VAR
FUNC selection     :  -> Selection      VAR
```

The coins inserted by the user and the user's selection are put in **coin** and **selection**, respectively. **control_state** is used to keep track of the control state of the vending machine. It is obvious that **control_state**, **coin** and **selection** must be variable in order to model the dynamic behaviour of the vending machine. Because the sorts **ControlState**, **Coin** and **Selection** are tailor-made for this application, it is not surprising that all values may actually arise (i.e. the **POST** sections of the procedures concerned do not exclude any value). However, restrictions that do not apply to all states may be expressed by means of an axiom. For **control_state**, for example, we have the axiom:

```
AXIOM INIT => control_state = idle
```

The use of **VAR** as function body is of course not restricted to nullary functions. For example, in the specification of a file system one could have the following function definitions:

```
FUNC contents : File # Nat -> Byte             VAR
FUNC offset   : File       -> Nat    PRE TRUE  VAR
```

Writing a byte at position i in the file f will modify the value of **contents** for the arguments f, i, i.e. **contents**(f, i). The value of **offset** for the argument f will be modified after the reading or writing of the current byte from the file f such that **offset**(f) indicates the position in the file where the next byte will be read or written. The pre-condition **TRUE** guarantees that **offset** has a value for every existing file.

If *fbody* is of the form **DEP** $e_1, \ldots, e_l$, then the definition introduces a function that is *variable*, but may only vary if at least one of the entities $e_1, \ldots, e_l$ changes. Such a state component is called a *dependent* variable state component. The function concerned can be further characterized by the pre- and post-condition of the definition or by axioms.

Entities are of the form v or $w(X)$, where v is a name of a variable sort, function or predicate and w is a name of a variable function or predicate. If an entity is a name v, it denotes the *entire* sort, function or predicate concerned. If an entity is of the form $w(X)$, it denotes the *restriction* of the function or predicate concerned to the tuples of objects which can be yielded by the expression X (in COLD-1, expressions yield tuples of objects).

Suppose that a one-byte cyclic redundancy check (crc) is associated with every file in the file system considered above. The `crc` function could, for example, be defined as follows:

```
FUNC crc : File -> Nat
IN   f
OUT  n
PRE  TRUE
DEP  contents(f,$)
POST n < 256
```

The kind of crc used is not fixed. According to the pre- and post-condition, crc may be any total function from `File` to `Nat` with results less than 256. The function body `DEP contents(f,$)` indicates that `crc(f)`, the crc for the file `f`, must remain the same if the contents of `f` is not affected. In COLD-1, the expression `$` yields an arbitrary object tuple of the type required by the context. In `contents(f,$)`, the type is `Nat`. So the entity `contents(f,$)` is `contents` restricted in the first argument to the single file `f` but not restricted in the second argument.

If *fbody* is of the form `IND A`, where A is an assertion, then the definition introduces a function which may be constant or variable. The function concerned is uniquely characterized by the assertion A: f is the smallest function that satisfies the assertion A, provided that it exists. This means that if there are other functions satisfying A then there are argument tuples for which they yield a value but the function f does not. However, the existence of a smallest function is not guaranteed for all assertions A (this point is returned to below). Definitions of this kind are called *inductive* definitions.

This kind of definition is usually found in specifications of primitive data types. The non-basic functions can be characterized by inductive definitions. For example, in a specification of naturals, where the basic functions `0` and `succ` are sufficient to generate all natural numbers, one could have the following function definition for addition:

```
FUNC + : Nat # Nat -> Nat
IND  FORALL m,n : Nat
     ( m + 0       = m
     ; m + succ(n) = succ(m + n)
     )
```

Inductive definitions are frequently used in mathematics.

If a function f is inductively defined by an assertion A, we can rewrite A to an assertion A' inductively defining a predicate `is.f` intended to correspond to f as follows: $f(x_1, \ldots, x_m)$ is the unique tuple of objects $y_1, \ldots, y_n$ such that `is.`$f(x_1, \ldots, x_m, y_1, \ldots, y_n)$ holds. Rewriting the assertion used in the inductive definition of addition results in the assertion

```
FORALL m,n,k : Nat
( is.+(m,0,m)
; is.+(m,n,k) => is.+(m,succ(n),succ(k))
)
```

If there exists a smallest predicate `is.`f satisfying A', then there exists a smallest function f satisfying A provided that `is.`f is functional (i.e. for each tuple $x_1, \ldots, x_m$, the corresponding tuple $y_1, \ldots, y_n$ is unique). In Section 3.4, a sufficient syntactic condition for the existence of a smallest predicate is given.

If *fbody* is of the form `DEF` X, where X is an expression, then the definition introduces a function which may be constant or variable. The function concerned is uniquely characterized by the expression X: f is the smallest function that satisfies the assertion

$$\text{FORALL } x_1 : T_1, \ldots, x_m : T_m, y_1 : V_1, \ldots, y_n : V_n$$
$$(\; f(x_1, \ldots, x_m) = y_1, \ldots, y_n \texttt{<=>} X = y_1, \ldots, y_n \;)$$

provided that it exists. This implies that $f(x_1, \ldots, x_m)$ does not yield a result if X does not yield unique $y_1, \ldots, y_n$ for $x_1, \ldots, x_m$. Definitions of this kind are called *algorithmic* definitions. The function concerned may additionally be characterized by the pre- and post-condition of the definition or by axioms, but this gives easily rise to inconsistencies.

This kind of definition is used, amongst other things, to describe implementations of functions in a functional programming style [15] – using programming languages such as Standard ML [16] and Haskell [17]. Often the function being defined is recursively used in the definition. Consider the following algorithmic definition of addition:

```
FUNC + : Nat # Nat -> Nat
IN   m,n
DEF  ( n = 0      ?; m
     | NOT n = 0 ?; succ(m + pred(n))
     )
```

For given arguments m and n, the value of `+` is m if n is zero and its value is `succ`$(m$ `+` `pred`$(n))$ otherwise. So the function `+` is recursively used in this definition.

On the whole, algorithmic definitions of functions are rather concrete and probably on that account they are generally regarded as being easy to read and write. The functions being defined are often of an auxiliary nature.

In the specification of `VENDING2`, given in Section 2.2, there is the following algorithmic function definition:

```
FUNC vend : Coin # Selection -> Product
IN   c,s
DEF  ( price(price_table,s) <= validate(value_table,c) ?
```

```
     ; yield(product_table,s)
     )
```

For a given coin and selection, **vend** yields the selected product if its price is not greater than the value of the coin. Otherwise, **vend** does not yield a result. So the function **vend** is not recursively used in this definition.

If *fbody* is of the form FREE, then the definition is a *forward* declaration: the actual definition of a function f from $T_1 \times \ldots \times T_m$ to $V_1 \times \ldots \times V_n$ is supposed to be given elsewhere, but its name may already be used. Definitions of this kind are called *free* definitions.

In the specification of VENDING2, all functions used in the definition of vend are supposed to be defined later:

```
FUNC validate : ValueTable # Coin      -> Value     FREE
FUNC price    : PriceTable # Selection -> Value      FREE
FUNC yield    : ProdTable  # Selection -> Product    FREE

FUNC value_table   : -> ValueTable   FREE
FUNC price_table   : -> PriceTable   FREE
FUNC product_table : -> ProdTable    FREE
```

The first three functions will turn out to be constant functions and the latter three functions will turn out to be variable functions. But the actual choices between constant function and variable function are postponed.

3.4   Patterns for Predicate Definitions

A predicate definition in COLD-1 has the following general form:

```
PRED r : T₁ # ... # Tₙ
IN    x₁, ..., xₙ
rbody
```

Here PRED $r : T_1 \# \ldots \# T_n$ ($n \geq 0$) introduces a name for the predicate being defined. The T_is are sort names introduced elsewhere. The keyword PRED is a qualifier indicating that r is the name of a predicate and the domain type $T_1 \# \ldots \# T_n$ indicates that it is a predicate on $T_1 \times \ldots \times T_n$. Dependent on the context where the name occurs, the qualifier and/or the domain type may or should be omitted.

The object names $x_1, \ldots, x_n$ listed in the IN section are names for the arguments of the predicate being defined. They can be used to refer to the arguments in the predicate body *rbody*, if it is present. The IN section is optional. If this section is not present, the objects concerned can not be denoted by a name in the remainder of the definition.

The general form of predicate definitions is similar to the general form of function definitions, but OUT, PRE and POST sections can not be used. The reason is that there is no undefinedness nor anything like yielding a result in the case of a predicate. For any argument tuple $x_1, \ldots, x_n$, the predicate r is simply either true or false.

The predicate body *rbody*, if present, has one of the following forms:

1. VAR

2. DEP $e_1, \ldots, e_l$

3. IND A

4. DEF A

5. FREE

So the possible forms of function bodies and predicate bodies are essentially the same. The only (and obvious) difference is that, in the case of an algorithmic definition, functions are defined by an expression and predicates by an assertion.

If no predicate body is present, then the definition introduces a predicate that is constant. The predicate concerned can be further characterized, in a not necessarily unique way, by axioms.

As for functions, this kind of definition is usually found in specifications of primitive data types. For example, in a specification of finite sets one finds predicate definitions such as:

```
PRED is_in : Item # Set
```

The axiom characterizing the predicate `is_in` will be:

```
AXIOM FORALL i,j : Item, s : Set
      ( NOT is_in(i,empty)
      ; is_in(i,ins(j,s)) <=> i = j OR is_in(i,s)
      )
```

This axiom covers all cases because an object of sort `Set`, i.e. finite sets with elements of sort `Item`, can always be constructed by a finite number of applications of the function `ins` – `ins`(j,s) adds the element j to the set s – starting from the empty set `empty`.

If *rbody* is of the form VAR, then the definition introduces a predicate that is variable and can vary independently of other variable state components. The predicate concerned can be further characterized by axioms.

Suppose that each file in the file system considered above is either read-only or not. This could, for example, be modelled by the variable predicate `read_only` defined by:

```
PRED read_only : File    VAR
```

Writing a byte in the file f is inhibited if `read_only`(f) is true.

In the above example, a variable predicate is used for a varying property of objects of some sort. The following example shows the use of a variable predicate for a varying relation between objects:

```
PRED connection : Line # Line    VAR
```

The variable predicate `connection` models connections between the incoming and outgoing lines of a switching system.

If *rbody* is of the form DEP $e_1, \ldots, e_l$, then the definition introduces a predicate that is variable, but may only vary if at least one of the entities $e_1, \ldots, e_l$ changes. The predicate concerned can be further characterized by axioms.

Suppose that executable files are distinguished by a special format. The dependent variable predicate `executable` defined by

```
PRED executable : File
IN   f
DEP  contents(f,$)
```

models this without fixing the special format of executable files.

If *rbody* is of the form IND A, where A is an assertion, then the definition introduces a predicate which may be constant or variable. The predicate concerned is uniquely characterized by the assertion A: r is the smallest predicate that satisfies the assertion A, provided that it exists. This means that if there are other predicates satisfying A then there are argument tuples for which they are true but the predicate r is not. However, the existence of a smallest predicate is not guaranteed for all assertions A (a sufficient syntactic condition is given below).

This kind of definition is usually found in specifications of primitive data types. The non-basic predicates are frequently characterized by inductive definitions. For example, in a specification of naturals one could have the following predicate definition for greater than:

```
PRED > : Nat # Nat
IND  FORALL m,n : Nat
     ( succ(m) > m
     ; m > n => succ(m) > n
     )
```

Inductive definitions of predicates are related to definitions of predicates in the logic programming language Prolog [18].

In COLD-1, there is the following sufficient syntactic condition for the existence of a smallest predicate: if a predicate r is inductively defined by an assertion A which is a conjunction of r-Horn clauses, the existence of a smallest predicate satisfying A is guaranteed. An *r-Horn clause* has the following general form:[*]

$$\text{FORALL } x_1 : T_1, \ldots, x_m : T_m \ (A_1 \text{ AND } \ldots \text{ AND } A_l => r(X_1, \ldots, X_n) \ )$$

Here each X_i is either an object name introduced by FORALL $x_1 : T_1, \ldots, x_m : T_m$ or any other expression provided that it always denotes an existing object in the context under consideration – such as the expression succ(m) in the above example. Moreover, each A_j is either an assertion not containing r or an assertion of the form $r(X'_1, \ldots, X'_n)$ where $X'_1, \ldots, X'_n$ are expressions. The existence of a smallest predicate satisfying A is also guaranteed if A is equivalent to a conjunction of r-Horn clauses obtained by distribution of the quantifier FORALL – such as the defining assertion in the above example.

In Prolog predicates are essentially defined by a conjunction of Horn clauses as well. For example, the inductive definition of > above could be mapped to Prolog as follows:

```
gt(succ(M),M).
gt(succ(M),N) :- gt(M,N).
```

The semantics of Prolog programs agrees with the interpretation of such definitions as inductive ones. Note that expressions are always denoting in Prolog, so a simpler definition of Horn clause can be given.

If *rbody* is of the form DEF A, where A is an assertion, then the definition introduces a predicate which may be constant or variable. The predicate concerned is uniquely characterized by the assertion A: r is the smallest predicate that satisfies the assertion

FORALL $x_1 : T_1, \ldots, x_n : T_n$ ($r(x_1, \ldots, x_n)$ <=> A)

provided that it exists.

Suppose that an end-of-file check (eof) is associated with every file in the file system. This could, for example, be modelled by the predicate eof defined by:

```
PRED eof : File
IN   f
DEF  NOT EXISTS i : Nat ( i >= offset(f) AND contents(f,i)! )
```

In COLD-1, the symbol ! is used for definedness of expressions. This means that the assertion contents(f,i)!, which is used above to define the predicate eof, holds if there is a byte at position i in file f. Algorithmic definitions of predicates can also be used to describe implementations of predicates.

In the case that they are variable, nullary predicates can be very useful. They can be viewed as a property of states. For example, when all outgoing lines of a switching system are in use then the system is blocked. A variable nullary predicate blocked with an algorithmic definition like

```
PRED blocked :
DEF  FORALL lo : Line
     ( outgoing(lo) => EXISTS li : Line ( connection(li,lo) ) )
```

could be used to model this.

If *rbody* is of the form FREE, then the definition is a *forward* declaration: the actual definition of a predicate r on $T_1 \times \ldots \times T_n$ is supposed to be given elsewhere, but its name may already be used.

Suppose that files can be shared, but that it is important to distinguish the uses of a file by sharing. This can be established by means of intermediate links. For each shared use, a new, unique link will be used. In order to

postpone the choice between taking this link from a fixed collection or creating
it dynamically, one could have the following preliminary predicate definition:

```
PRED is_new : Link    FREE
```

3.5   Patterns for Sort Definitions

A sort definition in COLD-1 has the following general form:

```
SORT T
sbody
```

Here SORT T introduces a name for the sort being defined. The keyword SORT
is a qualifier indicating that T is the name of a sort. Dependent on the context
where the name occurs, the qualifier may or should be omitted.

The general form of sort definitions is similar to the general form of predicate definitions, but IN sections can not be used. This difference is not surprising for sorts do not take arguments.

The sort body *sbody*, if present, has one of the following forms:

1. VAR

2. DEP $e_1, \ldots, e_l$

3. FREE

Inductive and algorithmic definitions of sorts can not be given. So the sort
concerned is never uniquely characterized by the definition.

If no sort body is present, then the definition introduces a sort that is
constant.

As for functions and predicates, this kind of definition is usually found in
specifications of basic data types such as Boolean values, natural numbers and
characters. For example, in the specification of Boolean values one finds the
sort definition:

```
SORT Bool
```

The objects of sort Bool should not be confused with the truth values. Objects
of sort Bool are not used to classify formulae, but unlike truth values, they can
be computed by means of operations defined on them. The sort Bool could be
uniquely characterized by the axiom:

```
AXIOM true!;
      false!;
      NOT true = false;
      FORALL b : Bool ( b = true OR b = false )
```

Sort definitions without a sort body also occur in specifications of application
specific data types such as queries in the case of database management systems:

```
SORT Query
```

Amongst the axioms characterizing the sort `Query` one could have

```
AXIOM FORALL p : Query, el : ExprList, q : Qual
      ( s_exprl(p) = el AND s_qual(p) = q <=>
        p = mk_query(el,q) )
```

to make sure that, for example, $mk\_query(el_1,q_1) \neq mk\_query(el_2,q_2)$ if $el_1 \neq el_2$ or $q_1 \neq q_2$.

If *sbody* is of the form `VAR`, then the definition introduces a sort that is variable and can vary independently of other state components. Variable sorts can grow dynamically, but they can not shrink. In most cases, a procedure for dynamic object creation will be associated with a variable sort. A typical use of the objects to be created is as elements of data structures that are built dynamically.

In the file system considered above, files are such objects. So the sort `File` is defined by:

```
SORT File   VAR
```

The axioms characterizing the sort `File` might include:

```
AXIOM FORALL f : File, i : Nat
      ( contents(f,i + 1)! => contents(f,i)! )

AXIOM INIT => NOT EXISTS f : File ()
```

If *sbody* is of the form `DEP` $e_1, \dots, e_l$, then the definition introduces a sort that is variable, but may only vary if at least one of the entities $e_1, \dots, e_l$ changes.

Suppose that directories can be nested, i.e. they map names to files and (sub-)directories. Sometimes, it is a nuisance if files and directories can not be treated on an equal footing. This can be remedied by introducing directory elements which combine files and directories. This could, for example, be modelled by the dependent variable sort `DirElem` defined by:

```
SORT DirElem   DEP File,Dir
```

If *sbody* is of the form `FREE`, then the definition is a *forward* declaration: the actual definition of a sort T is supposed to be given elsewhere, but its name may already be used.

For example, one should add the following preliminary sort definition to the preliminary definition of the predicate `is_new` given above:

```
SORT Link   FREE
```

3.6   Patterns for Procedure Definitions

A procedure definition in COLD-1 has the following general form:

```
PROC p : T₁ # ...# Tₘ -> V₁ # ...# Vₙ
IN    x₁, ... ,xₘ
OUT   y₁, ... ,yₙ
PRE   pre
pbody
POST  post
```

Here PROC $p : T_1$ # $\ldots$ # T_m -> V_1 # $\ldots$ # V_n $(m, n \geq 0)$ introduces a name for the procedure being defined. The T_is and V_is are sort names introduced elsewhere. The keyword PROC is a qualifier indicating that p is the name of a procedure. The domain type T_1 # $\ldots$ # T_m and the range type V_1 # $\ldots$ # V_n indicate that it is a procedure that takes argument tuples from $T_1 \times \ldots \times T_m$ and yields result tuples from $V_1 \times \ldots \times V_n$. Dependent on the context where the name occurs, the qualifier and/or the domain and range type may or should be omitted.

The object names $x_1, \ldots, x_m$ listed in the IN section are names for the arguments of the procedure being defined and the object names $y_1, \ldots, y_n$ listed in the OUT section are names for the results. The PRE and POST sections contain assertions *pre* and *post*, respectively, in which these names are generally used to refer to the arguments and the results. They can also be used for that purpose in the procedure body *pbody*, if it is present. The IN and OUT sections are both optional. If these sections are not present, the objects concerned can not be denoted by a name in the remainder of the definition.

Procedures defined in COLD-1 either succeed or fail. The PRE section is used to bound the circumstances under which the procedure p must succeed: the states s and argument tuples $x_1, \ldots, x_m$ for which the pre-condition *pre* holds are exactly those for which it must be the case that $p(x_1, \ldots, x_m)$ succeeds in s. The POST section is used to delimit the possible effects of p: if $p(x_1, \ldots, x_m)$ transforms state s to state t yielding the result tuple $y_1, \ldots, y_n$, then the post-condition *post* must hold between s, $x_1, \ldots, x_m$, t and $y_1, \ldots, y_n$. The PRE and POST sections are optional as well. If not present, no restrictions of the kind concerned have to be met.

The general form of procedure definitions is similar to the general form of function definitions. However, the possible forms of procedure bodies are different.

The procedure body *pbody*, if present, has one of the following forms:

1. SAT X

2. DEF X

3. FREE

The possible forms of procedure bodies do not include VAR and DEP $e_1, \ldots, e_l$. The reason is that procedures transform states to states, but they can not vary from state to state. Furthermore, inductive definitions of procedures can not be given. The form SAT X is completely new.

If no procedure body is present, then the definition introduces a procedure that must leave the state unchanged. The difference with a function is then that the procedure may be non-deterministic, i.e. it is not restricted to yield always the same result for the same arguments. The procedure concerned can be further characterized, in a not necessarily unique way, by the pre- and post-condition of the definition or by axioms.

So this kind of procedure definition is used instead of a function definition if non-deterministic behaviour is allowed. For example, in a specification of a file system one could have the following definition for a procedure to show a path from the root to the current working directory:

```
PROC pwd : -> Path
OUT  p
PRE  TRUE
POST dir(root,p) = working
```

Objects of sort `Path` can be viewed as sequences of names. They are paths leading from one directory to another directory or a file. In the post-condition, `dir` is a function used to map paths to the directory that they refer to and `root` and `working` are variable functions used to keep track of the root directory and the current working directory, respectively. According to the pre- and post-condition, `pwd` may be any procedure that always succeeds and returns a path from the root directory to the current working directory. With sharing of directories, it is essential to say *a* path because there may be several such paths.

In the specification of `PWD` (now for password), given in Section 4.3, there is a procedure definition in which both the procedure body and the `POST` section are not present:

```
PROC login : Code ->
IN   c
PRE  c = pwd.var
```

According to this definition, the `login` procedure succeeds if the code c used as password is the same as the code currently stored in the (hidden) variable `pwd.var` and fails otherwise.

If *pbody* is of the form `SAT` X, where X is an expression, then the definition introduces a procedure that may only have effects that X can have: if X can not transform state s to state t yielding the tuple of objects $y_1, \ldots, y_n$, then $p(x_1, \ldots, x_m)$ can not transform s to t yielding $y_1, \ldots, y_n$. The procedure concerned can be further characterized, in a not necessarily unique way, by the pre- and post-condition of the definition or by axioms.

A typical use of the `SAT` section is the expression of modification rights. For example, in a specification of a file system one could have the following definition for a procedure to change the current working directory:

```
PROC cd : Path ->
IN   p
```

```
PRE   dir(working,p)!
SAT   MOD working
POST  working = dir(working',p)
```

According to the pre- and post-condition, cd may be any procedure that terminates successfully with the current working directory (working) changed to the one that the given path p stands for if p leads to an existing directory. According to the SAT section, cd must additionally be a procedure that only modifies the current working directory.

Another example is the definition of the procedure select in the specification of VENDING3 (Section 2.2):

```
PROC select : Selection ->
IN    s
PRE   control_state = coin_checked
SAT   MOD selection,control_state
POST  selection = s AND control_state = product_selected
```

The selection of a product may only succeed if the coin inserted by the user has been checked for validity. In that case the user's selection and the control state are updated. The SAT section expresses that nothing else may be updated.

In the SAT section, SKIP may be used to express that the procedure being defined has no modification rights. This means that, from a semantic point of view, the absence of a procedure body is indistinguishable from SAT SKIP. For example, the earlier definition of the procedure login is semantically equivalent to the following definition with a procedure body of the form SAT X:

```
PROC login : Code ->
IN    c
PRE   c = pwd.var
SAT   SKIP
POST  TRUE
```

A POST section is added in addition to a SAT section. This can be done because the absence of a POST section is indistinguishable from POST TRUE.

If *pbody* is of the form DEF X, where X is an expression, then the definition introduces a procedure that is uniquely characterized by X. The procedure p is such that, for all tuples of existing arguments $x_1, \ldots, x_m$, $p(x_1, \ldots, x_m)$ can transform state s to state t yielding the tuple of results $y_1, \ldots, y_n$ if and only if X can transform s to t yielding $y_1, \ldots, y_n$. The procedure concerned may additionally be characterized by the pre- and post-condition of the definition or by axioms, but this gives easily rise to inconsistencies.

An example is the definition of an implementation of the procedure select, given above, in the specification of MACHINE (Section 2.4):

```
PROC select : Selection ->
IN    s
PRE   control_state = coin_checked
DEF   set_selection(s) ; set_control_state(product_selected)
```

This procedure `select` implements the earlier one by two assignments to programming variables in sequential order.

Algorithmic procedure definitions remain abstractions of those in the current imperative programming languages such as Pascal, C and Ada. But, if only the subset of COLD-1 is used that is called PROTOCOLD [19], they can be compiled and executed for prototyping and product design purposes.

If *pbody* is of the form FREE, then the definition is a *forward* declaration: the actual definition of a procedure *p* is supposed to be given elsewhere, but its name may already be used.

For example, the following preliminary procedure definition might be useful when specifying a spooler for a printer:

```
PROC new_paper : Nat ->   FREE
```

3.7   Axioms and Theorems

Axioms and theorems in COLD-1 have the following general forms:

```
AXIOM A
```

```
THEOREM A
```

Both axioms and theorems occur in the scope of certain definitions. They introduce properties of the sorts, functions, predicates and procedures concerned; and connections between them. An axiom AXIOM *A* introduces a postulated property: it excludes sorts, functions, predicates and procedures for which *A* does not hold in all states. A theorem THEOREM *A* introduces a conjectured property: it should follow from the definitions and axioms that *A* holds in all states. So axioms are used to characterize sorts, functions, predicates and procedures by stating some of their properties and theorems are used to indicate that other properties are to be expected from the characterized sorts, functions, predicates and procedures.

Axioms are usually found in specifications of primitive data types. Equations are frequently used as the basic constituents of axioms. For example, in a specification of natural numbers one could have the following axiom:

```
AXIOM 0!;
      FORALL m,n : Nat
      ( succ(m)!
      ; NOT succ(m) = 0
      ; succ(m) = succ(n) => m = n
      ; is_gen(n)
      )
```

where `is_gen` is a predicate inductively defined by:

```
PRED is_gen : Nat
IND  is_gen(0);
```

```
FORALL n : Nat ( is_gen(n) => is_gen(succ(n)) )
```

Note that the above axiom introduces a postulated property about the sort Nat as well as the functions 0 and succ. Such global properties can not be expressed in the definitions introducing Nat, 0 and succ. This situation does not only occur in the specification of static, functional data types. It also occurs in dynamic, state-based data types or systems.

Consider the dynamic data type of directories with variable sort Dir and variable functions file and dir:

```
SORT Dir                          VAR

FUNC file : Dir # Name -> File    VAR

FUNC dir  : Dir # Name -> Dir     VAR
```

The functions file and dir are used to select by name files and sub-directories, respectively, from a directory. Within any directory, a name does not refer to both a file and a directory. This is expressed by the axiom:

```
AXIOM FORALL d : Dir, n : Name
      ( NOT ( file(d,n)! AND dir(d,n)! ) )
```

For dynamic data types there may also be properties that must hold in the initial state only or before and after execution of certain procedures. This can be expressed as well. In the case of directories, for example, one could express by the following axiom that there are no directories initially:

```
AXIOM INIT => NOT EXISTS d : Dir ()
```

Theorems are useful in any specification. Consider again the file system example. From the axioms about files and the definition of the predicate eof given earlier, it should follow that offset(f) indicates a position at which a byte is stored if eof(f) is false. This is expressed by the theorem:

```
THEOREM FORALL f : File
        ( NOT eof(f) => contents(f,offset(f))! )
```

Theorems are often used to relate the dynamic behaviour of a system with the basic concepts underlying it. In the specification of VENDING3, given in Section 2.2, procedures insert, check, select and produce are defined in pre- and post-condition style to model the dynamic behaviour of a vending machine. In VENDING5, a theorem is added to VENDING3 to express that it should follow from the definitions and axioms concerned that for a given coin c and selection s, the sequential execution of these procedures in the order of their enumeration above yields the selected product, i.e. the product referred to by vend(c,s), provided that in the state in which the execution starts the vending machine is idle, the coin c is valid and has enough value to pay the price the product corresponding to the selection s. This is a theorem that relates the dynamic behaviour of a vending machine with the basic concept of vending.

3.8   Assertions

In COLD-1, assertions are primarily used in inductive definitions, definitions
in pre- and post-condition style, axioms and theorems. Assertions are mainly
taken from (many-sorted) classical first-order logic [20] and dynamic logic [21].

The assertions of the following forms correspond to formulae of classical
first-order logic:

```
TRUE
FALSE
NOT A
A₁ AND A₂
A₁ OR A₂
A₁ XOR A₂
A₁ => A₂
A₁ <=> A₂
FORALL x₁ : T₁, ... ,xₙ : Tₙ ( A )
EXISTS x₁ : T₁, ... ,xₙ : Tₙ ( A )
X₁ = X₂
r(X)
```

where A, A_1, A_2 are assertions, X, X_1, X_2 are expressions, $x_1, \ldots, x_n$ are object
names (object names are logical variables), $T_1, \ldots, T_n$ are sort names and r is
a predicate name. Expressions of the following forms correspond to terms of
classical first-order logic:

```
x
()
X₁,X₂
ƒ(X)
```

where X, X_1, X_2 are also of one of these forms, x is an object name and f is a
function name. Expressions of these forms are deterministic and have no side
effects. Other COLD-1 expressions are allowed as well. Non-determinism and
side-effects are dealt with as follows. For an assertion of the form $X_1 = X_2$ or
$r(X)$, the possible side-effects of the expressions X_1, X_2 and X are discarded.
Further, the assertion concerned is interpreted as false if one of the expressions
involved is non-deterministic, i.e. does not yield a unique result. Note that,
in COLD-1, the notation for tupling (X_1, X_2) is not only available in function
and predicate application. Expressions are treated in more detail in the next
section.

In assertions, "()" can be used instead of TRUE. ";" can be used instead of
AND, but its priority is lower than that of AND and the other connectives. In

the various forms of assertions and expressions given in the current section and the next one, sub-expressions and -assertions are sometimes enclosed in parentheses. Under certain circumstances, these parentheses are optional. Further details are given in Section A.4.

The assertions and terms of the above forms should be interpreted as usual, but with respect to a given state because sorts, functions and predicates may vary from state to state. Some remarks concerning the existence of objects are in order. Terms may fail to denote a tuple of existing objects. Such terms are *undefined*. A term of the form X_1, X_2 is interpreted as undefined if either X_1 or X_2 is undefined. Analogously, a term of the form $f(X)$ is interpreted as undefined if the term X is undefined. An assertion of the form $r(X)$ is interpreted as false if the term X is undefined. This is also the case for equality: an assertion of the form $X_1 = X_2$ is interpreted as false if either X_1 or X_2 is undefined. In FORALL and EXISTS assertions the object names range over existing objects of the sorts concerned only. In addition to the built-in existential equality predicate "=", there is a built-in (unary) *definedness* predicate "!". As a consequence there are also assertions of the following additional form:

X!

X! holds if X is defined, i.e. denotes a tuple of existing objects. Just as with other predicates, an assertion of the form X! is interpreted as false if the term X is undefined.

Some other predicates, which can be defined in terms of the two above-mentioned built-in predicates, are available as well, viz. "^", "==", "/=" and "/==". They can best be explained as abbreviations:

X^   stands for NOT X!
X_1 == X_2 stands for $X_1 = X_2$ OR X_1^ AND X_2^
X_1 /= X_2 stands for NOT $X_1 = X_2$
X_1 /== X_2 stands for NOT X_1 == X_2

Interesting is the non-existential equality predicate "==": X_1 == X_2 holds not only if $X_1 = X_2$ holds, but also if X_1 and X_2 are both undefined.

Many assertions used in specifications of static data types are of the forms that correspond to formulae of classical first order logic. In a specification of ordered pairs, for example, one finds axioms such as:

```
AXIOM FORALL i1,j1 : Item1, i2,j2 : Item2
     ( tup(i1,i2) = tup(j1,j2) => i1 = j1 AND i2 = j2 )
```

Assertions about variable sorts, functions and predicates can be of these forms as well, viz. the assertions expressing their state-independent properties.

For example, in the specification of VENDING6, given in Section 2.2, there is the following axiom:

```
AXIOM dom(price_table) = dom(product_table)
```

This axiom expresses that, in all states, the selections for which there are prices are exactly the selections for which there are products.

Properties of the initial state, state transitions, etc., in other words properties concerning dynamic behaviour, require assertions of additional forms if they have to be expressed as axioms or theorems.

The additional forms in COLD-1 are:

```
INIT
FIN X
AFTER X THEN A
PREV A
ISNEW X
```

where A is an assertion and X is an expression. In general, FIN and AFTER assertions are not very useful if the expressions concerned have no side-effects. This means that these expressions are usually statements (see Section 3.9).

FIN and AFTER assertions are taken from dynamic logic, where they are usually represented as $< X >$ TRUE and $[X] A$, respectively. PREV assertions are also found in several variants of temporal logic (see e.g. [22]), where they are usually represented as $\ominus A$. ISNEW assertions are loosely connected with both dynamic logic and temporal logic.

The interpretation of the assertions of these forms is as follows:

- INIT holds in a state if and only if that state is the initial state;

- FIN X holds in a state if and only if X can transform that state to the same or another state;

- AFTER X THEN A holds in a state if and only if A holds in all states to which that state can be transformed by X;

- PREV A, which can only be used in AFTER assertions and POST sections of procedure definitions, holds in a state if and only if A holds in the previous state;

- ISNEW X, which can only be used in AFTER assertions and POST sections of procedure definitions, holds in a state if and only if X denotes an existing object in that state but not in the previous state.

INIT, FIN and AFTER assertions allow to express properties of the initial state and state transitions which are either postulated properties that are not expressible in the PRE and POST sections of procedure definitions or conjectured properties. The specification of a file system could contain the axiom

```
AXIOM INIT => NOT root! AND NOT working!
```

for expressing that there exists neither a root directory nor a current working directory in the initial state of the file system.

FIN and AFTER assertions are closely related to pre- and post-conditions.
They are frequently used in theorems. An example is the following theorem,
which expresses that any of the file operations succeeds in a state where no
file satisfies the end-of-file condition:

```
THEOREM FORALL f : File ( NOT eof(f) ) =>
         ( FIN FLUSH create
         ; FIN FLUSH read($)
         ; FIN write($,$)
         ; FIN rewrite($)
         )
```

FLUSH expressions (see Section 3.9) are used here to discard the results yielded
by the statements create and read($). AFTER assertions can also be used to
strenghten post-conditions of procedures. For example, in the specification of
VENDING6, given in Section 2.2, there is the following axiom:

```
AXIOM control_state = coin_inserted =>
      AFTER check
      THEN  value > 0 => value_table = rem(value_table',coin)
```

When the procedure check was defined in VENDING3, only a preliminary definition of the sort ValueTable was available. Therefore, the possible effect of
this procedure on value_table could not be given there.

PREV assertions are closely related to the '-notation, e.g. PREV NOT eof(f)
is logically equivalent to NOT eof'(f).

ISNEW assertions are used to characterize procedures for dynamic object
creation:

```
PROC create : -> File
OUT  f
PRE  TRUE
SAT  MOD File ; $
POST ISNEW f; FORALL g : File ( ISNEW g  => f = g );
     FORALL i : Nat ( NOT contents(f,i)! ); offset(f) = 0
```

So create creates a new empty file with its own, unique identity.

3.9 Expressions

In COLD-1, expressions are primarily used in algorithmic definitions, definitions in pre- and post-condition style (in the SAT section) and, of course, in
assertions occurring in definitions, axioms and theorems. Three kinds of expressions can be distinguished: terms, algorithmic expressions and statements.
Terms must be deterministic and have no side-effects. Both other kinds of expressions may be non-deterministic and only statements may have side-effects.

The expressions of the following forms are terms provided that the sub-
expressions concerned are terms as well:

x
$()$
X_1 , X_2
$f(X)$
THAT $x_1 : T_1 , \ldots , x_n : T_n$ (A)
PREV X

where A is an assertion, X, X_1, X_2 are expressions, $x, x_1, \ldots, x_n$ are object names, $T_1, \ldots, T_n$ are sort names and f is a function name.

If the sub-expressions are terms as well, these expressions can be interpreted as terms. When interpreted as terms, the expressions of the first and fourth form should be interpreted as usual, but just as the others with respect to a given state. Expressions of the form X_1, X_2 denote tuples of objects in the obvious way. They are used for application of functions with more than one argument. () denotes the empty tuple. Expressions of the last two forms should be interpreted as follows:

- THAT $x_1 : T_1 , \ldots , x_n : T_n$ (A) denotes the unique tuple of objects $x_1, \ldots, x_n$ such that A holds (if there does not exist such a unique tuple, the term is undefined);

- PREV X, which can only be used in AFTER assertions and POST sections of procedure definitions, denotes the tuple of objects denoted by X in the previous state.

Under the general interpretation, a term can be viewed as a statement that does not transform the state concerned and yields a result that is unique for that state.

Terms of the form THAT $x_1 : T_1 , \ldots , x_n : T_n$ (A), which are known as *descriptions*, are present in many variants of classical first-order logic. The following description can be used to refer to the byte which usually represents the space character in a text file:

THAT b : Byte (nat(b) = 32)

Descriptions can always be eliminated from assertions.

Terms of the form PREV X are also found in a few variants of temporal logic. Just as assertions of the form PREV A, they are closely related to the '-notation, e.g. PREV file(d,n) is equivalent to file'(d,n).

Terms are preferred in assertions of the forms $X!$, $X_1 = X_2$ and $r(X)$. It is worth noticing again that expressions of other forms than the above-mentioned ones are syntactically permitted, in which case possible side-effects are discarded and the assertions do not hold if some of the expressions concerned are non-deterministic. For example, assuming the definitions of eof and create given before, neither create! nor eof(create) hold in any state. Assuming that f1 and f2 are object names, eof(f1 | f2) may hold in some state provided that f1 and f2 denote the same object or one of the two is undefined. The use of assertions like eof(f1 | f2) is certainly not recommended, because they may cause a lot of confusion.

The algorithmic expressions include all expressions of the above forms. If a sub-expression of the expression concerned is an algorithmic expression, the prevalent non-determinism is fully inherited. For example, $f(X)$ will yield the value of f for one of the results that can be yielded by X.

In addition, the expressions of the following forms are algorithmic expressions provided that the sub-expressions concerned are algorithmic expressions as well:

A ?; X
X_1 | X_2
SOME $x_1 : T_1 , \ldots , x_n : T_n$ (A)

where A is an assertion, X, X_1, X_2 are expressions, $x_1, \ldots, x_n$ are object names and $T_1, \ldots, T_n$ are sort names.

$ can be used instead of SOME $x : T$ (). This leads to an extreme overloading of $. How this is resolved is sketched in Section 5.6 by means of an example.

If the sub-expressions are algorithmic expressions as well, these expressions can be interpreted as algorithmic expressions. When interpreted as algorithmic expressions, the expressions of these forms should be interpreted as follows:

- A ?; X yields a result if and only if A holds and X yields that result;

- X_1 | X_2 yields a result if and only if either X_1 or X_2 does so;

- SOME $x_1 : T_1 , \ldots , x_n : T_n$ (A) yields an arbitrary tuple of objects $x_1, \ldots, x_n$ for which A holds.

Under the general interpretation, an algorithmic expression can be viewed as a statement that does not transform the state concerned. Viewed as statements, expressions of the form A ?; X are of the more general form X_1 ; X_2 because A ? has a meaningful interpretation as a statement.

Algorithmic expressions are mainly used in algorithmic definitions of functions. They support function definition in a functional programming style. Various constructs for conditional evaluation can be regarded as abbreviations built from algorithmic expressions of the forms A ?; X and X_1 | X_2:

if A then X_1 else X_2

can be viewed as an abbreviation for

(A ?; X_1 | NOT A ?; X_2)

An example is the following definition of the factorial function:

```
FUNC fac : Nat -> Nat
IN   n
DEF  ( n = 0      ?; 1
     | NOT n = 0 ?; n * fac(n - 1)
     )
```

Algorithmic expressions of the forms $X_1 \mid X_2$ and SOME $x_1 : T_1, \ldots, x_n : T_n (A)$ can also be used to introduce non-determinism in order to postpone implementation details. For example, an arbitrary sequence of all integers in a set s is described by:

```
SOME l : IntSeq ( elems(l) = s )
```

Thus the order in which the elements are put in the sequence is not fixed. For another example, consider again the file system. The following expression stands for an arbitrary name that is not used in the directory d:

```
SOME n : Name ( NOT file(d,n)! AND NOT dir(d,n)! )
```

The statements include all expressions of the above forms. If a sub-expression of the expression concerned is a statement, its side-effects are fully inherited. For example, $f(X)$ can transform a state to another state if and only if X can do so.

In addition, the expressions of the following forms are statements:

```
MOD e₁, ... ,eₙ
NEW T₁, ... ,Tₙ
p(X)
A ?
X₁ ; X₂
X₁ | X₂
X *
FLUSH X
```

where A is an assertion, X, X_1, X_2 are expressions, $e_1, \ldots, e_n$ are entities, $T_1, \ldots, T_n$ are sort names and p is a procedure name.

STOP and SKIP can be used instead of FALSE? and TRUE?, respectively.

The expressions of the first three forms are the basic modification statements of COLD-1 and the expressions of the remaining forms are used to build composite statements from them. The interpretation of the expressions for basic modifications is as follows:

- MOD $e_1, \ldots, e_n$ succeeds in every state, it can transform that state to any other state wherein all entities but $e_1, \ldots, e_n$ are left unchanged and it does not yield a result – or more precisely an empty tuple of results;

- NEW $T_1, \ldots, T_n$ succeeds in every state, it can transform that state to any other state wherein the variable sorts $T_1, \ldots, T_n$ have been changed by adding a new object to each of these sorts and it yields a tuple of the added objects (where the ith object is the new object of sort T_i);

- $p(X)$ can transform a state to another state and yield a tuple of objects if and only if p can do so for some tuple of objects that can be yielded by X in the former state.

In programming languages, an expression of the form $p(X)$ is known as a *procedure call* and an expression of the form MOD $e_1, \ldots, e_n$ is known as a *random assignment*.

Statements are not only used in algorithmic definitions of procedures, but also in procedure definitions in pre- and post-condition style. In the latter case a statement appears in the SAT section. That statement is often just a random assignment statement. For example, in the definition of the procedure select in the specification of VENDING3 (Section 2.2), the following SAT section is given:

```
SAT  MOD selection,control_state
```

This expresses the modification rights of select: it may only update the variable functions selection and control_state. NEW statements can be viewed as MOD statements specialized for modifying variable sorts; they appear in the SAT section of procedures for dynamic object creation. The following definition of the procedure create is equivalent to the definition given earlier, but uses a NEW statement in the SAT section instead of a MOD statement:

```
PROC create : -> File
OUT  f
PRE  TRUE
SAT  NEW File
POST FORALL i : Nat ( NOT contents(f,i)! ) ; offset(f) = 0
```

Note that the POST section is simpler as well. Dynamic object creation occurs in more ways than is usually realized. For example, copying a file is an instance of dynamic object creation:

```
PROC cp : File -> File
IN   f1
OUT  f2
PRE  TRUE
SAT  NEW File
POST FORALL i : Nat ( contents(f1,i) == contents(f2,i) );
     offset(f2) = 0
```

The interpretation of the expressions of the forms meant for building composite statements, is as follows:

- A ? succeeds in a state if and only if A holds in that state, it does not transform that state and it does not yield a result – or more precisely an empty tuple of results;

- X_1 ; X_2 can transform a state to a second state if and only if X_1 can transform the first state to an intermediate state and X_2 can transform that intermediate state to the second state and it yields the concatenation of the results yielded by X_1 and X_2;

- $X_1 \mid X_2$ can transform a state to another state yielding a result if and only if either X_1 or X_2 can do so;

- $X * $ can transform a state to another state if and only if zero or more repetitions of X can do so (X is not allowed to yield a result).

So statements of the form A ?, including STOP and SKIP, have no side-effects. If statements without side-effects are combined using ";" or "|", then the resulting statements have no side-effects as well. Statements of the form A ?, including STOP and SKIP, are also deterministic. If deterministic statements are combined using ";", then the resulting statements are deterministic as well.

In programming languages, an expression of the form A ? is known as a *guard*, an expression of the form X_1 ; X_2 as a *sequential composition*, an expression of the form X_1 | X_2 as a *non-deterministic choice* and an expression of the form $X * $ as a *repetition*. The **if** and **while** statements from most programming languages can be regarded as abbreviations built from expressions of these forms:

if A **then** X_1 **else** X_2 and   **while** A **do** X

can be viewed as abbreviations for

(A ?; X_1 | NOT A ?; X_2)   and   (A ?; X) * ; NOT A ?

respectively. Note that sequential composition of statements that yield results leads to concatenation of the results.

In the following algorithmic procedure definition, guards, sequential composition and repetition are used:

```
PROC clear : File ->
IN   f
DEF  write(f,THAT b : Byte ( nat(b) = 0 )) * ; eof(f) ?
```

For a given file f, clear changes all bytes in f from the current offset till the end of the file to null bytes. A non-deterministic choice is used in the following statement:

```
( eof(f)      ?; THAT b : Byte ( nat(b) = 0 )
| NOT eof(f) ?; read(f)
)
```

It yields the next byte of the file f and increments the current offset if the end-of-file condition does not hold and yields a null byte without having any side-effect otherwise.

Guards permit to move the post-condition of a procedure definition from the POST section to the SAT section provided that it only refers to the current state. For example, the following definition of the procedure create is semantically equivalent to the previous one:

```
PROC create : -> File                          % not recommended
```

```
OUT   f
PRE   TRUE
SAT   ( NEW File
      ; FORALL i : Nat ( NOT contents(f,i)! ) AND offset(f) = 0 ?
      )
```

However, such practice is not recommended.

The interpretation of the expressions of the form FLUSH X is as follows:

- FLUSH X can transform a state to another state if and only if X can do so, but FLUSH X does not yield a result.

Expressions of the form FLUSH X are rather unusual and not found in programming languages, but their effect occurs implicitly in several programming languages (in C, for example, it is called "voiding"). A FLUSH expression is used to discard the result yielded by some statement. Its main use is in theorems about state transitions. An example is the following theorem, which expresses that in any state of the vending machine specified in VENDING3 (Section 2.2) one of its procedures succeeds:

```
THEOREM FIN ( insert
            | check
            | select
            | FLUSH produce
            )
```

Here we want to forget about the result yielded by produce, because otherwise the non-deterministic choice is meaningless.

In addition to the kinds of expressions treated above, there are expressions for giving names to objects. They can be used as sub-expressions in terms, algorithmic expressions and statements. They can even be used as sub-assertions in assertions. The constructs of the following forms are for giving names to objects:

$$\text{LET } x_1 : T_1, \ldots, x_n : T_n$$
$$x_1 : T_1, \ldots, x_n : T_n := X$$
BEGIN X END   (or BEGIN A END)

where A is an assertion, X is an expression, $x_1, \ldots, x_n$ are object names and $T_1, \ldots, T_n$ are sort names.

Constructs of the form LET $x_1 : T_1, \ldots, x_n : T_n := X$ can be used instead of the composition of the corresponding constructs of the first two forms.

The interpretation of the constructs of these forms is as follows:

- LET $x_1 : T_1, \ldots, x_n : T_n$ does the same as SKIP but in addition it introduces $x_1, \ldots, x_n$ as names for objects of the sorts $T_1, \ldots, T_n$;

- $x_1 : T_1, \ldots, x_n : T_n := X$ can do the same as X but it binds the names $x_1, \ldots, x_n$ to the elements of the tuple of objects yielded by X instead of

yielding that tuple if no objects are already bound to these names and
fails otherwise;

- BEGIN X END only differs from X in that it makes the object names
  visible in X externally invisible (BEGIN A END differs from A in the same
  way).

The algorithmic definition of the procedure clear given above is equivalent
to the following definition wherein a name is introduced for the null byte:

```
PROC clear : File ->
IN   f
DEF  LET nb : Byte := THAT b : Byte ( nat(b) = 0 ) ;
     write(f,nb) * ; eof(f) ?
```

Of course, giving names to objects is more useful if one has to refer to the
same object several times in a definition, axiom or theorem as in the following
example:

```
PROC read : File -> Byte
IN   f
OUT  b
PRE  NOT eof(f)
SAT  MOD offset(f) ; $
POST LET i : Nat := offset'(f) ;
     b = contents(f,i) ;
     offset(f) = i + 1
```

Giving names to objects is often needed when expressing a property of a non-
deterministic procedure that yields a result as in the following theorem:

```
THEOREM AFTER LET f : File := create THEN eof(f)
```

As explained in Section 3.8, eof(create) does not hold in any state because
create is non-deterministic. Use is made of the fact that f is an object name
with extendible scope; this fact permits its use in eof(f).

The rules governing scope extension for object names are as follows. LET
constructs, FORALL assertions, EXISTS assertions, THAT expressions and SOME
expressions all introduce object names. An object name so introduced has
limited visibility. The places where the object name is visible constitutes its
scope. If the object name is introduced by a FORALL assertion, the scope is
precisely the FORALL assertion concerned. Otherwise, the scope may extend
beyond the construct where the object name is introduced. The rules are such
that the scope extends where the existence of the object concerned may be
assumed without more ado. If the object name is visible in an assertion A_1 or
expression X_1 that does not terminate its scope, then its scope extends to a
textually following assertion A_2 or expression X_2 in the following cases:

A_1 AND A_2
A_1 ; A_2

$A_1 \Rightarrow A_2$
AFTER X_1 THEN A_2
X_1, X_2
$X_1 ; X_2$

Only assertions and expressions of the following forms do not terminate the scope of the object names visible inside them:

A_1 AND A_2
$A_1 ; A_2$
EXISTS $x_1 : T_1, \ldots, x_n : T_n$ (A)
PREV A
X_1, X_2
THAT $x_1 : T_1, \ldots, x_n : T_n$ (A)
PREV X
SOME $x_1 : T_1, \ldots, x_n : T_n$ (A)
A ?
$X_1 ; X_2$
FLUSH X

In Section 5.6, an algorithmic definition is given of a function **rem** which removes a set of elements from the domain of a map. That definition is equivalent to the following one which exhibits scope extension for the object name j:

```
FUNC rem : Map # Set[Item1] -> Map
IN   m,s
DEF  ( s = empty     ?; m
     | NOT s = empty ?;
         SOME j : Item1 ( is_in(j,s) ) ; rem(rem(m,j),diff(s,j))
     )
```

It is often useful to combine giving names to objects with decomposing tuples of results. Suppose that a display is modelled by the two variable nullary functions defined by:

```
FUNC screen : -> Text       PRE TRUE   VAR
FUNC cursor : -> Nat # Nat   PRE TRUE   VAR
```

One could have the following definition for a procedure corresponding to carriage return:

```
PROC cr : ->
PRE   TRUE
SAT   MOD cursor
POST LET i,j : Nat := cursor' ; cursor = (i,0)
```

To resolve type ambiguities, expressions of the following form are also provided:

$X :: T$

$X :: T$ has the same meaning as X. Such "casting" is only permitted if T is one of the possible types of X. Casting must not be confused with type conversion. If a type conversion is needed, it has to be defined as a function. See further Section 5.3, where also an example of casting can be found. In practice, it is seldom needed.

3.10   Concluding Remarks

In this chapter, the language constructs of COLD-1 for characterizing the states and state-transformers of a system are presented – like in programming languages, the state-transformers are called procedures in COLD-1. We see that the whole supports many existing styles of specification such as specification in equational style, specification in pre- and post-condition style, inductive definitions, algorithmic definitions in functional as well as imperative style, etc. Moreover, property-oriented, algebraic specification can be combined with model-oriented, state-based specification. All this means that systems can be described at many levels of detail, in any appropriate combination of styles and according to various paradigms.

Chapter 4
Patterns for Components

Today the factor of economy makes rationalization imperative in rental hous-
ing. On the other hand, the increased complexity of our requirements demands
flexibility. The future will have to reckon with both. For this purpose skeleton
construction is the most suitable system. It makes possible rationalized building
methods and allows the interior to be freely divided.

(Mies van der Rohe)

4.1   Introduction and Motivation

The objective of this chapter is to present the language constructs for modularization as provided by COLD-1. Focus will be on their form, the intended use,
and typical examples. Most examples will be taken from the vending machine
case of Chapter 2 and from the standard library of Appendix B. After reading
the chapter, the reader will have seen all relevant constructs of the language.

Components are units containing the definitions of sorts, functions, predicates, procedures, axioms and theorems, possibly importing other components
and with a certain degree of abstraction and information hiding. In principle, a system can be described as a long list of sorts, functions, predicates,
procedures, axioms and theorems, using the patterns for definitions presented
in Chapter 3. But this is not the right way to go: organizing things into
components brings structure into the system's description.

4.2   Basic Pattern

In order to write down components, there are typical patterns with keywords
such as COMPONENT, ABSTRACT, EXPORT, IMPORT, CLASS and END. This is helpful
for organizing all facts and dependencies of a component in a structured way.
A *component* is a module which has a name and a specification, possibly
different from its implementation(s). A typical component definition (with no
implementation) has the following form:

```
COMPONENT C[u₁,...,uₖ] SPECIFICATION
ABSTRACT A₁,...,Aₗ
EXPORT S
IMPORT B₁,...,Bₘ
CLASS D₁ ... Dₙ
END
```

The first line, COMPONENT $C[u_1,\ldots,u_k]$, introduces a component name which can be used later as a unique symbol to identify this component. The identifiers $u_1,\ldots,u_k$ are formal parameters. After the keyword SPECIFICATION, there are four optional sections which together constitute the specification of C.

The ABSTRACT section refers to components $A_1,\ldots,A_l$ which must contain specifications of the parameters (the $u_1,\ldots,u_k$), defining them as sorts or operations and stating further properties they must satisfy. The EXPORT section contains a list S of the names of the sorts and operations provided by C. S is the export signature of the component (the word *signature* comes from algebraic specification theory and it means "set of names"). All sorts and operations introduced by the two subsequent sections in so far as they are not exported remain local; they are said to be *hidden*. The IMPORT section lists the other components (the $B_1,\ldots,B_m$) which provide sorts and operations that can be used. Finally, the CLASS section contains a list of definitions (the $D_1,\ldots,D_n$), defining sorts, functions, predicates, procedures, axioms and theorems, all in the notations of Chapter 3.

By way of example we present a component HSVAR[Item], built according to the above pattern. The example is similar to the component SVAR presented in Section 2.3.1, except that it has a history variable counting the invocations of **set**. This procedure **set** has a non-trivial pre-condition, implying that it can be called at most 10 times; upon subsequent invocations it fails.

```
COMPONENT HSVAR[Item] SPECIFICATION
ABSTRACT
  ITEM
EXPORT
  FUNC var : -> Item
  PROC set : Item ->
IMPORT
  NAT
CLASS
  FUNC var : -> Item VAR
  FUNC his : -> Nat  VAR

  AXIOM INIT => his = 0

  PROC set : Item ->
  IN   i
  PRE  his < 10
  SAT  MOD var, his
```

```
        POST var = i;
             his = his' + 1
END
```

We can make distinct instantiations like HSVAR'[Nat] or HSVAR'[Bool], at least if we are in a context where the components providing Nat or Bool have been imported, as for example in the following import list:

```
IMPORT
  NAT,
  BOOL,
  HSVAR'[Nat],
  HSVAR'[Bool]
```

Next we discuss the purpose of the ABSTRACT section, the EXPORT section, and IMPORT section, comparing HSVAR with several alternative component definitions.

The ABSTRACT section of HSVAR refers to a component ITEM, which states that Item must be a sort. This prevents nonsense instantiations like HSVAR[10], where it is tried to use an operation as an actual parameter (assuming 10 refers to the operation FUNC 10: -> Nat). The instantiation HSVAR'[Bool] is equivalent to a non-generic component HSVARBOOL which could be defined directly as follows:

```
COMPONENT HSVARBOOL SPECIFICATION
EXPORT
  FUNC var : -> Bool
  PROC set : Bool ->
IMPORT
  BOOL,
  NAT
CLASS
  FUNC var : -> Bool VAR
  FUNC his : -> Nat  VAR

  AXIOM INIT => his = 0

  PROC set : Bool ->
  IN   i
  PRE  his < 10
  SAT  MOD var, his
  POST var = i;
       his = his' + 1
END
```

The EXPORT section of HSVAR is interesting because it does not contain his. It means that his is hidden, and when employing an instance of HSVAR, the history can not be observed directly. Yet the effect of his is still present, for only a limited number of sets can be done. Therefore the above definition is equivalent to the following, where a slightly different way of counting is adopted, viz. from 1 to 11, instead of from 0 to 10:

```
COMPONENT HSVAR_[Item] SPECIFICATION
ABSTRACT
  ITEM
EXPORT
  FUNC var : -> Item
  PROC set : Item ->
IMPORT
  NAT
CLASS
  FUNC var : -> Item  VAR
  FUNC his : -> Nat    VAR

  AXIOM INIT => his = 1

  PROC set : Item ->
  IN   i
  PRE  his < 11
  SAT  MOD var, his
  POST var = i;
       his = his' + 1
END
```

In general two components are equivalent if there is no difference in the set of facts (theorems) that follow from their definitions, provided we consider only those facts which can be expressed using the exported names only. So of course the fact INIT => his = 0 holds in HSVAR and not in HSVAR_, but this fact can not be expressed using exported names only because his is hidden. But facts like:

```
INIT => AFTER set(i); set(i); set(i); set(i); set(i);
              set(i); set(i); set(i); set(i); set(i);
              set(i)
        THEN FALSE
```

hold both for HSVAR and HSVAR_. Although the latter fact is a consequence of the way his is used, its formulation does not mention his. Facts of the latter kind determine the equivalence or non-equivalence of component definitions.

Hiding is a powerful specification technique; it allows us to write a model-oriented specification first and then remove the irrelevant facts by choosing the right export list.

The IMPORT section of HSVAR refers to the standard component NAT. Of course we could add the definitions of Nat and its operations together with appropriate axioms as a part of HSVAR instead, but importing NAT avoids such unnecessary duplication of information. In other words, HSVAR is equivalent to the much longer NATHSVAR given below.

```
COMPONENT NATHSVAR[Item] SPECIFICATION
ABSTRACT
  ITEM
EXPORT
  FUNC var : -> Item
  PROC set : Item ->
CLASS
  SORT Nat
  FUNC zero :        -> Nat
  FUNC succ : Nat -> Nat

  DECL m,n,q,r : Nat

  PRED is_gen: Nat
  IND  is_gen(zero);
       is_gen(m) => is_gen(succ(m))

  AXIOM
  {NAT1} zero!;
  {NAT2} succ(m)!;
  {NAT3} succ(m) /= zero;
  {NAT4} succ(m) = succ(n) => m = n;
  {NAT5} is_gen(n)

  PRED < : Nat # Nat
  IND  m < succ(m);
       m < n => m < succ(n)

  FUNC + : Nat # Nat -> Nat
  IND  m + zero = m;
       m + succ(n) = succ(m + n)
  % etc.

  FUNC var : -> Item   VAR
  FUNC his : -> Nat    VAR

  AXIOM INIT => his = 0

  PROC set : Item ->
  IN   i
  PRE  his < 10
  SAT  MOD var, his
  POST var = i;
       his = his' + 1
END
```

4.3   Using Components

When a component occurs in an abstraction or import list, it can be referenced,
by which we mean that parameters can be filled in and that further export
restrictions and renamings can be applied. In its simplest form, a reference to a
component is just a component name like NAT or BOOL as shown in the examples
of Section 4.2. However, there is a more general format, where most of the
sections are optional. When all sections are present, a component reference
looks as follows:

$$C' [v_1, \ldots, v_k] \text{ EXPORTING } \mathcal{S}$$
$$\text{RENAMING } \mathcal{R}$$
$$\text{QUALIFYING } a$$
$$\text{END}$$

It means: take a fresh copy of C, choosing actual parameters $v_1, \ldots, v_k$, exporting only $\mathcal{S}$, changing certain names (the renaming given by $\mathcal{R}$, see Section 4.5)
and such that all sort and operation names are prefixed by "a.". It is allowed
to omit the quote, in which case no copying takes place and C can be shared.

We give an example first. Consider the component PWD for "password"
given below, which uses an instance of SVAR. Recall from Section 2.3.1 that
the component SVAR has a variable function var and an update procedure
set. PWD can be interpreted as a conditional-access unit where a code can be
entered by a procedure called pwd.set and where the success or failure of a
login procedure depends on the login code and the code entered earlier. If c
is one of the codes 0, 1, 2, 3, 4, 5, 6, 7, 8, or 9, then execution of the sequence
pwd.set(c); login(c) terminates successfully, whereas for a code $d \neq c$, we
find that pwd.set(c); login(d) fails.

```
COMPONENT PWD SPECIFICATION
EXPORT
  PROC pwd.set : Code ->
  PROC login   : Code ->
IMPORT
  NAT' EXPORTING Nat,0,1,2,3,4,5,6,7,8,9
       RENAMING Nat TO Code
       END,
  SVAR'[Code] QUALIFYING pwd END
CLASS
  PROC login : Code ->
  IN   c
  PRE  c = pwd.var
END
```

There are two imported components, NAT and SVAR, each of which is used in
a particular way. Let us discuss the way NAT is referenced first:

```
NAT' EXPORTING Nat,0,1,2,3,4,5,6,7,8,9
```

```
RENAMING Nat TO Code
END
```

The quote after NAT indicates that we import a *copy* of NAT, which is the same as making another textual copy. So the codes 0, 1, 2, etc. are not just aliases of the natural numbers 0, 1, 2, etc. but they are elements of a disjoint set Code, which happen to have the same identifiers. The effect of the EXPORTING section is that only the names Nat and 0, 1, 2, 3, 4, 5, 6, 7, 8, 9, from NAT' are visible. So in the context of PWD, expressions like 5 + 6 can not be written down for codes. This is an additional narrowing of the export list of NAT, because NAT has already an export list of its own. The effect of the RENAMING section is that the identifier Nat is replaced by Code. In the CLASS section of PWD the resulting sort Code is used.

Next let us discuss the way SVAR is referenced:

```
SVAR'[Code] QUALIFYING pwd END
```

The copying (' notation) ensures that we get a storage cell as described by set and var of SVAR which is not shared by other components. For a detailed discussion on the copy operator (' notation) we refer to Section 4.8.

The parameter list [Code] indicates that Code is the actual parameter which comes instead of the formal parameter Item. This can be done because earlier in the same import list there is a renamed copy of NAT which provides this sort Code. Note that ITEM puts no other requirements upon Item (to be viewed here as requirements upon Code), except for the requirement that it must be a sort, and not an operation. The QUALIFYING section has the effect that all names defined in and exported by SVAR'[Code] are prefixed by "pwd."; the example is slightly artificial, but sometimes the feature of qualifying is convenient for avoiding name-clashes. A name is said to be *defined* in a component C if either its definition is contained in the CLASS section of C, or the name is defined in a copied component imported into C. (Note the recursion in this definition). Therefore set and var are turned into pwd.set and pwd.var respectively, whereas Code (which comes from the renamed NAT) is unaffected.

Now, we must have a closer look at the list of actual parameters $v_1, \ldots, v_k$. It occurs as $C'[v_1, \ldots, v_k]$ or $C[v_1, \ldots, v_k]$, which is only syntactically correct if C is a component defined as $C[u_1, \ldots, u_k]$, i.e. as a component with the same number of formal parameters. The formal parameters $u_1, \ldots, u_k$ must be viewed as unknowns, or placeholders, which are filled in during instantiation. The name v_1 replaces u_1, v_2 replaces u_2, etc.

Let us consider an instantiation $C'[v_1, \ldots, v_k]$ which occurs as a part of an IMPORT section and assume that $A_1, A_2, \ldots$ are the component references that precede it, in the sense that they occur earlier in the abstract section or import section of the component being defined. Then for each of the actual parameters (which is either a sort, a function, a predicate, or a procedure) it must be clear exactly where it is defined. There are two possibilities: either it is defined in one of the $A_1, A_2, \ldots$, or it is in the CLASS section of the component being defined. The following example shows both possibilities:

```
COMPONENT NAT_AND_CODE_VARS SPECIFICATION
EXPORT
  FUNC var : -> Nat,
       var : -> Code
  PROC set : Nat ->,
       set : Code ->
IMPORT
  NAT,
  SVAR'[Nat],
  SVAR'[Code]
CLASS
  SORT Code
  % ... (operations on Code)
END
```

The generic component SVAR[Item] is instantiated twice. The first instantiation has actual parameter Nat. So we should ask exactly where this Nat comes from. The answer is that is comes from NAT, because a reference to NAT occurs earlier in the same import list. The second instantiation has actual parameter Code. This Code comes from the CLASS section of NAT_AND_CODE_VARS itself, which is the second option mentioned above.

Some care is needed, because the order of component references in the import list is relevant. For example, the following is not in order, because the instantiation SVAR'[Nat] is not preceded by a component that provides the sort Nat.

```
COMPONENT NAT_VARS SPECIFICATION
EXPORT
  FUNC var : -> Nat
  PROC set : Nat ->
IMPORT
  SVAR'[Nat],                                          % wrong
  NAT
END
```

The mechanism of instantiating generic components with sorts or operations to be defined is very convenient. The following is an example of its use. We want to define a data type with constants r, g, b, p, y, w and we want these to be distinct values. Of course we could write $r \neq g$, $r \neq b$, etc. but the $5 + 4 + 3 + 2 + 1$ inequalities needed are a nuisance. The idea is to employ the standard data type SET which amongst other things has an insert operation ins, and a cardinality operation card. In practice we would define colours by reusing ENUM6 but the technique is worth remembering nevertheless.

```
COMPONENT COLOUR SPECIFICATION
EXPORT
```

```
     SORT Colour
     FUNC r : -> Colour,
          g : -> Colour,
          b : -> Colour,
          p : -> Colour,
          y : -> Colour,
          w : -> Colour
   IMPORT
     NAT,
     SET[Colour]
   CLASS
     SORT Colour

     FUNC r : -> Colour % red
     FUNC g : -> Colour % green
     FUNC b : -> Colour % blue
     FUNC p : -> Colour % pink
     FUNC y : -> Colour % yellow
     FUNC w : -> Colour % white

     AXIOM card(ins(r,ins(g,ins(b,ins(p,ins(y,ins(w,empty))))))) = 6
   END
```

There is a restriction which applies when a generic component is instantiated
with an operation defined in the CLASS section: in the actual parameter list of
a component name we may use any operation name that has been imported
"so far" (in either an abstraction or import list) or that has been defined
in the CLASS section, provided that the completed name of this operation
does not contain any sort names not yet imported or defined. We illustrate
this by means of an example referring to HASHMAP defined in Section 2.3.3
as HASHMAP[Item1,Item2,max,hash], where Item1 and Item2 must be sorts,
max must be a nullary function of type Nat and where hash is a unary function
from Item1 to Nat.

```
   COMPONENT USE_HASHMAP SPECIFICATION
   IMPORT
     NAT,
     HASHMAP[Nat,Nat,77,f]
   CLASS
     FUNC f : Nat -> Nat
     IN   n
     DEF  mod(n,77)
   END
```

The above is correct because the sort Nat and the constant 77 are introduced by
NAT, which precedes the instantiation HASHMAP [Nat,Nat,77,f]. Furthermore
the function f is defined in the CLASS section, and the sorts occurring in its full
name f : Nat -> Nat are also defined at the point preceding the instantiation.

We also give an example of incorrect use. In this example it is tried to construct a hashmap, mapping sequences of Booleans (bitstrings) to Booleans. The hash function f is defined as the number of **true** values modulo 77. The function **sum** is an auxiliary function which is defined recursively. It counts the number of **true** values.

```
COMPONENT WRONG_USE_HASHMAP SPECIFICATION
IMPORT
  BOOL,
  SEQ[Bool] EXPORTING Seq, hd, tl, empty END,
  HASHMAP[Seq,Bool,m,f],                                    % wrong
  NAT
CLASS
  FUNC sum : Seq -> Nat
  IN   s
  DEF  ( s  = empty ? ; 0
       | s /= empty ? ; ( hd(s) = false ? ; sum(tl(s))
                        | hd(s) = true  ? ; sum(tl(s)) + 1
       )                )

  FUNC m : -> Nat
  DEF  77

  FUNC f : Seq -> Nat
  IN   s
  DEF  mod(sum(s),m)
END
```

This is not in order because the names m and f used in HASHMAP[Seq,Bool,m,f] are not known at the point where HASHMAP[Seq, Bool,m,f] occurs. The reason is that the sort Nat is not known at this point. Of course the error is easy to repair: put NAT before HASHMAP in the import list.

4.4 Signatures

A signature is a set of names, typically arising as an export list, i.e. in an EXPORT section (see Section 4.2 on the basic pattern) or in an EXPORTING section (see Section 4.3 on instantiating components). A signature, indicated as S in Sections 4.2 and 4.3, is a set of names, where it is understood that names include their typing information (functionality) and instantiation information. In general, a signature is of the following form:

$name_1$,
$name_2$,
  $\vdots$
$name_k$,
SIG $A_1, \ldots, A_l$

where each $name_i$ $(1 \leq i \leq k)$ is a sort, function, predicate, or procedure name, and where each A_i $(1 \leq i \leq l)$ is a component name.

A signature must be understood as a set of complete names, but for user convenience there are certain rules that allow us to omit redundant information. For example `SORT Nat`, `SORT Set[Item]`, `FUNC + : Nat # Nat -> Nat` and `FUNC empty : -> Set[Nat]` are complete names. But of course, most of the typing information and the instantiation information can be omitted, provided they can be restored in a unique way (writing `Nat`, `Set`, `+` and `empty` respectively). Signatures are always complete with respect to sort names, by which we mean the following: if an operation name is included in a signature, then the sort names in the domain and range types of the operation are automatically included with it. This also holds for sort names which are implicit, i.e. which have been omitted from the domain and range types of operations. Furthermore, it is not necessary to repeat the keywords `SORT`, `FUNC`, `PRED` and `PROC`; e.g. after the first sort name, more incomplete sort names may follow (their `SORT` remaining implicit).

Consider the export list of the following example, adapted from Section 2.4. `VENDING6` provides the information to complete the export signature.

```
COMPONENT MACHINE
SPECIFICATION
EXPORT
  PROC insert,
       check,
       select,
       produce
IMPORT
  VENDING6
END
```

This can be used to illustrate the remarks made before on omitting keywords and on sort name completion. So `check`, `select` and `produce` are `PROC`s as well. Furthermore the completed export signature contains also the sorts `Coin`, `Selection` and `Product`, because `Coin` and `Selection` occur in the domain types of certain operations and `Product` occurs in the range type of an operation. In this way we find that the following is an alternative definition of `MACHINE`:

```
COMPONENT MACHINE
SPECIFICATION
EXPORT
  SORT Coin
  SORT Selection
  SORT Product
  PROC insert  : Coin       ->
  PROC check   :             ->
  PROC select  : Selection  ->
```

```
    PROC produce :                -> Product
IMPORT
   VENDING6
END
```

As a matter of fact, a very short version of **MACHINE** can be given, by omitting *all* redundant information.

```
COMPONENT MACHINE
SPECIFICATION
EXPORT
   insert, check, select, produce
IMPORT
   VENDING6
END
```

However, in most situations it is an advantage to have a clear overview of the operations provided by a component, including the typing information. For the prefered version of the machine's export list we refer to Section 2.4.

Next, let us illustrate the remarks made before on omitting instantiation information, when it can be restored uniquely. Consider the example TUP2 below, which has been taken from the standard library. It uses the standard **ITEM1** and **ITEM2** (which require **Item1** and **Item2** to be sorts). TUP2 specifies the parametrized data type of 2-tuples. Its interpretation is as follows: Tup2 is the set of tuples of objects of types **Item1** and **Item2**. $\text{tup}(i_1, i_2)$ is the tuple consisting of i_1 and i_2, $\text{proj1}(t)$ is the first element of tuple t, and similarly $\text{proj2}(t)$ is the second element of tuple t. This data type can be generalized in a straightforward way to the case of n-tuples $(n > 0)$.

```
COMPONENT TUP2[Item1,Item2] SPECIFICATION
ABSTRACT
   ITEM1,
   ITEM2
EXPORT
   SORT Tup2
   FUNC tup    : Item1 # Item2 -> Tup2,
        proj1 : Tup2 -> Item1,
        proj2 : Tup2 -> Item2
CLASS
   SORT Tup2  DEP Item1,Item2
   FUNC tup : Item1 # Item2 -> Tup2

   DECL t     : Tup2,
        i1,j1 : Item1,
        i2,j2 : Item2

   PRED is_gen : Tup2
   IND  is_gen(tup(i1,i2))
```

```
AXIOM
{TUP1} tup(i1,i2)!;
{TUP2} tup(i1,i2) = tup(j1,j2) => i1 = j1 AND i2 = j2;
{TUP3} is_gen(t)

FUNC proj1 : Tup2 -> Item1
IND  proj1(tup(i1,i2)) = i1

FUNC proj2 : Tup2 -> Item2
IND  proj2(tup(i1,i2)) = i2
END
```

The same could have been described more explicitly by restoring the missing
instantiation information [Item1,Item2]. It is all right to omit that, when
Tup2[Item1,Item2] is the only version of Tup2 visible. After completion of
the export list, we find that TUP2[Item1,Item2] is the same as:

```
COMPONENT TUP2[Item1,Item2] SPECIFICATION
ABSTRACT
  ITEM1,
  ITEM2
EXPORT
  SORT Tup2[Item1,Item2]
  FUNC tup : Item1 # Item2 -> Tup2[Item1,Item2],
       proj1 : Tup2[Item1,Item2] -> Item1,
       proj2 : Tup2[Item1,Item2] -> Item2
CLASS
  SORT Tup2  DEP Item1,Item2
  FUNC tup : Item1 # Item2 -> Tup2
  % ... (as before)
END
```

The idea is that each instantiation of TUP2 gives rise to another data type;
when we need 2-tuples of natural numbers and when we also need 2-tuples of
Booleans, then there are two versions of Tup2. One way to keep them apart is
to rename them immediately to NatsTup and BoolsTup, respectively.

```
COMPONENT TUP_INSTANTIATIONS SPECIFICATION
EXPORT
  SORT NatsTup,
       BoolsTup
  FUNC tup : Nat # Nat -> NatsTup,
       tup : Bool # Bool -> BoolsTup,
       proj1 : NatsTup -> Nat,
       proj2 : NatsTup -> Nat,
       proj1 : BoolsTup -> Bool,
       proj2 : BoolsTup -> Bool
IMPORT
  NAT,
```

```
        BOOL,
        TUP2[Nat,Nat] RENAMING Tup2 TO NatsTup END,
        TUP2[Bool,Bool] RENAMING Tup2 TO BoolsTup END
    END
```

Another, equally valid approach is to use instantiation information, and when
TUP_INSTANTIATIONS is used, write Tup2[Nat,Nat] and Tup2[Bool,Bool] to
keep the two versions of Tup2 apart. The following alternative definition of
TUP_INSTANTIATIONS is based on this approach.

```
    COMPONENT TUP_INSTANTIATIONS SPECIFICATION
    EXPORT
      SORT Tup2[Nat,Nat],
           Tup2[Bool,Bool]
      FUNC tup   : Nat # Nat       -> Tup2[Nat,Nat],
           tup   : Bool # Bool     -> Tup2[Bool,Bool],
           proj1 : Tup2[Nat,Nat]   -> Nat,
           proj2 : Tup2[Nat,Nat]   -> Nat,
           proj1 : Tup2[Bool,Bool] -> Bool,
           proj2 : Tup2[Bool,Bool] -> Bool
    IMPORT
      NAT, BOOL, TUP2[Nat,Nat], TUP2[Bool,Bool]
    END
```

But it is easy to see that the export list can be significantly simplified. First
of all, the sorts need not be mentioned separately, for they occur in the function types and are exported anyway. Secondly, the two functions tup can be
distinguished by their input types. Continuing along these lines we can write:

```
    COMPONENT TUP_INSTANTIATIONS SPECIFICATION
    EXPORT
      FUNC tup   : Nat # Nat  -> Tup2,
           tup   : Bool # Bool -> Tup2,
           proj1 : Tup2 -> Nat,
           proj2 : Tup2 -> Nat,
           proj1 : Tup2 -> Bool,
           proj2 : Tup2 -> Bool
    IMPORT
      NAT, BOOL, TUP2[Nat,Nat], TUP2[Bool,Bool]
    END
```

In this case, we can *not* go further and omit the typing information, because
this leads to undistinguishable occurrences of tup, proj1 and proj2. In other
words, the following is not in order:

```
    COMPONENT TUP_INSTANTIATIONS SPECIFICATION
    EXPORT
      tup, proj1, proj2                                    % wrong
    IMPORT
      NAT, BOOL, TUP2[Nat,Nat], TUP2[Bool,Bool]
```

END

Finally we mention a convenient way of including the entire set of names exported by some component. In particular, SIG $A_1, \ldots, A_l$ refers to the union of the export signatures of the components $A_1, \ldots, A_l$. For example, if we want TUP_INSTANTIATIONS to export the sorts Nat, Bool and the operations associated with them, we only have to write:

```
COMPONENT TUP_INSTANTIATIONS SPECIFICATION
EXPORT
  FUNC tup : Nat # Nat -> Tup2,
       tup : Bool # Bool -> Tup2,
       proj1 : Tup2 -> Nat,
       proj2 : Tup2 -> Nat,
       proj1 : Tup2 -> Bool,
       proj2 : Tup2 -> Bool
  SIG NAT, BOOL
IMPORT
  NAT, BOOL, TUP2[Nat,Nat], TUP2[Bool,Bool]
END
```

The SIG notation should be used with care because of the following possible disadvantages. First of all, the export list does not give a direct overview of the signature any more. In the example the export list refers to NAT and BOOL instead, the signatures of which must be looked for elsewhere. Secondly, it becomes difficult to analyse the dependencies amongst components in a large specification or in a large design when there are many different paths along which sorts and operations are provided.

4.5   Renamings

A renaming describes a systematic change of names. It occurs in a RENAMING section (see Section 4.3 on using components). A typical renaming was indicated as $\mathcal{R}$ in Section 4.3. Renamings are very similar to signatures with respect to omitting typing information, instantiation information and repeated keywords. In general, a renaming is of the following form:

$name_1$ TO new_name_1,
$name_2$ TO new_name_2,
$\vdots$
$name_k$ TO new_name_k

where each $name_i$ ($1 \leq i \leq k$) is a sort, function, predicate, or procedure name, and where each new_name_i is a *symbol*, i.e. a name without instantiation information, typing information or keyword (SORT, FUNC, PRED or PROC). The latter kinds of information and the keyword follow already from the corresponding

old *name*$_i$ and the systematic change applied to other names. Allowing them
to be mentioned explicitly in the new name would easily lead to inconsistencies.

When a sort is renamed, all occurrences of that sort name in function,
predicate and procedure types are automatically renamed as well. Consider
the following example, where the sort Tup2 is renamed to NatsTup, and where
the functions proj1 and proj2 are renamed to first and second. The fact
that Tup2 is renamed to NatsTup, implies that the function tup : Nat # Nat
-> Tup2 is changed to tup : Nat # Nat -> NatsTup and similarly that the
functions proj$i$: Tup2 -> Nat ($i = 1, 2$) are changed to first : NatsTup ->
Nat and second : NatsTup -> Nat respectively. This is also clear from the
export list.

```
COMPONENT NATTUP SPECIFICATION
EXPORT
   FUNC tup    : Nat # Nat -> NatsTup,
        first  : NatsTup   -> Nat,
        second : NatsTup   -> Nat
IMPORT
   NAT,
   TUP2'[Nat,Nat] RENAMING Tup2 TO NatsTup,
                           proj1 TO first,
                           proj2 TO second
                  END
END
```

The use of renamings is a powerful specification technique, because it makes
it possible to reuse existing components and to adapt them. For example, the
above NATTUP can be defined also by another much larger component, by textually including the adapted version of TUP2 (instead of referring to the existing
TUP2). The following is obtained by unfolding the usage of the instantiation
TUP2[Nat,Nat], substituting actual parameters for formal parameters and by
performing the name changes of the above RENAMING section.

```
COMPONENT NATTUP SPECIFICATION                  % unfolded version
EXPORT
   FUNC tup    : Nat # Nat -> NatsTup,
        first  : NatsTup   -> Nat,
        second : NatsTup   -> Nat
IMPORT
   NAT
CLASS
   SORT NatsTup
   FUNC tup : Nat # Nat -> NatsTup

   DECL t     : NatsTup,
        i1,j1 : Nat,
        i2,j2 : Nat
```

```
PRED is_gen : NatsTup
IND  is_gen(tup(i1,i2))

AXIOM
{TUP1} tup(i1,i2)!;
{TUP2} tup(i1,i2) = tup(j1,j2) => i1 = j1 AND i2 = j2;
{TUP3} is_gen(t)

FUNC first : NatsTup -> Nat
IND  first(tup(i1,i2)) = i1

FUNC second : NatsTup -> Nat
IND  second(tup(i1,i2)) = i2
END
```

Next we make some remarks to further clarify how renamings work. The instantiation part of a name can not be renamed, in the sense that one can not write RENAMING Tup2[Nat,Nat] TO Tup2[Number,Number], because the instantiation part is filled in when the component is instantiated (by instantiating TUP2 as TUP2[Nat,Nat], it follows that Tup2[Item,Item] becomes Tup2[Nat,Nat]). One can achieve the effect of changing Tup2[Nat,Nat] to Tup2[Number,Number], just by writing RENAMING Nat TO Number.

Very much in the same way, the functionality part of a name can not be renamed: one can not write things like RENAMING + : Nat # Nat -> Nat TO + : Number # Number -> Number. Yet, one can achieve the effect of changing + : Nat # Nat -> Nat to + : Number # Number -> Number, again by just writing RENAMING Nat TO Number. Of course the latter renaming does much more: it turns *all* operations on Nat into operations on numbers.

Finally we mention an obvious restriction on renamings: all names mentioned in a renaming should be different and be exported from the component that is being renamed.

4.6   More on Component Definitions

In Section 4.2 we showed the basic pattern to define a component. There are two more variations with respect to this pattern, so there are three kinds of component definitions. They are useful for indicating the rôle of the components involved with respect to their context. Each component is either:

- a specification component, or
- a specification-and-implementation component, or
- an abbreviation.

The basic pattern of Section 4.2 corresponds with a particular form of a specification component. A specification component, should be used to define a reusable design unit, for which it must be assumed that one or more implementations are available elsewhere, or will become available later. A specification-and-implementation component, defined by an extended pattern to be given in Section 4.6.2, should be used to define a reusable design unit, for which one implementation is already explicitly present; the component definition contains both a specification and an implementation. An abbreviation only serves to introduce a name for a description; this should be used to define a parameter restriction, or any other description which is not meant as a reusable design unit. Formally there is no semantic difference between a specification component and an abbreviation, but they express a methodological difference.

4.6.1   Specification Components

A specification component has a name and a specification, which is possibly different from its implementation(s). Its implementations are not included; they are elsewhere, or are assumed to come later. A specification component has the following form:

```
COMPONENT  C[u_1,...,u_k]
SPECIFICATION
    description
```

where the *description* can be a reference to another component (e.g. NATTUP), or can be given by the usual pattern consisting of four optional sections:

```
ABSTRACT  A_1,...,A_l
EXPORT  S
IMPORT  B_1,...,B_m
CLASS  D_1 ... D_n
END
```

We give a typical example, which is concerned with the dynamic data type of arrays with an index range that is a subrange of a (linearly ordered) sort. Its parameter restriction refers to WLORANGE, which requires <= to be a "weak linear order" on Item1 such that min and max are two Item1 constants satisfying min <= max. More details of WLORANGE will appear in Section 4.6.3.

```
COMPONENT ARRAY[Item1,<=,min,max,Item2] SPECIFICATION
ABSTRACT
   WLORANGE RENAMING
               SORT Item TO Item1
               FUNC lwb  TO min,
                    upb  TO max
            END,
   ITEM2
EXPORT
   SORT Array
```

```
FUNC min    :                              -> Item1,
     max    :                              -> Item1,
     val    : Array # Item1       -> Item2
PROC create :                              -> Array,
     upd    : Array # Item1 # Item2 ->
CLASS
  SORT Array                       VAR
  FUNC val : Array # Item1 -> Item2  VAR

  DECL i: Item1,
       b: Array
  AXIOM INIT => NOT EXISTS b ()

  PROC create : -> Array
  OUT  a
  PRE  TRUE
  SAT  NEW Array
  POST FORALL i ( val(a,i)^ )

  PROC upd : Array # Item1 # Item2 ->
  IN   a,n,i
  PRE  min <= n AND n <= max
  SAT  MOD val(a,n)
  POST val(a,n) = i
END
```

Its interpretation is as follows: Item1 is the set of objects acting as array indices; min is the minimal value that can be used for indexing and max is the maximal index; Item2 is the set of objects acting as values of array elements; Array is the set of arrays; create creates a new array; $val(a,i)$ is the value of the element with index i of array a; $upd(a,i,v)$ assigns the value v to the element with index i of array a.

The above specification component is a model of a module that provides a useful collection of facilities for program design. One can very well imagine that a memory management package, in combination with computer hardware realizes, or at least approximates the operations described. Therefore it is appropriate to view ARRAY[Item1,<=,min,max,Item2] as a design unit, and cast its description into the form of a specification component.

4.6.2 Specification-and-implementation Components

A specification-and-implementation component has a name, a specification, and one explicitly modelled implementation. It serves to define a reusable design unit, which has two views: an external view, usually a property-oriented and abstract specification, and an internal view, usually devised with efficiency considerations in mind. It has the following form:

```
COMPONENT  C [u₁,...,uₖ]
SPECIFICATION
   description₁
IMPLEMENTATION
   description₂
```

where each *description*$_i$ $(i = 1, 2)$ can be a reference to another component, or can be given by a pattern already discussed in Section 4.6.1, which consists of the four optional sections starting with ABSTRACT, EXPORT, IMPORT, and CLASS.

The following two requirements establish an *implementation relation* between the two descriptions:

- the signature exported by the SPECIFICATION part must be a subset of the signature exported by the IMPLEMENTATION part;
- all facts and properties described by the SPECIFICATION part must be logical consequences of the definitions given in the IMPLEMENTATION part.

The first of these requirements is of a syntactical nature. The check could be built into a typechecker (as has been done in Philips' TYCOON tool). The requirement says that the implementation provides everything promised by the specification (possibly more, but no less). The second requirement is called component "correctness" and it deals with the *meaning* of the descriptions involved. Component correctness checking requires logical reasoning and in its general form, this check is undecidable and can not be fully automated.

The following example has been adapted from Section 2.4.

```
COMPONENT MACHINE

SPECIFICATION
EXPORT
  PROC insert  : Coin        ->,
       check   :             ->,
       select  : Selection ->,
       produce :             -> Product
IMPORT
  VENDING6
END

IMPLEMENTATION
IMPORT
  COIN,
  VALUE,
  SELECTION,
  PRODUCT,
  HASHMAP'[Selection,Product,max2,hash2]
  % etc.
END
```

The vending machine is a design unit for which two distinct views exists, corresponding to two distinct descriptions. The SPECIFICATION part of MACHINE describes what the machine does, in terms of three sorts and four procedures only. The IMPLEMENTATION part of MACHINE describes how the machine does this, in terms of technical implementation modules, based on efficiency considerations. The implementation relation gives rise to proof obligations.

The above-mentioned implementation relation can be replaced by other, more liberal, relations if necessary. For example, in practice it could be justified to accept a procedure as an implementation of a function (but only if the procedure does not change the specified variables).

4.6.3   Abbreviation Components

An abbreviation only serves to introduce a name for a description. It has the following form:

LET $C[u_1, \ldots, u_k]$:=
   description

where the *description* again is a reference, or is built from the ABSTRACT, EXPORT, IMPORT, and CLASS sections of Section 4.6.1.

We give an example, which is the frequently used ITEM. It is usually employed as a parameter restriction of generic components such as stacks, sets, sequences, bags, or similar data types which are parametrized with respect to a single sort. This may be a variable sort, i.e. even dynamic object creation of the sort is allowed, which explains the keyword VAR.

```
LET ITEM :=
CLASS
    SORT Item VAR
END
```

It does not make sense to view ITEM as a reusable design unit: it is hard to imagine an engineer going to his boss and say: "well now we have a fine key-component to be used in some of our products, for *I have implemented* ITEM!".

Another example is WLO, which describes a weak linear ordering relation. Like ITEM, it is meant to be used as a parameter restriction in ABSTRACT clauses.

```
LET WLO :=
CLASS
    SORT Item    VAR
    PRED <= : Item # Item

    DECL i,j,k : Item

    AXIOM
    {WLO1} i <= i;
```

```
{WLO2} i <= j AND j <= i => i = j;
{WLO3} i <= j AND j <= k => i <= k;
{WLO4} i <= j OR j <= i
END
```

The axioms WLOi $(1 \leq i \leq 4)$ require that the relation <= is reflexive (1), anti-symmetric (2), transitive (3) and linear (4).

Yet another example is WLORANGE, which describes a weak linear order <= on a set Item with two constants called lwb and upb (typically used in array-indexing applications as lowerbound and upperbound).

```
LET WLORANGE :=
EXPORT
  FUNC lwb : -> Item,
       upb : -> Item
  PRED <=  : Item # Item
IMPORT
  WLO
CLASS
  FUNC lwb : -> Item
  FUNC upb : -> Item

  AXIOM lwb <= upb
END
```

4.7   Structure of Complete Descriptions

In this section we discuss how to put the components together. A complete multi-component description consists of three parts: an operator clause, a list of components, and finally a system description. Often it is appropriate to consider such a complete multi-component description as a *design*, i.e. the decomposition of a system, including all relevant details of specifications, implementations, and the structural relations that hold between them. So the pattern for such a description is as follows.

> *operator clause*
> *component*$_1$
> *component*$_2$
> $\vdots$
> *component*$_k$
> SYSTEM *description*

where the *description* can be a reference to a component introduced before, or can be given by the usual pattern consisting of four optional sections:

> ABSTRACT $A_1, \ldots, A_l$
> EXPORT $\mathcal{S}$

```
IMPORT  B₁, ..., Bₘ
CLASS  D₁ ... Dₙ
END
```

The operator clause is optional. If the list of components is empty, the keyword
SYSTEM may be omitted as well. The full details of the syntax will be given in
an appendix. As can be seen there, it is also possible to have nested designs,
since a multi-component description is allowed within the SPECIFICATION part
or IMPLEMENTATION part of a component. This generality will rarily be needed.

The operator clause contains information of a purely syntactic nature. It
is used for parsing assertions and expressions in the description to which the
clause is attached. We give an example.

```
OPERATORS
    PREFIX          -,    '
    INFIX LEFT      *,    /
    INFIX LEFT      +,    -
    INFIX           <,   >,   <=,   >=
```

This means that the unary operators - and ' have the same priority, which is
higher than the priority of *, /, + etc. Similarly * and / have the same priority,
which is higher than the priority of +, binary -, and <, ..., >=. Finally <, >, <=
and >= have the lowest priority. The keyword LEFT means that the operators
following it associate to the left. This operator clause allows us to write - (a
+ b + c * d), which is parsed as - (((a + b) + (c * d))).

The list of components represents a collection of design units, where possibly some components refer to other components. It is organized as a list,
although in practice, one might decide to store each component in a separate
file, for example VENDING1 in a file vending1.comp, NAT in a file nat.comp,
and so on. In order to avoid cyclic reference patterns, the following restriction
has to be respected: for the component list

$$component_1$$
$$component_2$$
$$\vdots$$
$$component_k$$

it is required that each component name is introduced before it is used. Each
$component_i$ $(1 \leq i \leq k)$ is either of the form LET C_i [$u_1, ..., u_k$] := description
or of the form COMPONENT C_i [$u_1, ..., u_k$] SPECIFICATION description (with
possibly also an implementation). Now it is required that instantiations of C_i
occur only in components named C_j for $j > i$.

The description that follows SYSTEM can refer to all of the C_i. This description must be viewed as the description of the product itself, whereas the
components preceding it are its building blocks. We give an example, which
is adapted from Section 2.4. To simplify the presentation, we have omitted
components like ITEM, ITEM1, ITEM2, NAT, SEQ and MAP which are taken from
the standard library.

```
COMPONENT VENDING1    SPECIFICATION ...
COMPONENT VALUE       SPECIFICATION ...
COMPONENT VENDING2    SPECIFICATION ...
COMPONENT VENDING3    SPECIFICATION ...
COMPONENT VENDING4    SPECIFICATION ...
COMPONENT VENDING5    SPECIFICATION ...
COMPONENT VENDING6    SPECIFICATION ...
COMPONENT SVAR[Item] SPECIFICATION ...
COMPONENT STRING      SPECIFICATION ...
LET HASHPARAMETERS[Item] := ...
COMPONENT HASHMAP[Item1,Item2,max,hash] SPECIFICATION  ...
COMPONENT COIN        SPECIFICATION ...
COMPONENT SELECTION   SPECIFICATION ...
COMPONENT PRODUCT     SPECIFICATION ...
COMPONENT SVALUE      SPECIFICATION ...
COMPONENT CONTROL_STATE SPECIFICATION ...
COMPONENT MACHINE       SPECIFICATION ... IMPLEMENTATION ...
SYSTEM MACHINE
```

Next we explain how to interpret applied occurrences of component names, depending on their context. For specification components and for abbreviation components this is clear: such components have precisely one description associated with their name, so any reference to such a component refers to that single description. For a reference to a specification-and-implementation component, the situation is more complicated. Such a component C has two descriptions associated with it, viz. the SPECIFICATION part of C and the IMPLEMENTATION part of C. Which of them is meant depends on the rôle of the reference. There are two such rôles:

- a specification rôle, which arises when a reference to C occurs in an ABSTRACT section, or in the SPECIFICATION part of a component;
- an implementation rôle, which arises when a reference to C occurs in any other place.

The situation will be clarified by the following example. Suppose that we add another component definition DUO_MACHINE at the end of the component list of the previous example.

```
COMPONENT DUO_MACHINE
SPECIFICATION
IMPORT
  MACHINE' RENAMING insert TO insert_mark,  ... END,
  MACHINE' RENAMING insert TO insert_dollar, ... END
CLASS
  ...
END
```

Each instantiation MACHINE' of the machine component in the above import list refers to the SPECIFICATION part of the machine's definition, and not to its

IMPLEMENTATION part. In general, a reference to a component in a specification rôle means that the component is used as a theory, for reasoning purposes. But a reference to a component in an implementation rôle will be resolved during the process of system building (code generation); in that process all IMPLEMENTATION parts are brought together and at the end there will be a long list of definitions (sorts, functions, predicates etc.) which can be executed or used for further transformation and translation. Obviously, a reference to a single-description component always refer to its single description – for reasoning and for system building.

4.8   More on Instantiating Components

This section will be devoted to the optional quote following the component name. It is a kind of postfix operator acting upon the component name C; it will be referred to as the *copy operator*. The meaning of the copy operator is that $C'[v_1, \ldots, v_k]$ refers to a fresh copy of C whereas $C[v_1, \ldots, v_k]$ without ' refers to the original text of C directly. One might guess that this makes no difference, but in COLD-1 it does because sort and operation names always carry implicit origin information with them. This is necessary for the proper treatment of shared components, see also Secton 9.4. The *origin* of a name is a unique label for the defining occurrence of the name. It is easy for a tool like a type checker to attach such labels to all names and it is convenient to think of these labels as pairs $\langle l, c \rangle$ consisting of a line number l and a column number c. A function f which is defined in line l at position c can be uniquely identified as $f_{\langle l,c \rangle}$. In this way distinct fs can be distinguished, even if all of them are refered to in the formal text as f. We shall explain the difference using an example COUNTER[Item] concerning a collection of counters, (one for each item).

```
COMPONENT COUNTER[Item] SPECIFICATION
ABSTRACT
  ITEM
EXPORT
  FUNC cnt  : Item -> Nat
  PROC tick : Item ->
IMPORT
  NAT
CLASS
  FUNC cnt : Item -> Nat VAR
  AXIOM INIT => FORALL i : Item ( cnt(i)^ )

  PROC tick : Item ->
  IN   i
  PRE  TRUE
  SAT  MOD cnt(i)
```

```
      POST cnt'(i)^ => cnt(i) = 0;
           cnt'(i)! => cnt(i) = cnt'(i) + 1
  END
```

If we assume that the line numbering starts at the first line of the first component that is not in the standard library, we find that the counter defined here is cnt$_{(10,6)}$ and that the tick procedure is tick$_{(13,6)}$. This is so because FUNC cnt is on the 10-th line and begins in column 6. Now we use COUNTER to make a model of a personnel database for a particular sales organization. The database consists of two parts. The first part records for each employee e the number of products sold by e. This first part is called SALES.

```
  COMPONENT SALES SPECIFICATION
  EXPORT
    PRED sales_ok    : Employee
    PROC sales_tick : Employee ->
  IMPORT
    NAT,
    CHAR,
    SEQ[Char] RENAMING Seq TO Employee END,
    COUNTER[Employee]
  CLASS
    PRED sales_ok : Employee
    IN   e
    DEF  cnt(e) > 100

    PROC sales_tick : Employee ->
    IN   e
    DEF  tick(e)
  END
```

The second part of the database records the number of complaints filed against each of the employees. This second part is called COMPLAINTS.

```
  COMPONENT COMPLAINTS SPECIFICATION
  EXPORT
    PRED complaints_ok   : Employee
    PROC complains_tick : Employee ->
  IMPORT
    NAT,
    CHAR,
    SEQ[Char] RENAMING Seq TO Employee END,
    COUNTER'[Employee]
  CLASS
    PRED complaints_ok : Employee
    IN   e
    DEF  cnt(e) < 10

    PROC complaints_tick : Employee ->
```

```
    IN    e
    DEF   tick(e)
END
```

The two parts of the database are packaged into a component PERSONNEL, which provides two ok predicates, viz. sales_ok and complaints_ok as well as two tick procedures, to wit sales_tick and complaints_tick. Clearly it is the purpose of the database to keep track of sales and complaints separately. For an employee e who has sold 200 units, and against whom no complaints are filed, the fact sales_ok(e) should hold, but clearly complaints_ok(e) should hold too.

```
COMPONENT PERSONNEL SPECIFICATION
IMPORT
  SALES,
  COMPLAINTS
END
```

In the above specification it was essential to have a fresh copy of COUNTER in COMPLAINTS. Otherwise the same counter variable cnt would be used for both parts of the database, clearly leading to completely wrong ok values for the employees.

Renaming the counters into cnt1 and cnt2 say, turns them into two distinct variables too, but there always remains the danger that subsequent renamings in higher-level components cause a name clash (and hence undesired sharing). Therefore it is better to use the copy operator.

To explain better how the mechanism of origins prevents the two counters being confused, a transformed version of SALES and COMPLAINTS is given below. The reference to COUNTER'[Employee] is replaced by a reference to a fresh copy of COUNTER, named _COUNTER_ANONYMOUS. The origins are attached to the defining occurrences of the functions and procedures involved. For each applied occurrence the origin has been traced back and has been made explicit too. The line numbers and a line with numbers facilitating column counting have been added.

```
    12345678901234567890123456789012345678901234567890123456789012345678901234567890123456
001   COMPONENT COUNTER[Item] SPECIFICATION
002   ABSTRACT                                    % transformed version
003     ITEM                                      % with explicit origins
004   EXPORT
005     FUNC cnt  : Item -> Nat
006     PROC tick : Item ->
007   IMPORT
008     NAT
009   CLASS
010     FUNC cnt (10,6) : Item -> Nat VAR
011     AXIOM INIT => FORALL i : Item ( cnt (10,6)(i)^ )
012
```

```
013       PROC tick(13,6) : Item ->
014       IN   i
015       PRE  TRUE
016       SAT  MOD cnt(10,6)(i)
017       POST cnt(10,6)'(i)^ => cnt(10,6)(i) = 0;
018            cnt(10,6)'(i)! => cnt(10,6)(i) = cnt(10,6)'(i) + 1
019       END
020
021       COMPONENT SALES SPECIFICATION
022       EXPORT
023         PRED sales_ok   : Employee
024         PROC sales_tick : Employee ->
025       IMPORT
026         NAT,
027         CHAR,
028         SEQ[Char] RENAMING Seq TO Employee END,
029         COUNTER[Employee]
030       CLASS
031         PRED sales_ok : Employee
032         IN   e
033         DEF  cnt(10,6)(e) > 100
034
035         PROC sales_tick : Employee ->
036         IN   e
037         DEF  tick(13,6)(e)
038       END
039
040       COMPONENT _COUNTER_ANONYMOUS[Item] SPECIFICATION
041       ABSTRACT
042         ITEM
043       EXPORT
044         FUNC cnt  : Item -> Nat
045         PROC tick : Item ->
046       IMPORT
047         NAT
048       CLASS
049         FUNC cnt(49,6) : Item -> Nat VAR
050         AXIOM INIT => FORALL i : Item ( cnt(49,6)(i)^ )
051
052         PROC tick(52,6) : Item ->
053         IN   i
054         PRE  TRUE
055         SAT  MOD cnt(49,6)(i)
056         POST cnt(49,6)'(i)^ => cnt(49,6)(i) = 0;
057              cnt(49,6)'(i)! => cnt(49,6)(i) = cnt(49,6)'(i) + 1
058       END
059
```

```
060    COMPONENT COMPLAINTS SPECIFICATION
061    EXPORT
062      PRED complaints_ok    : Employee
063      PROC complaints_tick : Employee ->
064    IMPORT
065      NAT,
066      CHAR,
067      SEQ[Char] RENAMING Seq TO Employee END,
068      _COUNTER_ANONYMOUS[Employee]
069    CLASS
070      PRED complaints_ok : Employee
071      IN   e
072      DEF  cnt(49,6)(e) < 10
073
074      PROC complaints_tick : Employee ->
075      IN   e
076      DEF  tick(52,6)(e)
077    END
```

Once the effect of the copy operator has been simulated by inserting an additional anonymous "fresh copy" component and the origins have been made explicit, it is clear that there are two distinct counters involved: the first of these is $cnt_{(10,6)}$, which is used in the definition of sales_ok and of $tick_{(13,6)}$, which at its turn is used in the definition of sales_tick. The second counter is $cnt_{(49,6)}$, which is used in the definition of complaints_ok and of $tick_{(52,6)}$, which at its turn is used in the definition of complaints_tick.

The situation is somewhat similar to the way persons are identified by their name. Usually a family name and a Christian name are enough, but in particular situations a person must show his passport where additional origin information is made explicit: the place and date of birth. For example, there are many Dutchmen called Jan Jansen, but when we write for example

Jan Jansen$_{(Amsterdam, 4-12-1960)}$,
Jan Jansen$_{(Tuitjenhorn, 4-8-1918)}$

they can be distinguished.

Another way of explaining how the copy operator makes a difference is to show the import structures as diagrams, as in Figures 4.1 and 4.2. Figure 4.1 shows the situation as defined in the above example. There are two COUNTER components, each with similar internal details, but acting as two distinct storages. But Figure 4.2 shows what happens if the quote after COUNTER in the import list of COMPLAINTS is omitted. In that case SALES and COMPLAINTS will share a single instance of COUNTER. There are many useful applications of this kind of module sharing, but it is undesired in the database example because the sales and the complaints countings would be confused. Actually it would be better to use a *copy* of COUNTER in SALES too, but this was not shown in order to keep the transformation process in the example as simple as possible.

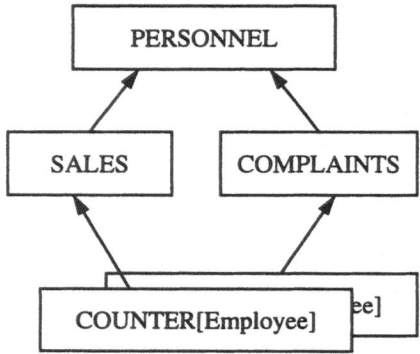

Figure 4.1: Import structure: COMPLAINTS imports COUNTER'[Employee].

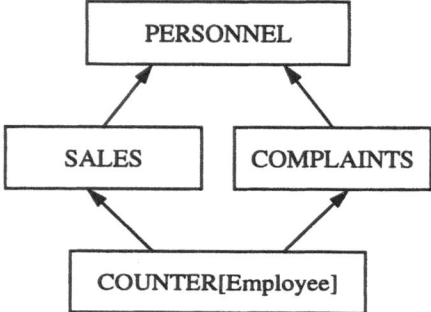

Figure 4.2: Import structure: COMPLAINTS imports COUNTER[Employee].

It should be clear that the copy operator (indicated by a quote behind a component name) is a powerful mechanism that avoids a lot of text copying that would be needed otherwise.

4.9 Concluding Remarks

Now the details have been explained, let us look back and make the advantages of the proposed structuring mechanisms explicit.

First of all, each module is a context for the designer, or put in other words, a kind of "closed world model". A designer which is reading, writing, or modifying a component C can have a clear focus: there is a well-defined set of names which can be used, which are introduced only via the parameters, the import list, and the own CLASS section of C. Any assumptions or facts about the parameters are made explicit as well: they are put together in the ABSTRACT section.

Giving a name to something is the ultimate form of abstraction, and it allows us to draw high-level box-diagrams and import graphs. The names of the components are the handles for the planning and management of the design process. It makes sense for a boss to ask an engineer "well, how long did it take you to make that implementation of HASHMAP? ".

A component is a unit of reusability and of course the probability that a component will be reused by somebody else is larger if the component is more general, and can be adjusted to specific needs. That is why the language supports *generic* components: a component $C[u_1,\ldots,u_k]$ has k parameters which can be filled-in when the component is instantiated. The ABSTRACT section makes it possible to reason about the restrictions and assumptions about the $u_1,\ldots,u_k$, avoiding confusion in the sense that the provider of the component and the user of the component have different ideas about the parameters. The language constructs of Section 4.3 are meant for instantiating reusable components. Making a copy, choosing actual parameters, hiding, renaming and qualifying are different ways of adjusting C to specific needs.

Another advantage of the basic pattern of Section 4.2 is that it supports information hiding; hiding by means of EXPORT removes unnecessary details and makes it possible to write model-oriented specifications and then remove the irrelevant details by choosing the right export list. This was shown by the example of Section 4.2 concerning HSVAR and HSVAR_. Usually it is much easier to write such model-based specifications than to write axiomatic and property-oriented specifications. In particular, this often holds for designers which already have much programming experience, but are new in the field of logical specification. Moreover, the EXPORT section of a component is useful (even if no hiding takes place), for it acts as a compact overview of the sorts and operations provided by the component.

It should be noted that components can be *shared*. If the state-based component SVAR is imported by two distinct user components UC1 and UC2, then these refer to the same storage cell (and not to two copies of them with possibly distinct storage contents). But if we want to have two or more identical copies of a state-based component, this can be arranged as well. The copy operator has the same effect as writing the definitions of the component another time, which implies that all variables are declared twice.

Component definitions support different views. In particular, when employing a specification-and-implementation component, there are two views. This makes it possible to distinguish the *what* from the *how* and it frees the user of a module from all details and efficiency tricks used in the implementation of the module. He can rely on the SPECIFICATION part only (at least if the component is correct). Moreover the EXPORT clause can be used to give a compact summary of the names of all sorts and operations provided.

The explicit structure of a design built from a well-organized collection of components can be of help in understanding a complex system and managing its complexity. Practice has shown that individual sort, operation and axiom definitions are too small as units for understanding a design. Modern programming languages offer modularization or packaging constructs at the same level of granularity as presented in this chapter. When using pictorial representations in combination with tools for generating and manipulating them, it is easy to visualize the structure of a design. In this way it becomes possible to have a clear overview of large specifications and designs.

Chapter 5
Mechanisms for Naming

Nomen est omen. (Plautus)

5.1 Introduction and Motivation

In COLD-1, one may overload the symbols that serve the purpose of names for sorts and operations. This means that the same symbol may be used for different things. By doing so, we introduce the problem that the symbol alone does not suffice to trace back the corresponding definition. In order to resolve this problem, symbols have to be completed with qualifiers, domain types and range types just as in the definitions concerned. If a unique completion can not be derived from the context, this must be done explicitly. In this way it is guaranteed that the corresponding definition can be traced back. However, there remains a problem with parametrized component definitions: the same symbol may still be used for sorts or operations from different instantiations. If the instantiation concerned can not be derived from the context, the actual parameters of the component concerned must be added to resolve this problem.

All this means that complete names for sorts and operations are not just symbols, but it is often allowed to omit some or all other parts. In this way, advantage is taken of two conflicting ideas:

- the first idea is that one wants to extract as much information from a name as possible (its domain type, its range type, etc.);
- the other idea is that it is convenient to have names which are short, because this is easier for writing and managing the texts.

The conflict between these two ideas is resolved by using information from the context. This context-dependency gives rise to certain locality principles associated with modules which help in avoiding undesirable overloading. This chapter presents the structure of complete names for sorts and operations and explains the possibilities to omit parts of them. Object names, which are handled in much the same way as sort and operation names, are also covered.

COLD-1 has a strong type discipline. This means that every well-formed expression has a unique type. The type of an expression depends upon the

domain and range types of the symbols occurring in it. There is a complication due to overloading of symbols: typing and overloading resolution are
interdependent. Therefore, the typing of expressions is explained as well.

Occurrences of names of sorts and operations can amongst other things
be found in the instantiation part of names of other sorts and operations.
They can also be found in the instantiation part of names of the parametrized
components concerned. Those occurrences give rise to additional problems
with overloading. These problems and their solutions will also be treated.

The last three sections of this chapter explain how name clashes arise and
how they can be avoided, how the usual notations for numbers and strings are
treated as names, and how some purely syntactic issues related to names are
dealt with.

5.2   Structure of Names

A complete *name* for a sort, predicate, function or procedure in COLD-1
consists of the following:

1. a *qualifier* indicating whether the name is a sort, predicate, function or
   procedure name;
2. a *symbol* which is a string of letters, digits and special characters;
3. an *instantiation* which is a list of names corresponding to the actual
   parameters of the component defining the name;
4. for names of operations, a *functionality* which consists of the *domain* type
   and, in so far as appropriate, the *range* type of the operation concerned.

An example of a complete name is:

    PRED is_in[Item] : Item # Set[Item]

where:

PRED	is the qualifier,
is_in	is the symbol,
[Item]	is the instantiation,
: Item # Set[Item]	is the functionality of the name.

The symbol is always required, but the other parts may be omitted when it
is clear from the context which complete name is meant. Certain parts even
must be omitted in some contexts.

The instantiation part must be omitted in the defining occurrence of a
name. This is natural because the defining occurrence of a name does not
originate from a particular instantiation of the component defining the name.
The defining occurrence of the name from the example above could have been:

    PRED is_in : Item # Set

or

```
PRED is_in : Item # Set[Item]
```

but not

```
PRED is_in[Item] : Item # Set[Item]                    % wrong
```

The qualifier part must be omitted in the applied occurrences of a name in assertions and expressions. For example, the following is wrong:

```
FORALL n : Item
( EXISTS s : Set[Item]
  ( PRED is_in[Item] : Item # Set[Item](n,s)           % wrong
) )
```

The following is right:

```
FORALL n : Item ( EXISTS s : Set[Item] ( is_in(n,s) ) )
```

The qualifier part is omitted as required here and no confusion about which name is meant can arise by leaving out the instantiation part and the functionality part as well.

The applied occurrences of a name are not limited to assertions and expressions; they can also be found in, for example, signatures and renamings. The above-mentioned restriction concerning the qualifier part does not apply to these remaining occurrences. In a specification of finite sets one could have the following signature in the EXPORT section:

```
SORT Set
FUNC empty  :                  -> Set
FUNC ins    : Item # Set -> Set
FUNC union  : Set  # Set -> Set
FUNC diff   : Set  # Set -> Set
PRED is_in  : Item # Set
PRED subset : Set  # Set
```

All parts but the symbol part must be omitted in the applied occurrences of a name as a new name in renamings. So the RENAMING section of the component references

```
SET[Nat] RENAMING Set TO NatSet END
```

and

```
SET[Nat] RENAMING SORT Set TO NatSet END
```

are in order, but the RENAMING section of the following component reference is not:

```
SET[Nat] RENAMING SORT Set TO SORT NatSet END          % wrong
```

5.3   Names in Definitions and Axioms

In each definition, a name is introduced for the sort or operation being defined.
Such an occurrence of a name is called its defining occurrence. In various
sections of the definition concerned there may be occurrences of names in
assertions and expressions. Such occurrences of names are examples of applied
occurrences.

It is quite natural and very useful to have defining occurrences of names that
are as complete as possible. Without the qualifier part and the functionality
part, it may become very difficult or even impossible to determine what is
being defined in the remainder of the definition concerned. For example, in
the specification of HASHPARAMETERS, given in Section 2.3, there is the following
function definition:

```
FUNC hash : Item1 -> Nat
IN   i
PRE  TRUE
POST hash(i) < max
```

From the IN, PRE and POST sections of this definition, it can only be determined
that hash is the name of a function or a procedure. The domain type of hash
can not be determined at all (but this could be resolved by using the following
IN section: IN i : Item1).

On the other hand, it becomes rather inconvenient to have to write the
qualifier and functionality parts for each occurrence of a name in an assertion
or expression while it is clear what is meant when they are omitted. The
assertion in the POST section of hash looks as follows after the addition of the
appropriate functionality part to each occurrence of a name:

```
hash : Item1 -> Nat (i : Item1) < : Nat # Nat max : -> Nat
```

This is difficult for the writer and not very intelligible for the reader. It would
be worse if the appropriate qualifier parts were added as well. However, as
mentioned before, this is not allowed in assertions and expressions. This restriction works against bad naming habits such as using the same symbol for
a function and a procedure with the same functionality.

In a specification of stacks in a parametrized component definition, the
procedure push could be defined by:

```
PROC push : Stack # Item ->
IN   s,i
PRE  TRUE
SAT  MOD seq(s)
POST seq(s) = cons(i, seq'(s))
```

where Item is the parameter. In this case, the assertion in the POST section
looks even worse after the addition of the functionality parts:

```
seq : Stack[SORT Item] -> Seq[SORT Item] (s : Stack[SORT Item]) =
```

```
cons : Item # Seq[SORT Item] -> Seq[SORT Item]
( i : Item
, seq' : Stack[SORT Item] -> Seq[SORT Item] (s : Stack[SORT Item])
)
```

Notice that there are applied occurrences of names in the instantiation part of other names. These applied occurrences are treated in the same way as those in signatures and renamings. This means that in the above post-condition SORT may be omitted from each occurrence of SORT Item. This example further shows that a "'" is always put after the symbol part of the name, even if there is also a functionality part present.

Typing and overloading resolution are interdependent. An expression of the form $f(X)$ always occurs as a constituent of another COLD-1 construct which may put requirements upon the possible types of the whole expression. In certain cases this means that its type can be inherited from this enclosing construct. Furthermore, a collection of possible types can be synthesized from the subexpression X. From the context of the expression, we can further extract the collection of complete names that are visible in the expression. Together this is used to resolve overloading. So typing is involved in overloading resolution. Only in certain cases the type of $f(X)$ can be inherited from the enclosing construct. In the remaining cases, if f is overloaded, the type can only be determined after overloading resolution. Consequently, overloading resolution is involved in typing as well.

Two types can be combined in a union type which is essentially the collection of all objects of the two types. However, explicit embedding is needed because of the strong type discipline of COLD-1. In a specification of unions of types in a parametrized component definition, the same symbol may be used for the two embeddings involved. The complete names of the embedding could be:

```
FUNC union2 : Item1 -> Union2
FUNC union2 : Item2 -> Union2
```

One could also have the following axiom:

```
AXIOM FORALL i1,i2 : Item1 ( union2(i1) = union2(i2) <=> i1 = i2 )
```

Consider the expression union2(i1). It is a constituent of an equation. This requires that it has the same type as the expression union2(i2). So the type of union2(i1) can not be inherited. The subexpression i1 has only one possible type, viz. Item1. union2 is overloaded, but this information is enough to derive that only FUNC union2 : Item1 -> Union2 could have been meant. Herewith the overloading has been resolved and it can now be established that the type of union2(i1) is Union2. In the same way it can be determined that the type of union2(i2) is Union2 as well. This means that union2(i1) and union2(i2) have the same type, so the above-mentioned well-formedness requirement on the equation is met.

In a specification of finite maps in a parametrized component definition, the same symbol may be used for two functions for removing elements from their domains. The complete names of the these functions could be:

```
FUNC rem : Map # Item1       -> Map
FUNC rem : Map # Set[Item1] -> Map
```

The first function removes one element from the domain of a map and the second function removes a set of elements. One could have the following inductive definition of the second function:

```
FUNC rem : Map # Set[Item1] -> Map
IND  FORALL m : Map
     ( rem(m,empty) = m
     ; FORALL i : Item1, s : Set[Item1]
       ( rem(m,ins(i,s)) = rem(rem(m,i),s) )
     )
```

Consider the expression `rem(rem(m,i),s)`. Just like in the previous example, the type of `rem(rem(m,i),s)` can not be inherited. The possible types of the subexpression `rem(m,i)` are obtained by first deriving the possible domain types of this occurrence of `rem` from the possible types of `m` and `i` and then taking the range types of the names that match with these domain types (only `FUNC rem : Map # Item1 -> Map` matches). This results in one possible type for `rem(m,i)`, viz. `Map`. Furthermore, it is clear that `Set[Item1]` is the only possible type of `s`. These two pieces of information are enough to derive that only `FUNC rem : Map # Set[Item1] -> Map` could have been meant with the outer occurrence of `rem`. Consequently, the type of the subexpression `rem(m,i)` is `Map`. This information turns out not to contribute at all to the overloading resolution for the inner occurrence of `rem`, but the possible types of `m` and `i` are enough to derive that only `FUNC rem : Map # Item1 -> Map` could have been meant with this occurrence of `rem`. Herewith the overloading of both occurrences of `rem` has been resolved and the type of the subexpression `rem(m,i)` has been established as well. The type of `rem(rem(m,i),s)` can now directly be determined (this type is also `Map`).

In a specification of finite bags in a parametrized component definition, a component `SET[Item]` may be imported, for example, in order to define a function for turning bags into corresponding sets. The symbol used for the empty bag may be the same as the imported symbol for the empty set. The complete names could be:

```
FUNC empty : -> Set
FUNC empty : -> Bag
```

There could additionally be overloading of the symbol `is_in`:

```
PRED is_in : Item # Set
PRED is_in : Item # Bag
```

The following axiom must not be used in that case:

```
AXIOM FORALL i : Item ( NOT is_in(i,empty) )              % wrong
```

The overloading of **empty** and **is_in** can not be resolved in this case. One solution is to complete the incomplete name **empty**:

    AXIOM FORALL i : Item (NOT is_in(i,empty : -> Bag))

Another solution is to cast the expression **empty**:

    AXIOM FORALL i : Item (NOT is_in(i,empty :: Bag))

Recall that an expression may always be casted in one of its possible types (see Section 3.9).

5.4   Names in Signatures and Renamings

In signatures and renamings, names can be grouped by qualifier. For example, the signature for the **EXPORT** section of a specification of finite sets given in Section 5.2 can also be written as follows:

```
SORT Set
FUNC empty :                    -> Set,
     ins   : Item # Set -> Set,
     union : Set  # Set -> Set,
     diff  : Set  # Set -> Set
PRED is_in  : Item # Set,
     subset : Set  # Set
```

Since a signature is used to sum up the names provided by a component, it is generally considered to be useful to have complete names in signatures. Grouping names by qualifier avoids needless repetition of the qualifiers. Although it is not recommended, parts of the names may be omitted if a unique completion can be derived from the context. A very short, but not very informative version of the above signature is:

    Set, empty, ins, union, diff, is_in, subset

As a matter of fact an even shorter signature is possible, viz.:

    empty, ins, union, diff, is_in, subset

That is, the sort name **Set** may even be omitted. The sort names occurring in the domain types and range types of the operations in a signature may be omitted, because the signature is automatically complemented by these sort names. In other words, signatures are closed with respect to sort names. If this was not automatically done, it would have to be enforced by a well-formedness requirement.

The following signature consists of the names that could be provided by the component concerning finite maps mentioned earlier:

```
SORT Map
FUNC empty :                        -> Map,
     add   : Map # Item1 # Item2 -> Map,
```

```
        rem    : Map # Item1              -> Map,
        rem    : Map # Set[Item1]         -> Map,
        app    : Map # Item1              -> Map,
        dom    : Map                      -> Set[Item1],
        ran    : Map                      -> Set[Item2],
        restr  : Map # Set[Item1]         -> Map
   PRED submap : Map # Map
```

Here it is assumed that two instantiations of the component SET have been imported, viz. SET[Item1] and SET[Item2]. In order to distinguish between the sorts Set from these two instantiations, the instantiation part is used in this signature where Set occurs. This signature is actually the one appearing in the EXPORT section of the component MAP from the standard library of Appendix B. The component XMAP used in the specification of VENDING6 (Section 2.2) is the same as MAP, except for the replacement of app by the infix operator @.

In the specification of VENDING6, there is the following component reference in the IMPORT section:

```
XMAP[Selection,Value] RENAMING Map TO PriceTable, @ TO price END
```

The RENAMING section is in order, but it might be made somewhat more informative:

```
XMAP[Selection,Value]
  RENAMING
    SORT Map                              TO PriceTable
    FUNC @ : Map # Selection -> Value TO price
  END
```

Recall that all parts but the symbol part must be omitted in the occurrences of a name as a new name in renamings.

In the following component reference, there is an EXPORTING section as well as a RENAMING section. It exhibits grouping of names in both the signature and the renaming concerned:

```
SEQ'[Char]
  EXPORTING
    SORT Seq
    FUNC empty :                 -> Seq,
         seq   : Char            -> Seq,
         cat   : Seq  # Seq -> Seq,
         len   : Seq            -> Nat,
         sel   : Seq  # Nat -> Seq
  RENAMING
    SORT Seq TO String
    FUNC seq TO ',
         cat TO +
  END
```

The above component reference could occur in the IMPORT section of a specification of strings. In the EXPORT section, the following signature could occur:

```
SORT String
FUNC empty :                        -> String,
     '       : Char                 -> String,
     +       : String # String -> String,
     len     : String           -> Nat,
     sel     : String # Nat     -> String
SIG STRING_NOTATION[Char]
```

The component name STRING_NOTATION[Char] is used in the last line of this signature to include the set of all names provided by that component (see also Section 4.4). The Incremental Generic Library of Objects (IGLOO) [23], from which a number of components have been selected in the standard library of Appendix B, contains a component STRING with an EXPORT section in which SIG STRING_NOTATION[Char] occurs. STRING_NOTATION[Char] provides the usual notation for strings (see further Section 5.8).

5.5   Names in Instantiations

The instantiation part of a name may be needed if the component defining the name is parametrized and the same symbol is used for sorts or operations from different instantiations. If the instantiation concerned can not be derived from the context, the instantiation part of the name – i.e. the actual parameter list of the component concerned – must be added to resolve this problem. This means that instantiation parts of names are essentially lists of names for sorts and operations. They are similar to signatures in the sense that there are no differences with signatures with respect to what may or must be omitted in names occurring in instantiations. But note that, unlike signatures, the order of the names is important. Besides, because they play different parts, instantiations are not automatically closed with respect to sort names.

In the example about finite maps presented in Section 5.4, it was assumed that two instantiations of the component SET had been imported, viz. SET[Item1] and SET[Item2]. In order to distinguish between the sorts Set from these two instantiations, the instantiation part was used in the functionality parts of names where Set occurred:

```
dom : Map -> Set[Item1]
ran : Map -> Set[Item2]
```

The following would also be in order but it is not particularly useful:

```
dom : Map -> Set[SORT Item1]
ran : Map -> Set[SORT Item2]
```

In the specification of MACHINE, given in Section 2.4, there are among other things the following component references in the IMPORT section:

```
HASHMAP'[Selection,Product,max2,hash2]
  RENAMING
    lookup TO yield,
    exists TO exists_product
  END

HASHMAP'[Selection,Value,max2,hash2]
  RENAMING
    lookup TO price,
    exists TO exists_price
  END
```

In the definition of one of the operations of MACHINE, the assertion

```
exists_price(selection)
```

is used. A name clash for exists has been prevented by applying a renaming to the instantiations of HASHMAP. Instead the appropriate instantiation part could have been added to occurrences of exists. In that case, the above-mentioned assertion would most likely become:

```
exists[Selection,Value,max2,hash2](selection)
```

Although it is not recommended, the following is not prohibited:

```
exists                                          % not recommended
[ SORT Selection,
       Value
  FUNC max2  :                -> Nat,
       hash2 : Selection -> Nat
]
(selection)
```

There is no essential difference between the instantiation part of a name for a sort or operation and the instantiation part of the name for the component concerned. However, where component names occur, it is generally more difficult to trace back where the actual parameters come from. The way in which this is done, restricts the names that may be used as actual parameters in the instantiation part of a component name. They are restricted to the names made available by the components referred to so far in the ABSTRACT and IMPORT sections of the component in which the component name occurs and the names defined in the CLASS section of that component. In the latter case, the functionality of the name concerned may not contain sort names not yet imported or defined (this is further explained in Section 4.3).

Consider, for example, the following component reference from the IMPORT section of MACHINE (Section 2.4):

```
HASHMAP'[Selection,Value,max2,hash2]
  RENAMING
    lookup TO price,
    exists TO exists_price
```

END

The names **Selection** and **Value** come from SELECTION and VALUE, which occur earlier in the IMPORT section concerned. The names **max2** and **hash2**, which are defined in the CLASS section, depend on the sort names **Selection** and **Nat**, which are already imported as both names are made available by SELECTION. Figure 5.1 clarifies the situation.

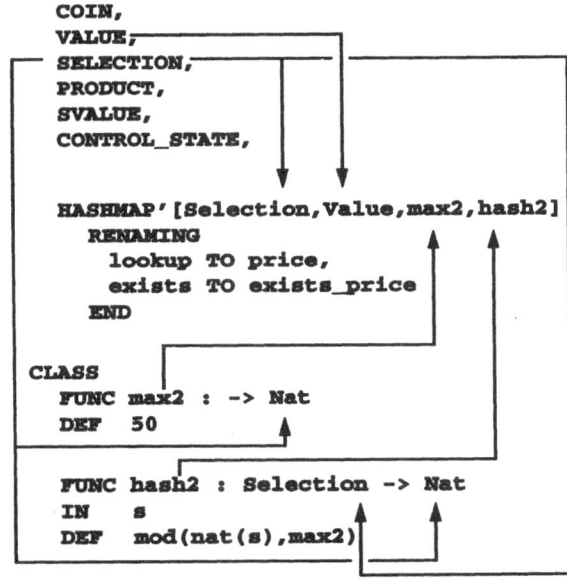

Figure 5.1: Where the actual parameters come from.

Tracing back the component from which a sort or operation name originates, is not needed if the originating component is mentioned in a FROM clause. For example, the previous component reference could as well be written as follows:

```
HASHMAP'[Selection FROM SELECTION,Value FROM VALUE,max2,hash2]
   RENAMING
      lookup TO price,
      exists TO exists_price
   END
```

Obviously, this is not required in the IMPORT section of MACHINE as explained above. FROM clauses can be viewed as an additional part of a complete name which must be omitted everywhere but in the instantiation part of component names. Grouping by originating component is also allowed.

5.6   Object Names

Object names are used in assertions and expressions to refer to objects.[1] They
are introduced in FORALL and EXISTS assertions, THAT and SOME expressions,
LET constructs in assertions and expressions, and in the IN and OUT sections
of operation definitions. Object names are treated in much the same way
as sort and operation names. A complete object name consists of a symbol
part and functionality part (the latter part consists of a range type only). An
instantiation part is needless because an object name is always local to a CLASS
section. A qualifier part is never present – not even in a complete object name.

It has been mentioned before (Section 5.3) that one should not use the same
symbol for a function and a procedure with the same functionality, because
such overloading is unresolvable in assertions and expressions. For the same
reason one should not use the same symbol for a nullary function and an object
with the same functionality.

Declarations are provided for two purposes. One purpose is to make it
possible to omit the types of object names where these names are introduced in
FORALL and EXISTS assertions, THAT and SOME expressions, and LET constructs
that do not bind the names concerned to objects, i.e. constructs of the following
form:

LET $x_1 : T_1, \ldots, x_n : T_n$

A declaration has the following general form:

DECL $x_1 : T_1, \ldots, x_n : T_n$

The scope of a declaration is restricted to the CLASS section in which it appears.
Consider the declaration:

DECL m : Map, i : Item1, s : Set[Item1]

In the scope of this declaration, the following definition of the function rem is
equivalent to the definition given earlier (Section 5.3):

```
FUNC rem : Map # Set[Item1] -> Map
IND  FORALL m
     ( rem(m,empty) = m
     ; FORALL i, s ( rem(m,ins(i,s)) = rem(rem(m,i),s) )
     )
```

The other purpose of declarations is to allow for implicit universal quantification in inductive definitions, axioms and theorems. For example, the
previous definition can be further simplified to:

```
FUNC rem : Map # Set[Item1] -> Map
IND  rem(m,empty) = m;
     rem(m,ins(i,s)) = rem(rem(m,i),s)
```

---

[1]Object names are frequently called logical variables in mathematics and logic. But,
unlike programming variables, they are of a static nature.

The implicit universal quantification proceeds as follows. Let A be an assertion in which object names occur free. A has the general form A_1 ; ... ;
A_n, where $n \geq 1$. An object name that occurs free for the first time in A_i
$(1 \leq i \leq n)$ is made bound by universal quantification over A_i ; ... ; A_n.
This implicit universal quantification only works for assertions in inductive
definitions, axioms and theorems.

Using declarations, many inductive definitions, axioms and theorems given
earlier can be simplified. In Section 3.7, an inductive definition of a predicate
is_gen on natural numbers and an axiom about natural numbers are given.
This can also be written as follows:

```
DECL m,n : Nat

PRED is_gen : Nat
IND  is_gen(zero);
     is_gen(n) => is_gen(succ(n))

AXIOM zero!;
      succ(m)!;
      NOT succ(m) = zero;
      succ(m) = succ(n) => m = n;
      is_gen(n)
```

The following example is a simple, but complete component specification. In
this example, the occurrences of n and b in the axiom are implicitly typed on
the basis of the declaration and the assertion concerned is moreover implicitly
universally quantified. However, the type of n in the IN section of the definition
of byte is determined by the domain type of byte and the assertion in the PRE
section of this definition is not implicitly quantified.

```
COMPONENT BYTE_ SPECIFICATION
EXPORT
  SORT Byte
  FUNC byte : Nat  -> Byte,
       nat  : Byte -> Nat
IMPORT
  NAT
CLASS
  SORT Byte

  DECL n : Nat, b : Byte

  FUNC byte : Nat  -> Byte
  IN   n
  PRE  n < 256

  FUNC nat  : Byte -> Nat
  PRE  TRUE
```

```
AXIOM n < 256 => nat(byte(n)) = n;
      byte(nat(b)) = b
END
```

Object names are not only introduced in FORALL and EXISTS assertions, THAT and SOME expressions, and "proper" LET constructs. Additionally, they are introduced in IN and OUT sections of definitions (as in the previous example), and in LET constructs of the form

LET $x_1 : T_1, \ldots, x_n : T_n := X$

which bind the names concerned to objects as well. Other occurrences of an object name than its introducing occurrence are generally occurrences as expressions. There is one exception: object names introduced in expressions of the form LET $x_1 : T_1, \ldots, x_n : T_n$ may also occur at the left-hand side of expressions of the form

$x_1 : T_1, \ldots, x_n : T_n := X$

which bind the names introduced earlier to objects. In all these additional cases, the types of the object names concerned may be omitted – just as in the cases mentioned before. However, the types concerned are derived in a different way.

The types of object names in IN and OUT sections are derived from the domain type and range type, respectively, of the operation being defined. Instead of the earlier inductive definition of rem, the following algorithmic definition could be given:

```
FUNC rem : Map # Set[Item1] -> Map
IN   m,s
DEF  ( s = empty      ?; m
     | NOT s = empty ?;
       LET i := SOME j : Item1 ( is_in(j,s) ) ;
       rem(rem(m,i),diff(s,i))
     )
```

The object names m and s are introduced in the IN section to be used in the function body to refer to the arguments of the function. So according to the domain type m must have type Map and s must have type Set[Item1].

The types of the object names $x_1, \ldots, x_n$ in expressions of the form

LET $x_1, \ldots, x_n := X$

are derived from the type of the expression X which must have only one possible type. In the algorithmic definition of rem the type of i is Item1 because it is the unique type of SOME j : Item1 (is_in(j,s)).

For expressions of the form

$x_1, \ldots, x_n := X$

the normal overloading resolution applies: the types concerned are derived in essentially the same way as for the equation $x_1, \ldots, x_n = X$. Consider the following lemma, which could be used to prove the theorem from the CLASS section of the component VENDING5 presented in Section 2.2:

```
DECL s : Selection

THEOREM control_state = coin_checked =>
            AFTER
              LET p : Product ;
              select(s) ;
              p := produce
            THEN
              p = yield(product_table,s)
```

Product is amongst the possible types of the object name p in p := produce – it occurs in the scope of LET p : Product – and it is the only one possible type of the expression produce. Because it is required that p and produce have the same type, this is enough to derive that only the object name p : Product could have been meant.

Recall that $ abbreviates SOME $x : T$ () for some T. This leads to an extreme overloading of $. It is interesting to explain how this is resolved by means of an example. Consider the following alternative to the SAT section used in the definition of the procedure PROC produce : -> Product from the CLASS section of VENDING3 (Section 2.2):

```
SAT  MOD control_state ; $
```

The possible types of this occurrence of $ can not be synthesized from any subexpression. This means that any type is a possible type. As a consequence, the type of this $ must be inherited from the type of the enclosing expression MOD control_state ; $. From its context, it can be extracted that the type of this expression is Product (the range type of the procedure produce). Because MOD control_state has type (), i.e. the type with the empty tuple as sole element, this leaves Product as the only type for this occurrence of $. Herewith the overloading has been resolved: $ stands for SOME x : Product (). So the type of both $ and MOD control_state ; $ is Product. The well-formedness requirement that the type Product must be included in the possible types of MOD control_state ; $ is trivially met.

5.7   Name Clashes

A simple name clash occurs if the same name is introduced several times in the CLASS section of a component. However, name clashes may also occur when one or more components are imported into another component: the same name may be provided by several components. The following cases must be distinguished:

1. the name concerned can be traced back to exactly one definition that is not a forward declaration;
2. the name concerned can be traced back to more than one definition that is not a forward declaration.

Recall that a forward declaration is indicated by the keyword FREE. In case 2, it is assumed that the same name is used for different things. This is considered to be an erroneous situation which can be avoided by adding a RENAMING or QUALIFYING section to the component names concerned. In case 1, it is assumed that the name is not used for different things. This might be as intended or not. If it is not intended, this identification can be prevented by applying the copy operator "'" to the component names concerned.

The following example (adapted from [24]) describes a situation where the identification is intended. The example is given because it illustrates how exactly such situations arise. A COLD-1 specification of a relational database management system could include components TUPLE, RELATION, DATABASE, TUPLESTRUCT, RELSCHEMA and DBSCHEMA. In the relational data model [25], a tuple is a map from attributes to values, a relation is a set of tuples with the same set of attributes as domain and a database is a map from relation names to relations. Clearly, RELATION is imported into DATABASE.

```
COMPONENT DATABASE SPECIFICATION
EXPORT
  SORT Database
  FUNC empty   :                                    -> Database,
       put_rel : Database # RelName # Relation -> Database,
       get_rel : Database # RelName            -> Relation,
       del_rel : Database # RelName            -> Database,
       rel_nms : Database                      -> Set[RelName]
IMPORT
  RELNAME,
  RELATION,
  MAP'[RelName,Relation] RENAMING Map TO Database END,
  SET[RelName]
CLASS
  % details omitted here
END
```

A relation schema presents intra-relational constraints on a relation and a database schema presents intra-relational constraints on the relations in a database as well as inter-relational constraints on the database. Relation schemas are used to present the intra-relational constraints. For this reason, RELSCHEMA is imported into DBSCHEMA.

```
COMPONENT DBSCHEMA SPECIFICATION
EXPORT
  SORT DbSchema
  FUNC empty        :                              -> DbSchema,
```

```
            put_relsch : DbSchema # RelName # RelSchema -> DbSchema,
            get_relsch : DbSchema # RelName          -> RelSchema,
            del_relsch : DbSchema # RelName          -> DbSchema,
            add_constr : DbSchema # InclConstraint   -> DbSchema
      PRED is_valid_instance : Database # DbSchema
   IMPORT
      RELNAME,
      RELSCHEMA,
      MAP[RelName,RelSchema],
      INCLCONSTRAINT,
      TUP2'[Map,InclConstraint] RENAMING Tup2 TO DbSchema END,
      DATABASE
   CLASS
      % details omitted here
   END
```

Suppose further that RELSCHEMA contains the definition of a predicate on relations and relation schemas to check whether a relation is a valid instance
of a relation schema or not and that DBSCHEMA contains the definition of a
similar predicate on databases and database schemas (already anticipated in
the presentation of DBSCHEMA just given). This requires that RELATION is also
imported into RELSCHEMA and that DATABASE is also imported into DBSCHEMA.

```
   COMPONENT RELSCHEMA SPECIFICATION
   EXPORT
      SORT RelSchema
      FUNC mk_relsch : TupleStruct # Set[Key] -> RelSchema,
           structure : RelSchema             -> TupleStruct,
           keys      : RelSchema             -> Set[Key]
      PRED is_valid_instance : Relation # RelSchema
   IMPORT
      TUPLESTRUCT,
      KEY,
      SET[Key],
      TUP2'[TupleStruct,Set] RENAMING Tup2 TO RelSchema END,
      RELATION
   CLASS
      % details omitted here
   END
```

The import structure is shown in Figure 5.2. RELATION is indirectly imported
into DBSCHEMA twice, viz. via RELSCHEMA and via DATABASE. Consequently, the
importation of RELSCHEMA and DATABASE into DBSCHEMA causes name clashes
for the names provided by RELATION. These clashes are dealt with in COLD-1
as intended in this case: sorts or operations denoted by the same name in
RELSCHEMA and DATABASE are considered to be identical in DBSCHEMA if they
originate from RELATION.

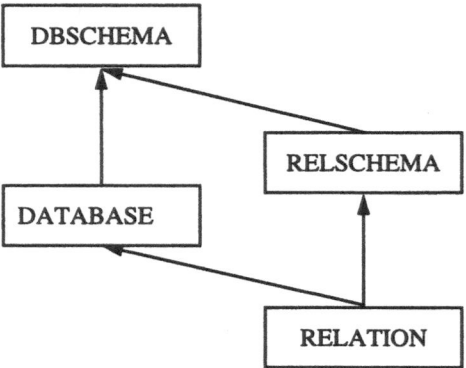

Figure 5.2: Import structure of database schema.

In other situations, the above-mentioned identification might not what is intended. In the component TUPLE mentioned above, it is likely that tuples will be modelled by maps. This means that the component MAP[Attr,Val] is imported. Besides, the sort Map will probably be renamed to Tuple (some operations might be renamed as well):

```
MAP[Attr,Val] RENAMING Map TO Tuple END
```

When importing TUPLE elsewhere, Tuple might be renamed again; even to Map. Tuple is just an alias for Map – introduced to avoid unwanted name clashes. So the renaming in the component TUPLE does not guarantee that tuples are not identified with their representation outside TUPLE. This can be guaranteed by importing

```
MAP'[Attr,Val] RENAMING Map TO Tuple END
```

into TUPLE instead. In other words, the copy operator is used here to enforce that tuples and the particular representation chosen for them are not mixed up. For similar reasons, the copy operator is used in the import sections of the components DATABASE, RELSCHEMA and DBSCHEMA presented above.

For a quite different example, consider the following component definition whose use provides another reason for applying the copy operator:

```
COMPONENT TOGGLE SPECIFICATION
EXPORT
  SORT Toggle
  PROC new :          -> Toggle,
       on  : Toggle ->,
       off : Toggle ->
CLASS
  SORT Toggle    VAR

  AXIOM INIT => NOT EXISTS t : Toggle ()
```

```
    PRED flag : Toggle   VAR                % TRUE is on, FALSE is off

    PROC new : -> Toggle
    PRE  TRUE
    SAT  NEW Toggle
    POST NOT flag(t)

    PROC on : Toggle ->
    IN   t
    PRE  NOT flag(t)
    SAT  MOD flag(t)
    POST flag(t)

    PROC off : Toggle ->
    IN   t
    PRE  flag(t)
    SAT  MOD flag(t)
    POST NOT flag(t)
END
```

In a specification of, for example, a pinball machine, one can find several specializations of toggles, such as buttons, solenoids and detectors. If TOGGLE is imported into components BUTTON, SOLENOID and DETECTOR without copying, then renaming can not preclude that these components will share the variable state component flag – which may lead to unwanted side-effects.

If a name that is provided by several components can be traced back to more than one definition that is not a forward declaration, then this is considered to be an erroneous situation. It has been mentioned before that this can be avoided by adding a RENAMING or QUALIFYING section to the component names concerned. If TOGGLE is imported into BUTTON, this could be done as follows:

```
TOGGLE'
  RENAMING
    Toggle TO Button,
    on     TO press,
    off    TO release
  END
```

This does not only prevents name clashes, but it also takes care of suitable names. However, if several kinds of buttons are needed then it might become difficult to find suitable but different names for each kind. In that case qualifying is useful:

```
BUTTON' QUALIFYING kind1 END
```

Assuming that Button, press and release are the only names defined in and exported by BUTTON, this could alternatively be written:

```
BUTTON'
```

```
RENAMING
  Button  TO kind1.Button,
  press   TO kind1.press,
  release TO kind1.release
END
```

In the following description, the parametrized component SVAR concerning simple programming variables (presented in Section 2.2) is used to store three stacks. The description can be viewed as the IMPLEMENTATION part of a component that maintains a sequence of strings which can be shuffled. The implementation employs one stack of strings, called main_stack, to maintain the sequence concerned and two auxiliary stacks of strings, called aux1_stack and aux2_stack, to implement the shuffle (see further Section 7.6).

```
IMPORT
  BOOL,
  STRING,
  RANDOM[Bool],
  STACK[String],
  SVAR'[Stack]
    RENAMING var TO main_stack, set TO set_main_stack END,
  SVAR'[Stack]
    RENAMING var TO aux1_stack, set TO set_aux1_stack END,
  SVAR'[Stack]
    RENAMING var TO aux2_stack, set TO set_aux2_stack END
CLASS
  % details omitted here
END
```

The copy operator is applied here to achieve that three distinct programming variables are obtained. Each occurrence of the component name SVAR'[Stack] in the IMPORT section provides the two names FUNC var[Stack] : -> Stack and PROC set[Stack] : Stack ->, but either of both names is used for a different operation in each occurrence of SVAR'[Stack] due to the repeated application of the copy operator. This makes directly clear why renamed versions of SVAR'[Stack] are needed.

5.8   Names and Notational Conventions

There are special notations to denote constants of *number* and *string* sorts.

For number sorts, such as the sort Nat from the component NAT given in the standard library of Appendix B, the usual sequences of digits are made available. For example, in the assertion

```
n < 256
```

the sequence of digits 256 corresponds to the complete name

```
FUNC 256 : -> Nat
```

(assuming that the type of n is Nat) which denotes the natural number 256.

For string sorts, such as the sort String from the component STRING provided by the IGLOO library, the usual sequences of characters enclosed by double quotes are made available. In the specification of a file system one could have the following expression in the body of procedures with paths as arguments (see, for example, Section 3.6):

```
"No such file or directory"
```

The corresponding complete name is

```
"No such file or directory" : -> String
```

which denotes a certain string of length 25.

The special notations for constants of number sorts and string sorts must explicitly be imported into a component. This is generally done by importing a component that exports the notation concerned, such as the components NAT and STRING mentioned above.

Operation applications are by default of the form $o(X)$ where o is the name of a function, predicate or procedure. However, prefix or postfix notation is more usual for certain symbols used for unary operations and so is infix notation for certain symbols used for binary operations. For example, it is out of the common to write <(0,+(n,1)). Usually, infix notation is used for both + and < such that the more familiar assertion 0 < n + 1 can be produced. Prefix, postfix and infix notation can be introduced for certain symbols in COLD-1 by means of *operator clauses*. To each complete description – consisting of zero, one or more component definitions and a system description – an operator clause may be attached. In the operator clause, one may declare certain symbols as infix, prefix or postfix operator. In order to avoid excessive use of parentheses, priorities and associativities must be assigned to these operators (associativities only to the infix operators) as well. All this is explained in Section 4.7. The operator clause applies only to the description to which it is attached.

In addition to the operators declared by the specifier for (unary and binary) functions, predicates and procedures, there are many operators that have been built in COLD-1. The priorities and associativities of the latter operators are given in Section A.4.

This means amongst other things that the parentheses in the assertion

```
FORALL n : Nat ( n = n )
```

are mandatory, but that the parentheses in the assertion

```
FORALL n : Nat ( n >= 0 )
```

may be omitted. In practice, the enclosing parentheses can seldom be omitted in FORALL and EXISTS assertions. Therefore, enclosing parentheses were treated as mandatory when the various forms of assertions were outlined in Section 3.8. The same was done for several other forms of assertions and expressions.

5.9   Concluding Remarks

In this chapter it is explained that, instead of demanding of the specifier to provide all occurrences of the symbols that are used to refer to sorts and operations with all syntactic attributes relevant to the issues of well-formedness and meaning, COLD-1 takes over this burden as much as possible. Only if relevant attributes can not be derived from the context, they need to be supplied by the specifier. We see that this approach thus allows, among other things, overloading of symbols to the highest possible degree under a strong type discipline.

Another thing is that undesirable clashes may occur: different occurrences of the same symbol may still refer to different things when all their syntactic attributes are taken into account. These are considered to be erroneous situations and this chapter explains how they arise. We also see how easy they can be avoided with powerful facilities for modular structuring.

Chapter 6
The Automatic Railway Case

Experimentum solum certificat in talibus. (Albertus Magnus)

6.1 Objectives

The objective of the present chapter is to show how the notations presented before can be put to work and be used fruitfully. To that end a case study will be performed in this chapter. After all, "in such things, only the experience gives certainty" as the above citation says.

The case study concerns a computer-based railway system with electrically controlled trains and a specific automatic train braking system. The realization described here is for model trains, but the principles could be applied to a full-scale railway network as well. Railways are safety-critical systems. Automatic train braking is used in modern railway systems to combine the flexibility of human operators with the vigilance of automated equipment. Technically the approach chosen here deviates from what most railway companies have adopted. The novel approach guarantees that the case study is not a reverse engineering of a system already proven. In the devising of a model railway the space limitations call for additional flexibility. The assumption that neither the driver nor the safety-equipment is on-board (both being located at fixed off-track positions) gives rise to additional problems and technical options. These problems and options tend to increase the complexity of the case study, which makes it even more interesting. An essential part of the system is the embedded software, whose specification and design are far from trivial and which will be discussed in the present chapter.

A model railway system similar to the one described here has been realized for the well-known H0 type of model trains (A track width). By using detectors, a few switching relays and a stored-program computer, it is possible to realize a *virtual train connection*. This is a principle which assumes a one-to-one correspondence between users and trains. Each user ("driver") has access to an adjustable power supply. The system maintains the one-to-one correspondence by enforcing an invariant, which among other things implies that at any time there is at most one train in each section. Sections (blocks) are electrically separated parts of the rails, each section having its own power supply wire.

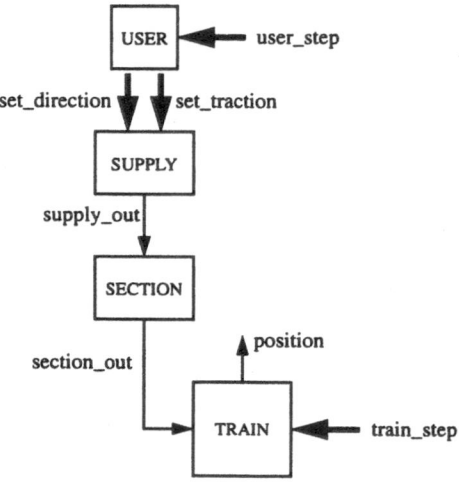

Figure 6.1: Simple railway system with one train.

Figure 6.1 shows the architecture of the simplest kind of model railway system: there is one user who controls a switch button and knob at a power supply. The switch button serves to set the direction of the train to either "normal" or "reversed", while the knob serves to set the traction level of the train. The output of the supply is fed into the railway, which consists of one section. The train obtains its voltage, and hence its power from this section. The train has a variable position, which changes according to mechanical and electrical laws, depending on the mass of the train, the voltage applied and the motor characteristics. In Section 6.2 the data types needed to describe such a simple railway system will be presented. In Section 6.3 its main components will be presented: a user, a power supply, a section and a train.

The architecture of the multi-train railway system to be developed in the present chapter is much more complicated. A diagram of this architecture is given in Figure 6.2. There are three independent users, each controlling one train by means of a power supply and a (virtual) connection. The connection is realized by means of stopper relays, selector relays and of course the railway sections. Furthermore there are devices to inform the controller about the positions of the trains: detectors and a detector multiplexer. The controller activates and deactivates the relays. In Sections 6.4 and 6.5 we return to the requirements and the architecture of the system.

In Section 6.6 the additional components necessary for the multi-train railway system are presented: stoppers, selectors, detectors and a controller. That is followed by several sections devoted to the design of the controller software.

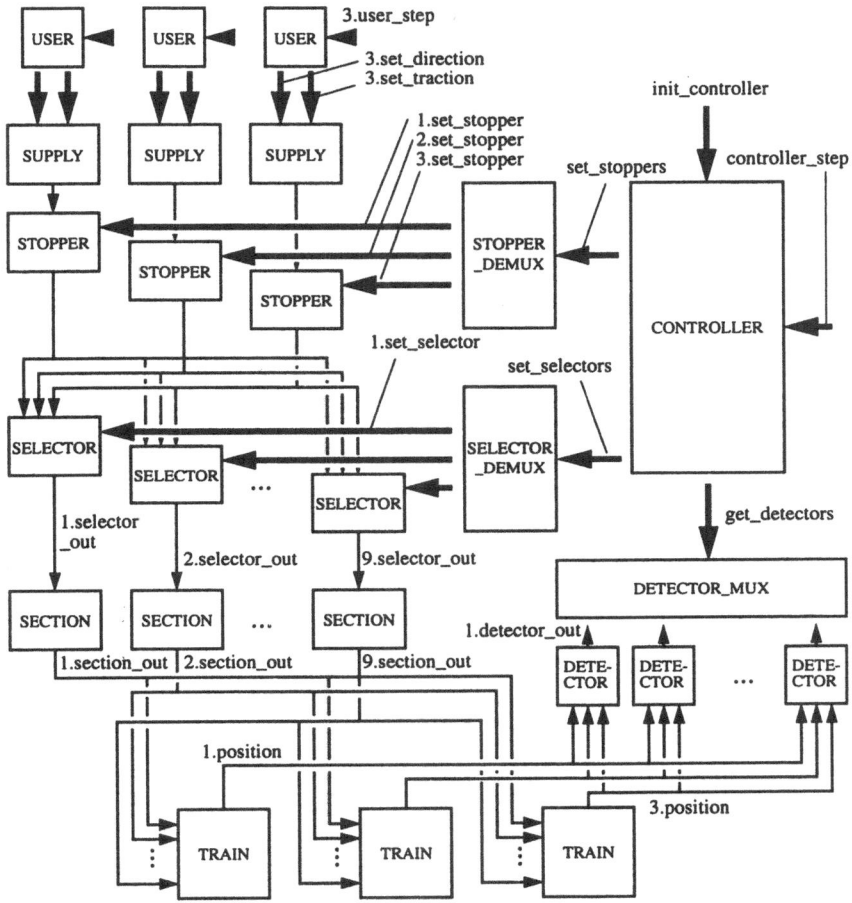

Figure 6.2: Architecture of the automatic railway system.

The controller software can be viewed as a special operating system, monitoring and allocating certain scarce resources. In this case, the scarce resources are the railway sections. They are scarce in the following sense: first, if there are never two trains in one section, then this fact implies a certain safety (no collisions); secondly, if two trains get their power from one and the same section, it is impossible to control them in an independent way.

A classical operating system can offer a *virtual memory*, that is, a memory which behaves like one large linearly ordered memory, whereas in reality there are only several smaller pieces of memory available, which are dynamically allocated in an automatic way, without explicit user intervention. Analogously, the multi-train railway system of this case study offers a *virtual train connection*. For example, there may be three trains acting upon the output of a power supply. Each train behaves as if it were connected to its power supply by a flexible wire. In reality there are switches wired to the sections, which are dynamically allocated in an automatic way. The user will notice that the train is blocked every now and then, but he will never lose control entirely; if his train can not move forwards, it can still be reversed and move backwards.

The practical details and the assumptions concerning user requirements and hardware availability are taken from a personal model railway project done in 1982 and first described in [26].

6.2   Vocabulary of the Application Domain

The concepts of directions, traction levels and voltages will be introduced first. After that the concepts of position, ordering of positions, distance between positions, time and speed will be discussed. These concepts should be viewed as data types, or sorts. Most of their properties are described by algebraic means, i.e. by equations and inductive definitions. Standard data type components are used frequently, notably BOOL, NAT, INT, SET, SEQ and various enumerated data types ENUMi, for example ENUM3 and ENUM4. The component XSEQ (of extended sequences) is assumed to be the same as SEQ, except for the addition of the infix operator @, which offers the notation s @ i for selection in addition to sel(s,i).

6.2.1   Directions

The electrical power is transferred to the trains via the rails. The track consists of two rails. One of these is "earthed" ("grounded"), which means that its potential serves as a reference potential. Let us assume that the earthed rail is always at the left-hand side of the train. The other rail can have a positive or a negative potential, or voltage, with respect to the ground. If it is positive, the train will move forwards. If it is 0 Volt, the train will stop within e.g. 0.5 s If the potential is negative, the train will move backwards. The component DIRECTION describes the sort Direction, which has two elements.

```
COMPONENT DIRECTION SPECIFICATION
EXPORT
  SORT Direction
  FUNC forward   : -> Direction,
       backward  : -> Direction,
       reverse   : Direction -> Direction
IMPORT
  ENUM2' RENAMING Enum2 TO Direction,
                  x0     TO forward,
                  x1     TO backward
          END
CLASS
```

```
        FUNC reverse : Direction -> Direction
        IND  reverse(forward)  = backward;
             reverse(backward) = forward
    END
```

The standard data type ENUM2 is used. It provides the sort Enum2 and the constants x0 and x1.

6.2.2 Traction Levels

The users have access to control knobs that serve to indicate the desired motor power of the trains. The term "traction" refers to a user's view of this motor power.

```
COMPONENT TRACTION SPECIFICATION
EXPORT
  SORT Traction
  FUNC nat   : Traction -> Nat,
       level : Nat -> Traction
  PRED <=    : Traction # Traction
IMPORT
  NAT,
  NAT' RENAMING Nat TO Traction END
CLASS
  FUNC level : Nat -> Traction
  IN   k
  DEF  ( k = 0 ? ; 0
       | k > 0 ? ; 1 + level(k - 1)
       )

  FUNC nat : Traction -> Nat
  IN   t
  DEF  THAT k : Nat (t = level k)
END
```

In the above specification traction levels are introduced as the elements of a sort Traction. See also Figure 6.3. In practice we do not use the traction levels beyond level 9, but in a mathematical sense they exist as values. In Section 6.3.2 a power supply will be presented whose control knob has 10 positions, labelled 0 .. 9.

We ought to mention that there are several useful alternative approaches to the specification of Traction. First of all, it can be noted that level and nat define an isomorphism between Traction and Nat. Since the task of describing such isomorphisms occurs more than once (later we will describe a sort Dis of distances similarly), it may be convenient to use a component ISONAT which should export both Nat and Isonat say together with the morphism functions between them. But in order to keep the appendix with the standard components as simple as possible, ISONAT, ISOINT etc. have not been included.

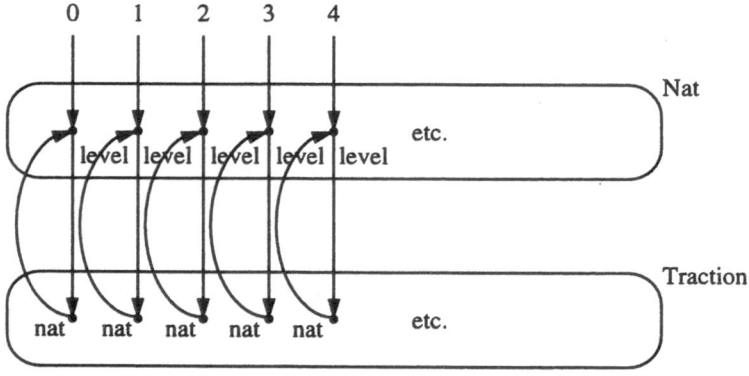

Figure 6.3: The sort of `Traction`.

Another alternative is to use a generic component SUBNAT[lwb,upb] of
subranges of Nat and to instantiate it here as SUBNAT'[0,9]. This would be
closer to the reality of the power supplies used, but again we would have to
include SUBNAT in the library.

6.2.3 Voltages

The component VOLTAGE describes the sort Voltage. The operator Volt must
be declared as a postfix operator.

```
COMPONENT VOLTAGE SPECIFICATION
EXPORT
  SORT Voltage
  FUNC int  : Voltage -> Int,
       Volt : Int -> Voltage
  PRED <    : Voltage # Voltage,
       >    : Voltage # Voltage,
       <=   : Voltage # Voltage,
       >=   : Voltage # Voltage
IMPORT
  INT,
  INT' RENAMING Int TO Voltage END
CLASS
  FUNC Volt : Int -> Voltage                         % postfix
  IN   i
  DEF  ( i < 0 ? ; (i + 1) Volt - 1
       | i = 0 ? ; 0
       | i > 0 ? ; 1 + (i - 1) Volt
       )

  FUNC int : Voltage -> Int
```

```
IN    v
DEF   THAT i : Int (v = i Volt)
END
```

The standard data type INT is used. It provides the sort Int, the constants denoted by the special number notations 0, 1, 2, ..., + for addition, − for subtraction, and the binary relations <, <=, > and >=.

In the above specification voltages are introduced as the elements of a sort Voltage. This sort is isomorphic to the sort of integer numbers. The DEF clause of Volt defines the isomorphism recursively. If $i < 0$ then the definition of i Volt is reduced to the simpler case of $(i + 1)$ Volt, by subtracting 1 from that. The integer 0 is mapped to the voltage 0, which defines the base case of the recursion. And for $i > 0$, we find that i Volt is equal to $1 + ((i - 1)$ Volt$)$.

In physics it is useful to model voltages as real numbers, but for the present case study the discrete model satisfies our purposes well enough. See also Figure 6.4. Voltages below −9 Volt or above 9 Volt will not be used.

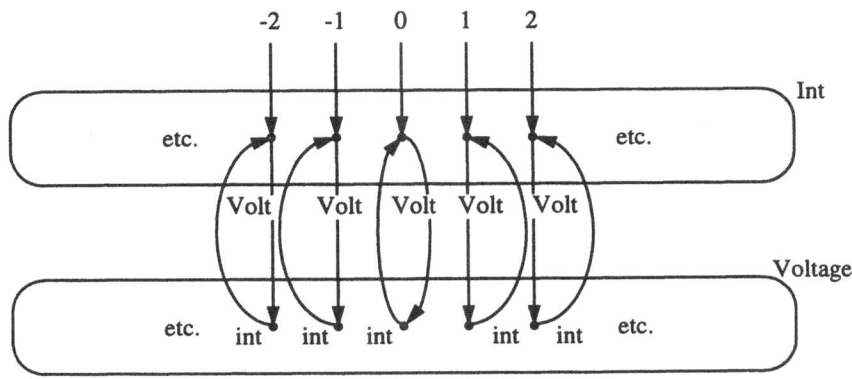

Figure 6.4: The sort of Voltage.

Again we ought to mention an alternative approach to the specification of Voltage. We could have defined a general-purpose component ISOINT and replaced the definition of VOLTAGE by:

```
COMPONENT VOLTAGE SPECIFICATION                          % alternative
EXPORT
  % as before
IMPORT
  INT,
  ISOINT' RENAMING Isoint TO Voltage,
                   isoint : Int -> Isoint TO Volt
            END
END
```

6.2.4 Positions

The component NETWORK describes the sort Pos of positions and the operations that model the essential connection information of a railroad network.
The operators ++ and -- must be declared as postfix operators. For each position p there is a next position p++ and a previous position p--. The former
corresponds to the forward direction, the latter to the backward direction.

No railway crossings will be considered here and it is also assumed that no
turning-loops occur (note that a turning-loop may short-circuit the supply).
The positions are supposed to cover both the positions of the railway as well
as one or more "off-track" positions, modeling the points reached by the train
if it does not stop in time at the end of the track. A point (a switch towards
a siding) is viewed as a position with a modifiable ++ or --.

More network properties will be added in Section 6.7.6 when the particular
railway network of this case study will be presented.

```
COMPONENT NETWORK SPECIFICATION
EXPORT
  SORT Pos
  FUNC ++ : Pos -> Pos,
       -- : Pos -> Pos
  PRED is_point  : Pos
  PROC mod_point : Pos ->
CLASS
  SORT Pos

  FUNC ++ : Pos -> Pos PRE TRUE VAR              % postfix
  FUNC -- : Pos -> Pos PRE TRUE VAR              % postfix

  PRED is_point : Pos

  PROC mod_point : Pos ->
  IN   p
  PRE  is_point(p)
  SAT  MOD p++ | MOD p--
END
```

The network concepts are illustrated in three figures. Figure 6.5 shows a
straight railway segment, which is linearly ordered in the sense that a movement backwards can be undone by a movement forwards, and vice versa.
Figure 6.6 shows several positions, one of which is a point. The predicate
is_point, shown as an area, holds for one position. In the case of a movement backwards, following the -- arrows, there is a joining of two straight
segments. But in the case of a movement forwards, following the ++ arrows,
there is choice. In the state of Figure 6.6 the choice is to the left. Execution
of mod_point could result in another state, as shown in Figure 6.7.

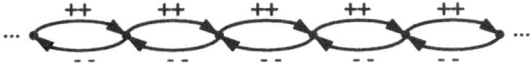

Figure 6.5: Straight segment.

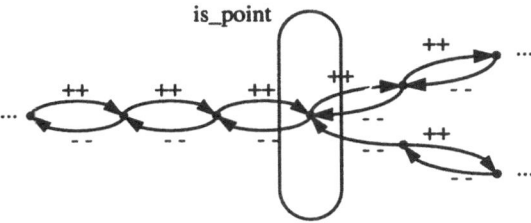

Figure 6.6: A point set to the left.

6.2.5   Ordering Properties

Next we will aim at the definition of an ordering relation (<) on positions. If $p < q$ this means roughly that p comes before q (when a train moves forward).

First we have to give a very generic description of a section as an arbitrary subset of all positions, characterized by a predicate (sec). This is necessary to specify the parameters of the "<" concept, which depend on the set of positions considered and on the network connections considered. The predicate sec characterizes such sets, while prv (for previous) characterizes the network connections. When used, the "previous" function prv can be either -- or ++.

```
LET SECTION :=
EXPORT
  sec, prv
IMPORT
  NETWORK
CLASS
  PRED sec : Pos
  FUNC prv : Pos -> Pos
END
```

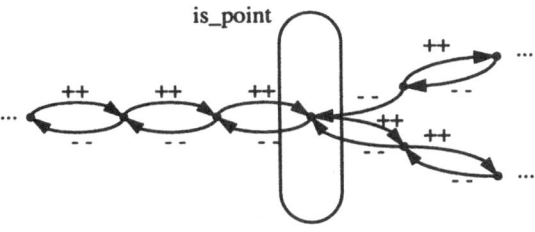

Figure 6.7: A point set to the right.

The above generic SECTION is only used for specification purposes, as a parameter restriction. In Section 6.3.3 we will describe specific properties of real railway sections, like the fact that they can convey the electricity to the trains.

In general, it does not make sense to ask "does position p come before position q ?", because there may be cycles in the relations induced by ++ or --. But for restricted sets of positions the question may make sense. This motivates the ordering relations < and <= introduced in ORD below.

```
LET ORD[sec,prv] :=
ABSTRACT
  SECTION
EXPORT
  PRED <    : Pos # Pos,
        <=  : Pos # Pos
IMPORT
  NETWORK
CLASS
  DECL p,q : Pos

  PRED <= : Pos # Pos
  IND  sec(p)  =>  p <= p;
       p <= q AND sec(prv(p))  =>  prv(p) <= q

  PRED < : Pos # Pos
  IN   p,q
  DEF  (p <= q) AND (p /= q)
END
```

When employing ORD[sec,--], we find that $p <= q$ holds if within sec position p is reached by driving a train in the -- direction, starting from q. (This is the intended use. ORD[sec,++] is analogous, but then it is necessary to rename < to > and <= to >=). In the typical applications of "<" or "<=", for example considering the positions p for which sec(p) holds, we can import ORD[sec,--] and then we can write axioms such as

```
sec(p) => (first <= p AND p <= last)
```

to fix certain positions (first and last) within the given section, as sketched in Figure 6.8.

6.2.6 Metric Properties

It makes sense to ask "how far is position p away from position q ?". An obvious idea is to introduce a metric, which is a distance function D, such that $D(p,q)$ is the distance between p and q. But some care is needed because there may be several alternative routes from p to q (or from q to p). There are two special notions of distance which can be defined easily; they are denoted as Df and Db. Df is called the "forward distance" and Db is the "backward distance".

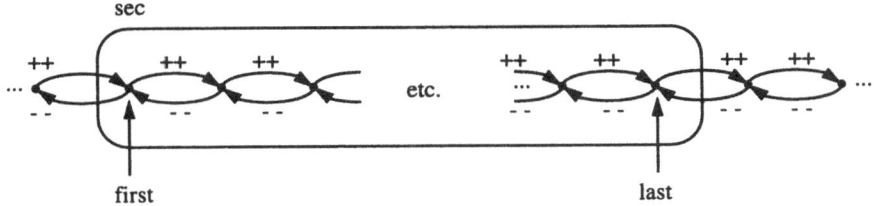

Figure 6.8: Function graph of a straight section.

For positions p and q with a linearly organized set of positions between them, which means that ++ and -- are each other's inverses, it can be shown that $Df(p,q) = Db(q,p)$.

Distances are nothing but natural numbers, but in order to arrive at a kind of dimension checking, they are modelled as elements of a separate sort Dis. The operators nm, um and mm must be declared postfix operators. They denote nanometres (nm), micrometres (μm) and millimetres (mm), respectively. In this way COLD-1 expressions like 5 mm, or 5000 um can be used to indicate a distance of 5 mm. The remark relating to the use of an auxiliary component (ISONAT) made for the sorts Traction and Voltage applies here as well.

```
COMPONENT DIS SPECIFICATION
EXPORT
  SORT Dis
  FUNC nm  : Nat -> Dis,
       um  : Nat -> Dis,
       mm  : Nat -> Dis,
       nat : Dis -> Nat,
       +   : Dis # Dis -> Dis
  PRED <   : Dis # Dis,
       <=  : Dis # Dis,
       >   : Dis # Dis,
       >=  : Dis # Dis
  FUNC Df : Pos # Pos -> Dis,
       Db : Pos # Pos -> Dis
IMPORT
  NAT,
  NETWORK,
  NAT' RENAMING Nat TO Dis END
CLASS
  FUNC nm : Nat -> Dis                                  % postfix
  IN   k
  DEF  ( k = 0 ? ; 0
       | k > 0 ? ; 1 + (k - 1) nm
       )

  FUNC um : Nat -> Dis                                  % postfix
```

```
IN    k
DEF   (k * 1000) nm


FUNC mm : Nat -> Dis                                   % postfix
IN    k
DEF   (k * 1000) um


FUNC nat : Dis -> Nat
IN    d
DEF   THAT k : Nat (d = k nm)


FUNC Df : Pos # Pos -> Dis
IN    p,q
DEF   ( p = q ?  ; 0 nm
      | p /= q ? ; (nat(Df(p++,q)) + 1) nm
      )


FUNC Db : Pos # Pos -> Dis
IN    p,q
DEF   ( p = q ?  ; 0 nm
      | p /= q ? ; (nat(Db(p--,q)) + 1) nm
      )
END
```

The notion of "forward distance" is illustrated by Figure 6.9. Note that the familiar formula Df(p,q) <= Df(p,r) + Df(r,q) holds, provided that the distances Df(p,q), Df(p,r) and Df(r,q) are defined. In the same way, Db(p,q) <= Db(p,r) + Db(r,q) holds. But in the presence of points (see Figure 6.42), the formula Df(p,q) = Db(q,p) does *not* hold in general. It is also interesting

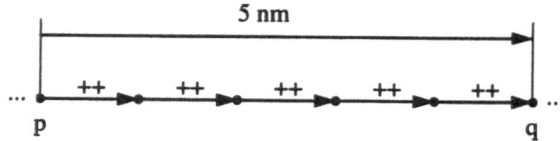

Figure 6.9: Forward distance Df(p,q) = 5 nm.

to see how the COLD-1 concept of undefinedness works for the given definition of Df: if q can not be reached from p, then Df(p,q) is undefined, that is, NOT Df(p,q)! holds.

We would like to add a few remarks concerning the distinction between ordering and metric properties. The ordering properties of sections and other special areas and of the relationships that exist between them are in a sense the deepest geometric properties; they are preserved under a wide class of transformations of the railway system, such as the stretching or reducing of distances.

The metric properties represent a more detailed view of a railway than the ordering properties. Metric properties concern distance, so they are indispensable in modeling the dynamic behaviour of a train: its speed, its inertia and the accelerating effects of its motor. If it would be possible to stop a train instantaneously, a railway safety system could be devised without including metric properties in the vocabulary. But since it takes some time for a train to stop, the length of the braking trajectory must be taken into account.

6.2.7 Time

The classical theory of movement and acceleration is known as Newtoneon mechanics. It is based on the assumption that position, speed (velocity) and acceleration are functions of time. The set of time values is taken to be $\mathbb{R}$ and the analysis of the position of an object from a given acceleration history requires the calculus of differentiation and integration. This is not an easy thing to describe in COLD-1 and here we adopt another model, assuming a discrete time-axis. The sort Time introduced below should be interpreted as relative time or duration, not as absolute time.

```
COMPONENT TIME SPECIFICATION
EXPORT
  SORT Time
  FUNC msec : Nat -> Time,
       nat  : Time -> Nat,
       +    : Time # Time -> Time
  PRED <    : Time # Time
IMPORT
  NAT,
  NAT' RENAMING Nat TO Time END
CLASS
  FUNC msec : Nat -> Time                                    % postfix
  IN   n
  DEF  ( n = 0 ? ; 0
       | n > 0 ? ; 1 + (n - 1) msec
       )

  FUNC nat : Time -> Nat
  IN   t
  DEF  THAT n : Nat (t = n msec)
END
```

The operator msec must be declared a postfix operator.

6.2.8 Speed

We model the behaviour of a moving train by assuming that its speed and position are variables which are modified by a procedure called train_step.

It is assumed that the latter procedure is executed at regular intervals: 1000 times every second. The notion of "speed" is viewed as distance per execution of `train_step`. The unit of time (a "step") is 1 ms

```
COMPONENT SPEED SPECIFICATION
EXPORT
  SORT Speed
  FUNC mmpersec : Int -> Speed,
       int : Speed -> Int,
       *   : Time # Speed -> Dis
  PRED <   : Speed # Speed,
       >   : Speed # Speed,
       <=  : Speed # Speed,
       >=  : Speed # Speed
IMPORT
  INT,
  DIS,
  TIME,
  INT' RENAMING Int TO Speed END
CLASS
  FUNC umpersec : Int -> Speed                        % postfix
  IN  i
  DEF ( i < 0 ? ; (i + 1) umpersec - 1
      | i = 0 ? ; 0
      | i > 0 ? ; 1 + (i - 1) umpersec
      )

  FUNC mmpersec : Int -> Speed                        % postfix
  IN  i
  DEF (i * 1000) umpersec

  FUNC int : Speed -> Int
  IN  s
  DEF THAT i : Int (s = i umpersec)

  FUNC * : Time # Speed -> Dis
  IN  t,s
  DEF (nat(t) * abs(int(s))) nm
END
```

The operator `umpersec` must be declared a postfix operator. It denotes μm/s, or nm per train step, which is the same. Similarly, `mmpersec` denotes mm/s, which is the same as μm/ms This `mmpersec` is a postfix operator too.

6.3   Analysis of the Application Domain

The concepts of users, power supplies, sections and trains are introduced next. Most of these are physical components which will be modelled in a component-oriented way. An alternative approach would have been to employ an object-oriented style, where each user, each supply, etc. would be modelled as an object, that is, a value carrying attributes (for more information on that style see Sections 9.7 and 9.8). In the present approach, however, one component in COLD-1 corresponds to one physical component. When more than one physical component of a certain kind is needed, for example three trains, the component copy operator (') must be used, together with QUALIFYING or RENAMING clauses. This approach is fine when describing a fixed design, such as the present case study. When a higher degree of reusability and ease of adaptation are important, the object-oriented approach may offer the additional flexibility needed. COLD-1 supports both approaches.

The physical and abstract interconnections of the components are described using the origin mechanism of the language. For example, consider the FREE definitions of set_direction and set_traction of USER in Section 6.3.1 below. In Section 6.3.2 these will be defined as operations of SUPPLY. Such common operations of USER and SUPPLY will be unified as soon as they are put together by means of IMPORT.

6.3.1   A User

The component USER models the behaviour of one user. There are two actions that can be performed by a user: setting the direction to either forward or backward, and setting the traction level.

```
COMPONENT USER SPECIFICATION
EXPORT
  PROC set_direction : Direction ->,
       set_traction  : Traction ->,
       user_step     : ->
IMPORT
  DIRECTION,
  TRACTION
CLASS
  PROC set_direction : Direction -> FREE
  PROC set_traction  : Traction  -> FREE

  PROC user_step : ->
  DEF  set_direction($) | set_traction($)
END
```

The "abstract hardware diagram" (or "box diagram") of USER is given in Figure 6.10. This kind of diagram will be given for most components of the case study. The thick arrows are commands (procedures). In other diagrams thin arrows will be used too; they are wires (functions), as can be seen in Figure 6.11. These diagrams can be assembled to show the interconnections of the entire system, as in Figure 6.2. Of course it is possible to eliminate the

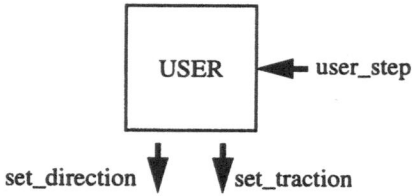

Figure 6.10: Abstract hardware diagram of a user.

"free" definitions, for example by adding SUPPLY to the import list. Throughout this case however we will show the main components of the railway system architecture as independent units. That way we can present diagrams such as Figures 6.10 and 6.11 in a very systematic manner (this will be discussed further in Sections 8.5 and 8.6).

6.3.2   A Power Supply

The component SUPPLY models a power supply with adjustable direction and traction level. One supply provides the electrical power needed for one train. For example, when three trains are used, three supplies are needed. The precondition of set_traction restricts the traction level to values less than or equal to level 9.

```
COMPONENT SUPPLY SPECIFICATION
EXPORT
  PROC set_direction : Direction  ->,
       set_traction  : Traction ->
  FUNC supply_out    : -> Voltage
IMPORT
  NAT,
  INT,
  DIRECTION,
  TRACTION,
  VOLTAGE
CLASS
  FUNC direction : -> Direction PRE TRUE VAR
  FUNC traction  : -> Traction  PRE TRUE VAR

  AXIOM INIT => direction = forward AND traction = level 0

  PROC set_direction : Direction ->
  IN  p
  PRE  TRUE
```

```
SAT  MOD direction
POST direction = p

PROC set_traction : Traction ->
IN   t
PRE  t <= level 9
SAT  MOD traction
POST traction = t

FUNC supply_out : -> Voltage
DEF  ( direction = forward  ? ;  int(nat(traction)) Volt
     | direction = backward ? ;  (-int(nat(traction))) Volt
     )
END
```

The abstract hardware diagram of this specification is given in Figure 6.11.

Common realizations for a model train supply include a multi-voltage transformer followed by a rotary switch and a rectifier which serves to turn the alternating current (AC) of the transformer into the direct current (DC) needed by the train. More sophisticated realization techniques yield a pulsed output with an adjustable duty cycle. This results in improved motor characteristics, but has the disadvantage that electronic circuitry including switching transistors or thyristors is needed.

A possible front of the power supply control is shown in Figure 6.12; it shows a state with direction = forward and traction = level 3.

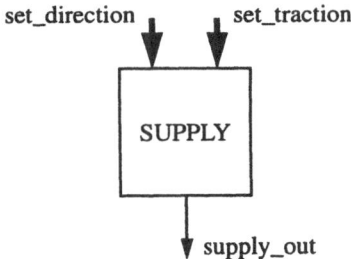

Figure 6.11: Abstract hardware diagram of a power supply.

6.3.3   A Section

A section (or "block") is a piece of railway track which is electrically isolated from its neighbouring sections. It has an electrical supply line, which comes from a supply, possibly through a stopper and a selector. There are different types of sections, two of which are included here: SECTION_S, which is a straight section, and SECTION_Y1, which is a section with one point.

COMPONENT SECTION_S SPECIFICATION

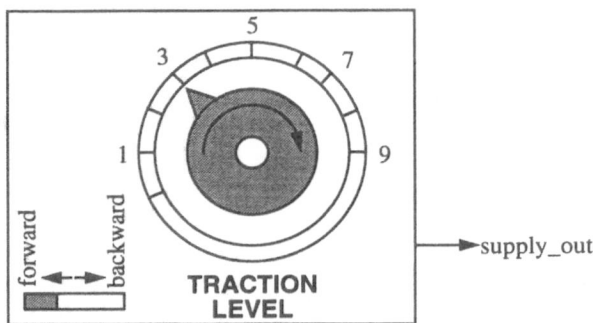

Figure 6.12: Front view of a power supply.

```
EXPORT
  FUNC section_in  : -> Voltage,
       section_out : -> Voltage
  PRED sec    : Pos
  FUNC first : -> Pos,
       last  : -> Pos
IMPORT
  NETWORK,
  VOLTAGE,
  ORD[sec,--]
CLASS
  FUNC section_in  : -> Voltage FREE
  FUNC section_out : -> Voltage DEF section_in

  PRED sec : Pos

  DECL p : Pos

  AXIOM sec(p) => (p++)-- = p AND (p--)++ = p AND NOT is_point(p)

  FUNC first : -> Pos
  FUNC last  : -> Pos

  AXIOM first = THAT p (sec(p) AND NOT sec(p--));
        last  = THAT p (sec(p) AND NOT sec(p++))

  AXIOM sec(p)  =>  first <= p AND p <= last
END
```

The functions section_in and section_out model the transfer of voltage.
In particular, section_in is supposed to be the output wire of a previous
component, and hence it acts as an input for SECTION_S.

The first axiom describes the organization of the positions, which is that
there are no joints or forkings. The second axiom states that first and last

are the first and the last position in the section. The last axiom states that the ordering <= is total.

The abstract hardware diagram, covering the voltage transfer aspects of this specification, is given in Figure 6.13. Additional diagrams are given in Figures 6.14 (topological aspects) and 6.15 (physical aspects).

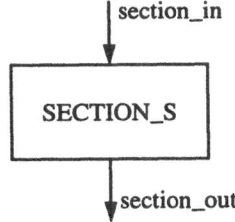

Figure 6.13: Abstract hardware diagram of a straight section.

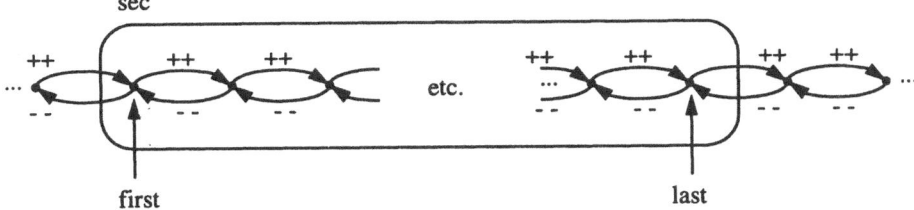

Figure 6.14: Function graph of a straight section.

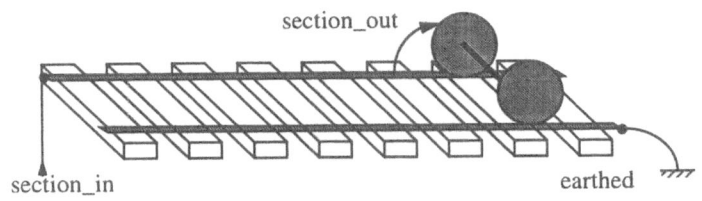

Figure 6.15: Voltage transfer of a section (physical view).

```
COMPONENT SECTION_Y1 SPECIFICATION
EXPORT
   FUNC section_in  : -> Voltage,
        section_out : -> Voltage
   PRED sec   : Pos
   FUNC first : -> Pos,
        last1 : -> Pos,
        last2 : -> Pos
```

```
IMPORT
  NETWORK,
  VOLTAGE,
  ORD[sec,--]
CLASS
  FUNC section_in  : -> Voltage FREE
  FUNC section_out : -> Voltage DEF section_in

  PRED sec : Pos

  DECL p,q : Pos

  FUNC point : -> Pos
  PRE  TRUE
  DEF  THAT p (sec(p) AND is_point(p))

  AXIOM sec(p) => (p++)-- = p;
        sec(p) AND p-- /= point  =>  (p--)++ = p

  FUNC first : -> Pos
  FUNC last1 : -> Pos
  FUNC last2 : -> Pos

  PRED is_last : Pos
  IN   p
  DEF  sec(p) AND NOT sec(p++)

  AXIOM first = THAT p (sec(p) AND NOT sec(p--))

  AXIOM last1 /= last2;
        is_last(last1) AND is_last(last2);
        is_last(p)  =>   p = last1 OR p = last2

  AXIOM sec(p)  =>  first <= p AND (p <= last1 OR p <= last2)
END
```

The functions section_in and section_out model the transfer of voltage.
The first axiom describes the organization of the positions: except for one
point there are no joints or forkings. The second and the third axioms explain
how first, last1 and last2 are the first and the last positions in the section.
The last axiom describes the ordering <= by means of an auxiliary predicate
is_last.

Figure 6.16 shows the section in a state in which the point is set to the left.

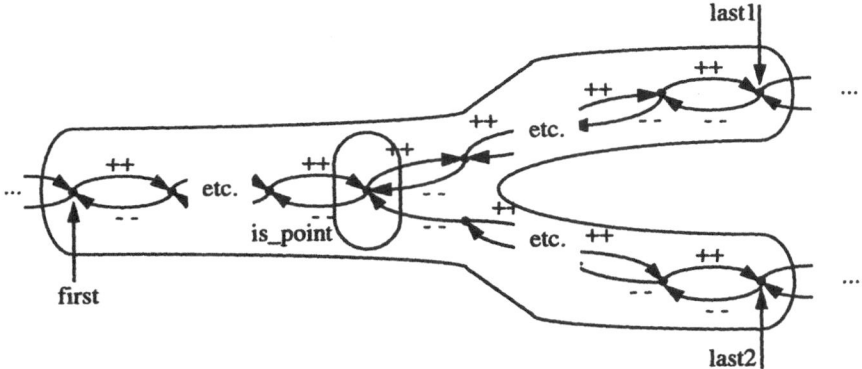

Figure 6.16: Function graph of a section with one point.

6.3.4   A Train

Trains may have different motor characteristics and different braking performances. Therefore the component TRAIN introduced below is parametrized, with two parameters, called s_max and t_max. The former indicates the maximal speed of the train, while the latter indicates the maximum time required to stop (braking time).

```
LET TRAIN_PARAMS :=
EXPORT
  FUNC s_max : -> Speed,
       t_max : -> Time
IMPORT
  TIME,
  SPEED
CLASS
  FUNC s_max : -> Speed PRE TRUE
  FUNC t_max : -> Time  PRE TRUE
END
```

The table of Figure 6.17 shows the intended interpretation of the units adopted. The table of Figure 6.18 shows the intended interpretation and a typical value for each train parameter. It is easy to see that if s_max = 50 mm/sec and t_max = 500 msec, the product t_max * s_max = 25 mm is an upperbound to the maximum stopping-distance.

The units and the typical values shown apply to a model railway. It is assumed that the trains are operated at voltages whose absolute values do not exceed 9 Volt. Here we describe a parametrized component; for the instantiations we refer to Section 6.7.5.

The specification is tuned to an application in which the train runs on a railway system with at most 9 sections. It must be admitted that it is not elegant that the description of a general-purpose train shows such details of

concept	unit
speed	1 mmpersec
train step (time)	1 msec

Figure 6.17: Units of train parameters.

parameter	interpretation	typical value
s_max	max speed	50 mm/sec
t_max	max braking time	500 msec

Figure 6.18: Interpretation of train parameters.

the railway. On the other hand, it is true that a train will obtain its electricity
from one of the 9 sections; which one depends on the precise position of the
train. Again, the "free" definitions could be removed by putting 9 sections
into the import list.

```
COMPONENT TRAIN[s_max,t_max] SPECIFICATION
ABSTRACT
  TRAIN_PARAMS
EXPORT
  FUNC 1.section_out : -> Voltage,
       2.section_out : -> Voltage,
       % etc.
       9.section_out : -> Voltage
  PRED 1.sec : Pos,
       2.sec : Pos,
       % etc.
       9.sec : Pos
  PROC train_step : ->
  FUNC position   : -> Pos,
       speed      : -> Speed
  PROC brake_time : -> Time
IMPORT
  NAT,
  INT,
  DIS,
  TIME,
  SPEED,
  NETWORK,
  VOLTAGE
CLASS
  FUNC 1.section_out : -> Voltage FREE
  FUNC 2.section_out : -> Voltage FREE
       % etc.
```

```
FUNC 9.section_out : -> Voltage FREE

PRED 1.sec : Pos FREE
PRED 2.sec : Pos FREE
     % etc.
PRED 9.sec : Pos FREE

FUNC voltage : -> Voltage
DEF  ( 1.sec(position) ? ; 1.section_out
     | 2.sec(position) ? ; 2.section_out
       % etc.
     | 9.sec(position) ? ; 9.section_out
     )

FUNC position : -> Pos    PRE TRUE VAR
FUNC speed    : -> Speed PRE TRUE VAR

AXIOM abs(int(speed)) <= (abs(int(s_max))::Nat)

AXIOM INIT => speed = 0 mmpersec

PROC adapt_position : ->
PRE  TRUE
SAT  MOD position
POST (speed >= 0 mmpersec) =>
     Df(position',position) = (1 msec) * speed;
     (speed <= 0 mmpersec) =>
     Db(position',position) = (1 msec) * speed

PROC adapt_speed : ->
PRE  TRUE
SAT  MOD speed
POST speed = f(voltage,speed')

DECL v,w : Voltage, s,t : Speed

FUNC f : Voltage # Speed -> Speed

AXIOM {1} f(0 Volt,0 mmpersec) = 0 mmpersec;
      {2} s > 0 mmpersec  =>  f(0 Volt,s) < s;
      {3} s < 0 mmpersec  =>  f(0 Volt,s) > s;
      {4} s > 0 mmpersec  =>  NOT f(v,s) < 0 mmpersec;
      {5} s < 0 mmpersec  =>  NOT f(v,s) > 0 mmpersec;
      {6} s <= t AND v <= w  =>  f(v,s) <= f(w,t)

PROC train_step : ->
DEF  adapt_speed; adapt_position
```

```
PROC brake_time : -> Time
DEF  ( speed  = 0 mmpersec ? ; 0 msec
     | speed /= 0 mmpersec ? ; adapt_speed; (1 msec) + brake_time
     )

AXIOM {7} voltage = 0 Volt  =>  brake_time < t_max
END
```

The reader might ask: "how are you sure the function **voltage** is defined?".
Well, we can not be sure, for this depends on the railway topology: for example,
if there are positions p for which none of $1.\mathtt{sec}(p)$, $2.\mathtt{sec}(p),\ldots$, $9.\mathtt{sec}(p)$
holds, then the voltage is not defined for such positions p. If the train is
off-track it will not pick up any voltage.

We would like to add some explanation concerning clauses {1} to {7} of
the axioms. The first axiom gives constraints for the function **f**, which is the
functional relation between voltage, speed and "new" speed.

1. braking a train which is already at speed 0 again yields speed 0;
2. braking a train moving forwards yields a reduced speed;
3. braking a train moving backwards yields a reduced speed;
4. if a (forward) change of direction occurs, there is a point of speed 0;
5. if a (backward) change of direction occurs, there is a point of speed 0;
6. the function is covariant in both arguments; feeding less voltage into a
   train, or into a slower train, can not make the train go faster (i.e. faster
   than it would go without lowered voltage or lowered speed);
7. if the train gets a voltage of 0 Volt, then the train will return to a zero
   speed within the maximum brake-time of **t_max** train steps.

It may be helpful to regard the quantity $\mathtt{f}(v,s) - s$ as $\frac{\Delta \text{ speed}}{\Delta t}$, where Δ
speed is the speed increment and where Δt is the unit time step.

If we consider the function $\mathtt{f}_{\text{voltage}}$, which for a given voltage is **f** as a
function from **Speed** to **Speed**, then it is easy to see that the fixed points of
$\mathtt{f}_{\text{voltage}}$ correspond to stationary situations. In other words: if $\mathtt{f}_{\text{voltage}}(s) = s$,
then the train will keep its speed s as long as the voltage is kept constant.

The definition of **brake_time** can also be read as follows: $\mathtt{brake\_time} =$
$min\ n \cdot [\mathtt{f}_{\text{voltage}}^{n}(\mathtt{speed}) = 0]$, where we use the notation of exponentiation to
indicate repeated function application.

Clauses {4} and {5} guarantee that the definition of **brake_time** works as
expected. Due to the discreteness of the notions of distance and speed, {4}
and {5} do not hold automatically. The situation should be compared with the
case of $\mathbb{R}$-valued functions. For such functions there is a theorem put forward
by Bolzano (1781 – 1848), which says that for a continuous real function S,
defined at the interval $[0, 1]$ such that $S(0) < 0 < S(1)$, there is a t in $[0, 1]$ for
which $S(t) = 0$. Here we need a similar property for the speed as a function of

time: when the train brakes, there must be a point in time for which "speed" = 0.

The abstract hardware diagram of this specification is given in Figure 6.19. See also Figure 6.20.

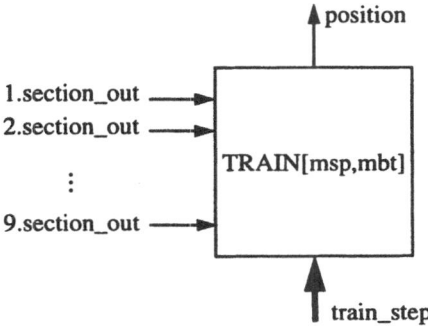

Figure 6.19: Abstract hardware diagram of a train.

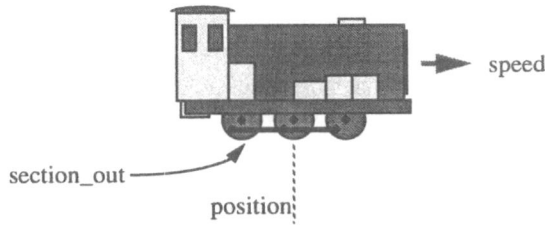

Figure 6.20: A train (physical view).

6.4   System Requirements

Throughout this case study we will adopt the requirement that the railway system accommodates several trains which are controllable simultaneously while the overall track length is very limited, maybe even a few metres only. This requirement is justified by space limitations. The railway is realized as a model system which must easily fit in a normal home. Therefore the safety system described in the present chapter will sometimes allow trains to be located in adjacent sections. When there are no space limitations there is an easy solution, which is that each pair of trains has at least one free section between them. But here we will avoid the use of additional free sections, even if this will give rise to complex tracking and allocation algorithms. Also for reasons of space we will accept the restriction to use very short trains only; a typical train consists of just one locomotive.

We will adopt the requirement that the trains must always be movable: a driver may notice that a train is blocked every now and then, but he will never lose control entirely. If his train can not move forwards it can still be reversed and move backwards. When playing with a model railway system this is a fine property, because there is always something which can be done.

Another requirement is that each train must be a passive device without any on-board control buttons, switches, signal decoders or train identification circuitry. Instead, the voltage of the rails is fed directly into the motor of the train. The polarity of the voltage simply determines the direction in which the train moves. The users (drivers, players) operate remotely; they set the traction level and direction of power supplies using one supply for each train. The system must provide the virtual train connection. This ensures that any standard low-budget type of model trains can be used without modifications, except for the magnets.

6.5   The Architecture of Safety

6.5.1   Survey

Figure 6.21 gives a survey of the railway system. The principal ideas behind the system architecture will be mentioned here; the details will be explained later. The architecture is described for the specific case of three trains and nine sections, but it can easily be adapted to any other number of trains and sections if desired.

The three users are shown at the top of Figure 6.21 Each user has access to its own supply, upon which two operations can be performed. Each supply has one output, carrying a voltage to be fed into the corresponding train. The intention is that the first user has a virtual train connection to the first train while the second and third users similarly have connections to the second and third trains, respectively. There are 3 stoppers, one for each train. Roughly speaking, a stopper is a switch which can be opened to disrupt the supply of electricity to the corresponding train. This can be used to guarantee safety: if a train is about to enter a section in which there is already another train, then the former train must be stopped. The stoppers can be controlled by a central controller via a component called STOPPER_DEMUX, which abbreviates "stopper demultiplexer". The idea is that the controller sends the control data for all stoppers at once, for example using one output line instead of a separate output line for each stopper. Three control data are multiplexed onto one line. The stopper demultiplexer translates such multiplexed data into three simple actions for the individual stoppers.

The railway has 9 sections, and therefore there are 9 selectors. The first selector can connect the input of the first section to one of the outputs of the stoppers, and hence to one of the supplies. Like the stoppers, the selectors can be controlled by the controller via a component called SELECTOR_DEMUX.

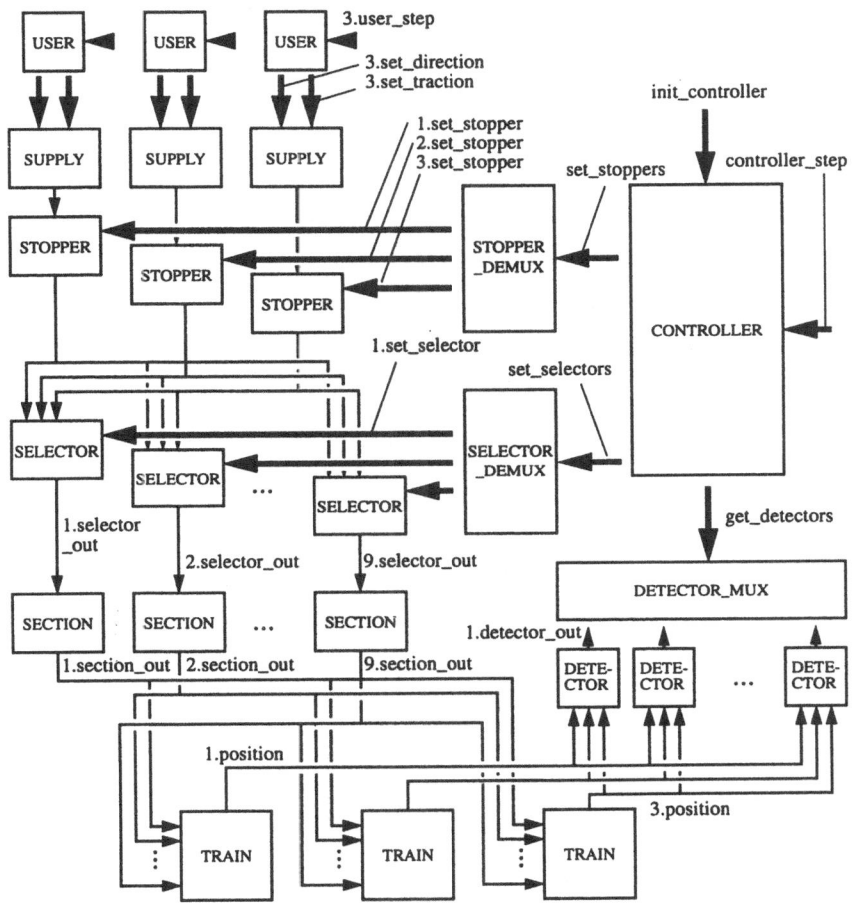

Figure 6.21: Abstract hardware diagram.

The railway consists of 9 sections and 29 detectors. Again, the design can be adapted to an arbitrary number of sections and detectors. There is a detector somewhere near the beginning and a detector near the end of every section; except for certain short sections, most sections also have one or more detectors in the central area of the section. Each detector has an output connection, which carries true if there is a train near the detector, and false otherwise. Again, these data are multiplexed to enable them to be transferred to the controller in an efficient way.

The three trains are shown at the bottom of Figure 6.21. The position of each train is shown as an output; this output is not realized as a wire, but as a moving magnetic field because the trains carry little magnets whose fields are sensed by the detectors.

Finally the controller is the "intelligent box", containing a computer and a stored program. It reads the detectors and calculates suitable control data for the stoppers and the selectors.

6.5.2 The Sort of "Stopperstate"

The sort StopperState is an enumerated data type with four distinct values. Each value is a possible state of a stopper (to be described in Section 6.6.1).

```
COMPONENT STOPPERSTATE SPECIFICATION
EXPORT
  SORT StopperState
  FUNC full_stop     : -> StopperState,
       non_stop      : -> StopperState,
       forward_stop  : -> StopperState,
       backward_stop : -> StopperState
IMPORT
  ENUM4' RENAMING Enum4 TO StopperState,
                  x0    TO full_stop,
                  x1    TO non_stop,
                  x2    TO forward_stop,
                  x3    TO backward_stop
         END
END
```

The value full_stop corresponds to the situation in which the supply of electrical power to the train is completely interrupted. Conversely, non_stop means that the stopper does not block the electrical power at all. The values forward_stop and backward_stop correspond to a one-directional blocking of the power supply.

6.5.3 Enumerating the Devices

Several enumerated data types (sorts) are introduced, first for enumerating the various devices involved, and later for use in the implementation of the controller's data structures.

Most enumerated data types have a value nil, which is useful for special purposes (as explained in Sections 6.7.6 and 6.12). There is no enumerated data type user, because the principle of the virtual train connection presumes a one-to-one correspondence between users and trains. Actually there are only 3 trains. The value of t4 can be viewed as a "dummy train" which need not exist physically (explained in Section 6.12).

```
COMPONENT TRAIN_SORTS SPECIFICATION
IMPORT
  STOPPERSTATE,
  ENUM10' RENAMING Enum10 TO Section,
                   x0 TO nil,
```

```
                      x1 TO s1,
                      x2 TO s2,
                      % etc.
                      x9 TO s9
              END,
      ENUM30' RENAMING Enum30 TO Detector,
                      x0 TO nil,
                      x1 TO d1,
                      x2 TO d2,
                      % etc.
                      x29 TO d29
              END,
      ENUM5' RENAMING Enum5 TO Train,
                      x0 TO nil,
                      x1 TO t1,
                      x2 TO t2,
                      x3 TO t3,
                      x4 TO t4
              END,
      ENUM3' RENAMING Enum3 TO DetectorKind,
                      x0 TO entry,
                      x1 TO exit,
                      x2 TO mid
  END       END
```

The standard data type ENUM10 provides the sort Enum10, the constants x0, x1, ... x9 and, among other things, a successor operator succ. The other enumerations are similar.

From TRAIN_SORTS it is clear that there will be 9 sections, 29 detectors and 3 real trains (besides the fourth dummy train). There are three kinds of detectors: entry detectors, used near the beginning of a section, exit detectors, used near the end of a section, and mid detectors, positioned in the central area of a section, which is the area between the entry and the exit detector. The sort DetectorKind is useful for distinguishing these kinds.

When using COLD-1 in an engineering environment and for large applications it is advantageous not to write the full texts of the renamings applied to ENUM5, ENUM10, ENUM30 etc. Instead, generator tools can be used which expand a minimum input to both the full specification and an efficient implementation. In this book, however, we will just use the "% etc." notation.

6.6   Components for Safety and Reachability

Now it is time to give precise descriptions of the stoppers, the stopper demultiplexer, the selectors, the selector demultiplexer, the detectors and the detector multiplexer. We describes already STOPPERSTATE, which is a simple data type component needed in connection with the stoppers.

6.6.1   A Stopper

A simple stopper could be realized as a single switch. Here a more sophisticated kind of stopper is introduced which can put a diode in series with the
supply line. It is important to realize that there is a one-to-one correspondence between the polarity of the electricity fed through the stopper and the
direction of the train, at least for the DC kind of train motors, as described
by TRAIN.

```
COMPONENT STOPPER SPECIFICATION
EXPORT
  FUNC stopper_in  : -> Voltage,
       stopper_out : -> Voltage,
       state       : -> StopperState
  PROC set_stopper : StopperState ->
IMPORT
  INT,
  VOLTAGE,
  STOPPERSTATE
CLASS
  FUNC stopper_in : -> Voltage FREE

  FUNC state : -> StopperState PRE TRUE VAR

  PROC set_stopper : StopperState ->
  IN   s
  PRE  TRUE
  SAT  MOD state
  POST state = s

  FUNC stopper_out : -> Voltage
  DEF ( state = full_stop    ? ; 0 Volt
      | state = non_stop     ? ; stopper_in
      | state = forward_stop ? ;
                ( stopper_in >= 0 Volt ? ; 0 Volt
                | stopper_in <= 0 Volt ? ; stopper_in
                )
      | state = backward_stop ? ;
                ( stopper_in >= 0 Volt ? ; stopper_in
                | stopper_in <= 0 Volt ? ; 0 Volt
                )
      )
END
```

The abstract hardware diagram of this specification is given in Figure 6.22. An
electrical wiring diagram of a possible implementation with two diodes and two
switches is given in Figure 6.23. A diode is a simple electrical component which
lets a positive voltage pass, whereas it blocks a negative voltage. There are four

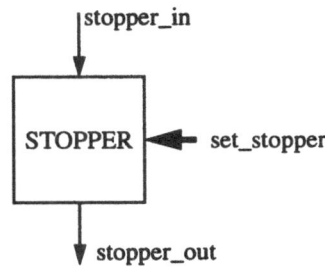

Figure 6.22: Abstract hardware diagram of a stopper.

possible states, one for each **StopperState** value. The procedure **set_stopper** activates or deactivates the switches. This can be realized using relays. The mapping from **StopperState** values to switch positions for this realization is given in the table of Figure 6.24. It can be seen that Figure 6.23 shows the stopper in **state = forward_stop**.

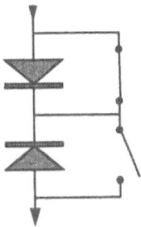

Figure 6.23: Realization of a stopper.

state	*upper switch*	*lower switch*
full_stop	open	open
non_stop	closed	closed
forward_stop	closed	open
backward_stop	open	closed

Figure 6.24: Table of switch positions for stopper.

6.6.2   A Stopper Demultiplexer

It is considered convenient if the controller can send the control data for all stoppers at once. STOPPER_DEMUX translates the multiplexed data into simple actions for the individual stoppers.

```
COMPONENT STOPPER_DEMUX SPECIFICATION
EXPORT
```

```
     PROC 1.set_stopper : StopperState ->,
          2.set_stopper : StopperState ->,
          3.set_stopper : StopperState ->
     PROC set_stoppers  : Seq[StopperState] ->
  IMPORT
    NAT,
    STOPPERSTATE,
    XSEQ[StopperState]
  CLASS
    PROC 1.set_stopper : StopperState -> FREE
    PROC 2.set_stopper : StopperState -> FREE
    PROC 3.set_stopper : StopperState -> FREE

    PROC set_stoppers : Seq[StopperState] ->
    IN   s
    PRE  len(s) = 3
    DEF  1.set_stopper(s @ 0);
         2.set_stopper(s @ 1);
         3.set_stopper(s @ 2)
  END
```

The data type XSEQ, when instantiated with the sort StopperState, provides
the sort Seq[StopperState], the constant empty and operations such as cons,
hd, tl, sel or @ for selection, and len.

The abstract hardware diagram of this specification is given in Figure 6.25.

Figure 6.25: Abstract hardware diagram of a stopper demultiplexer.

6.6.3 A Selector

A selector can connect the electrical input of a section to the output of a chosen
stopper.

```
  COMPONENT SELECTOR SPECIFICATION
  EXPORT
    FUNC 1.stopper_out : -> Voltage,
         2.stopper_out : -> Voltage,
         3.stopper_out : -> Voltage,
         selector_out  : -> Voltage
    FUNC switch        : -> Train
    PROC set_selector  : Train ->
```

```
IMPORT
  NAT,
  VOLTAGE,
  TRAIN_SORTS
CLASS
  FUNC 1.stopper_out : -> Voltage FREE
  FUNC 2.stopper_out : -> Voltage FREE
  FUNC 3.stopper_out : -> Voltage FREE

  FUNC switch : -> Train
  PRE  TRUE
  VAR

  PROC set_selector : Train ->
  IN   t
  SAT  MOD switch
  POST switch = t

  FUNC selector_out : -> Voltage
  DEF  ( switch = t1 ? ; 1.stopper_out
       | switch = t2 ? ; 2.stopper_out
       | switch = t3 ? ; 3.stopper_out
       )
END
```

The names of the input lines have been chosen such that the component fits directly into the architecture of Figure 6.21. From a reusability point of view this may be a bad idea because applications of SELECTOR could for example be envisaged, in which the inputs do *not* come from stoppers. In that case it would be a nuisance to see names 1.stopper_out, 2.stopper_out and 3.stopper_out. But in the context of the present case study it is an advantage, because frequent renamings can be avoided.

The abstract hardware diagram of this specification is given in Figure 6.26. An electrical wiring diagram with three switches is given in Figure 6.27. The

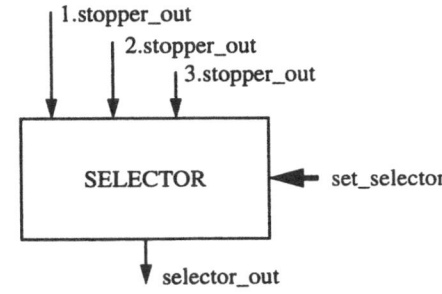

Figure 6.26: Abstract hardware diagram of a selector.

upper two switches are connected; this is easily realized if they are two switches
of one relay. There are three possible states, one for each `Train` value. The
realization could support four trains, but no use is made of that. The mapping
from `Train` values to switch positions is given in the table of Figure 6.28. It
can be seen that Figure 6.27 shows the stopper when `switch = t1`, which
means that `1.stopper_out` is selected. When the `Train` value is coded binary
(`t1` as 01, `t2` as 10 and `t3` as 11), its most significant bit controls the relay
of the lower switch and the least significant bit controls the relay of the upper
switches.

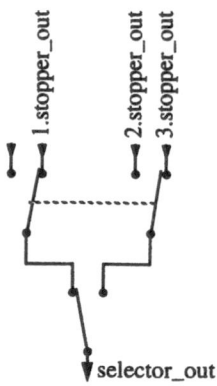

Figure 6.27: Realization of a selector.

switch	lower switch	upper switches
t1	left	right
t2	right	left
t3	right	right

Figure 6.28: Table of switch positions for a selector.

6.6.4   A Selector Demultiplexer

Like the stoppers, the selectors can be controlled by the controller via a demultiplexer component. It is called `SELECTOR_DEMUX`.

```
COMPONENT SELECTOR_DEMUX SPECIFICATION
EXPORT
  PROC 1.set_selector : Train ->,
       2.set_selector : Train ->,
       3.set_selector : Train ->,
       % etc.
```

```
              9.set_selector : Train ->
    PROC set_selectors  : Seq[Train] ->
IMPORT
  NAT,
  TRAIN_SORTS,
  XSEQ[Train]
CLASS
  PROC 1.set_selector : Train -> FREE
  PROC 2.set_selector : Train -> FREE
  PROC 3.set_selector : Train -> FREE
       % etc.
  PROC 9.set_selector : Train -> FREE

  PROC set_selectors : Seq[Train] ->
  IN   s
  DEF  1.set_selector(s @ 0);
       2.set_selector(s @ 1);
       3.set_selector(s @ 2);
       % etc.
       9.set_selector(s @ 8)
END
```

The abstract hardware diagram of this specification is given in Figure 6.29.

In terms of microprocessor I/O circuitry, the selector demultiplexer also serves to minimize the number of physical interconnections from the controller to the switch activator circuitry of the selectors. Note that a brute force parallel approach would require 2×9 wires. In a slower but more efficient approach, the controller outputs the 18 bits in a serial way. At the realization level the selector demultiplexer is a serial-to-parallel convertor, which is easily realized by means of a shift register, for example using transistor transistor logic (TTL) serial-in/parallel-out shift register integrated circuits (ICs) of type SN74164. The same technique can also be used for the stopper demultiplexer.

Figure 6.29: Abstract hardware diagram of a selector demultiplexer.

6.6.5 A Detector

A detector is described as a linearly ordered set of positions with a specified minimum length of 5 mm (see the third axiom below), ranging from a position called **first** to a position called **last**. If the position of one of the three trains is in this set, the value of **detector_out** is **true**. Otherwise it is **false**. The axiomatization of the topological properties is similar to that of **SECTION_S** in Section 6.3.3.

```
COMPONENT DETECTOR SPECIFICATION
EXPORT
  FUNC 1.position   : -> Pos,
       2.position   : -> Pos,
       3.position   : -> Pos
  FUNC detector_out : -> Bool
  PRED det : Pos
IMPORT
  NAT,
  DIS,
  BOOL,
  NETWORK,
  ORD[det,--]
CLASS
  FUNC 1.position : -> Pos FREE
  FUNC 2.position : -> Pos FREE
  FUNC 3.position : -> Pos FREE

  PRED det : Pos

  DECL p : Pos

  FUNC first : -> Pos
  DEF  THAT p (det(p) AND NOT det(p--))

  FUNC last  : -> Pos
  DEF  THAT p (det(p) AND NOT det(p++))

  AXIOM det(p)  =>  (p--)++ = p AND (p++)-- = p

  AXIOM det(p)  =>  first <= p AND p <= last AND NOT is_point(p)

  AXIOM Df(first,last) >= 5 mm

  FUNC detector_out : -> Bool
  PRE  TRUE
  POST detector_out = true <=> (  det(1.position)
                               OR det(2.position)
                               OR det(3.position)
                               )
END
```

The predicate **det** characterizes the set of positions for which a train will make the output **true**. This is the "range" of the detector. The positions in the range are ordered by the relation "<=", which is available here because ORD[det,--] has been imported. The first and the second axiom say that the ordering is linear.

The abstract hardware diagram of this specification is given in Figure 6.30. An electrical wiring diagram with one switch is given in Figure 6.31, where

Figure 6.30: Abstract hardware diagram of a detector.

one of the trains is shown too. An interesting option is to use a Reed-contact fixed between the rails and activated by small magnets attached to the trains. A Reed-contact is a switch, encapsulated in a small glass mounting, which is closed by putting it in a magnetic field. Although the model treats the

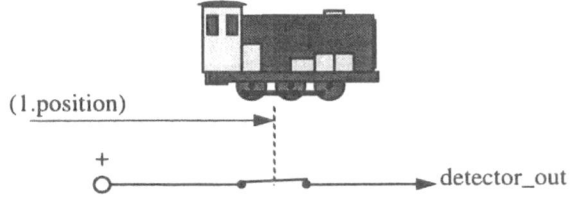

Figure 6.31: Detector activated by train t1.

trains as points rather than as objects with a given length, it can be shown that the approach of the present chapter and in particular the algorithms of Section 6.11 work for trains of non-zero lengths too, provided that this length is less than the distance between the detectors. Furthermore it is necessary to have several magnets attached to the trains, at least one at each end of the train.

6.6.6   A Detector Multiplexer

The detector multiplexer combines the 29 detector output values into a composite value which can be read by the controller using a single call of the operation **get_detectors**.

```
COMPONENT DETECTOR_MUX SPECIFICATION
EXPORT
   FUNC 1.detector_out  : -> Bool,
        2.detector_out  : -> Bool,
        3.detector_out  : -> Bool,
```

```
        % etc.
        29.detector_out : -> Bool
   PROC get_detectors    : -> Seq[Bool]
IMPORT
  NAT,
  BOOL,
  XSEQ[Bool]
CLASS
  FUNC 1.detector_out  : -> Bool FREE
  FUNC 2.detector_out  : -> Bool FREE
  FUNC 3.detector_out  : -> Bool FREE
        % etc.
  FUNC 29.detector_out : -> Bool FREE

  PROC get_detectors : -> Seq[Bool]
  OUT  y
  POST len(y) = 29;
       y @ 0  = 1.detector_out;
       y @ 1  = 2.detector_out;
       y @ 2  = 3.detector_out;
                    % etc.
       y @ 28 = 29.detector_out
END
```

The procedure `get_detectors` could have been modelled as a function. The
only reason for using a procedure is to obtain a uniformly organized interface
for the controller: 5 procedures (depicted as thick arrows in Figure 6.2). In
general, a procedure can have non-determinism and modification rights. The
procedure `get_detector` is a special case – it has neither.

The abstract hardware diagram of this specification is given in Figure 6.32.
A typical implementation technique is to organize the contacts of the detectors

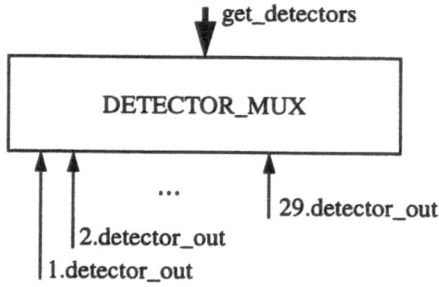

Figure 6.32: Abstract hardware diagram of a detector demultiplexer.

in a matrix configuration. For example, one could use 16 columns and 4 rows.
When executing `get_detectors`, each column is selected once and then 4
detector values can be scanned in parallel. In terms of microprocessor I/O

circuitry this can be done as follows: four bits are needed to be able to select 1 line out of 16 (e.g. using a TTL line selector IC of type SN74154). This means that an 8-bit parallel I/O port is sufficient to read up to 16 × 4 detectors, provided that 4 bits are configured as outputs and 4 bits as inputs.

6.6.7 A Controller

The controller is the "intelligent box", containing a computer and a stored program which must guarantee the safety of the railway system as a whole. Only a preliminary description of CONTROLLER can be given here.

```
COMPONENT CONTROLLER_DRAFT SPECIFICATION
EXPORT
  PROC get_detectors   : -> Seq[Bool],
       set_stoppers     : Seq[StopperState] ->,
       set_selectors    : Seq[Train] ->,
       init_controller  : Seq[Detector] ->,
       controller_step  : ->
IMPORT
  BOOL,
  XSEQ[Bool],
  TRAIN_SORTS,
  XSEQ[Train],
  XSEQ[Detector],
  XSEQ[StopperState]
CLASS
  PROC get_detectors : -> Seq[Bool]             FREE
  PROC set_stoppers  : Seq[StopperState] ->     FREE
  PROC set_selectors : Seq[Train] ->            FREE

  PROC init_controller : Seq[Detector] ->
  SAT  FLUSH get_detectors;
       set_stoppers($);
       set_selectors($)

  PROC controller_step : ->
  SAT  FLUSH get_detectors;
       set_stoppers($);
       set_selectors($)
  END
```

The above specification says that the controller offers two procedures, viz. init_controller and controller_step, which are supposed to manage the railway system through the exclusive use of get_detectors, set_stoppers and set_selectors.

The abstract hardware diagram of this specification is given in Figure 6.33. In Section 6.10.1 the controller will be further refined.

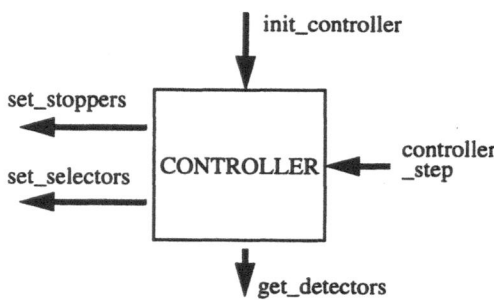

Figure 6.33: Abstract hardware diagram of controller.

6.7 Putting the Components Together

Now it is time to describe the various copies of USER, SUPPLY, STOPPER, etc. Three users are combined in a high-level architecture unit USERS (Section 6.7.1) and three supplies are combined in SUPPLIES (Section 6.7.2). STOPPERS contains three stoppers and a stopper demultiplexer (Section 6.7.3) and SELECTORS contains three selectors and a selector demultiplexer (Section 6.7.4). TRAINS contains three trains (Section 6.7.5). Finally the railway RAILWAY is composed of 9 sections, 29 detectors and one detector multiplexer (Section 6.7.6). In this way we arrive at a precise understanding of the abstract hardware diagram of Figure 6.34. Although this is a high-level diagram, it is still a very precise picture. Its components USERS, SUPPLIES, STOPPERS, etc. are well-specified and the rules for deriving the diagrams from the component specifications are explained in Sections 8.5 and 8.6.

6.7.1 The Users

Three qualified copies of USER are combined in USERS. One procedure is added, viz. users_step. No real abstraction is done here, only a grouping. The export list is omitted.

```
COMPONENT USERS SPECIFICATION
IMPORT
  USER' RENAMING set_direction TO 1.set_direction,
                 set_traction  TO 1.set_traction
        QUALIFYING 1
        END,
  USER' RENAMING set_direction TO 2.set_direction,
                 set_traction  TO 2.set_traction
        QUALIFYING 2
        END,
  USER' RENAMING set_direction TO 3.set_direction,
                 set_traction  TO 3.set_traction
        QUALIFYING 3
```

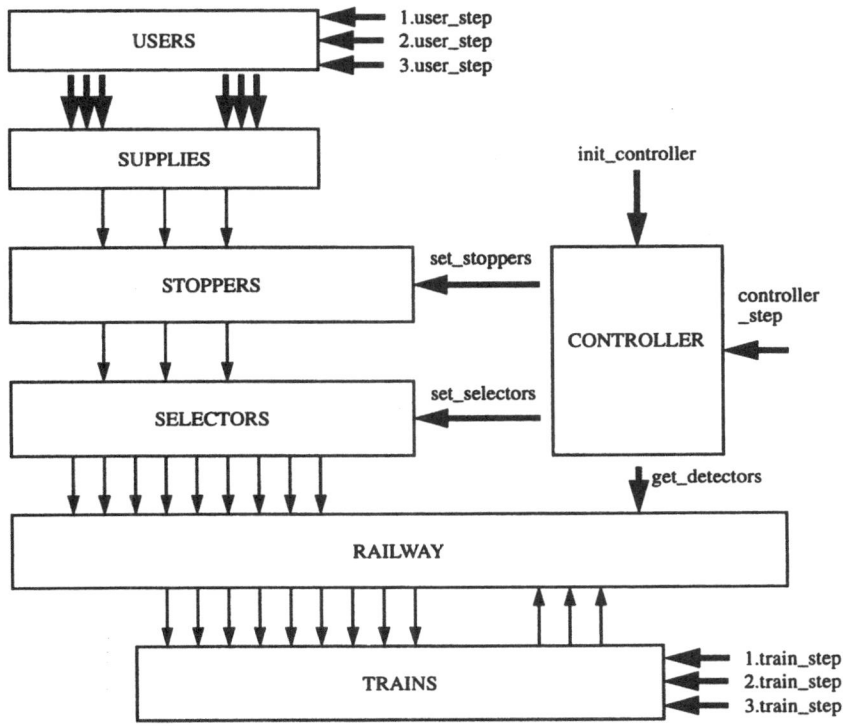

Figure 6.34: Survey of the automatic railway system.

```
        END
CLASS
  PROC users_step : ->
  DEF  1.user_step | 2.user_step | 3.user_step
END
```

The effect of the QUALIFYING clauses is that the names defined in USER are prefixed by 1., 2., etc. The FREE name must however be renamed explicitly.

6.7.2 The Power Supplies

The qualified copies of SUPPLY are combined in SUPPLIES.

```
COMPONENT SUPPLIES SPECIFICATION
IMPORT
  SUPPLY' QUALIFYING 1 END,
  SUPPLY' QUALIFYING 2 END,
  SUPPLY' QUALIFYING 3 END
END
```

6.7.3   The Stoppers

The qualified copies of STOPPER and a STOPPER_DEMUX are combined in one
component STOPPERS. Also, an auxiliary function called state is added for
reasoning purposes.

```
COMPONENT STOPPERS SPECIFICATION
IMPORT
  STOPPER' RENAMING stopper_in TO 1.supply_out QUALIFYING 1 END,
  STOPPER' RENAMING stopper_in TO 2.supply_out QUALIFYING 2 END,
  STOPPER' RENAMING stopper_in TO 3.supply_out QUALIFYING 3 END,
  STOPPER_DEMUX,
  TRAIN_SORTS
CLASS
  FUNC state : Train -> StopperState
  IN   t
  DEF  ( t = t1 ? ; 1.state
       | t = t2 ? ; 2.state
       | t = t3 ? ; 3.state
       )
END
```

6.7.4   The Selectors

The qualified copies of SELECTOR and one SELECTOR_DEMUX are put together in
one component SELECTORS. Also an auxiliary function called switch is added
for reasoning purposes.

```
COMPONENT SELECTORS SPECIFICATION
IMPORT
  SELECTOR' QUALIFYING 1 END,
  SELECTOR' QUALIFYING 2 END,
  SELECTOR' QUALIFYING 3 END,
           % etc.
  SELECTOR' QUALIFYING 9 END,
  SELECTOR_DEMUX,
  TRAIN_SORTS
CLASS
  FUNC switch : Section -> Train
  IN   s
  DEF  ( s = s1 ? ; 1.switch
       | s = s2 ? ; 2.switch
         % etc.
       | s = s9 ? ; 9.switch
       )
END
```

6.7.5   The Trains

The instantiations of TRAIN are combined in TRAINS. Several auxiliary functions are added.

```
COMPONENT TRAINS SPECIFICATION
IMPORT
  NAT,
  INT,
  TIME,
  SPEED,
  TRAIN_SORTS,
  TRAIN'[s_max,t_max] QUALIFYING 1 END,
  TRAIN'[s_max,t_max] QUALIFYING 2 END,
  TRAIN'[s_max,t_max] QUALIFYING 3 END
CLASS
  % train parameters :

  FUNC s_max : -> Speed DEF   50   mmpersec
  FUNC t_max : -> Time   DEF   500 msec

  PROC trains_step : ->
  DEF   1.train_step ; 2.train_step ; 3.train_step

  FUNC position : Train -> Pos
  IN    t
  DEF   ( t = t1 ? ; 1.position
        | t = t2 ? ; 2.position
        | t = t3 ? ; 3.position
        )

  FUNC speed : Train -> Speed
  IN    t
  DEF   ( t = t1 ? ; 1.speed
        | t = t2 ? ; 2.speed
        | t = t3 ? ; 3.speed
        )

  FUNC brake_time : Train -> Time
  IN    t
  DEF   ( t = t1 ? ; 1.brake_time
        | t = t2 ? ; 2.brake_time
        | t = t3 ? ; 3.brake_time
        )
  END
```

6.7.6   The Railway

The railway consists of sections and detectors satisfying additional layout properties which relate the positions of the detectors to the positions of the sections.
There are different kinds of sections, each with its own layout (TOPology):

- a straight section with two detectors (TOP_S_2),
- a straight section with four detectors (TOP_S_4),
- a section with one point and three detectors (TOP_Y1_3).

These layouts give rise to additional requirements that apply to the sections
and the detectors involved. These requirements could not be given as a part
of SECTION_S or SECTION_Y1, neither as a part of DETECTOR. Here they are
given in a generic form, to be instantiated later, when the particular railway
is described in RAILWAY.

```
COMPONENT TOP_S_2[sec,first,last,entry,exit] SPECIFICATION
ABSTRACT
  SECTION_S EXPORTING sec, first, last          END,
  DETECTOR  EXPORTING det RENAMING det TO entry END,
  DETECTOR  EXPORTING det RENAMING det TO exit  END
EXPORT
  PRED sec   : Pos,
       entry : Pos,
       exit  : Pos
  FUNC first : -> Pos,
       last  : -> Pos
IMPORT
  NAT,
  DIS,
  NETWORK,
  ORD[sec,--]
CLASS
  DECL p,q : Pos

  AXIOM {1} entry(p) => sec(p);
            exit(p)  => sec(p)

  AXIOM {2} entry(p) AND exit(q)  =>  p < q

  AXIOM {3} entry(p)  =>  Df(first,p) > 30 mm;
            exit(p)   =>  Df(p,last)  > 30 mm
END
```

The first two axioms introduce *ordering* properties (see Section 6.2.5). Axiom
{1} states that the detectors are contained in the section. Axiom {2} states
that the entry detector comes before the exit-detector, where the notion of
"before" is taken as <, provided by ORD[sec,--].

The third axiom concerns *metric* properties. (see Section 6.2.6). It states that the detectors are positioned at a certain distance from first and last; the distance must be more than 30 mm. This value of 30 mm is enough for a train to stop, because in TRAINS the parameters s_max and t_max are defined as 50 (mm/sec) and 500 (train steps of 1 msec), respectively, so 25 mm is already an upperbound to the distance a train can travel when it is stopped. The remaining 5 mm is a safety zone.

The axioms labelled {1}, {2}, and {3} are illustrated in the diagrams of Figure 6.35, Figure 6.36 and Figure 6.37, respectively. The function arrows of the "previous position" operator -- are shown In Figure 6.36. Note that the ordering relation <= was defined in Section 6.2.5 as the relation generated by --; then < was derived from <=. Of course it would not be hard to draw the function arrows of ++ because we know that $(p++)-- = p$ and $(p--)++ = p$. Figure 6.37 shows ++ (the definition of forward distance function Df refers to ++).

These diagrams are based on general principles for drawing Venn diagrams and function graphs, which will be discussed in Sections 7.3 and 7.8, respectively.

Figure 6.35: Venn diagram of TOP_S_2.

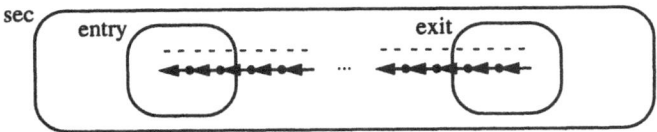

Figure 6.36: Function graph of TOP_S_2.

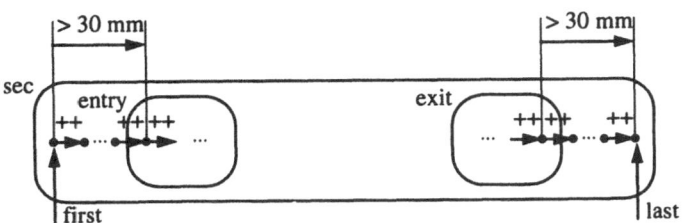

Figure 6.37: Function graph of TOP_S_2.

The layout of a straight section with four detectors is given below. TOP_S_4 describes the positions of these detectors in relation to the positions of the section. There is an entry detector, an exit detector and two additional detectors in the "mid" area.

```
COMPONENT TOP_S_4[sec,first,last,entry,mid1,mid2,exit] SPECIFICATION
ABSTRACT
  SECTION_S EXPORTING sec, first, last          END,
  DETECTOR  EXPORTING det RENAMING det TO entry END,
  DETECTOR  EXPORTING det RENAMING det TO exit  END,
  DETECTOR  EXPORTING det RENAMING det TO mid1  END,
  DETECTOR  EXPORTING det RENAMING det TO mid2  END
EXPORT
  PRED sec   : Pos,
       entry : Pos,
       exit  : Pos,
       mid1  : Pos,
       mid2  : Pos
  FUNC first : -> Pos,
       last  : -> Pos
IMPORT
  NAT,
  DIS,
  NETWORK,
  ORD[sec,--]
CLASS
  DECL p,q : Pos

  AXIOM {1} entry(p) => sec(p);
            exit(p)  => sec(p);
            mid1(p)  => sec(p);
            mid2(p)  => sec(p)

  AXIOM {2} entry(p) AND mid1(q) => p < q;
            mid1(p)  AND mid2(q) => p < q;
            mid2(p)  AND exit(q) => p < q

  AXIOM {3} entry(p)  =>  Df(first,p) > 30 mm;
            exit(p)   =>  Df(p,last)  > 30 mm
END
```

The axioms labelled {1}, {2} (the ordering properties) and {3} (the metric properties) are illustrated in the diagrams of Figure 6.38, Figure 6.39 and Figure 6.40, respectively. Axiom {3} states that the entry and exit detectors are positioned at a certain distance from first and last; again the distance must be more than 30 mm.

The layout of a Y-shaped section, which is a section with one point and three detectors, is given below:

Figure 6.38: Venn diagram of TOP_S_4.

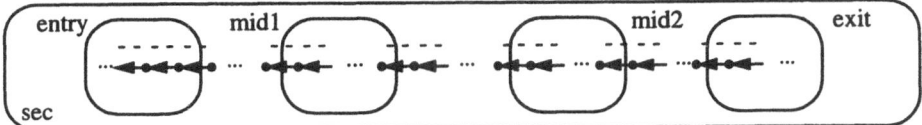

Figure 6.39: Function graph of TOP_S_4.

```
COMPONENT TOP_Y1_3[sec,first,last1,last2,entry,exit1,exit2]
SPECIFICATION
ABSTRACT
  SECTION_Y1 EXPORTING sec, first, last1, last2  END,
  DETECTOR   EXPORTING det RENAMING det TO entry END,
  DETECTOR   EXPORTING det RENAMING det TO exit1 END,
  DETECTOR   EXPORTING det RENAMING det TO exit2 END
EXPORT
  PRED sec   : Pos,
       entry : Pos,
       exit1 : Pos,
       exit2 : Pos
  FUNC first : -> Pos,
       last1 : -> Pos,
       last2 : -> Pos
IMPORT
  NAT,
  DIS,
  NETWORK,
  ORD[sec,--]
CLASS
```

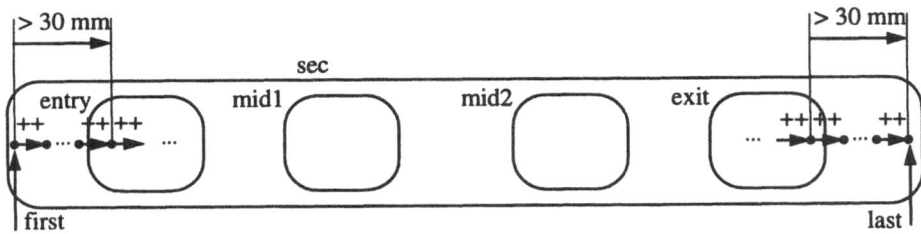

Figure 6.40: Function graph of TOP_S_4.

```
DECL p,q,r : Pos

AXIOM {1} entry(p) => sec(p);
          exit1(p) => sec(p);
          exit2(p) => sec(p)

AXIOM {2} entry(p) AND exit1(q)  =>  p < q;
          entry(p) AND exit2(q)  =>  p < q;
          exit1(p) AND exit2(q)  =>  NOT (  p < q
                                         OR p = q
                                         OR q < p
                                         )

AXIOM {3} entry(p)  =>  Df(first,p) > 30 mm;
          exit1(p)  =>  Df(p,last1) > 30 mm;
          exit2(p)  =>  Df(p,last2) > 30 mm
END
```

The axioms labelled {1}, {2} (the ordering properties) and {3} (the metric properties) are illustrated in the diagrams of Figure 6.41, Figure 6.42 and Figure 6.43 respectively.

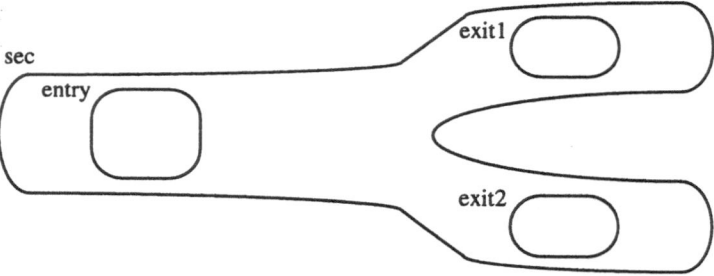

Figure 6.41: Venn diagram of TOP_Y1_3.

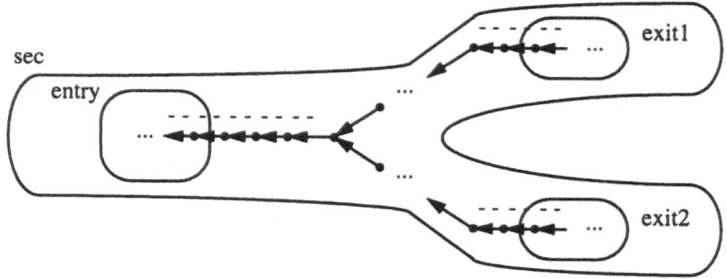

Figure 6.42: Function graph of TOP_Y1_3.

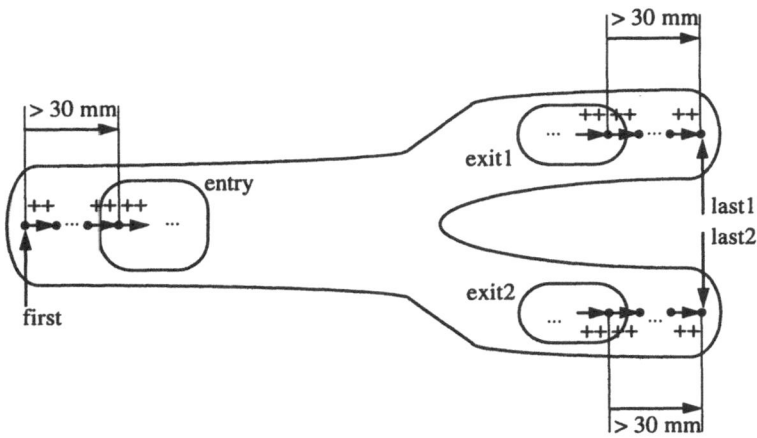

Figure 6.43: Function graph of TOP_Y1_3.

The railway consists of 9 sections, with a total of 29 detectors. It is described in RAILWAY and the resulting layout is shown in Figure 6.44.

```
COMPONENT RAILWAY SPECIFICATION
IMPORT
  NAT,
  NETWORK,
  XSEQ[Pos],
  VOLTAGE,
  XSEQ[Voltage],
  TRAIN_SORTS,

  SECTION_S' RENAMING section_in TO 1.selector_out QUALIFYING 1 END,
  SECTION_S' RENAMING section_in TO 2.selector_out QUALIFYING 2 END,
  SECTION_S' RENAMING section_in TO 3.selector_out QUALIFYING 3 END,
  SECTION_S' RENAMING section_in TO 4.selector_out QUALIFYING 4 END,
  SECTION_S' RENAMING section_in TO 5.selector_out QUALIFYING 5 END,
  SECTION_S' RENAMING section_in TO 6.selector_out QUALIFYING 6 END,
  SECTION_S' RENAMING section_in TO 7.selector_out QUALIFYING 7 END,
  SECTION_Y1' RENAMING section_in TO 8.selector_out QUALIFYING 8 END,
  SECTION_S' RENAMING section_in TO 9.selector_out QUALIFYING 9 END,

  DETECTOR' QUALIFYING 1 END,
  DETECTOR' QUALIFYING 2 END,
  DETECTOR' QUALIFYING 3 END,
  DETECTOR' QUALIFYING 4 END,
          % etc.
  DETECTOR' QUALIFYING 29 END,
  DETECTOR_MUX,
```

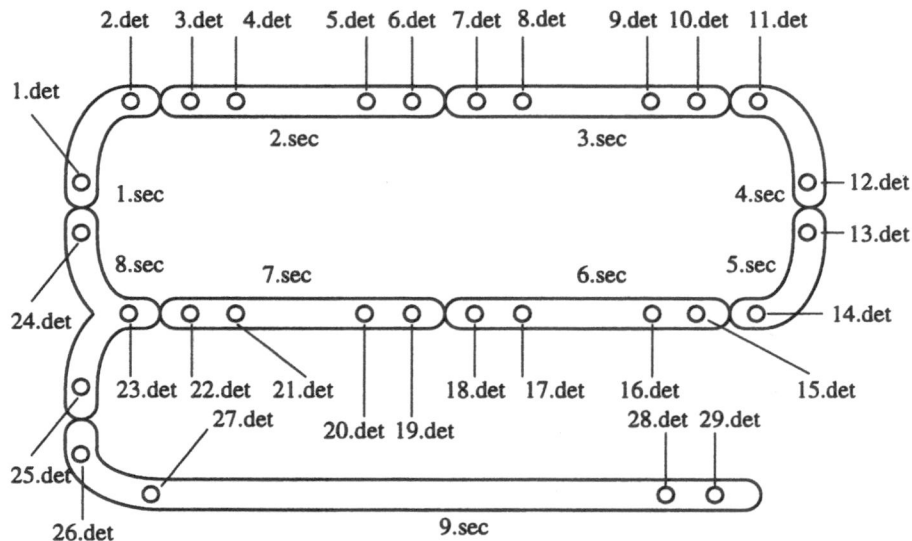

Figure 6.44: Railway layout.

```
TOP_S_2 [1.sec,1.first,1.last,1.det,2.det],
TOP_S_4 [2.sec,2.first,2.last,3.det,4.det,5.det,6.det],
TOP_S_4 [3.sec,3.first,3.last,7.det,8.det,9.det,10.det],
TOP_S_2 [4.sec,4.first,4.last,11.det,12.det],
TOP_S_2 [5.sec,5.first,5.last,13.det,14.det],
TOP_S_4 [6.sec,6.first,6.last,15.det,16.det,17.det,18.det],
TOP_S_4 [7.sec,7.first,7.last,19.det,20.det,21.det,22.det],
TOP_Y1_3 [8.sec,8.first,8.last1,8.last2,23.det,25.det,24.det],
TOP_S_4 [9.sec,9.first,9.last,26.det,27.det,28.det,29.det]

CLASS
   DECL d : Detector, p,q : Pos

   FUNC section : Pos -> Section
   IN  p
   DEF ( 1.sec(p)     ? ; s1
       | 2.sec(p)     ? ; s2
       | 3.sec(p)     ? ; s3
         % etc.
       | 9.sec(p)     ? ; s9
       | off_track(p) ? ; nil
       )

   PRED off_track : Pos
   IN  p
```

```
DEF  NOT (1.sec(p) OR 2.sec(p) OR 3.sec(p) OR
         4.sec(p) OR 5.sec(p) OR 6.sec(p) OR
         7.sec(p) OR 8.sec(p) OR 9.sec(p))


AXIOM section(p)!


% interconnections of the sections :


AXIOM 8.last2++ = 1.first AND 1.first-- = 8.last2;
      1.last++  = 2.first AND 2.first-- = 1.last;
      2.last++  = 3.first AND 3.first-- = 2.last;
      3.last++  = 4.first AND 4.first-- = 3.last;
      4.last++  = 5.first AND 5.first-- = 4.last;
      5.last++  = 6.first AND 6.first-- = 5.last;
      6.last++  = 7.first AND 7.first-- = 6.last;
      7.last++  = 8.first AND 8.first-- = 7.last;
      8.last1++ = 9.first AND 9.first-- = 8.last1;
      off_track(9.last++) AND     (p-- = 9.last => off_track(p))


% auxiliary definitions :


FUNC detector : Pos -> Detector
IN   p
DEF  ( 1.det(p)   ?  ; d1
     | 2.det(p)   ?  ; d2
       % etc.
     | 29.det(p)  ?  ; d29
     )


PRED env : Detector # Pos
IND  ( d = detector(p)  =>  env(d,p)
     ; env(d,p) AND p++ = q AND detector(q)^  =>  env(d,q)
     ; env(d,p) AND p-- = q AND detector(q)^  =>  env(d,q)
     ; env(d,p) AND p = q++ AND detector(q)^  =>  env(d,q)
     ; env(d,p) AND p = q-- AND detector(q)^  =>  env(d,q)
     )
END
```

We will add some explanation for the above RAILWAY. The function section
serves to partition the set of all positions into sections. The dummy value "nil"
of sort Section is associated with all positions which are factually off-track.
Later this will prove convenient: by allocating the dummy train t4 to the
section nil the safety requirement that none of t1, t2, t3 may run off-track
is reduced to a special case of another safety requirement, viz. that there is at
most one train in each section.

The axiom section(p)! guarantees that the function section is defined
for all p. From this follows the disjointness of the sections. This can be seen by

assuming for example that both $1.\mathtt{sec}(p)$ and $2.\mathtt{sec}(p)$ hold, which means that $1.\mathtt{sec}$ and $2.\mathtt{sec}$ are not disjoint. Then the DEF clause of section tells us that $\mathtt{section}(p) = \mathtt{s1}$ and $\mathtt{section}(p) = \mathtt{s2}$. This is a contradiction, so the assumption is false.

A new concept is introduced in RAILWAY: the environment of a detector. This is useful for expressing the idea that a train is supposed to be somewhere "near" the detector which last signalled true for this train. We can think of "$\mathtt{env}(d,p)$" as "$p \in \mathtt{env}(d)$" and then $\mathtt{env}(d)$ is the environment of d, which consists of all positions in d itself as well as those positions which can be reached without passing another detector. This is illustrated in Figure 6.45, which shows diagrams for the environments of detectors d6, d23 and d29. In each diagram the environment $\mathtt{env}(d)$ is shaded; more precisely, the positions p for which $\mathtt{env}(d,p)$ form the shaded area. A special case arises for detector d29: its environment extends to nil, which acts as a hypothetical section, containing off-track positions.

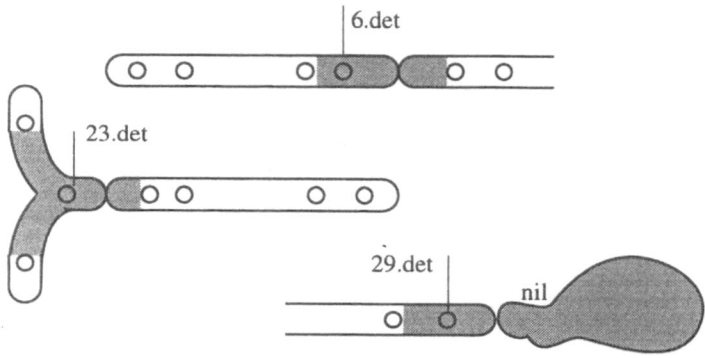

Figure 6.45: The environments of detectors d6, d23 and d29.

6.8   Refinements of the Safety Requirement

The component SAFETY describes the requirements already sketched in Section 6.1. We will make the simplifying assumption that there are always precisely three trains on the track and that each train is above one of the detectors during the initialization. It is not hard to relax these requirements, but these assumptions make the presentation of the controller simpler. The reachability requirements of the virtual train connection are not explicit here. But the algorithms of Section 6.11 will take care of these requirements too.

```
COMPONENT SAFETY SPECIFICATION
EXPORT
  PRED safe :,
       ready_to_go :
```

```
      FUNC inidata : -> Seq[Detector]
   IMPORT
     NAT,
     NETWORK,
     TRAINS,
     RAILWAY,
     TRAIN_SORTS,
     XSEQ[Detector]
   CLASS
     PRED safe :
     DEF  NOT off_track(1.position);
          NOT off_track(2.position);
          NOT off_track(3.position);
          section(1.position) /= section(2.position);
          section(2.position) /= section(3.position);
          section(3.position) /= section(1.position)

     PRED ready_to_go :
     DEF  safe;
          detector(1.position)!;
          detector(2.position)!;
          detector(3.position)!

     FUNC inidata : -> Seq[Detector]
     OUT  s
     PRE  ready_to_go
     POST len(s) = 3;
          s @ 0 = detector(1.position);
          s @ 1 = detector(2.position);
          s @ 2 = detector(3.position)
   END
```

We shall describe a *use case*, that is, a typical scenario of the system's operation. The reader may find it helpful to follow the use case by playing a token game on Figure 6.44. Consider an initial state in which train 1 is in section 3 above detector 9, train 2 is in section 5 above detector 14 and train 3 is in section 9 near detector 29 and in which all supplies have traction level 0. Initially the trains are not moving. The sequence inidata consists of d9, d14, and d29 in that order. The condition ready_to_go holds and init_controller must be called with inidata as an actual parameter.

Next the users adjust their supplies by doing 1.set_direction(forward), 2.set_direction(backward), 1.set_traction(2) and 2.set_traction(9). As a result the supply of train 1 has traction level 2 and direction = forward. The supply of train 2 has traction level 9 and direction = backward. The supply of train 3 has traction level 0, which is unchanged.

Without intervention, train 1 and train 2 will sooner or later collide. But it is too soon to stop either of them yet. Train 2 immediately leaves detector

14, followed by train 1 leaving detector 9. In the meantime, the controller has decided that section 3 is allocated to train 1, that section 5 is allocated to train 2 and that section 9 is for train 3. Actually section 6 is given to train 2 too. At regular intervals the controller executes:

```
set_selectors(⟨⊔,⊔,t1,⊔,t2,⊔,⊔,⊔,t3⟩)
```

that is, set_selectors(s) for a sequence of train values where the third value of s is t1, the fifth value of s is t2 and the ninth value of s is t3. All stoppers remain in state non_stop.

Let us assume that train 2 arrives at detector 13 *before* train 1 arrives at detector 10. Then this arrival is noticed by the controller, which regularly performs get_detectors (there are real-time requirements of course, see Section 6.13). The controller must act by allocating section 4 to train 2 too. Section 6 is released. For train 2 a kind of hand-over procedure from section 5 to section 4 begins.

When train 1 arrives above detector 10, the controller has no choice but to stop train 1. The controller executes set_stoppers(s) , where the first value of s is forward_stop and where the second value of s is non_stop. Train 1 stops while still in section 3.

In the meantime train 2 enters section 4, passes over detector 12 first and eventually arrives at detector 11. Now train 2 must be stopped too. Its stopper is put in state backward_stop. Train 2 stops while still in section 4. At the same time the controller finds that train 2 does not need section 5 any more. The hand-over of train 2 from section 5 to section 4 is completed.

The users have caused a dead-lock, but fortunately the dead-lock is easily resolved by either the first or the second user, who can reverse the direction of his train. Throughout the entire use case the safety requirements are respected.

6.9   Data Structures

Inside the controller there are data structures recording statuses of the detectors, storing estimations of the locations of the trains and storing the data to be transferred to the stoppers and the selectors. These data structures are organized as a number of arrays, and therefore we will start with a generic model of one-dimensional arrays.

6.9.1   An Array

An array is characterized by the domain Dom of index values and the range Ran of result values. Each instance of ARRAY1 is one array.

```
COMPONENT ARRAY1[Dom,Ran] SPECIFICATION
ABSTRACT
  ITEM RENAMING Item TO Dom END,
  ITEM RENAMING Item TO Ran END
```

```
EXPORT
  FUNC var : Dom -> Ran
  PROC set : Dom # Ran ->
CLASS
  FUNC var : Dom -> Ran
  PRE  TRUE
  VAR

  PROC set : Dom # Ran ->
  IN   i,k
  PRE  TRUE
  SAT  MOD var(i)
  POST var(i) = k
END
```

6.9.2 The Static Data

In order to be able to perform its task, the controller must "be aware of"
certain facts about the layout of the railway. Of course such knowledge can
be coded into the algorithms, but it is better to make the essential algorithms
independent of the layout. If we say that the control software is table-driven,
then the arrays of the present section are the "tables".

```
COMPONENT STATIC_DATA SPECIFICATION
EXPORT
  FUNC sect : Detector -> Section,
       next : Detector -> Section,
       kind : Detector -> DetectorKind
  PROC init_static_data : ->
  PRED static_data_ok  :
IMPORT
  TRAIN_SORTS,
  ARRAY1'[Detector,Section]
          RENAMING var TO sect, set TO set_sect END,
  ARRAY1'[Detector,Section]
          RENAMING var TO next, set TO set_next END,
  ARRAY1'[Detector,DetectorKind]
          RENAMING var TO kind, set TO set_kind END
CLASS
  PROC init_static_data : ->
  PRE  TRUE
  SAT  (set_sect($,$) | set_next($,$) | set_kind($,$))*
  POST static_data_ok

  PRED static_data_ok :
  DEF  sect(d1) = s1;  next(d1) = s8;  kind(d1) = entry;
       sect(d2) = s1;  next(d2) = s2;  kind(d2) = exit;
```

```
sect(d3)  = s2;  next(d3)  = s1;   kind(d3)  = entry;
sect(d4)  = s2;  next(d4)  = nil;  kind(d4)  = mid;
sect(d5)  = s2;  next(d5)  = nil;  kind(d5)  = mid;
sect(d6)  = s2;  next(d6)  = s3;   kind(d6)  = exit;
sect(d7)  = s3;  next(d7)  = s2;   kind(d7)  = entry;
sect(d8)  = s3;  next(d8)  = nil;  kind(d8)  = mid;
sect(d9)  = s3;  next(d9)  = nil;  kind(d9)  = mid;
sect(d10) = s3;  next(d10) = s4;   kind(d10) = exit;
sect(d11) = s4;  next(d11) = s3;   kind(d11) = entry;
sect(d12) = s4;  next(d12) = s5;   kind(d12) = exit;
sect(d13) = s5;  next(d13) = s4;   kind(d13) = entry;
sect(d14) = s5;  next(d14) = s6;   kind(d14) = exit;
sect(d15) = s6;  next(d15) = s5;   kind(d15) = entry;
sect(d16) = s6;  next(d16) = nil;  kind(d16) = mid;
sect(d17) = s6;  next(d17) = nil;  kind(d17) = mid;
sect(d18) = s6;  next(d18) = s7;   kind(d18) = exit;
sect(d19) = s7;  next(d19) = s6;   kind(d19) = entry;
sect(d20) = s7;  next(d20) = nil;  kind(d20) = mid;
sect(d21) = s7;  next(d21) = nil;  kind(d21) = mid;
sect(d22) = s7;  next(d22) = s8;   kind(d22) = exit;
sect(d23) = s8;  next(d23) = s7;   kind(d23) = entry;
sect(d24) = s8;  next(d24) = s1;   kind(d24) = exit;
sect(d25) = s8;  next(d25) = s9;   kind(d25) = exit;
sect(d26) = s9;  next(d26) = s8;   kind(d26) = entry;
sect(d27) = s9;  next(d27) = nil;  kind(d27) = mid;
sect(d28) = s9;  next(d28) = nil;  kind(d28) = mid;
sect(d29) = s9;  next(d29) = nil;  kind(d29) = exit
END
```

These static data represent an abstract topological view of the railway with
the following interpretation: sect gives the sections in which the detectors are
located; next gives the neighbouring sections for the entry and exit detectors;
kind classifies the detectors according to their positions within the sections.
With reference to Figure 6.44 it can be verified that the data are in accordance
with the facts in the following sense:

- if sect(d) = s and p is in the range of d, then p is in section s;
- if next(d) = s and kind(d) = "exit", then s is the first section that can
  be reached from an arbitrary p in d, going in the ++ direction;
- if next(d) = s and kind(d) = "entry", then s is the first section that
  can be reached from an arbitrary p in d, going in the -- direction;
- if kind(d) = "mid" then no other section can be reached, starting from
  a position in d, without passing at least one other detector.

6.9.3   The Dynamic Data

The tasks of the controller are to be aware of the most recent detection signals, to be aware of where the trains are located, to have at least estimates of their positions ("locations"), and to manage the mobility of the trains in a way which guarantees safety. Four array variables are available to help in performing these tasks.

```
COMPONENT DYNAMIC_DATA SPECIFICATION
EXPORT
   FUNC det : Detector  -> Bool,
        loc : Train      -> Detector,
        sel : Section    -> Train,
        stp : Train      -> StopperState
   PROC set_det : Detector # Bool        ->,
        set_loc : Train # Detector       ->,
        set_sel : Section # Train        ->,
        set_stp : Train # StopperState ->
IMPORT
BOOL,
TRAIN_SORTS,
ARRAY1'[Detector,Bool]       RENAMING var TO det, set TO set_det END,
ARRAY1'[Train,Detector]      RENAMING var TO loc, set TO set_loc END,
ARRAY1'[Section,Train]       RENAMING var TO sel, set TO set_sel END,
ARRAY1'[Train,StopperState] RENAMING var TO stp, set TO set_stp END
END
```

The variables and their interpretations are:

- $det(d)$: the output value of detector d,
- $loc(t)$: the location of train t (a detector near its current position),
- $sel(s)$: the selected train, which may be in section s,
- $stp(t)$: the stopperstate of train t.

6.10   Invariant Assertions

6.10.1   The Controller's Invariant

Returning to the controller, whose specification was started in Section 6.6.7, we will give a refinement next. The controller imports the static and dynamic data structures. The algorithms remain to be designed, which will be done in Section 6.11. Setting up a suitable invariant is the main step in deriving these algorithms; they will be treated in Section 6.10.2. INVARIANTS is supposed to define the invariant and ALGORITHMS the algorithms.

```
COMPONENT CONTROLLER SPECIFICATION
EXPORT
   PROC set_stoppers    : Seq[StopperState] ->,
```

```
              set_selectors   : Seq[Train] ->,
              get_detectors   : -> Seq[Bool],
              init_controller : Seq[Detector] ->,
              controller_step : ->
      IMPORT
        BOOL,
        XSEQ[Bool],
        TRAIN_SORTS,
        XSEQ[Train],
        XSEQ[Detector],
        XSEQ[StopperState],
        SAFETY,
        STATIC_DATA,
        DYNAMIC_DATA,
        INVARIANT,      % to be refined in 6.10.2
        ALGORITHMS      % to be refined in 6.11
      CLASS
        PROC set_stoppers  : Seq[StopperState] -> FREE
        PROC set_selectors : Seq[Train] ->        FREE
        PROC get_detectors : -> Seq[Bool]         FREE

        THEOREM {C1} controlled => safe

        THEOREM {C2} ready_to_go => AFTER init_controller(inidata)
                                    THEN  controlled

        THEOREM {C3} controlled => AFTER ( users_step
                                         ; trains_step
                                         ; controller_step
                                         )
                                   THEN  controlled
      END
```

The main invariant is called `controlled`. Theorem {C1} says that the safety requirement must be a logical consequence of `controlled`. Theorem {C2} concerns the initialization of the invariant. Theorem {C3} is the main invariance theorem. It is still too early to try to prove these theorems, for their truth depends on the definition of `controlled` (Section 6.10.2) and on algorithmic details which will not be presented until Section 6.11.

6.10.2   Refinements of the Invariant

The invariant `controlled` is a refinement of the safety requirement `safe`. The former assertion is stronger than the latter, partly because `controlled` will be defined in terms of the static and dynamic variables as well as in terms of the train positions.

The definition of the invariant given below explains the purpose of the

variables loc, sel and stp in a precise way. Moreover it paves the way for the
design of controller_step as a sequential algorithm. Of course the algorithm
performs an input-step which calls get_detectors to fill det, and there is an
output-step which transfers the values in sel to the selectors and the values
in stp to the stoppers. In the meantime, the essential steps of any operating
system must be taken:

1. assessing the state of the system and all explicit or implicit requests;
2. deciding upon the allocation of resources;
3. enforcing the allocation.

Roughly speaking, the first step calculates loc, which contains the locations
of the trains. The step is called estimation and its post-condition is a part
of the invariant called estimation_ok. There will also be a condition called
estimation_almost_ok, which is a weakened version of estimation_ok.[1]

The second step calculates sel, which contains the selections, i.e. the settings of the selectors; this step is called allocation and its post-condition is
a part of the invariant, called allocation_ok. Safety is a consequence of this
allocation_ok.

The third step calculates stp, which contains the settings of the stoppers;
this step is called intervention and its post-condition is a part of the invariant
called intervention_ok.

```
COMPONENT INVARIANT SPECIFICATION
IMPORT
  DIS,
  SPEED,
  NETWORK,
  STOPPERS,
  SELECTORS,
  USERS,
  RAILWAY,
  TRAINS,
  TRAIN_SORTS,
  STATIC_DATA,
  DYNAMIC_DATA
CLASS
  DECL p,q : Pos, d : Detector, t : Train, s : Section, x : Dis

  PRED controlled :
  DEF  static_data_ok;
       estimation_ok;
       allocation_ok;
```

---

[1] estimation_almost_ok holds when a train t leaves the environment of one detector,
say env(d_1), and enters the range of another detector d_2. Such a train step violates
estimation_ok but not in a severe way because it is still easy to make a new estimation:
take loc(t) = d_2.

```
      intervention_ok;
      output_ok

PRED env : Detector # Train
IN    d,t
DEF   env(d,position(t))


PRED real : Train
IN    t
DEF   t /= nil AND t /= t4


PRED estimation_ok :
DEF   FORALL t,d
      (real(t) AND loc(t) = d  =>  env(d,t))


PRED estimation_almost_ok :
DEF   FORALL t,d
      ( real(t) AND loc(t) = d  =>  (  env(d,t)
                                       OR detector(position(t))!
      )                                )


PRED env : Section # Train
IN    s,t
DEF   AFTER 1.set_stopper(full_stop);
            2.set_stopper(full_stop);
            3.set_stopper(full_stop)
      THEN EXISTS q,x
           ( section(q) = s
           ; x = brake_time(t) * speed(t) + 5 mm
           ; (  speed(t) >= 0 mmpersec AND Df(position(t),q) <= x
             OR speed(t) <= 0 mmpersec AND Db(position(t),q) <= x
           ) )


PRED allocation_ok :
DEF   sel(nil) = t4;
      FORALL s,t ( real(t)  =>  ( sel(sect(loc(t))) = t
                               ; env(s,t)  =>  sel(s) = t
                 )               )


PRED intervention_ok :
DEF   FORALL t
      (real(t) => (kind(loc(t)) = exit AND sel(next(loc(t))) /= t
                   =>  stp(t) = forward_stop;
                   kind(loc(t)) = entry AND sel(next(loc(t))) /= t
                   =>  stp(t) = backward_stop ) )


PRED output_ok :
```

```
DEF  FORALL s,t (real(t) => ( sel(s) = t => switch(s) = t
                              ; state(t) = stp(t)
               )              )
```

% preservation properties :

```
THEOREM estimation_ok => AFTER ( users_step
                                ; trains_step
                                )
                   THEN   estimation_almost_ok
```

```
THEOREM controlled => AFTER ( users_step
                             ; trains_step
                             )
                   THEN   allocation_ok
END
```

The first function env introduced above allows us to write env(d, t) as an abbreviation of env(d,position(t)).

The conditions estimation_ok and estimation_almost_ok assert the consistency of the estimations in loc with the factual situation of the trains which may or may not be in the environment of certain detectors. See Figure 6.45 to recall this notion of environment.

In addition to "the environment of a detector", a new concept is introduced here, viz. "the environment of a section". More precisely, we shall say that train t is in the environment of section s (env(s, t)) if the position p of t is close enough to s so that it would be possible to reach s from p – even after activation of the stoppers. Of course this depends on the position and the speed of the train. If we consider a train t with a given speed, then env(s, t) still depends on the position p of train t. The latter dependency is shown in Figure 6.46. The environment of s is shaded; more precisely, the shaded area contains the positions p for which position(t) = p implies env(s, t). A special case arises for the section nil, which takes the rôle of the area containing the off-track positions. Its environment extends to the exit area of section s9.

The concept of env(s, t) is used to define allocation_ok, which among other things requires that as soon as a train t is in the environment of a section s, that section must be allocated to the train, in the sense that sel(s) = t. Let us explain the DEF clause of allocation_ok in more detail. The first clause guarantees that nil is always allocated to the dummy train t4. The second clause applies to all the other trains, which explains the premise (real(t) =>). For a train t, first consider the section sect(loc(t)), which is the section containing the detector that most recently signalled t; since there is no evidence that t has left this section, it must be allocated to t. Therefore sel(sect(loc(t))) = t must hold. Next consider a section s for which env(s, t), which means that in principle t could enter s, as sketched in Figure 6.46; in that case s must be given to train t too.

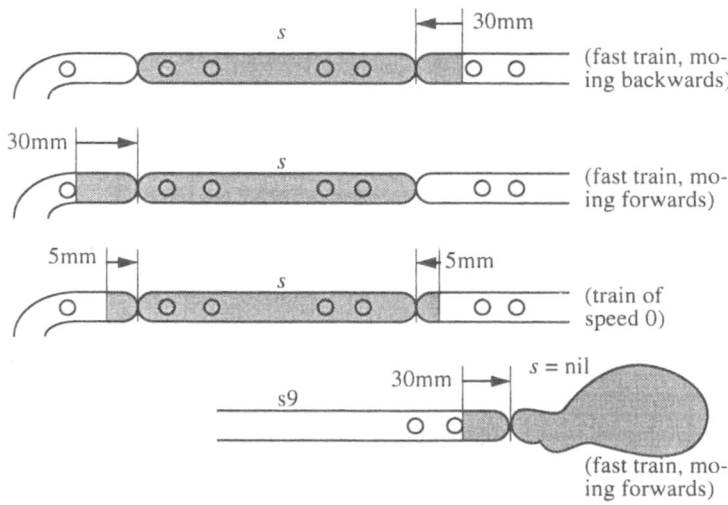

Figure 6.46: The environment of a section s for various train speeds.

Finally we will explain `intervention_ok`. If `kind(loc(t))` = `exit` this could mean that t is about to leave its section `loc(t)`; this is taken as an implicit request to get the next section, which is `next(loc(t))`. If the next section however has already been allocated to another train (`sel(next(loc(t)))` $\neq$ t) then the request is denied and t is not allowed to go further in the forward direction. In that case `stp(t)` = `forward_stop` must hold. The clause for `kind(loc(t))` = `entry` is analogous.

6.11   Algorithms

The heart of the `controller_step` is called `control` and it consists of three procedures, corresponding to the three essential steps of any operating system, as explained in Section 6.10.2. They read the static data and operate on the dynamic data. The control software is designed according to Wirth's paradigm: "algorithms + data structures = programs", [27]. The interaction between these procedures and the dynamic data is indicated in the data flow diagram of Figure 6.47. The procedures `input` and `output` are not detailed further here. Their implementation must be based on the technical details of the I/O ports of the processor used. We will leave `input` and `output` in a pre- and post-condition style.

```
COMPONENT ALGORITHMS SPECIFICATION
IMPORT
BOOL,
TRAIN_SORTS,
XSEQ[Detector],
```

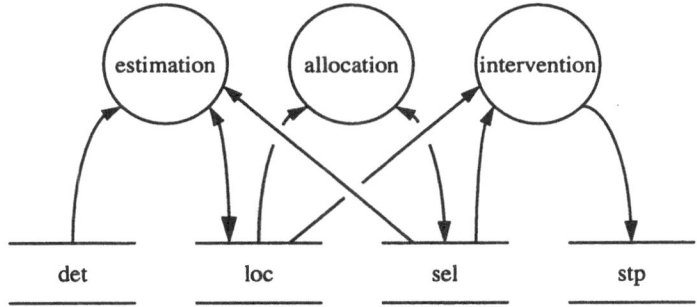

Figure 6.47: Algorithms and data structures.

```
STATIC_DATA,
DYNAMIC_DATA,
INVARIANT,

% loop counters :

SVAR'[Detector] RENAMING var TO D,  set TO set_D  END,
SVAR'[Train]    RENAMING var TO T,  set TO set_T  END,
SVAR'[Train]    RENAMING var TO Tb, set TO set_Tb END,
SVAR'[Section ] RENAMING var TO S,  set TO set_S  END,

% auxiliary array :

ARRAY1'[Section,Train] RENAMING var TO n_sel, set TO set_n_sel END

CLASS
  PROC set_stoppers  : Seq[StopperState] -> FREE
  PROC set_selectors : Seq[Train] ->        FREE
  PROC get_detectors : -> Seq[Bool]         FREE

  DECL t : Train, s : Section, d : Detector

  PROC init_controller : Seq[Detector] ->
  IN   s
  DEF  init_static_data;
       set_loc(t1, s @ 0);
       set_loc(t2, s @ 1);
       set_loc(t3, s @ 2);

       set_sel(nil,t4);
       set_T(nil);
       ( T /= t3 ?;
         set_T(succ(T));
```

```
            set_sel(sect(loc(T)),T)
        ) * ; T = t3 ? ;

        intervention;
        output

    PROC controller_step : ->
    DEF  input;
         control;
         output

    PRED input_ok :
    DEF  FORALL d
         ( det(d) = true <=> EXISTS t (detector(position(t)) = d) )

    PROC input : ->
    PRE  TRUE
    SAT  FLUSH get_detectors;
         set_det($,$) *
    POST input_ok

    PROC output : ->
    PRE  TRUE
    SAT  set_selectors($); set_stoppers($)
    POST output_ok

    PROC control : ->
    DEF  estimation;
         allocation;
         intervention

    PROC estimation : ->
    DEF  set_D(nil);
         ( D /= d29 ? ;
           set_D(succ(D));
           ( det(D) = true  ? ; set_loc(sel(sect(D)),D)
           | det(D) = false ? ; SKIP
           )
         ) * ; D = d29 ?

THEOREM static_data_ok
        AND input_ok
        AND estimation_almost_ok
        AND allocation_ok => AFTER estimation
                             THEN  estimation_ok

    PRED ELSE :
```

```
DEF  NOT sel(next(loc(T))) = T AND NOT n_sel(next(loc(T))) = nil

PROC allocation : ->
DEF  set_sel(nil,t4);

     set_S(nil);
     ( S /= s9 ? ;
       set_S(succ(S));
       set_n_sel(S,nil)
     ) * ; S = s9 ? ;

     set_T(nil);
     ( T /= t3 ?;
       set_T(succ(T));
       set_n_sel(sect(loc(T)),T);
       ( kind(loc(T)) /= mid ? ;
         ( sel(next(loc(T))) = T      ?; set_n_sel(next(loc(T)),T)
         | n_sel(next(loc(T))) = nil ?; set_n_sel(next(loc(T)),T)
         | ELSE                       ?; SKIP
         )
       | kind(loc(T)) = mid  ? ;
         SKIP
       )
     ) * ; T = t3 ? ;

     set_S(nil);
     ( S /= s9 ? ;
       set_S(succ(S));
       set_sel(S,n_sel(S))
     ) * ; S = s9 ?

THEOREM static_data_ok
        AND estimation_ok
        AND allocation_ok => AFTER allocation
                             THEN  allocation_ok

PROC intervention : ->
DEF  set_T(nil);
     ( T /= t3 ? ;
       set_T(succ(T));
       set_Tb(sel(next(loc(T))));
       ( kind(loc(T)) = mid      ? ; set_stp(T,non_stop)
       | kind(loc(T)) = entry    ? ;
                     ( Tb =  T ? ; set_stp(T,non_stop)
                     | Tb /= T ? ; set_stp(T,backward_stop)
                     )
       | kind(loc(T)) = exit    ? ;
```

```
                    ( Tb =  T ? ; set_stp(T,non_stop)
                    | Tb /= T ? ; set_stp(T,forward_stop)
                    )
          )
        ) * ; T = t3 ?

THEOREM static_data_ok
        AND estimation_ok
        AND allocation_ok => AFTER intervention
                             THEN  intervention_ok
END
```

We will explain the main algorithmic procedures next. In this explanation we will use square brackets for array indexing, which will help the intuition of readers familiar with Pascal or C. We write loc[t1] := d instead of set_loc(t1,d).

The procedure init_controller is given a sequence of detectors as its input parameter. These detectors describe the initial positions of the trains. Therefore the "location" array loc is filled first: the first position is stored in loc[t1], the second position in loc[t2] and the third in loc[t3]. After that, the "selection" array sel must be filled. If there is a train in a section then this train must be selected; in other words, the sections are allocated to the trains which are already in the sections. Note that for each train t the section in which it is located is given as sect[loc[t]]. So for each of the trains t1 ... t3 the assignment sel[sect[loc[T]]] := T must be performed, where T is the loop counter. Finally intervention and output are called.

The procedure estimation updates the "location" array loc. It is called "estimation" because it does not give the exact positions of the trains, but estimates of their positions (the environment in which the train is). All 29 detectors are checked. If detector D signals the presence of a train then for some train t the value of loc[t] can be updated. The detector does not provide information about the identity of the train, but fortunately the "selection" array sel in combination with the static data sect contains enough information to determine the identity of the train. If detector D, which is positioned in section sect[D], signals a train, then this must be the train selected by this section. There can be at most one train in that section, namely train sel[sect[D]]. So the update step for D is the assignment loc[sel[sect[D]]] := D.

The procedure allocation updates the "selection" array sel. The new selection depends on the old selection and the updated "location" array loc. The new selection is stored in the auxiliary array n_sel first. Therefore allocation consists of three main steps, each step containing a repetition. The first step is to fill n_sel with nil values. So first it is assumed that no sections are allocated to trains yet. The second step allocates sections to trains when this is obligatory, or when there is an implicit request to do so. It is obligatory to allocate the section sect[loc[T]] to train T, because T has already entered this section. There is an implicit request to allocate a section to T if this train approaches the section, which is the case for section next[loc[T]], provided

that loc[T] is an entry detector or an exit detector. The request is only
granted if it does not conflict with allocations already performed. Moreover,
the obligatory allocations have priority over the implicit requests. Finally the
third step copies the results from n_sel into sel.

The procedure **intervention** updates the "stopper" array stp. The body
of the repetition is executed for each train. For train T, interesting cases arise if
T is located at the entry or the exit of a section, for in the "mid" area it need not
be stopped. If T is the train processed in a certain step of the repetition then
Tb is the neighbouring train sel[next[loc[T]]], that is, the train to which
the neighbouring section next[loc[T]] has been allocated. For example, if
we assume that loc[T] is an exit detector then it may be necessary to perform
stp[T] := forward_stop. In particular, this is necessary if the neighbouring
section belongs to another train. But if Tb = T then this is not necessary:
stp[T] := non_stop is safe.

6.12   Proof Aspects

According to the Floyd-Hoare-Dijkstra approach to program correctness, any
non-trivial loop is to be accompanied by an invariant assertion. Below we
will give the loop invariant of **init_controller**. But first we must introduce
an auxiliary predicate to characterize the range of the main quantification of
the invariant. For an assertion A we can write FORALL t (t1_T(t) => A) to
express that A holds for all values (t) from t1 to T. Recall that T is the loop
counter.

```
DECL t : Train, d : Detector, s : Section

PRED t1_T : Train
IN   t
DEF  nat(t1) <= nat(t) AND nat(t) <= nat(T)
```

It is essential that the repetition of **init_controller** does not change loc; to
keep the presentation simple this fact has been ommited from the formulation
of the invariant:

```
static_data_ok;
estimation_ok;
T /= t4;
sel(nil) = t4;
FORALL t (t1_T(t) => sel(sect(loc(t))) = t)
```

Next we will turn our attention to the loop invariant of **estimation**. The
range of the main quantification is characterized by the predicate t1_t3 (holding for the **real** trains, not nil and not t4). Another auxilary predicate is
d1_D, which is used as the range of a THAT construct. The function active
is introduced to keep the invariant readable; for a train t, active(t) is the
unique detector in the range d1..D which is activated by t (if it exists; it is

otherwise undefined).

```
PRED t1_t3 : Train
IN   t
DEF  nat(t1) <= nat(t) AND nat(t) <= nat(t3)

PRED d1_D : Detector
IN   d
DEF  nat(d1) <= nat(d) AND nat(d) <= nat(D)

FUNC active : Train -> Detector
IN   t
DEF  THAT d (d1_D(d) AND det(d) = true AND t = sel(sect(d)))
```

We will write PREV loc(t) to refer to the value of loc(t) in the state *before* execution of estimation. The invariant is:

```
FORALL t (t1_t3(t) => ( active(t)!      => loc(t) = active(t)
                      ; NOT active(t)! => loc(t) = PREV loc(t)
         )                     )
```

The first repetition expression of allocation is simple; it fills the "new" selection array n_sel with nil values.

The second repetition expression of allocation is difficult. Below we will give the loop invariant which is useful for proving the theorem that allocation preserves allocation_ok. Two special train values are used: firstly, nil is used to indicate that a certain section has not been allocated to a train. Secondly train t4 need not exist physically, but because it is permanently allocated to the "section" nil of the off-track positions, the real trains will not run off-track. The invariant is:

```
static_data_ok;
estimation_ok;
allocation_ok;
T /= t4;
sel(nil) = t4;
FORALL t (t1_T(t) => n_sel(sect(loc(t))) = t AND
                     FORALL s (env(s,t) => n_sel(s) = t))
```

The third repetition expression of allocation is again easy. The train values selected for each section are copied from n_sel into sel.

The loop invariant of the repetition expression of intervention is:

```
static_data_ok;
estimation_ok;
allocation_ok;
T /= t4;
FORALL t (t1_T(t) =>
( LET Tb := sel(next(loc(t)));
  kind(loc(t)) = exit  AND Tb /= t  =>  stp(t) = forward_stop;
```

```
kind(loc(t)) = entry AND Tb /= t  =>  stp(t) = backward_stop ))
```

On the assumption that the AFTER-THEN style theorems which describe the estimation, allocation and intervention hold, it is still necessary to combine these theorems to prove the main invariance statement {C3}. The table of Figure 6.48 gives a survey of the most important steps and assertions.

In this table a "+" indicates that the step restores the assertion (under a certain pre-condition). A "−" indicates that the step may violate the assertion. A "□" indicates that the step preserves the assertion. The "-" symbol marked by [1] refers to the fact that trains_step violates estimation_ok, but still preserves estimation_almost_ok. The "-" symbol marked by [2] means that estimation does not violate allocation_ok, but because new requests are generated, a new allocation step is nevertheless required.

	stat ic_d ata_ ok	inpu t_ok	esti mati on_ ok	allo cati on_ ok	inte rven tion _ok	outp ut_ ok
users_step	□	□	□	□	□	□
trains_step	□	−	−[1]	□	□	□
input	□	+	□	□	□	□
estimation	□	□	+	−[2]	−	□
allocation	□	□	□	+	−	−
intervention	□	□	□	□	+	−
output	□	□	□	□	□	+

Figure 6.48: Survey of steps and assertions.

When assuming that the theorems concerning estimation, allocation, and intervention from ALGORITHMS have been verified already, the proof of {C3} (the main proof obligation)is relatively easy. The work really is in these AFTER-THEN style theorems concerning the procedures containing loops. The theorems about allocation and intervention are not hard if one assumes that the postulated loop invariants hold, but proving the theorem on estimation on the basis of its loop invariant is a bit difficult. Then it only remains to prove the postulated loop invariants correct. The most complicated of these is the loop invariant for allocation. The reader may wish to skip such proof details, but when needed one could go to the bottom. For the interested reader we will go into the details of proving the theorem on estimation on the basis of its loop invariant. This is our goal:

```
THEOREM static_data_ok
        AND input_ok
        AND estimation_almost_ok
        AND allocation_ok => AFTER estimation
                        THEN  estimation_ok
```

Assumptions: Assume an "old" state, henceforth called the PREV-state, in which the four "**ok**" assertions:

1. `static_data_ok` ,
2. `input_ok`,
3. `estimation_almost_ok` and
4. `allocation_ok`

all hold. Of these 1. and 2. are not endangered, but concerning 3. en 4. we only know that they hold in the PREV-state. Also assume that `estimation` preserves the following invariant:

```
FORALL t (t1_t3(t) => ( active(t)!    => loc(t) = active(t)
                      ; NOT active(t)! => loc(t) = PREV loc(t)
         )                )
```

with the given auxiliary definitions:

```
PRED t1_t3 : Train
IN   t
DEF  nat(t1) <= nat(t) AND nat(t) <= nat(t3)

PRED d1_D : Detector
IN   d
DEF  nat(d1) <= nat(d) AND nat(d) <= nat(D)

FUNC active : Train -> Detector
IN   t
DEF  THAT d (d1_D(d) AND det(d) = true AND t = sel(sect(d)))
```

If the loop terminates, we know that D = d29, which we can combine with the invariant which still holds too. In other words, in the new state we find that:

```
FORALL t (t1_t3(t) => ( active_1_29(t)!    => loc(t) = active(t)
                      ; NOT active_1_29(t)! => loc(t) = PREV loc(t)
         )                )
```

with the obvious auxiliary definitions obtained by taking d29 for D:

```
PRED d1_d29 : Detector
IN   d
DEF  nat(d1) <= nat(d) AND nat(d) <= nat(d29)

FUNC active_1_29 : Train -> Detector
IN   t
DEF  THAT d (d1_d29(d) AND det(d) = true AND t = sel(sect(d)))
```

In this way all the assumptions have been made explicit and we proceed stating the main assertion of the theorem.

To be shown: `estimation_ok` holds, that is:

```
FORALL t,d (real(t) AND loc(t) = d =>  env(d,t))
```

The proof will effectively use `static_data_ok` and `input_ok`, which means that the static data and the input data are according to the facts.

Proof. Pick an arbitrary train t for which `real(t)`. If we succeed in showing that $loc(t) = d \Rightarrow env(d,t)$ holds, we are done. We distinguish two cases.

Case 1. t is above a detector. Via `input_ok` we find that:

EXISTS d (det(d) = true)   "because t is above it"

In fact there is precisely *one* detector activated by t because the ranges of the detectors are disjoint. Consider this d. It is inside section `sect(d)` because the static data are according to the facts. So train t is in this section because it is in the range of d, which is contained in the section. Thus it is most certainly in the `env` of this section. So the last clause of `allocation_ok` tells that $sel(sect(d)) = t$. So now we have found an explicit expression for t, viz. $sel(sect(d))$. From the invariant we thus find that $loc(t) = d$ for this t. We also have that $env(d,t)$ holds. So $loc(t) = d \Rightarrow env(d,t)$ looks in order. At least: it looks in order *for this d*, but what about the other detectors, say d'? We know that there is no other d' for which $loc(t) = d'$, because `loc` is a function. Therefore it turns out that *for all d* in d1..d29 the implication $loc(t) = d \Rightarrow env(d,t)$ holds.

Case 2. t is not above a detector. Then `estimation_almost_ok` tells the following:

$loc(t) = d \Rightarrow env(d,t)$ (in the PREV-state of course).

In this case EXISTS d (det(d) = true AND t = sel(sect(d))) does not hold. The loop invariant states that $loc(t) = $ PREV $loc(t)$. And therefore $loc(t) = d \Rightarrow env(d,t)$ holds (because formally the train did not move during `estimation`). This completes the proof.

It is interesting to note that the proof steps are most often concerned with the railway itself rather than just with the algorithm. Maybe this is unusual, but in this case study it stems from the fact that the system's safety is a global system property. The algorithm is a piece of embedded software fulfilling its function only in cooperation with the sections, the trains, the selectors, the stoppers and the other physical and electronic system components.

6.13   Real-time Aspects

If we could assume that the time needed to execute `controller_step` is negligible compared with the unit step time of the train then it is sufficient to execute `controller_step` at regular intervals of 1 ms In our model we will assume that the user step takes zero time, although in reality it could be done concurrently with a train step.

Note that the real-time aspects of the behaviour of the train have been taken into account, on the basis of the assumptions concerning `adapt_position` and `adapt_speed`, as described in `TRAIN`. The formulation of the invariant `controlled` uses the concept of the environment of a section, which depends on train speed and brake time.

However, using a small microprocessor and low-cost multiplexers and de-multiplexers (details in Sections 6.6.6, 6.6.4, and 6.14) it turned out that it takes 20 msec to execute `controller_step`. It is executed in an infinite loop, with a polling-rate of 50 control steps per s During one control step 20 train steps take place.

This requires a further analysis, which will be conducted informally next. We know that one single train step disturbs `allocation_ok`, but still preserves `allocation_almost_ok`, which suffices to get the allocation `ok` again. But it is also easy to see that in 101 steps a train could pass a detector without being noticed. For in 100 steps of 1 ms a train moves at most $\frac{100}{1000} * $ `s_max` $= 5$ mm, which equals the guaranteed detector length. Similarly, the safety zone of 5 mm incorporated in to the definition of `env`(s,t) could be used up during a delay of 100 ms But it is more than sufficient to compensate for a delay of at most 20 ms The computer-controlled railway system still guarantees safety when the polling-rate of 50 control steps per s is used. In fact, a stronger version of the invariance theorem {C3} holds, as shown below. This holds because in 20 steps a train can not pass a detector without being detected.

```
PROC 20_trains_steps : ->
DEF  trains_step; trains_step; trains_step; trains_step;
     trains_step; trains_step; trains_step; trains_step;
     trains_step; trains_step; trains_step; trains_step;
     trains_step; trains_step; trains_step; trains_step;
     trains_step; trains_step; trains_step; trains_step

THEOREM {C3} controlled => AFTER ( users_step
                                 ; 20_trains_steps
                                 ; controller_step
                                 )
                          THEN  controlled
```

6.14   Realization Aspects

The algorithms can be translated to any imperative programming language. Some of them are shown in a Pascal-like notation below. To be able to compile them as part of a Pascal program, some renaming must be done first to resolve the overloading and to avoid using the reserved name `nil`.

```
procedure estimation;
begin
for D := d1 to d29 do
   if det[D] = true
   then loc[sel[sect[D]]] := D
```

```
end;

procedure allocation;
begin
sel[nil] := t4;
for S := s1 to s9 do
   n_sel[S] := nil;
for T := t1 to t3 do
  begin
  n_sel[sect[loc[T]]] := T;
  if kind[loc[T]] ≠ mid
  then if (sel[next[loc[T]]] = T)
       or (n_sel[next[loc[T]]] = nil )
       then n_sel[next[loc[T]]] := T
  end; {for}
for S := s1 to s9 do
   sel[S] := n_sel[S]
end;

procedure intervention;
begin
for T := t1 to t3 do
  begin
  Tb := sel[next[loc[T]]];
  case kind[loc[T]] of
      mid : stp[T] := non_stop;
      entry : if Tb = T
              then stp[T] := non_stop
              else  stp[T] := backward_stop;
      exit  : if Tb = T
              then stp[T] := non_stop
              else  stp[T] := forward_stop;
  end {case}
  end {for}
end;
```

The algorithms have been translated into assembly code and have been loaded in the program memory of a single-board Motorola 6802 computer. The computer has a parallel I/O port of type MC6820, which is used to read the detectors and to control the relays of the stoppers and the selectors. The interface between the computer and these peripherals presents no special electronic or algorithmic problems; the details are omitted here. Some of the details are given in [26]. See also the implementation remarks in Sections 6.6.6, 6.6.4 and 6.14. Although it is not presented as an explicit requirement, it can be verified that the points can be shifted while the system is operational without causing any problems. The system has been tested for a railway layout of greater complexity than discussed before; to simplify the presentation, the layout of Figure 6.44 was devised later.

6.15   Concluding Remarks

The entire control software is table-driven. If the topology of the railway is changed, only the contents of the arrays described in Section 6.9.2 need to be changed. If the detectors are not too close to the first and last points of their sections, the algorithms may remain unchanged.

When the approach of the present chapter is used for a larger railway system, the number of special components for safety and reachability does not grow too much. In particular, if T denotes the number of trains and S the number of sections then the number of switches needed is:

$$\# \text{switch} = 2 \times T + S \times (T - 1)$$

because for each train there must be two switches in the stopper and for each section there are $T - 1$ switches in the selector. If the number of relays is counted (coupled sets of switches), the growth of the number of selector relays is logarithmic:

$$\# \text{relay} = 2 \times T + S \times {}^2 \log T$$

Finally, the number of detectors needed is given by:

$$2 \times S \leq \# \text{detector} \leq 4 \times S$$

The case study shows how the COLD-1 language can be used to make a wide range of assumptions and design decisions explicit. It may well be the case that certain assumptions are *not* made explicit in particular software projects, but in the present case study the safety requirements and the way they are satisfied by the design are quite complex. On the assumption that for the automatic railway case it is important to have a detailed and explicit understanding of the essential assumptions and design decisions, it is shown that this can be done. Note that COLD-1 is essentially a logical language: there is not just one fixed model for the specifications of the present chapter. There are infinitely many railways that can satisfy the given axioms and there are many different implementations of **TRAIN**. But their restrictions and commonalities are given by the definitions and the axioms. The invariants given can be used to analyse the correctness of the algorithms in a rigorous way. Rigorous (manual) correctness proofs may still contain errors and in fact experience learns that large specifications often contain errors themselves, but if there is a suspect or weak spot, all the information required to perform a more detailed analysis is at least available.

The case study shows a variety of styles. The positions of the track, their ordering and their metric properties are described in an algebraic style and so are the standard data types of numbers and sequences which are used frequently. Physical components and arrays are modelled in a state-based component-oriented style. But for the sake of the controller software there are enumerated data types too, one for each category of physical components. The

COLD-1 language is used to introduce a collection of auxiliary concepts serving specification and reasoning purposes. But the data structures and algorithms themselves are also expressed in the language.

An interesting aspect of the case study is the relation between the "real world" and the dynamic model of that world as present in the data structures of the controller. In general it is tempting to think that the controller software manages a complete and truthful dynamic model of all the relevant facts in the real world, and uses this model to establish desired effects in the real world. The case study shows that this view is too simple. The controller can base its decisions on incomplete data only. The relation between the real world and the dynamic model involves many subtleties, as illustrated by the concepts of the environment of a detector (Section 6.7.6, Figure 6.45), and the environment of a section (Section 6.10.2, Figure 6.46). In fact, the computer never contains the data needed to tell which detector is closest to a certain train. Many times the computer can not even distinguish in exactly which section a train is situated. Establishing effects in the real world is not a supplement to gathering data. Without allocation and intervention, the estimation algorithm would be worthless.

Another interesting aspect of the case study is the treatment of real-time aspects. Although COLD-1 has no built-in concepts for modeling time or for reasoning about time, a simple assumption about the interpretation of train_step is all that is needed. We do not have any explicit or implicit claim that this is an efficient or easy way of dealing with real-time aspects. But the fact that it can be done is nice, and it has given many opportunities to show the language in action.

Chapter 7
Pictorial Representations

"Du brauchst ja nur auf die Figur ⊗⊗ *zu sehen, um zu sehen daß 2+2 =
4 ist." – Dann brauche ich nur auf die Figur* ⊗⊗ *zu schauen, um zu
sehen daß 2 + 2 + 2 = 4 ist.*   *(L. Wittgenstein)*

7.1 Survey

The objective of this chapter is to present several important types of pictorial
representations, their form and their meaning. After reading of this (and the
next) chapter, the reader will have an orderly overview of the most important
pictorial representations in software engineering and a precise understanding
of the correspondence between the pictures and their textual COLD-1 counterparts.

Most designers like to draw pictures when explaining their designs to other
people. Many people experience pictures as helpful when they try to understand a design made by someone else. There are differences amongst individ-
uals concerning the degree to which pictures are essential for them, but only
few people do not need them at all. Therefore it is no surprise that many software development methods have certain pictorial representations built-in, and
that some methods started as a pictorial representation, with the semantics,
methodology and tools added later.

This book will not propose new types of pictures but rather reuse existing
ideas. Two unifying frameworks are used. First, there is a syntactic one, based
on the form of the pictures, showing how pictures are built from lines, circles,
arrows etc. The other framework is a semantic one, based on COLD-1 which
is used to fill-in the fine details of the interpretation of the pictures. The
following subdivision of pictorial representations, based on their form, will be
adopted:

- area diagrams,
- graph diagrams,

- network diagrams,
- sequence charts,
- images,
- plot diagrams,
- matrix-like diagrams,
- formula-like diagrams,
- commuting diagrams.

Definitions of "area diagram", "graph diagram" etc. will be given in subsequent sections. Now about the semantic framework. Roughly speaking, there are two options for a certain picture. Either the picture represents some aspect of the *behaviour* of the system being designed, or the picture is about the *structure* of the system's description.

In case the picture is concerned with the behaviour of the system, we adopt a further subdivision into *static* behaviour and *dynamic* behaviour. By "static behaviour" we mean all facts that apply to an individual state, or that apply in a static world view. By "dynamic behaviour" we mean all aspects of system behaviour which are related to state transitions such as write operations on data structures, dynamic object creation, movement of physical devices, etc.

If the picture is concerned with the structure of the system, we adopt a further subdivision depending on the level of detail represented in the picture. This can be at the level of the *operations* (function and procedure definitions, but also assertions and expressions), or at the level of modules (components).

Let us give an example. Consider a simple graph diagram, as given in Figure 7.1. The graph allows a number of quite distinct interpretations, which are summarized in Figure 7.2.

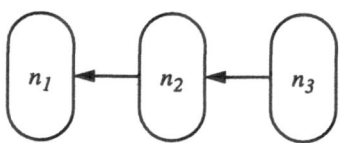

Figure 7.1: Simple graph diagram.

	node	edge	graph
behaviour (static)	value	"map to"	function
behaviour (dynamic)	state	"go to"	state machine
structure (1)	function	"use"	call graph
structure (2)	module	"import"	system structure

Figure 7.2: Distinct interpretations of graph diagram.

A first interpretation is that every node represents a value. In that case the diagram is concerned with a function on a three-valued data type which has the values n_1, n_2 and n_3. The collection of edges represents a function, f say, which satisfies the equations $f(n_2) = n_1$ and $f(n_3) = n_2$. In fact f is a *partial* function because $f(n_1)$ is not defined.

A second interpretation is that every node represents a state. In that case the diagram is concerned with a state space which has three states n_1, n_2 and n_3. The collection of edges represents a procedure p, with transitions from n_2 to n_1 and from n_3 to n_2. The graph diagram as a whole represents a finite state machine.

A third interpretation is that every node represents a function definition. In that case the diagram is concerned with three functions, called n_1, n_2 and n_3. The collection of edges indicate how one function is used by another. For example, there is a call of n_2 which occurs in n_1 and a call of n_3 which occurs in n_2. The graph diagram as a whole represents a call graph.

A fourth interpretation is that every node represents a module: the diagram is about a system with three modules, n_1, n_2 and n_3. The collection of edges indicates how one module is imported by another. For example, n_2 is imported into n_1, and n_3 is imported into n_2. The graph diagram as a whole represents the modular structure of a system.

The subdivision of the remainder of the present chapter into sections is based on the *form* of the pictures.

7.2 Area Diagrams: General

An area diagram is a system of closed curved lines which partition the two-dimensional space of the picture into areas.

In the subsequent sections we shall consider several kinds of area diagrams: Venn diagrams (Section 7.3), statecharts (Section 7.4), Nassi-Shneidermann diagrams (Section 7.5) and HOOD diagrams (Section 7.6).

7.3 Venn diagrams

Venn diagrams, named after J. Venn (1834-1923) are area diagrams where each area is interpreted as a set of values, or objects. Sometimes they are called Venn-Euler diagrams. The diagrams are useful for overviewing a state of affairs where a collection of objects is organized into sets, particularly when some of these sets have elements in common. Venn diagrams used to be very popular in textbooks on elementary mathematics using naive set theory. Sometimes they are used to explain the concepts of set union, intersection and complement. Referring to Figure 7.3, the shaded areas in (a) and (b) represent the union and intersection respectively of two sets p and q, whereas the shaded area in Figure 7.3 (c) is the complement of the set p. Note that the notion of *complement* of p (the set of objects which are not in p) assumes some given *universe*, which is the set of all objects being considered. In Figure 7.3 (c) the universe is shown as the area inside the outermost box.

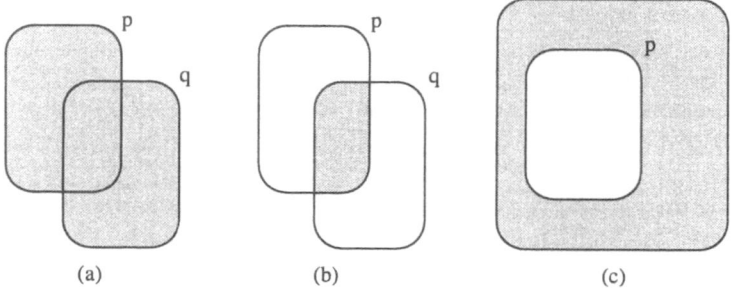

(a)   (b)   (c)

Figure 7.3: Venn diagrams for union, intersection and complement.

The following limitations of Venn diagrams should be mentioned. For certain applications care is needed to draw the "most general" situation; otherwise if, for example, the picture does not provide for an overlap of the areas of p and q, reasoning about the objects which are both in p and q could go wrong, or the case might just be forgotten. Secondly, the Venn diagrams work fine for sets, but they can not cope easily with Cartesian products, which are sets of pairs. Also nested sets (sets of sets etc.) do not fit in easily. When treating infinite sets with topological properties, questions like "does the boundary belong to the set?" deserve special care. Finally it is difficult to arrange a proper layout of the diagram when four or more sets are involved.

We assume that the reader has already an informal understanding of Venn diagrams and therefore the main issue to be addressed below is a systematic connection between the COLD-1 textual notation and Venn's diagrammatic notation. In particular we shall propose ways of drawing Venn diagrams for specifications using the following textual constructs:

- predicates of one argument (PRED),
- the standard data type of finite sets (SET).

A distinction will be made between "specific" Venn diagrams (Sections 7.3.1 and 7.3.3) and "generalized" Venn diagrams (Section 7.3.2 and 7.3.4). After that we shall also discuss some extensions: (1) Venn diagrams with arrows for functions, (2) statecharts.

7.3.1   Specific Venn diagrams for Predicates

A *specific* Venn diagram shows one particular state of affairs. All values are shown as dots (bullets), which are inside or outside the areas of the predicates, as appropriate. More precisely, consider a textual description of a component

C containing definitions of a sort S and one or more predicates $p_1, p_2, \ldots, p_n$ on S. This sort and these predicates could stem from the component's parameters, from its import list, or from its CLASS section. The predicates can be variable (VAR) or constant (not VAR). It does not matter if C is a SPECIFICATION, IMPLEMENTATION or LET-type component.

```
COMPONENT C SPECIFICATION
CLASS
   SORT S
   PRED p₁ :  S body of p₁
      ⋮
   PRED pₙ :  S body of pₙ
   axioms
   other sorts and operations
END
```

We can view C as the specification of a system which can go through a number of states. In principle there are many states in which the system can be. Each state is a "static world model", or "state of affairs". Even if there are no variables, the specification need not completely fix the state of the system and there may be many possible states. For each state we can draw one specific Venn diagram. The diagram has a number of areas, one for S and one for each of the predicates $p_1, p_2, \ldots, p_n$. The largest area is labelled S and all the other areas are enclosed in it. We focus our presentation of the drawing rules on situations where S contains only finitely many objects. Each object in the sort S is shown as a dot, possibly labelled with some term that refers to the object. Each object is shown once. The dot of an object x must be in the area of every p_i for which $p_i(x)$ holds ($1 \leq i \leq n$) in the state being considered. The dot of x should not be in the area of of a predicate p_i if $p_i(x)$ does not hold. It follows from these rules that whenever there exists an object x of sort S such that both $p_i(x)$ and $p_j(x)$ hold, then the areas of p_i and p_j must overlap. It is allowed to make the areas of p_i and p_j coincide, attaching two or more labels to the same area; this can only be done if both predicates hold for precisely the same objects. Very much in the same way, S and one or more of the p_i can coincide, provided this p_i holds for all objects of sort S. Every predicate has an area, even if there are no objects in it. If two predicates have no element in common, it is still allowed to show them by partially overlapping areas. Also if p_i holds for all objects that make p_j hold, the area of the former need not contain the area of the latter (it can be drawn that way, but it need not).

We consider two specific Venn diagrams for a sort S equivalent if the same predicates p_i and the same objects are shown and if furthermore in each diagram precisely the same objects are shown inside the area of each predicate. The structure of the diagrams with respect to equality, containment and disjointness of areas is considered irrelevant. This is illustrated in Figure 7.4 which shows several diagrams which are pairwise essentially the same. Figure 7.5

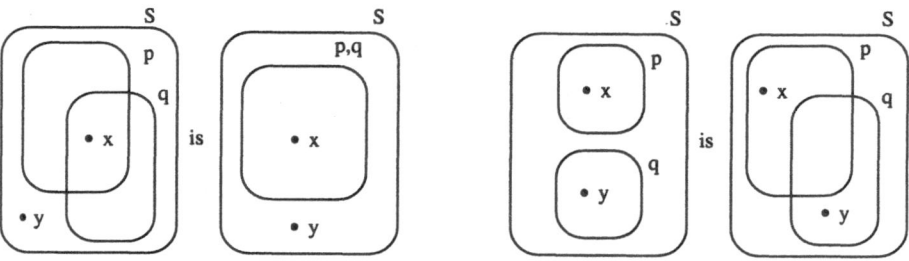

Figure 7.4: Equivalence of specific Venn diagrams.

shows several diagrams which can not be identified. Note that in Figure 7.5

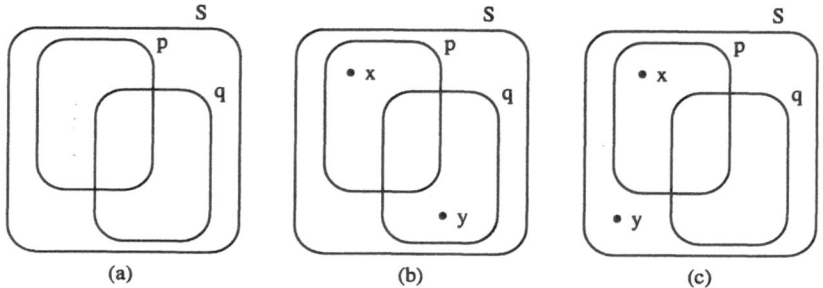

Figure 7.5: Three mutually distinct specific Venn diagrams.

(a) there are no objects at all. Clearly this differs from (b) and (c) which each show two objects x and y.

Next we present an example, which is about the contents of a simple data base concerning persons and the various types of driver licenses they have. The example builds upon the regulations of Dutch law, but the reader can easily translate it to his own national situation if he wishes to do so. In the Netherlands, a person can have an a-type license, which allows driving a motor cycle. A b-type license allows for driving a car, provided its weight, including the loading capacity, does not exceed 3.500 kilograms. A c-type license is for trucks. A d-type license is for buses. A person can have zero, one, two or more of these licenses. By Dutch law, a person can not have a truck license or a bus license unless he/she is already allowed to drive a normal car. In practice, there is just one exam to get the truck and bus-licenses together. So everybody who has a c-type license has a d-type license as well, and the other way around. The persons involved in the example are called Luke, Mike, Frits, Liz, Paul, Henk, Thijs, Anita, Guido, and Sue.

```
COMPONENT PERSON SPECIFICATION
IMPORT ENUM10'
    RENAMING Enum10 TO Person,
              x0      TO Luke,
              x1      TO Mike,
              x2      TO Frits,
              x3      TO Liz,
              x4      TO Paul,
              x5      TO Henk,
              x6      TO Thijs,
              x7      TO Anita,
              x8      TO Guido,
              x9      TO Sue
    END
END
```

The specification below is concerned with these ten persons and their status in 1994. Luke and Mike do not have a licence at all (they are too young). Frits only has an a-type license (he is happy with his Harley-Davidson). Liz, Paul and Henk only have a b-type license (they drive cars). Thijs, Anita and Guido have both an a-type and a b-type license (in the summer they prefer to go by motor, in the winter they use their cars). Sue has the b, c, and d-type licenses (she is a bus driver). This state of affairs is modelled by the following specification.

```
COMPONENT LICENSES_WORLD1994 SPECIFICATION
IMPORT
  PERSON
CLASS
  PRED a : Person
  IND  a(Fritz); a(Thijs); a(Anita); a(Guido)

  PRED b : Person
  IND  b(Liz);b(Paul);b(Henk);b(Thijs);b(Anita);b(Guido);b(Sue)

  PRED c : Person
  IND  c(Sue)

  PRED d : Person
  IND  d(Sue)
END
```

The specification LICENSES_WORLD1994 is complete in the sense that for all objects and for all predicates it is precisely fixed which facts about a, b, c and d hold and which do not. In that sense there is essentially only one state of affairs satisfying the specification. This state of affairs is shown by the specific Venn diagram of Figure 7.6. Next we rewrite the example to a more general form by introducing dynamical aspects. The licenses of the persons are made

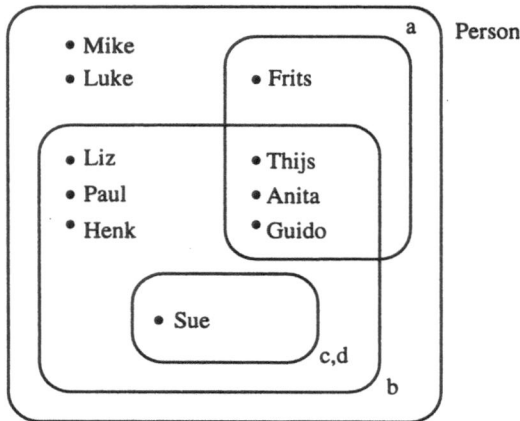

Figure 7.6: Specific Venn diagram for driver licenses (1994).

dependent on the year being considered (e.g. 1994 or 1995).

```
COMPONENT LICENSES_WORLD SPECIFICATION
IMPORT
  PERSON,
  NAT RENAMING Nat TO Year END
CLASS
  FUNC date : -> Year VAR

  PRED a : Person
  IND  a(Frits);
       a(Thijs);
       a(Anita);
       a(Guido);
       date = 1995 => a(Sue)

  PRED b : Person
  IND  b(Liz);b(Paul);b(Henk);b(Thijs);b(Anita);b(Guido);b(Sue)

  PRED c : Person
  IND  c(Sue)

  PRED d : Person
  IND  d(Sue)
END
```

Now let us consider the same group of persons in 1995. Sue has obtained the
a-type license at the beginning of this new year, whereas everything else has
remained the same. The new state of affairs can be shown by the specific Venn

diagram of Figure 7.7. It should be noted that in 1995 the set of persons which have c and d is a proper subset of the intersection of a and b. Therefore we could have drawn the c and d areas completely inside the overlap of a and b. But we took the other option which is all right too, viz. to not eliminate the overlap from the picture. To conclude this section we summarize the rules for

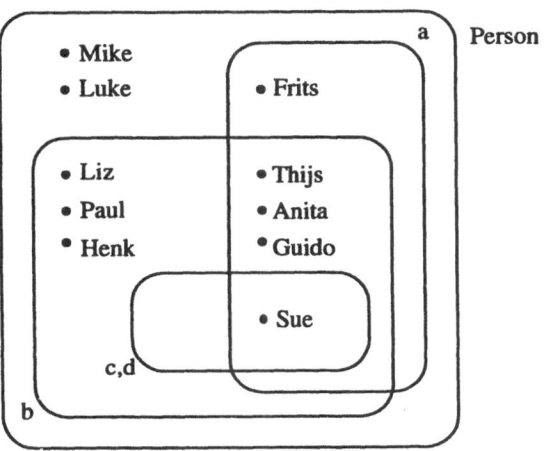

Figure 7.7: Specific Venn diagram for driver licenses (1995).

drawing a specific Venn diagram for a given state of affairs.

- the area for the sort S is the outermost area;
- all objects are shown as dots, possibly labelled;
- there is one area for each predicate p_i; two predicates which have the same thruth value for all objects, can be represented by one area; if there is a predicate which holds for all objects of the sort, it can be represented by the same area as the sort;
- if $p_i(x)$ holds for object x, then the dot of x is inside the area of p_i;
- otherwise it is outside the area.

7.3.2   Generalized Venn diagrams for Predicates

In contrast with the "specific" Venn diagrams of Section 7.3.1 there is another way of using almost the same diagrams, which we call *generalized* Venn diagrams. A generalized Venn diagram shows a number of facts (properties, requirements), about the possible states. The objects themselves are not shown. Consider again a textual description of a component C defining a sort S and one or more predicates $p_1, p_2, \ldots, p_n$ on S, as in Section 7.3.1.

We can view C as the specification of a system which can go through a number of states. There are many states in which the system can be, and the diagram serves to express facts concerning some collection of these states. One can decide to draw a diagram that applies to all states of the system, or to possible initial states, or to states satisfying an invariant. The notation of generalized Venn diagrams is of an assertional nature.

Each diagram has a number of areas, one for the sort S and one for each of the predicates $p_1, p_2, \ldots, p_n$. The largest area is labelled with the name of the sort, and all the other areas are enclosed in it. Again some of the predicate areas may coincide, and some of the predicate areas may coincide with the area of the sort. We consider two generalized Venn diagrams equivalent if they have the same structure with respect to equality, containment and disjointness of their areas. Other properties like size and relative positioning of the areas are considered irrelevant. This is illustrated in Figure 7.8 which shows several diagrams which are pairwise essentially the same. Figure 7.9 shows several

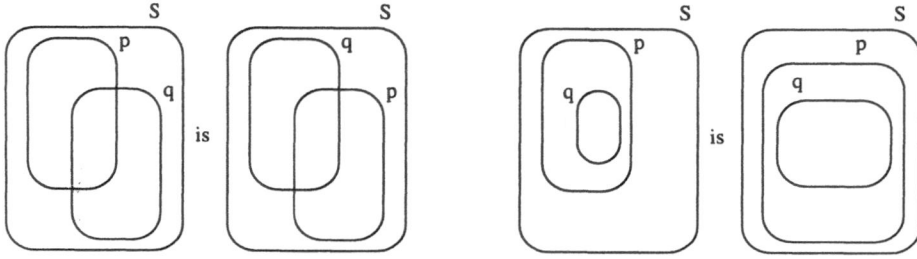

Figure 7.8: Equivalence of generalized Venn diagrams.

distinct diagrams which can not be identified – they have the same "signature" in the sense that each of them is about a sort S and two predicates p and q. If there are n predicates, and hence n "predicate areas", then because

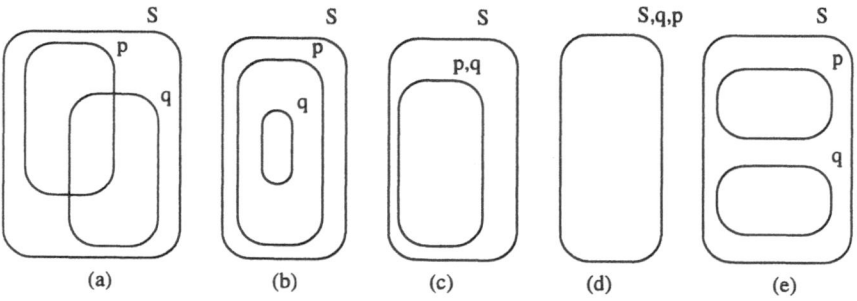

Figure 7.9: Five mutually distinct generalized Venn diagrams.

of the possibilities of overlapping, equality, containment and disjointness, the universe (the area of the sort) will be partitioned into at most 2^n smaller areas.

Some of these areas arise directly from one of the p_i, others are the overlap area of two or more predicate areas or their complements. Not all 2^n areas need to be present: by a suitable arrangement of the predicate areas, some of these areas will dissappear from the picture. The diagram in which all 2^n areas are present amounts to the TRUE assertion because the diagram shows "the most general" situation, as in Figure 7.9 (a) where $n = 2$. But the absence of a certain area means that the corresponding combination of truth values for the predicates can not occur.

For example, if the following follows from a certain specification for all states under consideration:

THEOREM $q(x)$ => $p(x)$

then the areas of p and q can be drawn such that the area of q is contained in the area of p. Here we assume that x is a logical variable which has been declared of type S, as can be done using the DECL construct. Recall that free logical variables in an axiom or theorem are implicitly universally quantified. So the above theorem should be read as FORALL x : S ($q(x)$ => $p(x)$). The resulting diagram is shown in Figure 7.9 (b). Very much in the same way, if the following holds for all states under consideration:

THEOREM $p(x)$ <=> $q(x)$

then it is allowed to make the areas of p and q coincide. This diagram is shown in Figure 7.9 (c). Also, if $p(x)$ holds for all x, then the area of p can coincide with the area of S. In Figure 7.9 (d) this is the case. And if we find that

THEOREM NOT ($p(x)$ AND $q(x)$)

then the areas of p and q can be drawn as disjoint areas, as in Figure 7.9 (e).

After these examples, we present the proper rule that describes which diagrams can be drawn for a given specification and a given collection of states. Suppose that the following holds:

THEOREM NOT (A_1 AND A_2 AND ... AND A_m)

where A_1, A_2, ..., A_m are assertions such that each A_k is either a predicate assertion $p_i(x)$ or its negation NOT $p_i(x)$. Then we are allowed to arrange the areas of the predicates such that there is no area common to the areas of the assertions in A_1, A_2, ..., A_m. Here we adopt the definition that the area of an assertion of the form NOT $p_i(x)$ is given as the area outside the area of p_i, i.e. the complement of p_i. Clearly not every theorem of the form NOT (A_1 AND A_2 AND ... AND A_m) can be arranged for in the style adopted here. In particular, if $m = 1$, a theorem like NOT $q(x)$ can not be represented because we have no explicit mechanism to draw the assertion that q is empty.

We shall illustrate the drawing rules by means of an example. It is about the regulations of Dutch law concerning the a, b, c and d-type driver licenses. Some of the principles involved are formalized below.

```
COMPONENT LICENSES_PRINCIPLES SPECIFICATION
CLASS
   SORT Person

   PRED a : Person VAR
   PRED b : Person VAR
   PRED c : Person VAR

   DECL x : Person

   AXIOM c(x) => b(x)

   PRED d : Person
   IN   x
   DEF  c(x)
END
```

The generalized Venn diagram which applies to all states of this specification is given in Figure 7.10.

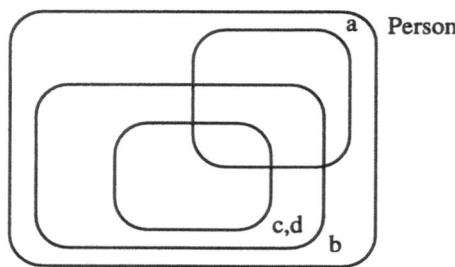

Figure 7.10: Generalized Venn diagram of licenses principles.

This example gives us the opportunity to discuss the relation between the specific Venn diagrams of Section 7.3.1 and the generalized Venn diagram presented here. A specific Venn diagram is said to "satisfy" a generalized Venn diagram if the former can be obtained from the latter by inserting dots corresponding to objects. For example, each of the diagrams presented in Figures 7.6 and 7.7 satisfies the diagram of Figure 7.10. This satisfaction relation between diagrams is consistent with the rules of drawing diagrams for given COLD-1 specifications. We find that the diagrams of Figures 7.6 and 7.7 satisfy the diagram of Figure 7.10. This is because the state of affairs for date = 1994 and the state of affairs for date = 1995 as specified in LICENSES_WORLD

obey the principles expressed by LICENSES_PRINCIPLES. In general, if we have
a given collection of states and draw a generalized Venn diagram $\mathcal{G}$ for it, and
if we also draw the specific Venn diagram $\mathcal{S}$ for one of these states, then $\mathcal{S}$
satisfies $\mathcal{G}$.

Some care is needed not to invert the definition of "satisfaction" by saying
that the generalized Venn diagram must be obtained by omitting the dots from
the specific Venn diagram. This is because in a specific Venn diagram the
structure with respect to equality, containment and disjointness is irrelevant.
It can be chosen as a matter of convenience. The only facts that matter are
the presence or non-presence of object dots in the areas.

There is an ordering relation on generalized Venn diagrams which arises in
a natural way, because for each generalized Venn diagram, there is a collection
of specific Venn diagrams: the diagrams that satisfy it. The inclusion relation
on these collections of specific diagrams gives rise to an "is-more-general-than"
relation on generalized Venn diagrams. For two generalized Venn diagrams $\mathcal{G}_1$,
$\mathcal{G}_2$ of the same signature we say that $\mathcal{G}_1$ is *more general than* $\mathcal{G}_2$ if each specific
Venn diagram satisfying $\mathcal{G}_2$, satisfies $\mathcal{G}_1$ too. The most general $\mathcal{G}$ arises as the
maximum element in this "is-more-general-than" relation; it is the diagram in
which all 2^n areas are present. For example, for $n = 2$ it is shown as the upper
diagram in Figure 7.11. For $n = 3$ the diagram is easy to draw too, whereas
for $n = 4$ – though technically still possible – the most general diagram is
already becoming complicated in a non-attractive way. Figure 7.11 shows
the generalized Venn diagrams for two predicates p and q together with their
ordering. They are organized into a Hasse diagram, that is, the most general
element is at the top, the least general element is at the bottom, and the
thin lines connect the diagrams to reflect the "is more general than" relation.
One might expect Figure 7.11 to have 2^{2^2} diagrams because each diagram is
obtained by omitting zero, one or more of the 2^2 areas shown in the most
general diagram. Half of these can not be drawn in the style adopted here (try
to omit the $\overline{p \cup q}$ area). They could easily be drawn however if one resorts to
the use of shading.

7.3.3   Specific Venn diagrams for Finite Sets

In this section we shall establish a connection between the standard data type
of finite sets and Venn diagrams. The diagrams are similar to the specific Venn
diagrams for predicates as presented in Section 7.3.1, in the sense that values
are shown as dots (bullets), which are inside or outside the areas of the sets
shown.

We start with a description of the standard data type of finite sets, which
is given by the parametrized component SET. The description is a stripped
version of the full component, given in the appendix. We give the ABSTRACT
clause and the EXPORT list first.

COMPONENT SET[Item] SPECIFICATION

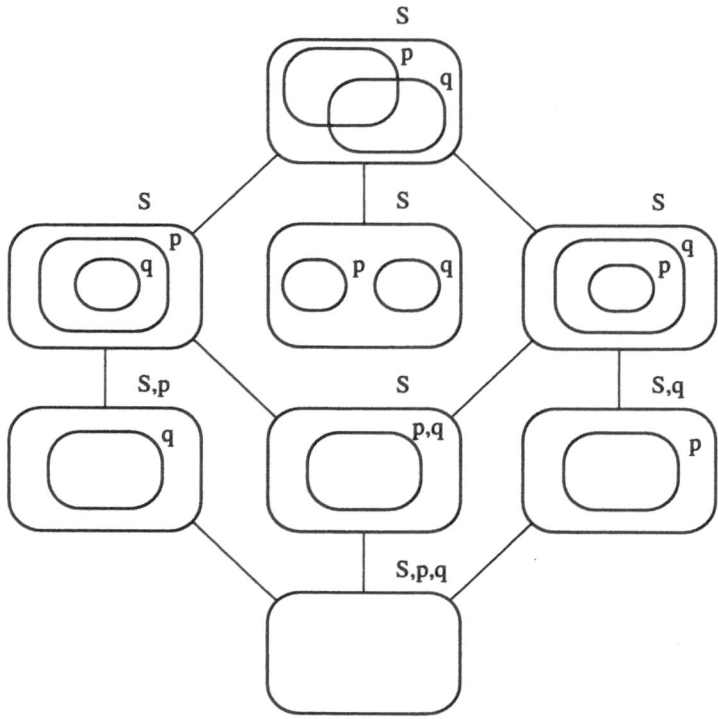

Figure 7.11: "Is-more-general-than" relation on generalized Venn diagrams.

```
ABSTRACT
  ITEM
EXPORT
  SORT Set
  FUNC empty  : -> Set,
       ins    : Item # Set -> Set,
       union  : Set  # Set -> Set,
       isect  : Set  # Set -> Set,
  PRED subset : Set  # Set,
       is_in  : Item # Set
```

The sort Item contains the objects which are, or are not, contained in the
various values of Set. If is_in(i,s) holds, this means that i is is an element
of s, or in mathematical notation, $i \in s$. empty is the empty set (or $\emptyset$),
ins(i,s) is the set s with i inserted (or $s \cup \{i\}$), union(s,t) is the union of
s and t (or $s \cup t$), isect(s,t) is the intersection of s and t (or $s \cap t$) and
subset(s,t) holds if s is a subset of t (or $s \subseteq t$).

Next we proceed with the CLASS ... END part of the component, which is
written in the algebraic style. The elementary operations is_in, empty and

ins are specified axiomatically in the axioms SET1 to SET7. The predicate
is_gen is an auxiliary predicate used in the last axiom. The other operations
for union, intersection and subset are defined inductively using the elementary
operations.

```
CLASS                                        % SET[Item] continued
  SORT Set    DEP Item
  PRED is_in : Item # Set
  FUNC empty :                -> Set
  FUNC ins    : Item # Set -> Set

  DECL s,t : Set,
       i,j : Item

  PRED is_gen : Set
  IND  is_gen(empty);
       is_gen(s) => is_gen(ins(i,s))

  AXIOM
  {SET1} empty!;
  {SET2} ins(i,s)!;
  {SET3} NOT is_in(i,empty);
  {SET4} is_in(i,ins(j,s)) <=> i = j OR is_in(i,s);
  {SET5} ins(i,ins(j,s)) = ins(j,ins(i,s));
  {SET6} ins(i,ins(i,s)) = ins(i,s);
  {SET7} is_gen(s)

  FUNC union : Set # Set -> Set
  IND  union(s,empty) = s;
       union(s,ins(i,t)) = ins(i,union(s,t))

  FUNC isect : Set # Set -> Set
  IND  isect(s,empty) = empty;
       isect(ins(i,s),ins(i,t)) = ins(i,isect(s,t));
       NOT is_in(i,s) => isect(s,ins(i,t)) = isect(s,t)

  PRED subset : Set # Set
  IND  subset(s,s);
       subset(s,t) => subset(s,ins(i,t))
END
```

If we consider a collection of sets s_i (values of Set), we can draw a specific
Venn diagram with one area for each set s_i. Each area is labelled by a term of
type Set denoting the set s_i, while containing dots for the objects x for which
is_in(x,s_i) holds. In other words, the diagram is similar to the specific Venn
diagrams of Section 7.3.1, provided we assume auxiliary predicates p_i (one for
each set s_i under consideration) defined as $p_i(x) \Leftrightarrow$ is_in(x,s_i). Although
one could draw the outermost area of the sort Item, it is sometimes better not

to show it, because if Item is infinite (as is Nat), the area is *not* a finite set, and hence is not a value of Set.

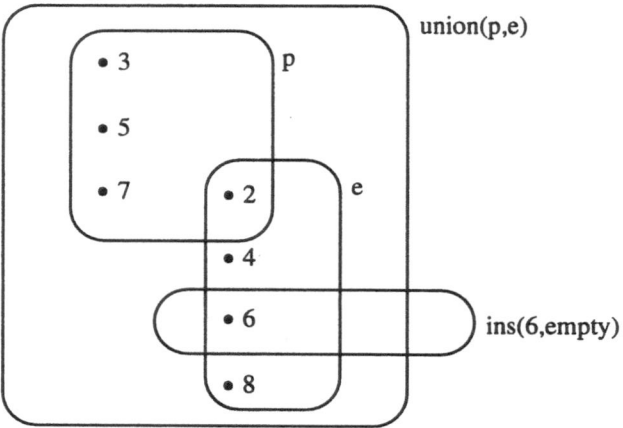

Figure 7.12: Specific Venn diagram with four finite sets.

We illustrate this with a simple example concerning finite sets of natural numbers.

```
COMPONENT SET_EXAMPLE SPECIFICATION
IMPORT
  NAT,
  SET[Nat]
CLASS
  DECL n,k : Nat

  FUNC p : -> Set
  DEF  ins(2,ins(3,ins(5,ins(7,empty))))

  PRED even : Nat
  IN   n
  DEF  EXISTS k (n = 2 * k)

  FUNC e : -> Set
  POST FORALL n ( is_in(n,e) <=> 0 < n AND n < 10 AND even(n) )
END
```

The set p is a small set of prime numbers, and e is the set of even numbers in the range 2..8. Two more sets are union(p,e) and ins(6,empty). The diagram of Figure 7.12 shows these four sets.

7.3.4 Generalized Venn diagrams for Finite Sets

Generalized Venn diagrams for finite sets are similar to the generalized Venn
diagrams for predicates, except for the fact that they do not show predicates,
but values of the data type **Set**. Again, the objects themselves are not shown.

We illustrate this with a simple example of a database with semantic constraints. The database contains data on the task assignments in a fictitious
software company concerned with employees (persons) and programs (tasks).

```
COMPONENT PERSON SPECIFICATION
CLASS
  SORT Person
  FUNC Lex     : -> Person
  FUNC Loe     : -> Person
  FUNC Paul    : -> Person
  FUNC Hans    : -> Person
  FUNC Gerard  : -> Person
  FUNC Roeland : -> Person
  %    etc.
END

COMPONENT TASK SPECIFICATION
CLASS
  SORT Task
  FUNC text_editor       : -> Task
  FUNC code_generator    : -> Task
  FUNC picture_tool      : -> Task
  FUNC module_normalizer : -> Task
  FUNC module_parser     : -> Task
  %    etc.
END
```

The tasks are programs to be specified and realized. Each program is allocated
to one programmer. Some programmers have a personal reviewer, whose task
it is to provide for consultancy and to detect potential errors.

```
COMPONENT DATABASE_CONSTRAINTS SPECIFICATION
IMPORT
  TASK,
  PERSON,
  SET[Person],
  MAP[Task,Person],
  MAP[Person,Person]
CLASS
  FUNC employees : -> Set[Person]
  PRE   TRUE

  FUNC programmer : -> Map[Task,Person]
  PRE   TRUE
```

```
VAR

FUNC reviewer : -> Map[Person,Person]
PRE   TRUE
VAR                                      % to be continued
```

As the specification shows, the set of hired employees is a constant, whereas the task assignment maps programmer and reviewer are dynamic notions, modelled as variables. For example, the database contents could contain the following set of empoyees:

employee
Paul
Roeland
Hans
Lex
Loe

or in other words, employee is the set containing Paul, Roeland, Hans, Lex and Loe. The database contents could contain the map programmer, given by the following table, which means that the text editor must be programmed by Loe, the code generator must be programmed by Paul, etc.

domain	range
text editor	Loe
code generator	Paul
picture tool	Roeland
module normalizer	Hans
module parser	Lex

and furthermore the map reviewer could be given by the following table, stating that the reviewer of Paul's work is Hans, the reviewer of Roeland's work is Loe, etc.

domain	range
Paul	Hans
Roeland	Loe
Hans	Gerard

Now let us assume that the company whose work assignment database we are discussing, has certain semantic constraints upon the database. The constraints are given by the following part of the specification.

% DATABASE_CONSTRAINTS continued

AXIOM subset(dom(reviewer),ran(programmer))

AXIOM subset(ran(programmer),employees)
END

We used the operations **dom** and **ran** on maps, as provided by the standard
data type module **MAP**. The first constraint states that it is useless to assign a
reviewer to someone who is not working on some program anyhow. The second
constraint states that only employees can be allocated to a programming task
(external reviewers are allowed however). In Figure 7.13 these constraints are
expressed in a generalized Venn diagram. We leave it to the reader to check if
the database contents sketched above (Paul, Roeland, Hans, etc.) satisfies the
constraints.

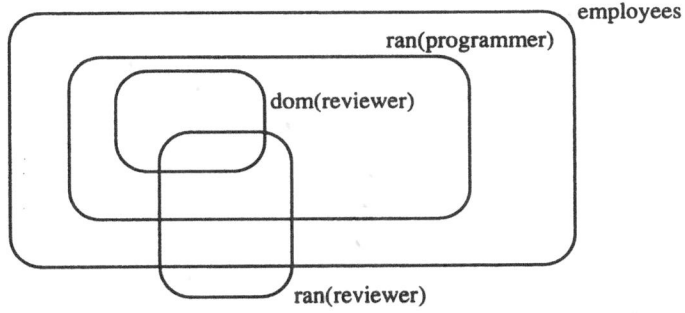

Figure 7.13: Generalized Venn diagram for programmers database.

7.3.5   Extended Forms: Venn diagrams with Arrows for Functions

We consider two variations of Venn diagrams: (1) Venn diagrams with arrows
for functions, (2) Harel's statecharts. We devote one section to each of these.

Specific Venn diagrams with arrows for functions are similar to the specific
Venn diagrams for predicates, or for finite sets, as presented in Sections 7.3.1
and 7.3.3 respectively, but one or more functions are shown too. Each function
is represented by a collection of arrows. The arrows must be labelled by the
name of the function. If f is a unary function, then there is an arrow labelled f
which starts at object a, pointing to object b, provided $f(a) = b$. There must
be no arrow starting at a if $f(a)$ is undefined. If f is binary, one must use
forking arrows, having two starting points. If more than one sort is involved,
for example because f is $f : S \rightarrow T$, then there is a separate area for each
of the sorts (S and T). We present an example which is closely related to the
specification **DATABASE_CONSTRAINTS** of Section 7.3.4. The main difference is

that here we used functions (which in principle could have an infinite domain), instead of finite maps.

```
COMPONENT PROGRAMMERS94 SPECIFICATION
IMPORT
  PERSON,
  TASK
CLASS
   PRED employee : Person
   IND  employee(Paul);
        employee(Roeland);
        employee(Hans);
        employee(Lex);
        employee(Loe)

   FUNC programmer : Task -> Person
   IND  programmer(text_editor)       = Loe;
        programmer(code_generator)    = Paul;
        programmer(picture_tool)      = Roeland;
        programmer(module_normalizer) = Hans;
        programmer(module_parser)     = Lex

   FUNC reviewer : Person -> Person
   IND  reviewer(Paul)    = Hans;
        reviewer(Roeland) = Loe;
        reviewer(Hans)    = Gerard
END
```

Note the inductive definition of employee. The keyword IND says that employee holds for the smallest set of persons which satisfy the given assertion, i.e. the assertion that employee must hold for Paul, Roeland, Hans, Lex, and Loe. This can be explained as follows. Consider another set, e.g. the set which contains Paul, Roeland, Hans, Lex, Loe and Gerard too. Then the assumption that employee holds for the latter set would still be consistent with the given assertion. But the set shown in Figure 7.14 is smaller than (= proper subset of) the set which contains Gerard. In fact it is smaller than *any* set which is all right for the given assertion. Therefore the set drawn in the diagram is the right interpretation of the predicate employee.

In the same way we can understand the keyword IND for the functions. For suppose that reviewer would be a function with more than three arrows, e.g. containing reviewer(Gerard) = Gerard too, than it would still be possible to satisfy the given assertions. Yet, this is not the right interpretation, because we must take the smallest function. The smallest function is the function with the smallest collection of arrows.

A diagram derived from PROGRAMMERS94 is given in Figure 7.14. The diagram has two collections of arrows: one for the function reviewer (3 arrows) and one for programmer (5 arrows).

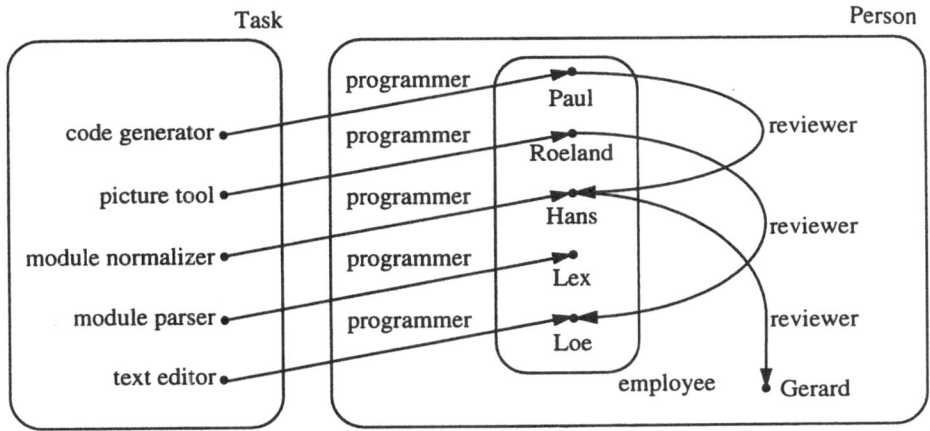

Figure 7.14: Venn diagram with arrows for functions of PROGRAMMERS94.

7.4   Statecharts

Statecharts are area diagrams extended with arrows. The areas are used to model sets of states, and the arrows model state transitions. In [28] they are introduced as an extension of conventional state transition diagrams with notions of hierarchy, concurrency and communication. Unlike the Venn diagrams, there are *two* ways of partitioning an area into subareas:

- **xor** (exclusive-or) decomposition, and
- **and** decomposition.

The **xor** decomposition of an area A is shown by enclosing two or more subareas in A, each with its own boundary, drawn in *solid* lines. If A has subareas $A_1, A_2, \ldots, A_n$, this means that whenever the system is in the state of A, it is in precisely one of the substates $A_1, A_2, \ldots, A_n$. A is said to be a superstate of $A_1, A_2, \ldots, A_n$.

The **and** decomposition of an area is shown by splitting A into two or more parts, separated by *dashed* lines. If A is split into $A_1, A_2, \ldots, A_n$ by dashed lines, this means that whenever the system is in the state of A, it is in all of its **and** components at the same time. A is said to be the orthogonal product of $A_1, A_2, \ldots, A_n$.

Labeled arrows are used to model state transitions and Harel has proposed a rich collection of facilities to model default states, history-dependent transitions, output actions, synchronization and communication. The interested reader is referred to [28]. Here we only give a small example, showing the main decomposition mechanisms for states.

The example is concerned with certain control aspects of a watch (in [28] a more complete analysis of a watch is made). The watch has two main states:

either the watch is off, which is the initial state, or it is on. It goes from off to
on by inserting a battery and from on to off by removing the battery. When
the watch is off, there are no interesting substates. But when it is on, the
watch can be viewed as consisting of two subsystems, which exist independently
(concurrently). They are called display and light. The display subsystem
keeps track of the time of day and of an alarm time; when the watch is on, one
of these is displayed. The light subsystem is for reading the display in the
dark; when the watch is on, either light_off holds, or light_on (but of course
these do not hold at the same time). The display and the light are orthogonal,
in the sense that the actual state on has four substates, characterized by the
combinations:

display	*light*
time_of_day	light_off
time_of_day	light_on
time_of_alarm	light_off
time_of_alarm	light_on

The state of the display can be modified by the procedure next, which toggles
between the time_of_day and the time_of_alarm. The state of the light can
be modified by two procedures, that correspond to pressing one user-button
on the watch. When the button is pushed (procedure push), the light goes
on. When the button is released, the light goes off. There is also an operation
goto_normal, made available to the user by means of another button. It
transfers the display to the time_of_day state and the light to the off state
simultaneously. This models two events, one in each subsystem, which are
synchronized.

```
COMPONENT WATCH SPECIFICATION
CLASS
   % decomposition of main state of WATCH :

   PRED off : VAR
   PRED on  : DEF   display AND light

   AXIOM off XOR on;
         INIT => off

   PROC insert_battery : ->
   PRE  off
   SAT  MOD off, time_of_day, light_off, time_of_alarm, light_on
   POST time_of_day AND light_off

   PROC remove_battery : ->
   PRE  on
```

```
SAT  MOD off, time_of_alarm, time_of_day, light_on, light_off
POST off


% decomposition of on :

PRED display : DEF time_of_alarm OR time_of_day
PRED light   : DEF light_on OR light_off


AXIOM display <=> light


% decomposition of display :

PRED time_of_alarm : VAR
PRED time_of_day   : VAR


AXIOM display => (time_of_alarm XOR time_of_day)


PROC next : ->
PRE  display
SAT  MOD time_of_alarm, time_of_day
POST time_of_alarm' => time_of_day;
     time_of_day' => time_of_alarm


% decomposition of light :

PRED light_on  : VAR
PRED light_off : VAR


AXIOM light => (light_on XOR light_off)


PROC push : ->
PRE  light_off
SAT  MOD light_on, light_off
POST light_on


PROC release : ->
PRE  light_on
SAT  MOD light_on, light_off
POST light_off


% synchronized action of display and light :

PROC goto_normal : ->
PRE  on
SAT  MOD time_of_alarm, time_of_day, light_on, light_off
POST time_of_day AND light_off
END
```

The above COLD-1 specification has been organized in such a way that a statechart can be drawn for it in a straightforward way. It is given in Figure 7.15. The uppermost arrow in the area of WATCH indicates the default state upon entry (off) of the topmost superstate.

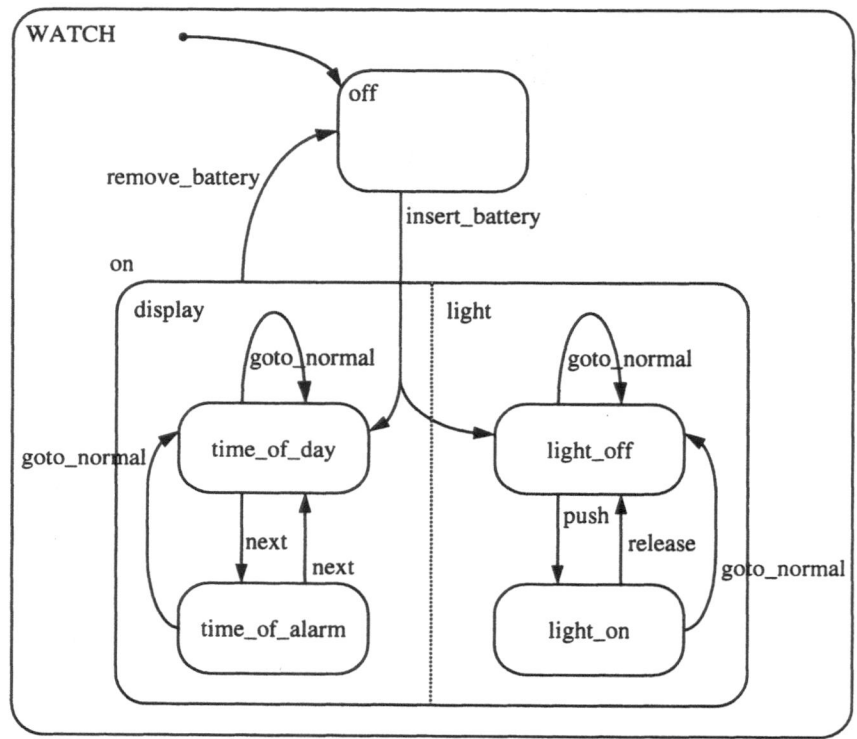

Figure 7.15: Statechart for WATCH.

An alternative statechart is shown in Figure 7.16; it is obtained by exploiting the fact that the transition goto_normal applies to *all* substates of display and light. In particular, the two arrows labelled goto_normal which start in time_of_day and in time_of_alarm can be combined into one arrow whose begin point is at the boundary of their enclosing area, which is display. In the same way, both arrows labelled goto_normal which start in light_off and light_on can be combined into one arrow whose begin point is at the boundary of the area of light.

Of course, the specification could have been set-up differently, e.g. by using variable functions ranging over suitably chosen enumerated data types, as follows:

```
FUNC state   : -> OnOff    VAR                        % alternative
FUNC display : -> DayAlarm VAR
FUNC light   : -> OnOff    VAR
```

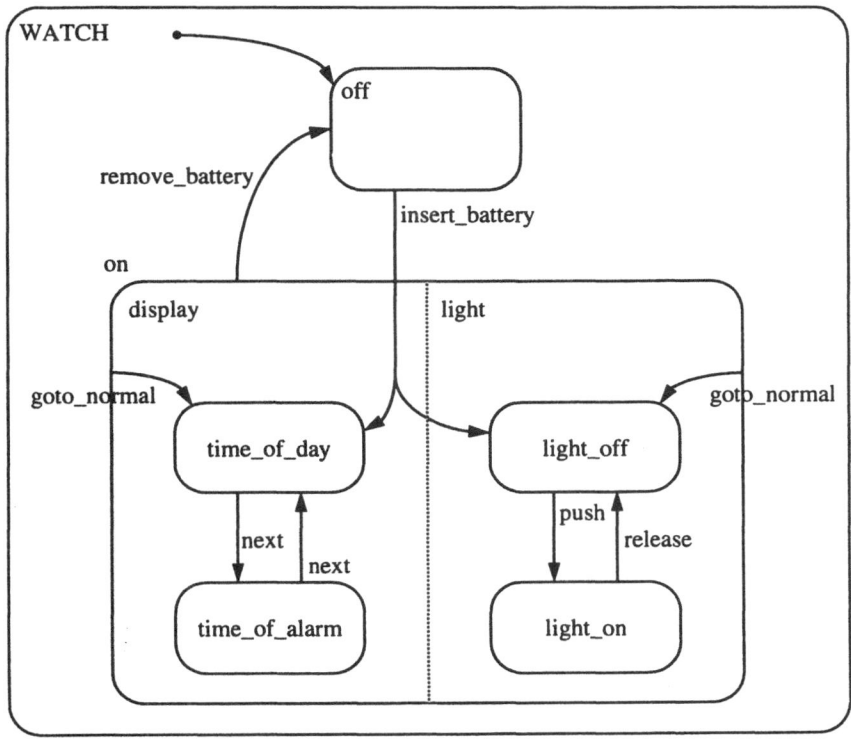

Figure 7.16: Alternative statechart for WATCH.

```
PROC remove_battery : ->
PRE   state = on
SAT   MOD state
POST state = off
```

Although this usage of functions leads to a more compact notation in COLD-1, than the usage of variable predicates, it makes the mapping from COLD-1 onto statecharts more complex.

It is interesting to note how the hierarchical state concept of statecharts makes it possible to zoom-in or zoom-out on a diagram. Consider the following specification, where all internal details of the on state are hidden.

```
COMPONENT WATCH_ SPECIFICATION
EXPORT
  PRED off :,
       on  :
  PROC insert_battery : ->,
       remove_battery : ->
IMPORT
```

```
WATCH
END
```

The above specification corresponds to the statechart where the internal details of on are removed. It is given in Figure 7.17. The statecharts approach has

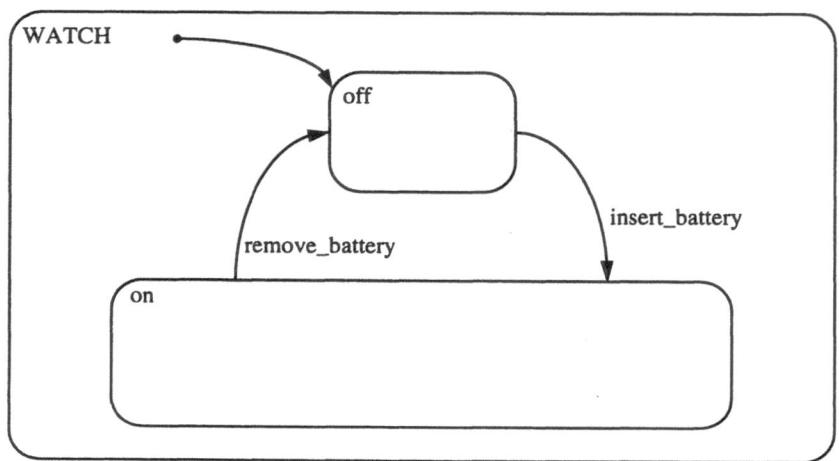

Figure 7.17: Statechart for WATCH (zoomed out).

been used as a basis for the commercial toolset STATEMATE of i-Logix. It is especially meant for designing the control aspects of *reactive* systems. It offers support for graphical editing, consistency checking and simulation of statecharts. STATEMATE also supports other diagrams, including activity-charts (a kind of data flow diagrams), and module-charts (a kind of network diagrams of the system structure).

7.5   Nassi-Shneidermann Diagrams

A Nassi-Shneidermann diagram is an area diagram, usually built from rectan-gular, triangular and special shapes, whose composition reflects the composi-tion of an expression (a program). For each operator in the expression language (programming language) there is a predefined shape. Sequential composition of two programs is modelled by stacking their pictures, and therefore Nassi-Shneidermann diagrams must be read from top to bottom. The diagrams were rather popular when "structured programming" reduced programming constructs to a few operators such as sequential composition and the ternary if ⊔ then ⊔ else ⊔ and the binary while ⊔ do ⊔. But the disadvantage is that the diagrams do not add much to the given program text: in fact they often consume more space, telling less. Also they do not really give an alternative view of the program.

The original reference is [29], but here we shall adapt the approach to the expression language of COLD-1. We define shapes and composition mechanisms for the following kinds of expressions:

$$
\begin{array}{|l|}
\hline
X \; ; \; Y \\
X \mid Y \\
X \; * \\
\textit{others} \\
\hline
\end{array}
$$

If X and Y are expressions, then $X \; ; \; Y$ is the sequential composition of X and Y. In operational terms, this means that first X is executed and after that Y is executed. If X and Y yield result values, then the result of $X \; ; \; Y$ is the tuple obtained by concatenating the results of X and the result of Y. The diagram for $X \; ; \; Y$ is obtained by stacking the diagram of Y on top of the diagram of X.

$X \mid Y$ is the alternative composition of X and Y. In operational terms, this means that either X is executed or Y is executed. Usually one of them fails in a given state, and if for example X fails and Y succeeds, then the effect of Y is established. In a practical execution model, this can be implemented by means of backtracking. When viewing an expression as a binary relation on states (a set of possible transitions), then $X \mid Y$ is the union of the relations of X and Y. The diagram for $X \mid Y$ is obtained by putting the diagram of Y to the right of the diagram of X.

$X \; *$ means the repetition of X for 0, 1 or more times. When viewing an expression as a binary relation on states, then $X \; *$ is the reflexive and transitive closure of the relation of X. Its diagram is obtained by enclosing the diagram of X in a special inversed-L shape with an asterisk.

All other expressions, e.g. the guard expression A ?, or the procedure call expression $p(x)$, are each shown as a box, containing that expression. Recall that if A is an assertion, then A ? is the expression which succeeds whenever A holds, and which fails otherwise. For the diagrams we also refer to Figure 7.18.

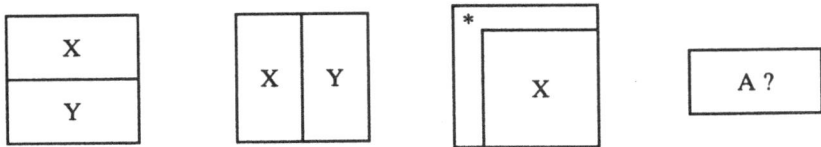

Figure 7.18: Nassi-Shneidermann diagrams for $X \; ; \; Y$, $X \mid Y$, $X \; *$, and A ?.

For example, consider the following program, where it is assumed that we have already specified two assignment procedures called set_r and set_q, operating on two variables r and q.

```
PROC divide : Nat # Nat ->
```

```
IN   x,y
PRE  y > 0
DEF  set_r(x);
     set_q(0);
     ( r >= y ?;
       set_r(r - y);
       set_q(q + 1)
     ) *;
     r < y ?
```

Then we can easily show the body of this procedure by means of a diagram, as given in Figure 7.19.

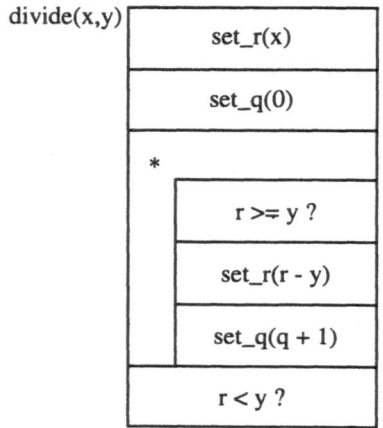

Figure 7.19: Nassi-Shneidermann diagram for body of `divide`.

As another example, consider the following function which serves to take maximum value of two natural numbers.

```
FUNC max : Nat # Nat -> Nat
IN   x,y
DEF  ( x > y      ? ; x
     | NOT x > y ? ; y
     )
```

Then we can easily show the body of this function by means of a diagram, as given in Figure 7.20 (note the ambiguity). Other forms of the diagrams are shown in Figure 7.21 (where the ambiguity has been removed). The areas of the two guards that occur in **max**, have been combined into a special shape. Two alternatives, with one guard being the negation of another guard, act as the COLD-1 form of an **if ⊔ then ⊔ else** construct.

In [30] a graphical language called POLAR is presented; the idea behind the Nassi-Shneidermann diagrams is employed at the level of modules instead of at

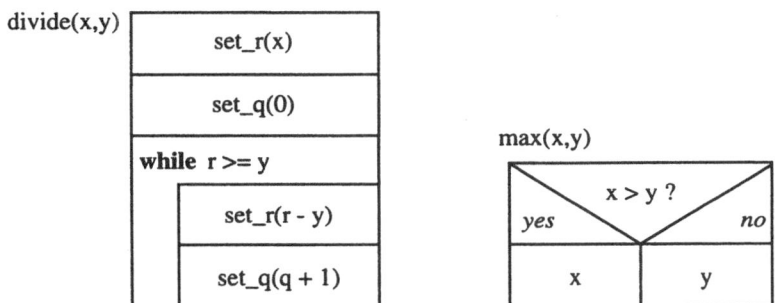

Figure 7.20: Nassi-Shneidermann diagram for body of **max**.

Figure 7.21: Alternative Nassi-Shneidermann diagrams for **divide** and **max**.

the level of the program statements. The pictures provide for a true abstraction step and they are much smaller in size than the formal text they represent. But this was done for COLD-K, which has orthogonal operators to compose modules. In COLD-1 we have the pattern-based approach of Chapter 4, which makes the whole idea less attractive.

7.6   HOOD diagrams

7.6.1   HOOD

A HOOD diagram is constructed from area diagrams, each having three (sometimes four) areas. The three or four areas are positioned according to a fixed pattern, as in Figure 7.22. Each area diagram represents one component, in [33] called an *object*. The top area is meant for the name of the component. The main area contains details about the internal construction of the component. The leftmost area contains a description of the external interface of the component. The small area at the left of the top area is optional. It can contain additional classification information about the component. In HOOD, this area can contain an "A", which means that the component is "active" (its actions are scheduled as a process), or an "E", which means that the component is part of the "environment". At a higher level, we also consider a graph structure, containing the area diagrams as nodes. Here we show the arrows as "is-part-of" connections, whereas in the original method they are drawn reversed, being considered as "is-decomposed-into" connections.

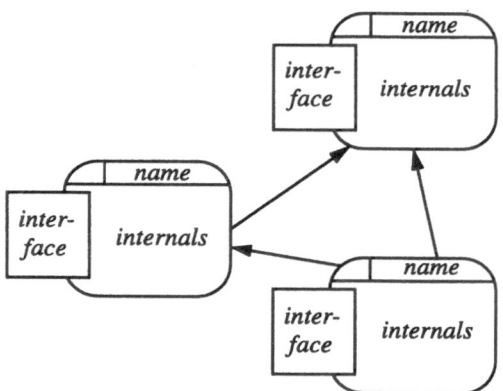

Figure 7.22: HOOD diagram for three components.

The diagrams are an essential part of the Hierarchical Object Oriented Design method HOOD, developed originally for the design of software for the European Space Agency. First the method was developed for Ada, later also a C++ version has been derived. We isolate one of the essential ideas from the HOOD context, relating it to the COMPONENT concept of COLD-1.

An important idea of HOOD is that each component has a name and a well-defined interface, such that users of the component do not have direct access to its internal structure but use the sorts and operations of the interface only. To clarify the concept of "interface" we must distinguish two aspects: syntax and semantics. If we focus on syntax only, the concept of "interface" can be understood as the set of names of the sorts and operations offered by a component. If we focus on semantics, the concept of "interface" can be understood as a set of guaranteed properties of a component concerning the sorts and operations offered by it. Therefore we propose two ways of using the diagrams.

- HOOD diagrams showing *export signatures* as interfaces;
- HOOD diagrams showing *specifications* as interfaces.

The next two sections are devoted to one of these approaches each.

7.6.2 HOOD diagrams for Export Signatures

Recall from Section 4.4 that a signature is set of names. When considering a module, it is important to know the names of the sorts and operations offered by it. When the module is used in another module, only these names are relevant when typechecking the latter module.

Consider a component C with no implementation, of the following form:

```
COMPONENT C[u₁,...,uₖ] SPECIFICATION
ABSTRACT A₁,...,Aₗ
EXPORT S
IMPORT B₁,...,Bₘ
CLASS D₁ ... Dₙ
END
```

or an abbreviation component of the form:

```
LET C[u₁,...,uₖ] :=
ABSTRACT A₁,...,Aₗ
EXPORT S
IMPORT B₁,...,Bₘ
CLASS D₁ ... Dₙ
END
```

We can draw an area diagram putting the name $C[u_1,\ldots,u_k]$ in the top area and the export signature S in the leftmost area of the diagram (the interface area). The remaining information, excluding the EXPORT clause, must be put in the main area. We refer to Figure 7.23. Furthermore it is allowed to omit the

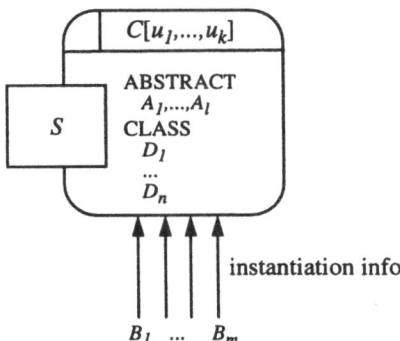

Figure 7.23: HOOD diagram for export signature.

IMPORT section, provided all components that were mentioned in the import list are shown with an arrow from each imported component to the importing component. At the lowest level of the hierarchy, one or more of the main areas can be left empty. In that case, the imports of the lowest-level component can be omitted too. Instantiation information must be put along the arrows. The effect of the copy operator (quote notation) however is shown by copying the diagram of the copied component.

We shall illustrate this with an example called STACK[Item] which is the dynamic data type of stacks. The procedure create serves to generate a new stack; push(s,i) has the effect of pushing item i onto stack s, whereas pop(s) removes the topmost item (if it exists). The function top(s) returns the item which is on top of the stack, not causing any side-effect, and finally the predicate is_empty(s) checks if stack s is empty.

```
COMPONENT STACK[Item] SPECIFICATION
ABSTRACT
  ITEM
EXPORT
  SORT Stack
  PROC create   : -> Stack,
       push     : Stack # Item -> ,
       pop      : Stack        ->
  FUNC top      : Stack        -> Item
  PRED is_empty : Stack
IMPORT
  NAT,
  SEQ[Item]
CLASS
  SORT Stack VAR
  FUNC seq : Stack -> Seq PRE TRUE VAR

  PRED is_empty : Stack
  IN   s
  DEF  seq(s) = empty

  FUNC top : Stack -> Item
  IN   s
  PRE  NOT is_empty(s)
  DEF  hd(seq(s))

  DECL s,t : Stack

  AXIOM INIT => NOT EXISTS s ()

  PROC create : -> Stack
  OUT  s
  PRE  TRUE
  SAT  NEW Stack
  POST seq(s) = empty

  PROC push : Stack # Item ->
  IN   s,i
  PRE  TRUE
  SAT  MOD seq(s)
  POST seq(s) = cons(i,seq'(s))

  PROC pop : Stack ->
```

```
IN   s
PRE  NOT is_empty(s)
SAT  MOD seq(s)
POST seq(s) = tl(seq'(s))
END
```

The information available in the above specification can be organized into the diagram of Figure 7.24. We have omitted some of the details of the CLASS section of STACK[Item]. In practice, one might use tools to zoom into the diagram and to scroll within an area, resolving the problem that the diagrams become too large.

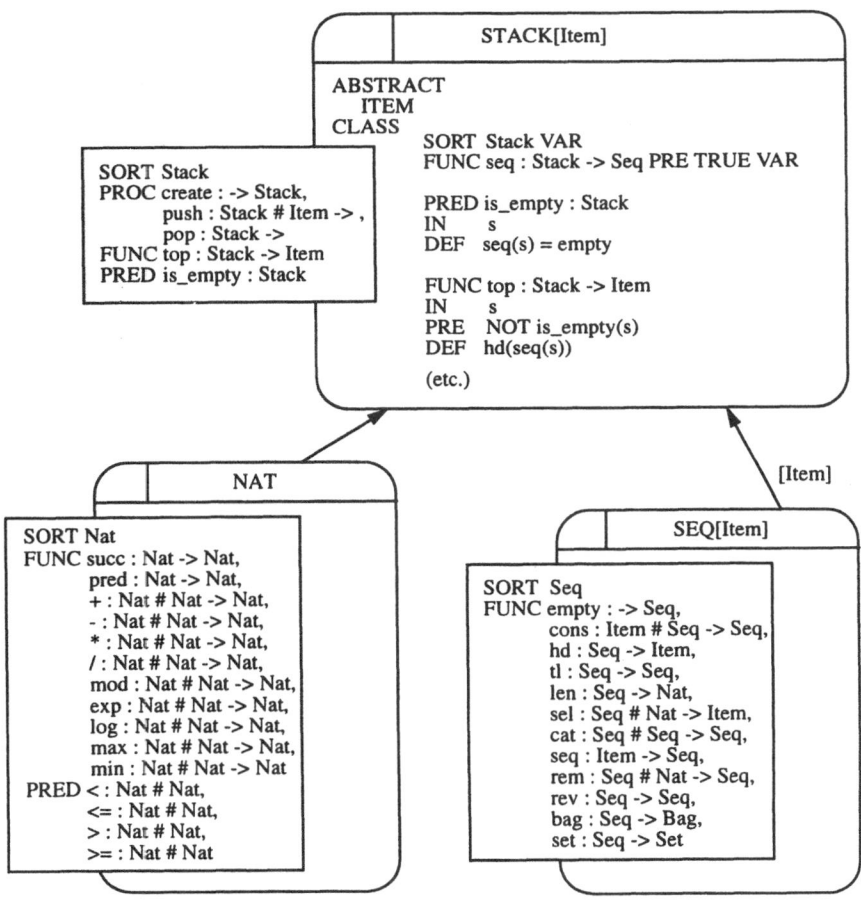

Figure 7.24: HOOD diagram for STACK[Item].

7.6.3   HOOD diagrams for Specifications

The approach of Section 7.6.2, where the concept of *interface* means "set of names", has a weakness: a name does not contain sufficient information to tell the effect of an operation. In fact, a user of a module must know the laws that hold for the data types offered by the module, as well as the pre- and post-conditions, modification rights, etc. of all procedures of the interface. In the approach of the present section, we assume that "interface" means "specification". Recall the specification-and-implementation components of Section 4.6.2, which have the following form:

```
COMPONENT  C[u₁,...,uₖ]
SPECIFICATION
    description₁
IMPLEMENTATION
    description₂
```

where each *description* is a reference to another component, or is given by ABSTRACT, EXPORT, IMPORT, and CLASS clauses. For this component C we can draw an area diagram, putting the name $C[u_1,\ldots,u_k]$ in the top area and the specification *description₁* in the interface area. The implementation *description₂* must be put in the main area. In the specification it is allowed to omit the IMPORT section, provided all components mentioned in the import list are shown as an area diagram too; there must be an arrow from each imported component to the interface area of the importing specification description. In the same way it is allowed to omit the imports from the implementation (the main area), in which case the arrows must point to the main area, containing the importing description. Instantiation information must be put along the arrows. The effect of the copy operator (quote notation) however is shown by copying the diagram of the copied component. We refer to Figure 7.25.

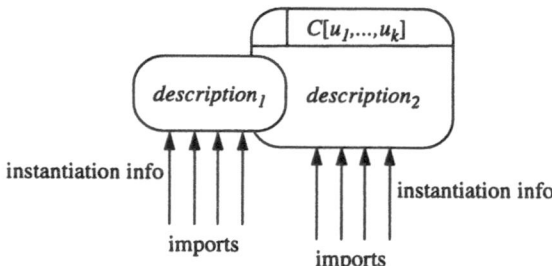

Figure 7.25: HOOD diagram for specification.

At the same time the idea of Section 7.6.2 can be applied to the export signature of the specification. This is particularly useful because of the fact that the specification part is usually quite large (probably still tools for zooming and scrolling are needed). We refer to Figure 7.26.

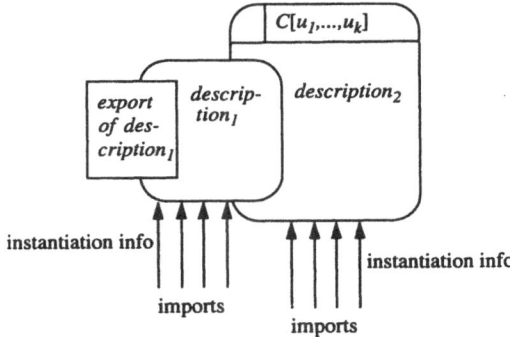

Figure 7.26: Combined HOOD diagram for export signature and specification.

We illustrate this with an example component COMMUNICATION_MANAGER, which is about a simplified kind of "personal communication and message system" for storage, translation, and retrieval of string objects called "letters". Its diagram is given in Figure 7.27. The specification of the component builds upon components called STRING and TRANSLATION, in addition to the standard data types of SEQ and BAG. In the design hierarchy shown in the diagram these appear at the lowest level of the hierarchy (in the sense that they have no imports themselves). In the COLD-1 text of STRING and TRANSLATION we have omitted a number of details. For the translation function, which maps strings to strings, it is assumed that there is an inverse translation too. This assumption is not essential, but later we shall find it convenient, when discussing the proof obligations that arise in connection with the correctness of the COMMUNICATION_MANAGER. By way of preparation for the communication manager's implementation we give a generic component RANDOM.

```
COMPONENT STRING SPECIFICATION
CLASS
  SORT String % details skipped here
END

COMPONENT TRANSLATION SPECIFICATION
EXPORT
  FUNC translation : String -> String
IMPORT
  STRING
CLASS
  FUNC translation : String -> String
  IN   s
  PRE  TRUE
  FUNC inverse : String -> String

  AXIOM FORALL s (inverse(translation(s)) = s)
```

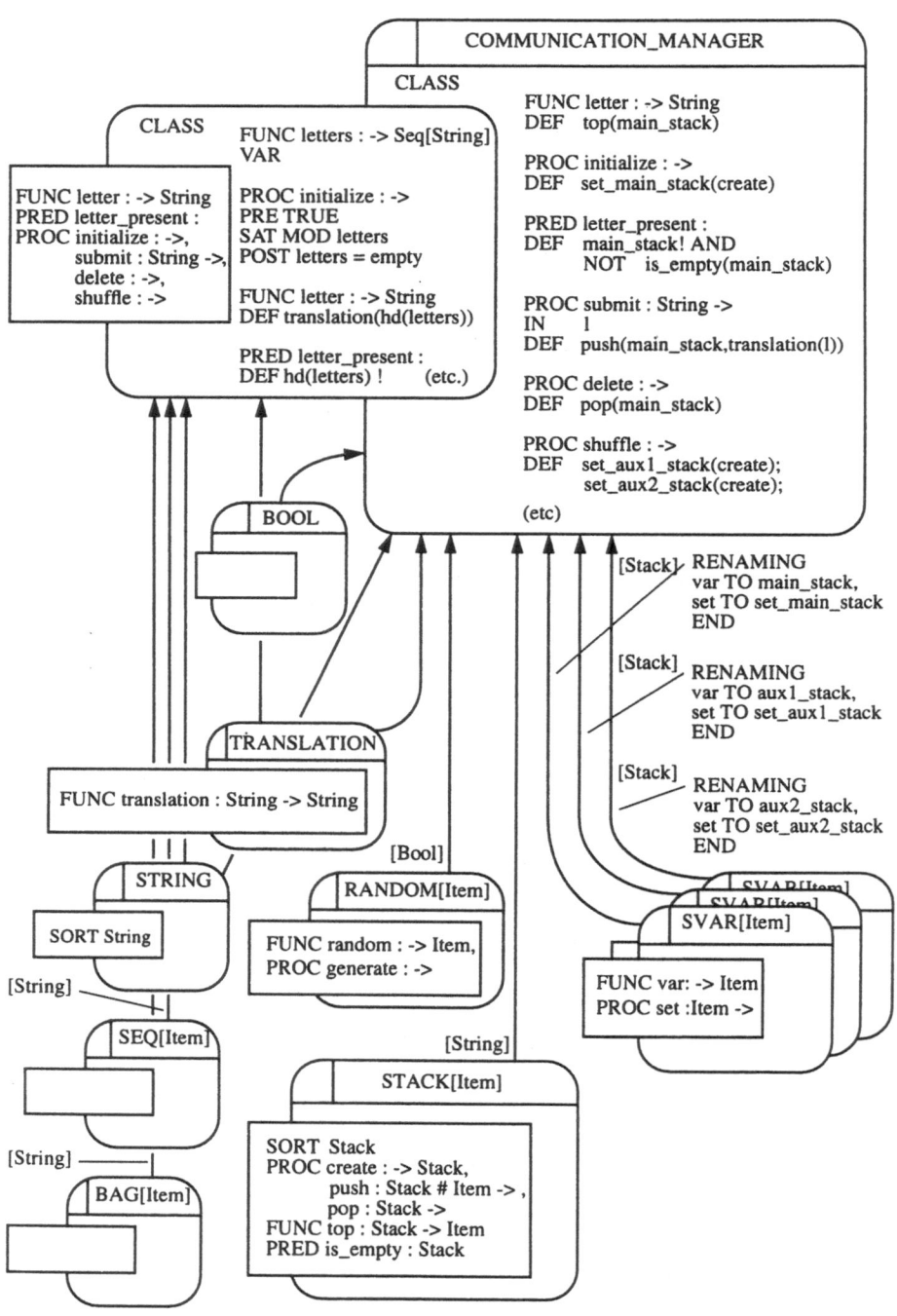

Figure 7.27: HOOD diagram for COMMUNICATION_MANAGER.

```
  % details skipped here
END

COMPONENT RANDOM[Item] SPECIFICATION
ABSTRACT
  ITEM
CLASS
  FUNC random : -> Item
  PRE  TRUE
  VAR

  PROC generate : ->
  SAT  MOD random
END
```

After these preparations we turn our attention to the main component of the
example: COMMUNICATION_MANAGER. As the reader will notice, it is a true toy
example.

The communication manager offers a function called letter, which is the
current letter to be read. This letter can be undefined, e.g. when no letter has
been submitted yet. If there is a letter, the predicate letter_present holds.
The procedure submit serves to enter a new letter into the system and delete
removes the current letter, replacing it by another one – if available. Conceptu-
ally, the system maintains a sequence of letters; only the head of this sequence
is visible as the translation of the current letter. It is not possible for the user
to access the whole sequence directly. It is possible to retrieve other letters
too, by means of the shuffle operation. This operation performs a (random)
permutation upon the sequence of letters stored. The system can be used to
store personal notes (things-to-do) and to retrieve them later. The default
retrieval mechanism is LIFO (last in, first out), but shuffling makes the order
of retrieval random. The complete description of COMMUNICATION_MANAGER
is given next. It has a specification part, which models the functionality as
explained above, and an implementation part, to be explained later.

```
  COMPONENT COMMUNICATION_MANAGER

  SPECIFICATION
  EXPORT
    FUNC letter : -> String
    PRED letter_present :
    PROC initialize : ->,
         submit    : String ->,
         delete    : ->,
         shuffle   : ->
  IMPORT
    STRING,
    TRANSLATION,
```

```
      SEQ[String],
      BAG[String]
   CLASS
     FUNC letters : -> Seq[String]
     VAR

     PROC initialize : ->
     PRE  TRUE
     SAT  MOD letters
     POST letters = empty

     FUNC letter : -> String
     DEF  translation(hd(letters))

     PRED letter_present :
     DEF  hd(letters) !

     PROC submit : String ->
     IN   s
     PRE  letters !
     SAT  MOD letters
     POST letters = cons(s,letters')

     PROC delete : ->
     PRE  letter_present
     SAT  MOD letters
     POST letters = tl(letters')

     PROC shuffle : ->
     PRE  letters !
     SAT  MOD letters
     POST bag(letters) = bag(letters')
   END

   IMPLEMENTATION
   IMPORT

   BOOL,
   STRING,
   TRANSLATION,
   RANDOM[Bool],
   STACK[String],
   SVAR'[Stack] RENAMING var TO main_stack, set TO set_main_stack END,
   SVAR'[Stack] RENAMING var TO aux1_stack, set TO set_aux1_stack END,
   SVAR'[Stack] RENAMING var TO aux2_stack, set TO set_aux2_stack END

   CLASS
```

```
FUNC letter : -> String
DEF  top(main_stack)

PROC initialize : ->
DEF  set_main_stack(create)

PRED letter_present :
DEF  main_stack! AND NOT is_empty(main_stack)

PROC submit : String ->
IN   l
DEF  push(main_stack,translation(l))

PROC delete : ->
DEF  pop(main_stack)

PROC shuffle : ->
DEF  set_aux1_stack(create);
     set_aux2_stack(create);

     ( NOT is_empty(main_stack) ? ;
       generate;
       ( random = true  ? ; push(aux1_stack,top(main_stack))
       | random = false ? ; push(aux2_stack,top(main_stack))
       ) ;
       pop(main_stack)
     ) * ; is_empty(main_stack) ? ;


     ( NOT is_empty(aux1_stack) ? ;
       push(main_stack,top(aux1_stack));
       pop(aux1_stack)
     ) * ; is_empty(aux1_stack) ? ;


     ( NOT is_empty(aux2_stack) ? ;
       push(main_stack,top(aux2_stack));
       pop(aux2_stack)
     ) * ; is_empty(aux2_stack) ?
END
```

The implementation is organized around a stack of strings, called `main_stack`.
When a letter is submitted, its translation is put onto the stack. The shuffle
operation employs two auxiliary stacks, called `aux1_stack` and `aux2_stack`.
Later we shall return to the the correctness of this implementation. The implementation uses `BOOL` and `RANDOM[Bool]` to accomplish the shuffling process:
the contents from the main stack is transferred to the auxiliary stacks in a

random way. The three simple programming variables (renamed versions of
SVAR'[Stack]) serve to store the stacks once they are created. Also STRING
and TRANSLATION are used.

The structure of COMMUNICATION_MANAGER is shown in the HOOD diagram
of Figure 7.27, which is a mixed approach, combining the techniques of Sections 7.6.2 and 7.6.3. We have omitted all details concerning the components
BOOL, SEQ, and BAG, which come from the standard library. It is important
to note that there is a structure clash between the specification and the implementation of COMMUNICATION_MANAGER. The specification refers to SEQ and
BAG, which are hidden, but which are nevertheless essential for the specification
of the componenet behaviour.

Since we have given a specification and an implementation for the communication manager, we should check if this implementation offers all sorts,
operations and properties specified. Therefore we note that the hidden variable letters of the SPECIFICATION part is referred to in most pre-conditions,
SAT clauses and post-conditions. But in the implementation it is not explicitly
present anymore (not even as a hidden function). Therefore we reconstruct
the letters from the main_stack of the implementation. This reconstruction
can be described by using the following abstraction procedure (it is like an
abstraction function, but because it refers to pop it must be a procedure):

```
PROC f : Stack -> Seq[String]
IN    s
DEF  ( is_empty(s)     ? ; empty
     | NOT is_empty(s) ? ; ( LET l:String;
                           ; l := translation^{-1}(top(s));
                           ; pop(s);
                           ; cons(l, f(s))
     )                     )
```

The implementation translates the letters immediately when they are submitted. This has been done for efficiency considerations: when the same letter
is observed often, it is a nuisance to have it translated each time, particularly
when this translation is a resource consuming process. This implies that the
abstract variable letters must be reconstructed from the inverse translation
of the letters on the main stack. Note that the implementation stacks contain
translated letters only and that translation is injective. The reconstructed
letters can be defined as:

```
FUNC letters : -> Seq[String]
DEF  f(main_stack)
```

(note that the side-effects in this function are "undone"). Now it is a routine
matter to check the properties specified. We take the definitions given in the
SPECIFICATION part of COMMUNICATION_MANAGER as proof obligations which
must be verified for the IMPLEMENTATION part. We treat PROC initialize

first. The first proof obligation is expressed as PRE TRUE, which means that initialize must always succeed (i.e. there must exist an end state t such that "current-state" → t is a transition of initialize). To verify this, we note that the DEF clause of the implementation refers to set_main_stack and create. Their properties can be found in SVAR (cf. set) and STACK respectively: both have pre-condition TRUE. Thus their composition has pre-condition TRUE too. The next proof obligation is expressed as SAT MOD letters, which means that letters is the only variable to be modified by initialize. Actually, letters is the *only* variable in the whole SPECIFICATION part, so that is easy. The third proof obligation for initialize is the clause POST letters = empty. From the implementation of initialize, we see that it stores a newly created stack in main_stack. From the specification of STACK we learn that is_empty holds for the newly created stack. This fact can be used to find the value of letters, which is given as f(main_stack), where f is the abstraction procedure given above. Since the body of f has two alternatives, and since the first alternative is guarded by is_empty(s), where s is main_stack, we find that letters is empty (which is the result of the first alternative). So the post-condition of initialize holds. Very much in the same way, we can check the proof obligations for the other operations: letter, letter_present, submit, delete, and shuffle.

For each of the three repetition constructs of the body of shuffle we mention the loop invariant. For the first and second repetition constructs this is bag(f(main_stack)) ∪ bag(f(aux1_stack)) ∪ bag(f(aux2_stack)) = bag(l'), where l' is the value of the sequence letters, immediately before execution of shuffle begins. Here ∪ is used as a shorthand for the union operation on bags. To get the loop invariant for the third repetition, we must add a conjunct is_empty(aux1_stack).

7.6.4   HOOD diagrams with Parent Components

In this section we add one more feature to the HOOD diagrams for export signatures, as presented in Section 7.6.2. The feature is to use *inclusion* as an alternative way of showing the "is-part-of" connections. This makes it possible to show explicitly that an anonymous copy of a component can only be accessed through the component in whose import list it occurs. Consider a component C with no implementation, of the following form:

```
COMPONENT C[u₁,...,uₖ] SPECIFICATION
ABSTRACT A₁,...,Aₗ
EXPORT S
IMPORT B₁,...,Bₘ
CLASS D₁ ... Dₙ
END
```

or an abbreviation component of the form LET $C[u_1,\ldots,u_k]$:= ..., then the import list $B_1,\ldots,B_m$ contains component references of two kinds:

- component references of the form C_i, where C_i is a component name;

- component references of the form $C_i\prime$, where C_i is a component name and where the quote ("'") is the *copy* operator;

in either case, there may or may not be subsequent EXPORTING, RENAMING, or QUALIFYING clauses.

An import of a component reference C_i of the first kind must be shown by an arrow from the diagram of C_i to the diagram of C. The imported component C_i must be positioned outside the area of C, because it can be shared by other components.

An import of a component reference $C_i\prime$ of the second kind can be shown by putting the imported copy inside the main area of C. No arrow is needed. In this way it is very explicit that because of the copying, the imported component $C_i\prime$ can not be shared by other components. C could be called the "parent component" of $C_i\prime$. By way of example, let us assume that we have three component definitions A, B, and C, which export sorts a, b, and c, respectively. Consider the parent component ABC_USER, for which the resulting diagram is shown in Figure 7.28.

```
COMPONENT ABC_USER SPECIFICATION
EXPORT
  a,b,c,d
IMPORT
  A',B',C
CLASS
  FUNC d : a # b -> c
END
```

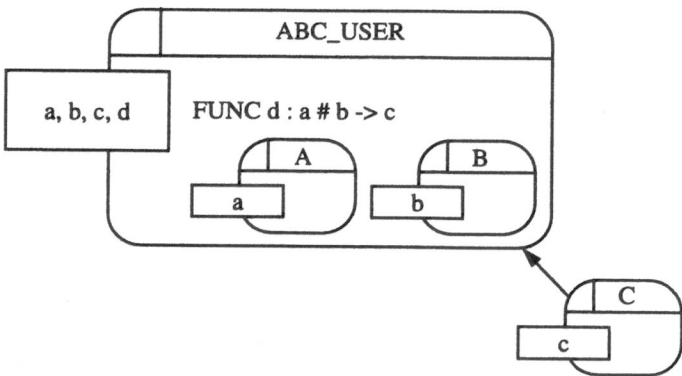

Figure 7.28: HOOD diagram for parent component.

7.7   Graph Diagrams: General

An *graph diagram* is a system of nodes and edges; the nodes are drawn as
circles, ovals, bullets, or boxes, whereas the edges are drawn as lines or arrows
going from one node to another. The edges may or may not be directed;
we shall confine ourselves to directed graphs, i.e. graphs with directed edges
(arrows).

In the subsequent sections we shall consider the following kinds of graph diagrams: function graphs (Section 7.8), state transition diagrams (Section 7.9),
call graphs (Section 7.10) and import graphs (Section 7.11).

7.8   Function Graphs

A function graph is a directed graph which serves to show how functions map
objects to objects. The nodes represent objects (values), and there is one edge
from x to y for each pair x, y such that $f(x) = y$. Each node will be shown as
a bullet. The edges are labelled with the names of the functions. Each function
is represented by a collection of edges. The rules for drawing a function graph
are:

- the objects are organized into disjoint areas, one for each sort;
- for a nullary function f, there is an arrow (not starting at any object)
  which ends at the object of f; but if f is undefined, that is f ^, there is
  no arrow;
- for a unary function f, there are arrows from x to y for all objects x, y
  such that $f(x) = y$;
- for a binary function f, there are fork-type arrows from x_1 and x_2 to y
  for all objects x_1, x_2 and y such that $f(x_1, x_2) = y$.

The cases for functions of three or more arguments are analogous to the above.
For a state-based specification, where some of the sorts and functions may be
state-dependent, each diagram applies to one state. Figure 7.29 shows the
various arrow types for nullary, unary and binary functions. Figure 7.30 shows

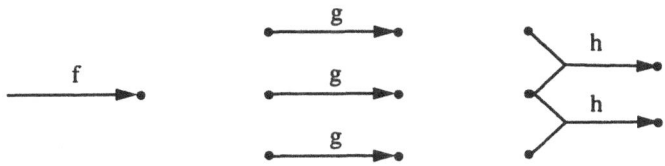

Figure 7.29: Arrow types for nullary f, unary g, and binary h.

a possible diagram for three functions with the following signature:

```
FUNC f :   -> S0
FUNC g : S0 -> S1
FUNC h : S1 -> S2
```

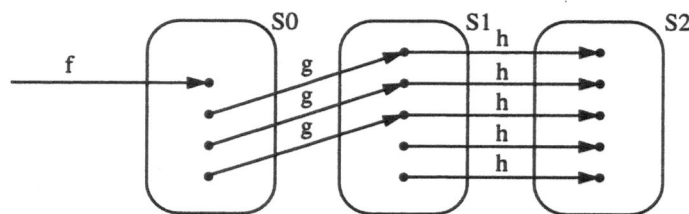

Figure 7.30: Function graphs for f, g, and h.

It should be noted that g in Figure 7.30 is *partial*, because g(f)^, or which is the same, NOT g(f)!. For the other objects in S0, g is defined however, so

```
FORALL x : S0 ( x /= f => g(x)! )
```

Function graph diagrams can easily be combined with Venn diagrams, as already shown in Section 7.3.5.

7.9   State Transition Diagrams

A state transition diagram is a directed graph which serves to show the states and state transitions of a dynamic system. The nodes represent states and the edges represent transitions. The nodes contain specific information about the variables in each state. Therefore the nodes are drawn as ovals (circles, boxes are all right too) in which this state information can be put. The edges are labelled with the names of the procedures. Each procedure is represented by a collection of edges, one for each transition. Note that if the states are structured into area diagrams, we get the statecharts of Section 7.4.

7.9.1   Basic Rules for Drawing Diagrams

We make some simplifying assumptions first: we consider only components which do not hide any variables, and also we assume that all sorts are constant (i.e. no SORT ... VAR definitions), and finally that all variables functions and predicates are nullary, or have a finite domain. Here are the basic rules:

- the initial state is marked as INIT;
- there must be one node for each state;
- for each variable function f, the node contains information about its value by means of an equation of the form $f = \ldots$, or by a set of equations of the form $f(x) = \ldots$; if the function is undefined, this is indicated by $f\,\widehat{}\,$, or $f(x)\,\widehat{}\,$;

- for each variable predicate p, the nodes contain information about its truth value by means of assertions, each of which is either p, or NOT p, or by a set of assertions which are either $p(x)$, or NOT $p(x)$;
- for each procedure p, the edges of all its possible transitions must be labelled with p, or by $p(e)$ where x is a term denoting the parameter value for that transition.

We illustrate the rules by the following example. It is about a very simple counter (count) which starts at zero, making increments of one. There is a second observer of this component, called turn which takes one of two values: black and white. If the system is used to count the number of moves made in a chess game, then turn tells the color of the next player to make a move. This turn is an abstract view on the variable count; it embodies an abstraction function.

```
COMPONENT BW_COUNTER SPECIFICATION
EXPORT
  SORT Color
  FUNC black : -> Color,
       white : -> Color
  FUNC count : -> Nat,
       turn  : -> Color
  PROC start : ->,
       next  : ->
IMPORT
  NAT,
  ENUM2 RENAMING Enum2 TO Color,
                 x0       TO black,
                 x1       TO white
        END
CLASS
  FUNC count : -> Nat VAR

  AXIOM INIT => NOT count!

  FUNC turn : -> Color
  DEF  ( mod(count,2) = 0 ?; white
       | mod(count,2) = 1 ?; black
       )

  PROC start : ->
  PRE   TRUE
  SAT   MOD count
  POST  count = 0

  PROC next  : ->
  PRE   count!
  SAT   MOD count
```

```
    POST count = count' + 1
END
```

Figure 7.31 gives the state transition diagram for one of the dynamic models that satisfies this specification. There are infinitely many states; we only show some of them, writing "etc." to indicate the others. Each of the two procedures **start** and **next** has a collection of transitions associated with it. The reader could check that all definitions and axioms of **BW_COUNTER** are true in this model.

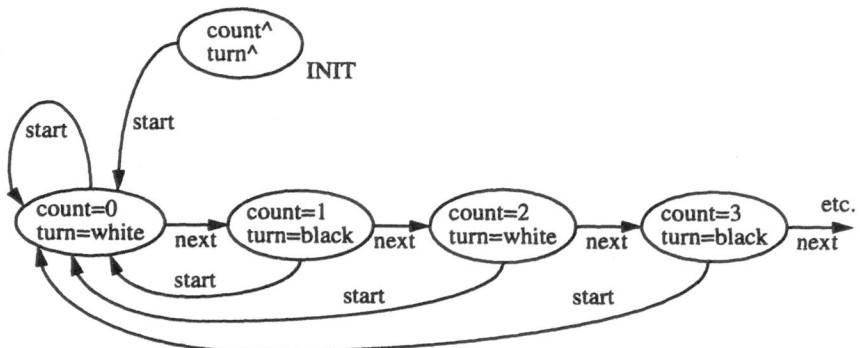

Figure 7.31: State transition diagram for BW_COUNTER.

7.9.2   Simplifying the Diagrams

For many systems the dynamic models are very complex in the sense that they have many states and transition patterns which can hardly be shown in a practical way. The example of BW_COUNTER has infinitely many states, but fortunately it is quite orderly. Many real systems are not orderly, a phenomenon sometimes referred to as "state-space explosion". Therefore we must look for ways to simplify the diagrams and the obvious idea is to remove some of the variables, keeping others, or keeping an "abstract view" only. We illustrate this using BW_COUNTER again (although in this example the diagram is already manageable without such simplification). The simplification will be explained as a two-step process. Let $v_1, \ldots, v_n$ be the variables to be removed (to be "forgotten"), then these two steps are:

1. consider a state transition diagram of the full specification and remove all information about $v_1, \ldots, v_n$ from the nodes;

2. identify all states which have the same values for the remaining variables. If s_1 and s_2 become part of one common state s', then this s' must have the incoming and outgoing transitions of s_1 and s_2.

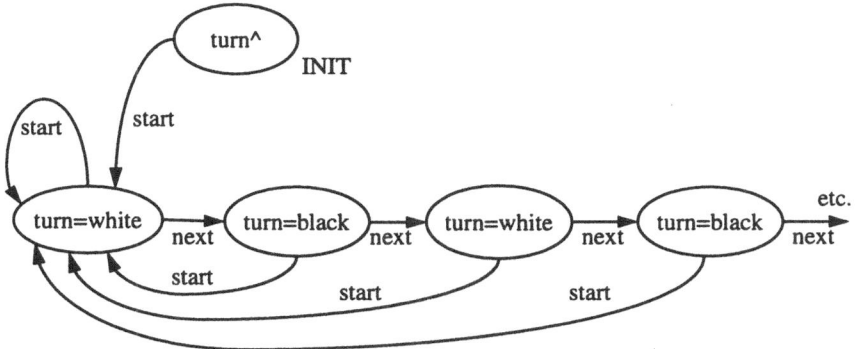

Figure 7.32: State transition diagram for BW_COUNTER, forgetting count.

Application of the first step to Figure 7.31, forgetting count, yields the diagram of Figure 7.32. From the latter diagram, observe that there are many states in which the remaining variable is essentially the same. For example, two states with turn = white are shown, and two states with turn = black. In fact, the "etc." represents infinitely many white and infinitely many black states. Next we perform the second step. After collecting all white states into one "super state", and doing the same for all black states too, we easily find the transitions between these super states: there is a next transition from at least one of the white states to at least one of the black states, and therefore there must be a next transition from the new white state to the new black state. In the same way we collect the other transitions, arriving at the diagram of Figure 7.33. The second step has turned the diagram into a finite state machine, for only

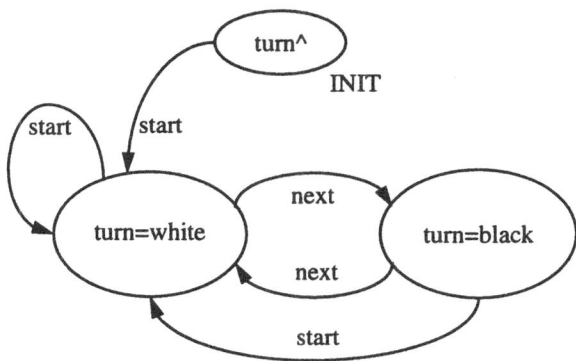

Figure 7.33: Simplified state transition diagram for BW_COUNTER.

three states are left. For purposes of playing chess, keeping track of who is to make the next move, the diagram indeed shows an aspect of the system's behaviour in a meaningful way.

7.9.3   Simplifying the Diagrams (Continued)

In this section we present a refinement of the approach of simplifying diagrams by unifying states. As it turns out, the approach of the previous section
is somewhat too naive. The problem is that certain states can have different
transition behaviours, even when they are the same with respect to their variables. In other words: the transition relations need not be compatible with a
straightforward identification of states.

The problem arises in the next example, called CM_MODEL, which is a Configuration Management model. The model describes a kind of lifecycle for a
single configuration item (e.g. a source file), which is constructed by a developer first. The developer has to hand it over to a system integrator, as
soon as it is ready. The system integrator then adopts responsibility for the
configuration item, a step called *take-over*. The integrator performs a quality
assessment upon the configuration item, giving it the status approved. The
developer can undo a hand-over, and the integrator at its turn can undo an
approval, but after the system integrator has done a take-over, the developer
will *not* get it back any more.

```
COMPONENT CM_MODEL SPECIFICATION
EXPORT
   FUNC owner      : -> Role,
        phase      : -> Maturity,
        quality    : -> Level
   PROC hand_over  : ->,
        take_over  : ->,
        approve    : Level ->,
        undo       : ->
IMPORT
   ENUM2' RENAMING Enum2 TO Role,
                   x0    TO developer,
                   x1    TO integrator
          END,
   ENUM2' RENAMING Enum2 TO Maturity,
                   x0    TO initial,
                   x1    TO final
          END,
   NAT' RENAMING Nat TO Level END
CLASS
   FUNC owner   : -> Role     VAR
   FUNC phase   : -> Maturity VAR
   FUNC quality : -> Level    VAR

   AXIOM INIT => owner = developer AND phase = initial AND quality^
```

```
PROC hand_over : ->
PRE  owner = developer AND phase = initial
SAT  MOD phase
POST phase = final

PROC take_over : ->
PRE  owner = developer AND phase = final
SAT  MOD owner, phase
POST owner = integrator AND phase = initial

PROC approve : Level ->
IN   n
PRE  owner = integrator AND phase = initial
SAT  MOD phase, quality
POST phase = final AND quality = n

PROC undo : ->
PRE  phase = final;
     owner = integrator => quality = 0
SAT  MOD phase, quality
POST phase = initial AND quality^
END
```

Note the pre-condition of undo, which says that "undoing" is prohibited for quality levels ≥ 1. This rule prevents integrators from too much backtracking in the development process of the configuration item. Only when quality = 0, the approval can be withdrawn. A number of aspects of this CM_MODEL have been taken from a real model used at Philips, although some details were added and others were simplified for the sake of the presentation. But the original model had the same kind of compatibility problems as the example given here (transition relations not being compatible with a straightforward identification of states). The state transition diagram is given in Figure 7.34. Now let us apply the simplification process of Section 7.9.2 to Figure 7.34, forgetting owner. This means that the difference between "developer" and "integrator" vanishes for the initial phases, so the two initial phase states turn into *one* state. Figure 7.35 shows the result. Actually the gain is only one state, but what is worse, the diagram is not a truthful model of the original specification any more. For example, according to to Figure 7.35, starting in the initial state, one can succesfully make the transitions hand_over, take_over, hand_over, in that order; this could *not* be done in Figure 7.34, and is not allowed by CM_MODEL (the post-condition of take_over contradicts the pre-condition of hand_over).

The right way to go is adopting a more cautious way of identifying states: before two states can become one, it must be checked that they have both the same variables and moreover, have essentialy the same outgoing transitions. This idea will be made more precise below, looking for a relation $\leftrightarrow$ that relates

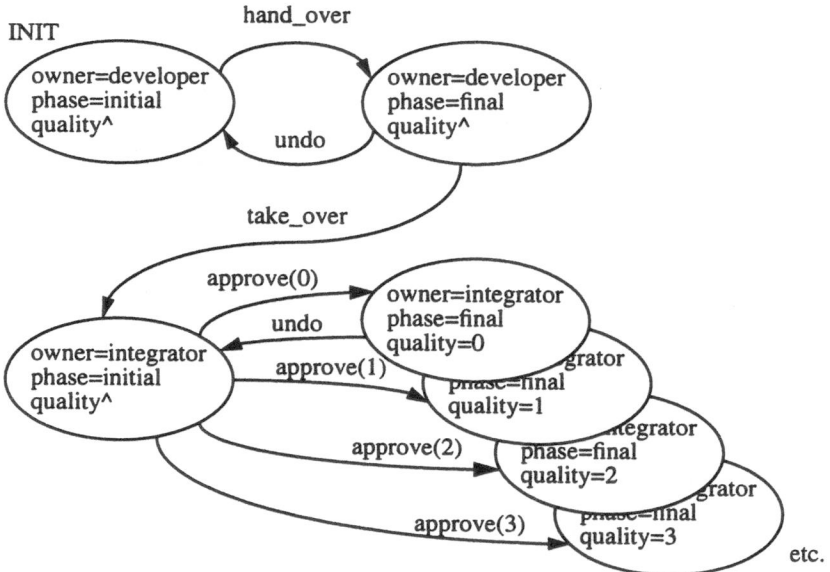

Figure 7.34: State transition diagram for CM_MODEL.

states which are identifiable. Such related states will be called "similar". When forgetting **owner** from Figure 7.34, we must keep two distinct states with **phase** = **initial** and **quality^**; the right model is given in Figure 7.36. If we want to simplify a state transition diagram S, for which straightforward removal of certain variables yields diagram S^-, then we must try to find a binary relation $\leftrightarrow$ on the nodes of S^-, such that:

- if $s \leftrightarrow t$ then $t \leftrightarrow s$,
- for each node s, we find that $s \leftrightarrow s$,
- if $s \leftrightarrow t$ then each variable in s is the same as in t,
- if a procedure p has a transition from s to s', and $s \leftrightarrow t$, then p must have a transition from t to t' with $s' \leftrightarrow t'$ too.

In general, one can imagine several distinct relations that satisfy the checks given above (for example, say that each s is similar to itself only). But for purposes of simplification, we should make $s \leftrightarrow t$ hold for as much pairs s and t as possible. The technical term for such a relation is an *auto-bisimulation*, and for the mathematical backgrounds we refer to [31] and [3]. If we apply this approach to Figure 7.34, forgetting **owner**, we find the assumption that the two leftmost states of Figure 7.34 are similar, wrong; it is in conflict with the third requirement for $\leftrightarrow$. It must be concluded that the best $\leftrightarrow$ can only relate states to itself, as in Figure 7.36.

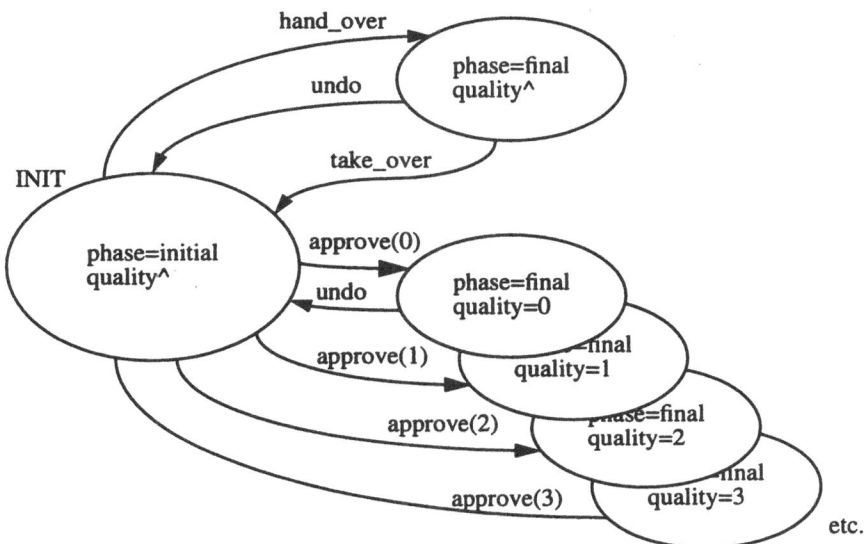

Figure 7.35: Naively simplified diagram for CM_MODEL, forgetting owner.

If we look back to the simplification which led to Figure 7.33, we see that it boils down to the definition that $s \leftrightarrow t$ if turn in s has the same color as turn in t.

Finally we shall apply the approach to Figure 7.34 of CM_MODEL, forgetting the variable quality. First we remove quality from all nodes, and then we look for a suitable relation $\leftrightarrow$. We could try to make $s \leftrightarrow t$ hold for states s and t from the group of states with owner = integrator and phase = final. But this can not be done, because the uppermost of these nodes has an outgoing undo transition, whereas the other nodes have not. However, this is the only problem, so we arrive at the simplified diagram of Figure 7.37.

7.9.4   Hiding

After the presentation of techniques for state transition diagram simplification of Section 7.9.2 and 7.9.3, it is interesting to explain the relation between these techniques and the notion of *hiding*, as embodied by an EXPORT clause. A function, predicate or procedure name is said to be *hidden* if it is present in the ABSTRACT, IMPORT or CLASS section, but does not occur in the EXPORT list. Hiding works as follows: consider a specification (without hiding); it has many possible dynamic models, which can be shown as state transition diagrams $S_1, S_2, \ldots$. Now if we apply hiding, the result is a new collection of dynamic models, having state transition diagrams $S_1^-, S_2^-, \ldots$ (one for each S_i). The

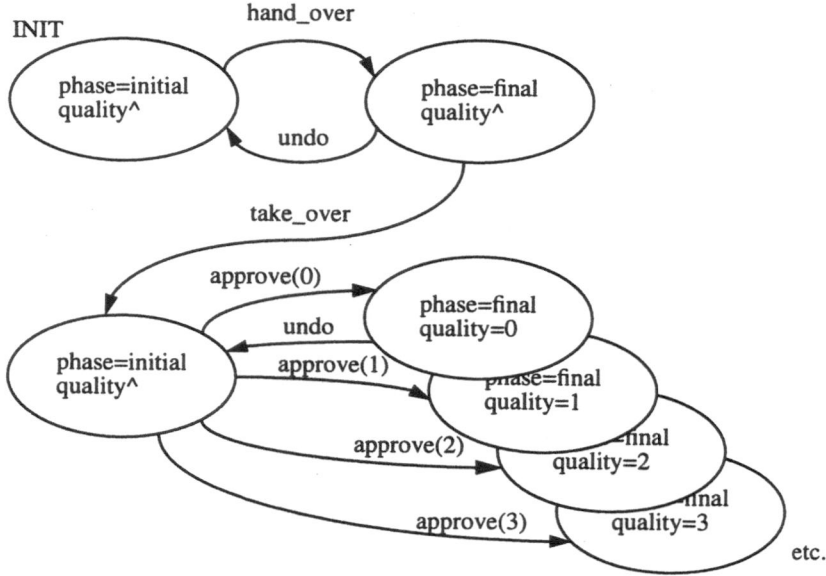

Figure 7.36: "Simplified" diagram for CM_MODEL, forgetting owner.

latter models are obtained by transforming each S_i into a S_i^- as follows:

- for each hidden variable, remove that variable from each node (as in the first step mentioned in Section 7.9.2);

- for each hidden procedure, remove all transition arrows of that procedure from the diagram.

Usually, many of the resulting state transition diagrams have many states which can be considered similar (in the sense that a non-trivial relation $\leftrightarrow$ can be found). One or more diagrams can be shown, but it makes sense to simplify them first, using the approach of Section 7.9.3. In the terminology of [3] this simplification means to consider *canonical* models only. For example, the specification BW_MOVER below is obtained by hiding count from BW_COUNTER. Therefore Figures 7.32 and 7.33 represent models of BW_MOVER, but only Figure 7.33 is a canonical model.

```
COMPONENT BW_MOVER SPECIFICATION
EXPORT
  SORT Color
  FUNC black : -> Color,
       white : -> Color
  FUNC turn  : -> Color
  PROC start : ->,
```

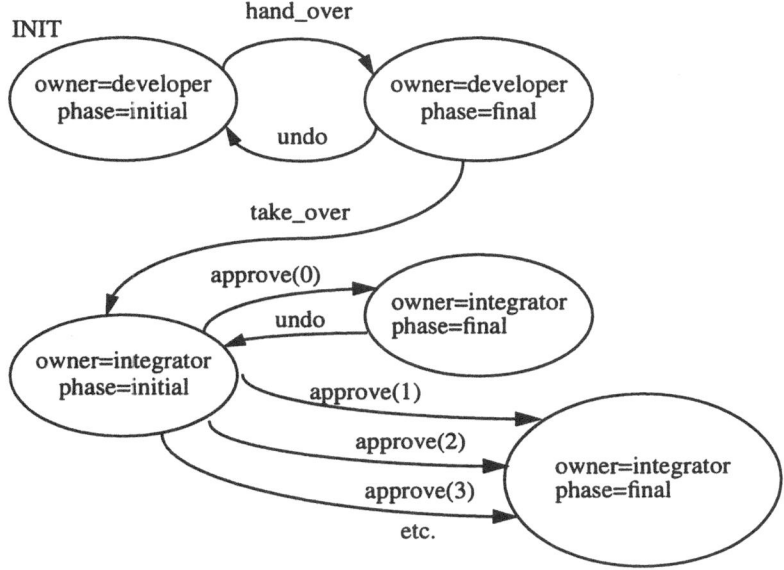

Figure 7.37: Simplified diagram for CM_MODEL, forgetting quality.

```
       next  : ->
IMPORT
  BW_COUNTER
END
```

As another example, the specification CM_PHASING is obtained by hiding owner from CM_MODEL, so Figure 7.36 represents a model of CM_PHASING.

```
COMPONENT CM_PHASING SPECIFICATION
EXPORT
  FUNC phase     : -> Maturity,
       quality   : -> Level
  PROC hand_over : ->,
       take_over : ->,
       approve   : Level ->,
       undo      : ->
IMPORT
  CM_MODEL
END
```

As yet another example, CM_NO_QUALITY is obtained by hiding quality from CM_MODEL. Figure 7.37 represents a model of CM_NO_QUALITY.

```
COMPONENT CM_NO_QUALITY SPECIFICATION
EXPORT
```

```
  FUNC owner    : -> Role,
       phase    : -> Maturity
  PROC hand_over : ->,
       take_over : ->,
       approve  : Level ->,
       undo     : ->
IMPORT
  CM_MODEL
END
```

Finally, we show an example where a procedure is hidden too. CM_FORWARD is obtained by hiding both **quality** and **undo**. The fact that **undo** is absent has made it possible to unify *all* states with **owner = integrator** and **phase = final**. Therefore Figure 7.38 represents a model of CM_FORWARD. Instead of having infinitely many transitions labelled **approve(0)**, **approve(1)**, etc., we have combined them, showing one arrow labelled **approve(n)**.

```
COMPONENT CM_FORWARD SPECIFICATION
EXPORT
  FUNC owner    : -> Role,
       phase    : -> Maturity
  PROC hand_over : ->,
       take_over : ->,
       approve  : Level ->
IMPORT
  CM_MODEL
END
```

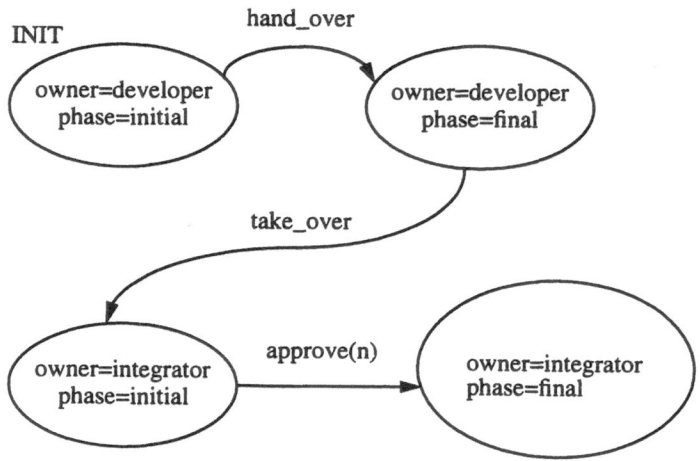

Figure 7.38: State transition diagram for CM_FORWARD.

7.10   Call Graphs

A call graph represents the "is-called-by" relation on functions, predicates and procedures. The nodes represent operations, and there is an arrow from p_1 to p_2 if p_1 is called by p_2. The principle is well-known for programming languages. But in this book we are dealing with COLD-1, which essentially is a *logical* language, and the is-called-by relation as such is not a-priori clear. The main complication is that an operation definition can consist of a number of distinct clauses, each with its own purpose and own interpretation.

A function definition can contain a pre-condition (PRE clause), a function body (DEF, IND, DEP, VAR, or FREE clause), and a post-condition (POST clause). The notion of "is-called-by" depends on an operational interpretation, which at its turn assumes a certain execution model. Several distinct execution models for COLD-1 can be devised, and for most of them (e.g. PROTOCOLD 1.1, or a straightforward mapping to C), an operation p_1 is said to be called by p_2 if p_1 occurs somewhere in the DEF clause of p_2 – even if no run-time invocation occurs, as is the case for p_1 in (FALSE ?; p_1 | TRUE ?; q_1).

A predicate definition can contain no pre- or post-condition; it only has a predicate body (DEF, IND, DEP, VAR, or FREE clause).

A procedure definition can contain a pre-condition (PRE clause), a procedure body (DEF, SAT, or FREE clause), and a post-condition (POST clause). For predicates and procedures, the most obvious notion of is-called-by corresponds to occurring in the body (particularly the DEF clause when taking a PROTOCOLD 1.1 or C-like execution model, and the IND clause when taking a Prolog-like execution model for predicates).

A more cautious approach is to adopt several relations: an occurs-in-the-pre-condition-of relation, an occurs-in-the-body-of relation, and an occurs-in-the-post-condition-of relation. We propose to use the notations $\rightarrow_{pre}$, $\rightarrow_{body}$ and $\rightarrow_{post}$ respectively (one could even go one step further by distinguishing $\rightarrow_{sat}$, $\rightarrow_{dep}$, etc. as variations of $\rightarrow_{body}$). In this way the graphs can have three kinds of arrows. The above-mentioned is-called-by relation is nothing but $\rightarrow_{body}$.

A third approach is to consider the "is-used-by" relation defined as the union of the three sets of arrows: $\rightarrow_{pre} \cup \rightarrow_{body} \cup \rightarrow_{post}$.

So there are three alternative approaches. When dealing with programs which have algorithmic definitions only we find that pre- and post-conditions are absent and that the three approaches are essentially the same. When dealing with specifications however, the second approach puts most information into the diagrams, whereas the third approach is the easiest one (the first approach fails in that case). For every diagram it should always be clear which approach is used. Summarising the approaches:

1. the graph shows $\rightarrow_{body}$ (is-called-by), or
2. the graph shows three relations $\rightarrow_{pre}$, $\rightarrow_{body}$ and $\rightarrow_{post}$, or
3. the graph shows $\rightarrow_{pre} \cup \rightarrow_{body} \cup \rightarrow_{post}$ (is-used-by).

We call the results "call graphs", "differentiated call graphs" and "generalized call graphs" respectively. We consider an example, for which Figure 7.39 shows the graphs. The nodes for the nullary functions 0 and 10 have been omitted.

```
FUNC f : Nat -> Nat
IN   x
PRE  x > 0
DEF  x + 10
POST x > 10

PROC p : Nat ->
IN   x
PRE  f(x) > 0
DEF  h(x); h(x)

PROC h : Nat ->
PRE  TRUE
POST TRUE
```

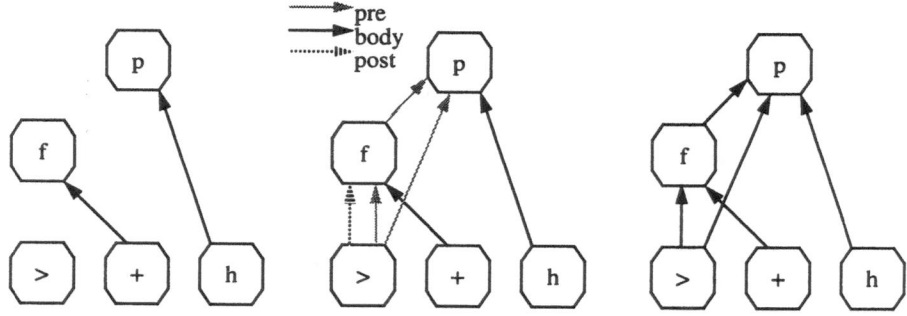

Figure 7.39: Call graph, differentiated call graph, and generalized call graph.

7.11   Import Graphs

An import graph represents the "is-imported-by" relation on components. The nodes represent components, and there is an arrow from C_1 to C_2 if C_1 is imported by C_2. In this section we shall restrict ourselves to components with no implementation, which are of the following form:

```
COMPONENT C_i[u_1,...,u_k] SPECIFICATION
ABSTRACT  A_1,...,A_l
EXPORT S
IMPORT B_1,...,B_m
CLASS D_1 ... D_n
END
```

Essentially, the same options and problems exist as for call graphs, see Section 7.10: a component definition has several clauses with distinct purposes and interpretations. The ABSTRACT clause is for a component what the precondition is for an operation, and the IMPORT clause is for a component what the body is for an operation. In the exported signature S, there can be one or more SIG clauses, for easy reference to the entire signature of other components. We propose to use the obvious notations $\rightarrow_{\text{abstract}}$, $\rightarrow_{\text{export}}$ and $\rightarrow_{\text{import}}$.

A classical import graph is nothing but the graph of $\rightarrow_{\text{import}}$. Again, it is an option to show all relations. And one can draw the is-used-by relation defined as the union of the three sets of arrows: $\rightarrow_{\text{abstract}} \cup \rightarrow_{\text{export}} \cup \rightarrow_{\text{import}}$. The latter approach has been taken for the preprocessor of the TEDDY graphical design browser [32]. We consider an example, for which Figure 7.40 shows the resulting graphs under the assumption that C3 and C4 are non-parametrized components and that C5 has an ABSTRACT clause mentioning ITEM.

```
COMPONENT C1[Item] SPECIFICATION
ABSTRACT  ITEM
EXPORT    f,g,h, SIG C3
IMPORT    C3,C4
CLASS
   ...
END

COMPONENT C2[Item] SPECIFICATION
ABSTRACT  ITEM
EXPORT    p,q
IMPORT    C3,C5[Item]
END
```

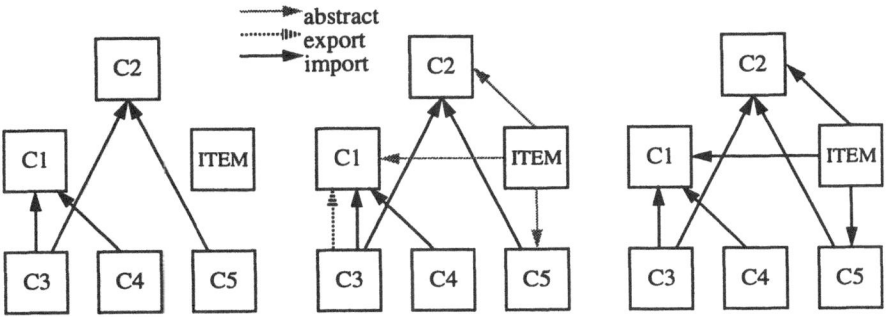

Figure 7.40: Import graph, differentiated import graph, and generalized import graph.

Various combinations can be made of the concepts proposed in the present section and in Section 7.6.3. For example, also in import graphs, it is an option to show the effect of the copy operator (quote notation) by copying the node of the copied component. This has been done in Figure 2.16.

7.12   Concluding Remarks

We can classify the picture kinds addressed in the present chapter according
to the nature of their interpretation. We refer to the classification scheme of
Section 7.1.

picture kind	form	interpretation
Venn diagram	area diagram	behaviour (static)
statechart	area+graph diagram	behaviour (dynamic)
Nassi-Shneidermann diagram	area diagram	structure (1)
HOOD diagram	area+graph diagram	structure (2)
function graph	graph diagram	behaviour (static)
state transition diagram	graph diagram	behaviour (dynamic)
call graph	graph diagram	structure (1)
import graph	graph diagram	structure (2)

Figure 7.41: Picture kinds presented in this chapter.

Other forms of pictorial representations (network diagrams and sequence
charts) will be addressed in the next chapter.

Chapter 8
More Pictorial Representations

For centuries painters composed by natural form and colour; at present the composition itself is the plastic expression, the image. (P. Mondrian)

8.1 Network Diagrams: General

A *network diagram* is a system of nodes and connections, also called devices and wirings respectively. The nodes are drawn as circles or boxes whereas the connections are drawn as connected systems of lines or arrows. Each node has an ordered collection of connection points on its boundary. The endpoints of a connection (wiring) can be tied to the connection points of the nodes. We shall restrict ourselves to directed networks, i.e. networks where each connection is a system consisting of arrows. Figure 8.1 illustrates the difference between a

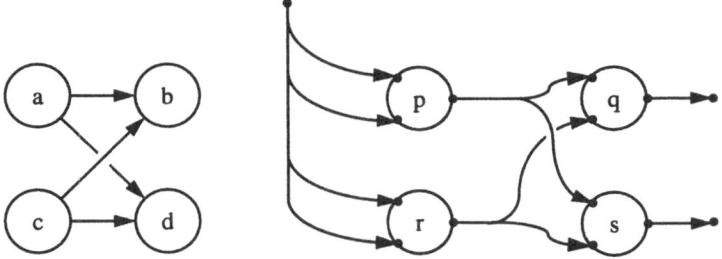

Figure 8.1: Graph and network.

graph and a network. The graph has four nodes a, b, c, and d and four directed edges. Each edge goes from one node to one other node. The network has four nodes p, q, r and s, and five connections (wirings). The first wiring feeds from a loose outermost connection point into the two input connection points of p as well as the two input connection points of r. Then there is a connection that feeds the output of p into the upper inputs of q and s. Another connection feeds the output of r into the lower inputs of q and s. Finally there are two connections with a loose end.

In the subsequent sections we shall consider the following kinds of network diagrams: data flow diagrams (Sections 8.2 and 8.3), flow charts (Section 8.4), abstract hardware diagrams (Section 8.5), state-based abstract hardware diagrams (Section 8.6) Petri nets (Section 8.7) and SDL-like diagrams (Section 8.8).

Sections 8.9, 8.10 and 8.11 are concerned with sequence charts.

8.2   Data Flow Diagrams

A data flow diagram (DFD) is a network in which the nodes represent operations and the connections describe how the outputs of certain operations are used as inputs for other operations The diagrams can be nested in the sense that one or more of the nodes can be refined to reveal an internal structure, which again takes the form of a data flow diagram. The external connection points of the node must match with the unbound ends of the connections of its internal data flow diagram. Examples of data flow diagrams are given in Figures 1.3, 2.1, 2.3, 2.5, 2.12 and 6.47.

Data flow diagrams are of course well-known from the structured methods such as Yourdon's Structured Analysis, DeMarco and Hatley/Pirbhai, see e.g. [34], [7] or [35]. For a survey of research on the integration of formal and structured methods we refer to [36]. In this section we begin by restricting ourselves to the functional aspects of data flow diagrams, postponing the discussion of "stores" to the next section.

The next example of an invoice system has a function `bill_for_service` with five parameters, named `customer_name`, `hours_of_labour` etc. It is assumed that we have the sorts `Nat`, `Dollar`, `String`, `Material` and furthermore the data types obtained by importing `SEQ[String]`, `SEQ[Material]`, and `MAP[Material,Dollar]`. The example has been adapted from [34].

```
FUNC bill_for_service : String
                      # Nat
                      # Map[Material,Dollar]
                      # Seq[Material]
                      # Dollar -> Seq[String]
IN   customer_name,
     hours_of_labour,
     price_file,
     materials_list,
     prepayment
OUT  complete_invoice
```

In Figure 8.2 the function is shown as a single node with five connection points which are directed inwards and one connection point which is directed outwards. The inward connection points have been labelled with the name and type of each of the parameters. The order of the connection points should match the order of the formal parameters of the COLD-1 function definition, considering the connection points in a clockwise manner.

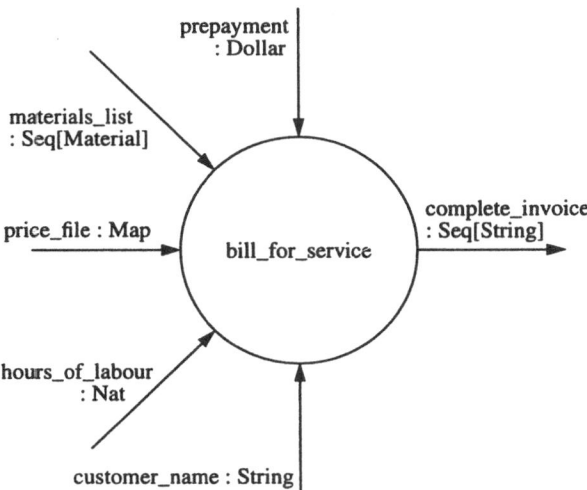

Figure 8.2: Data flow diagram of bill_for_service (external view).

Next we can decompose the "bill for service" function. Assume that we have functions bill_for_labour (transforming natural numbers into amounts of dollars), bill_for_materials (with domain sorts Map[Material,Dollar] and Seq[Material] and with range Dollar) and finally a function layout (transforming a string and two amounts of dollars to a sequence of strings). The "bill for labour" function defines the bill for labour based on the hours of labour, e.g. by multiplication with a certain rate. It is easy to imagine a "bill for materials" function which applies the map of the price file to each material in the list and sums the results. Also assume that we can subtract amounts of dollars. In this billing system, the amount of prepayment applies to the materials only.

```
FUNC bill_for_service : ...                          % as above
IN   customer_name, ...                              % as above
DEF  layout(customer_name
            ,bill_for_labour(hours_of_labour)
            ,bill_for_materials(price_file,materials_list)
            - prepayment
           )
```

In Figure 8.3, the decomposed function is shown as a data flow diagram. The diagram is an alternative presentation of the function body. The ends of the connections are tied to the nodes in the same order as the connection points of their single-node representation. Note that in general the order of the inward arrows is relevant, but for commutative operations, such as * and +, there is no harm in permuting the inputs for layout improvement.

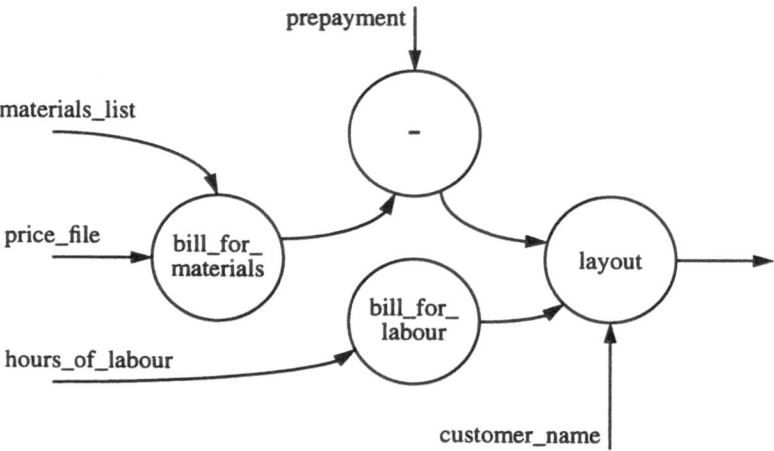

Figure 8.3: Data flow diagram of bill_for_service (internal view).

Data flow diagrams abstract from the dynamic aspects of system behaviour. Questions like "how often is the described input-output transformation performed?" and "exactly what conditions trigger it?" are not addressed. The diagrams are useful for at least the following purposes:

- for the analysis and top-down decomposition of the functional behaviour of systems during the phases of requirements analysis and architectural design;

- for the design and implementation of systems in those technologies which provide physical building blocks with input/output behaviour: electronic amplifiers, logical gates, dedicated arithmetical units, transputers, etc.

The example of Figures 8.2 and 8.3 covers the representation of functions: the external view can be drawn to show the function, giving its name, input type(s), output type(s) and optionally the parameter names. The internal view can be drawn for a function with an algorithmic body which is given by an IN clause and a DEF clause.

Next we discuss drawing data flow diagrams for predicates too. Recall the major distinction between a function and a predicate. Application of a function yields a value (an object), whereas application of a predicate yields a logical value, which is either TRUE or FALSE. In the structured methods it is customary to employ a variation of the data flow diagram, called "control flow diagram" to distinguish discrete-valued control signals from the other data signals. At the syntactic level the difference is usually indicated by using dashed arrows for the control flow diagrams. Here we employ the option of dashing arrows to mark those connections which have a logical value instead of a normal value associated with them. This is useful because it clearly distinguishes the value-oriented connections from the "logical" connections without forcing us to introduce a sort name for the latter connections (like Logical, or TrueFalse), which would be misleading with respect to the logic of COLD-1. In Figure 8.4 we present the pictorial representation of some of the operators built into COLD-1. The operators "^" and "!" denote undefinedness and definedness respectively. They match all types. In terms of data flow, these two operators can be explained as follows: "^" yields TRUE if no value at its input is available, FALSE otherwise. Definedness ("!") is the converse: it yields TRUE iff there is a value at its input. The absence of an input value can arise if a preceding operation is applied to a value outside the range of the pre-condition. For example 1/0 is undefined, and if we consider a data flow diagram with a node for /, then offering 0 at the second input does not give any result value at the output. The operator "=" denotes equality; it returns TRUE if both inputs

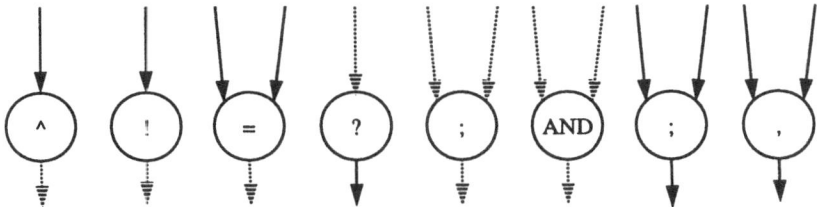

Figure 8.4: Data flow diagrams for COLD-1 operators.

are defined and are equal. The following default rule applies: if one or both of the inputs are not available (are undefined), then the output is FALSE. In fact, there are several such default rules, which we sometimes call *strictness* principles; we will summarize them below.

The operator "?" yields an output iff its input is TRUE. The output – if any – is of the empty type, which means that its output is the empty sequence of values. But in COLD-1, the empty sequence is considered defined, which is often exploited in combination with the strictness of the concatenation operators ";" and "," to write **if-then-else** like expressions. The operators ";" and "AND" are logical operators, having logical values at their inputs and outputs. Actually, they have the same meaning, the difference being that ";" is parsed with a low priority and "AND" is parsed with a high priority.

The operators "," and ";" are the same too (concatenation of sequences of values), but again ";" has a lower priority than ",". There are two operators denoted as ";", one on logical values and one on (sequences) of normal values.

Next we list the strictness principles for functions, predicates, and built-in operators. They are principles of COLD-1, rather than properties of the diagrams, but the data flow approach is a nice occasion to state them in terms of defaults for missing inputs. Figure 8.5 lists the defaults. Of course "^" is an exception to the last rule, (and so are "/=", "==" and "=/=").

node	result kind	example	default
function	value	`bill_for_service`	no output
predicate	truth value	">" and "<"	FALSE
built-in operator	value	";" and ","	no output
built-in operator	truth value	"="	FALSE

Figure 8.5: Strictness: defaults on one or more missing input.

8.3 Data Flow Diagrams with Stores

A data flow diagram can also be used to show a procedure together with its connection points (its parameters) labelled with parameter names and types. There is a special kind of nodes called "stores" (representing variables), which are connected to the procedure by means of directed edges. These edges indicate that the procedure has read- or write-access to the stores. Only the external view of the procedure is shown here – one could also add data flow connections between procedures.

Consider the definition of a procedure p in COLD-1 with a SAT MOD clause, referring to the variable functions v and w such that there are two distinct variable functions that appear quoted in the post-condition, viz. u and w. These u' and w' in the post-condition refer to the previous values of the variables. Actually, for u it does not matter if we write u, or u' in the post-condition, for p does not modify u. The intuition is that the values of u and w influence the behaviour (effect/result) of p.

```
FUNC u : ... -> ... VAR
FUNC v : ... -> ... VAR
FUNC w : ... -> ... VAR

PROC p : T₁ # ... # Tₘ -> V₁ # ... # Vₙ
IN   ...
OUT  ...
PRE  TRUE
SAT  MOD v, w
POST post(u', w')
```

Then we can draw a data flow diagram for p, as given in Figure 8.6. Each variable is shown as a pair of parallel lines with the name of the variable between them. For each variable which occurs in the SAT MOD clause there is an arrow from the procedure to the variable. For each variable which appears quoted in the post-condition there is an arrow from the variable to the procedure. Two opposite arrows are combined into one.

The above form of p with variables u, v and w represents a fairly large class of procedure definitions. Of course, there need not be precisely three variables, but the extension to fewer, or more variables will be obvious: all

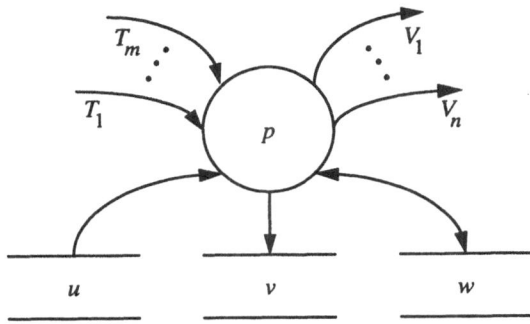

Figure 8.6: Data flow diagram for procedure p.

variables which appear (either quoted or unquoted) in the post-condition, but are not modified must be treated like u; all variables which are mentioned in the SAT MOD clause, but which do not appear quoted in the post-condition, must be treated like v; finally, all variables which are modified and appear quoted in the post-condition too, must be treated like w.

Next some further refinements and generalizations are presented. First, we allow for variable predicates too, showing them as dashed stores, and dashing the arrows to and from these stores. Secondly, we allow for non-trivial pre-conditions, adopting the convention that variables which occur in the pre-condition are treated in the same way as variables which occur quoted in the post-condition: there must be an arrow from the store symbol of the variable to the node of the procedure. Finally, it is convenient to combine the external views of several procedures, and put them in one diagram, showing how a group of procedures has read- or write-access to a group of variables.

The following simple example uses these refinements and generalizations. The resulting picture is Figure 8.7.

```
SORT Index

PRED bitmap : Index VAR
PRED saved  : Index VAR

PROC toggle : Index ->
IN   i
PRE  TRUE
SAT  MOD bitmap(i)
POST bitmap(i) <=> NOT bitmap'(i)

PROC backup : ->
PRE  EXISTS i : Index (bitmap(i))
SAT  MOD saved
POST FORALL j : Index (saved(j) <=> bitmap(j))
```

```
PROC restore : Index ->
IN   i
PRE  TRUE
SAT  MOD bitmap(i)
POST bitmap(i) <=> saved(i)
```

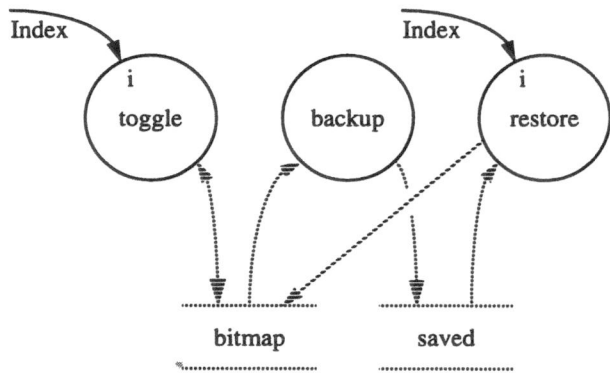

Figure 8.7: Data flow diagram for toggle, backup and restore.

8.4   Flow Charts

A flow chart is a network where some of the nodes represent elementary statements and where special nodes together with the connections show how the elementary statements are composed. Elementary statements are expressions with side-effects – assignments and procedure calls. A flow chart has one or more entry points and one or more exit points such that every path through the flow chart represents an execution sequence of the composite statement ("program") represented by the entire network.

As such, flow charts are concerned with the operational interpretation of programming language constructs. For the early imperative programming languages like assembly languages and FORTRAN they were used to have an alternative representation of the goto-structure present in certain programs. For COLD-1 there is no unique way of drawing the diagrams, because this depends on the *execution model* chosen. Examples are the PROTOCOLD 1.1 execution model [19] and the execution model obtained by a direct translation of COLD-1 to C. Here we show the latter choice.

In Figure 8.8 the principles of such a direct translation are given. One must add obvious translation rules for assertions, e.g. translating NOT A to ! A and translating A_1 AND A_2 to A_1 && A_2. Some care is needed because the translation is correct under certain conditions only (for example in X ; Y, the execution of X and Y may not fail). In Figure 8.9 the special nodes and

COLD-1 construct	C construct
$X \; ; \; Y$	$translation(X) \; translation(Y)$
p	$p()$;
$p(e)$	$p(e)$;
$e_1 = e_2$	$e_1 \;$ == $\; e_2$

(A ? ; X
 | NOT A ? ; Y
)
	if (A)
	    { $translation(X)$ }
	    else { $translation(Y)$ }

(A ? ; X) * ; NOT A ?	while (A) { $translation(X)$ }

Figure 8.8: Direct translation of COLD-1 to C.

connection patterns to represent sequential composition, the if-construct and the while-construct are given. The rhombic shape that appears in Figure 8.9 (b) and (c) is a special node called a *branch*. During execution, if A holds for a branch labelled A the outgoing connection labelled *yes* is taken, otherwise the *no*-connection is taken. A is said to be the *condition* of the branch.

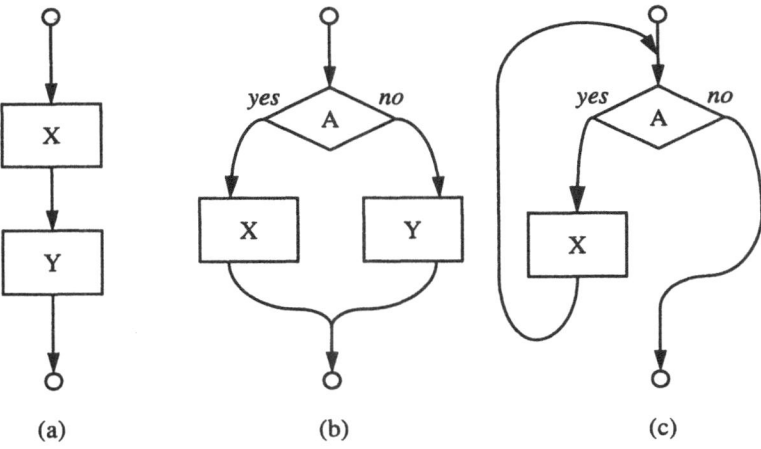

(a)   (b)   (c)

Figure 8.9: Flow chart patterns for sequential composition, if and while.

The diagrams give us a nice occasion to explain a proof technique due to Floyd [37]. Consider a program for which it must be proved that, assuming a certain pre-condition *pre* upon program entry, a given post-condition *post* holds upon program termination. Floyd's technique requires the usage of an assertion language to annotate (label) the input and output connection points of the nodes of the flow chart of the program. The assertions of COLD-1 can be used for that purpose. Usually it is not sufficient to work with logical connectives

only (AND, OR, NOT, etc.) because quantifiers are required when reasoning about
arrays or other non-trivial data structures. The entry connection point(s) of
the flow chart must be labelled with *pre*. The exit connection point(s) of the
flow chart must be labelled with *post*. A labeling must be found for all other
input and output connection points, such that the following rules are obeyed:

- if a connection point labelled A is connected to another connection point
  labelled B (the arrow pointing from the former to the latter), then A =>
  B must hold;

- if a node depicts a procedure call then the procedure must transform each
  state in which the assertion of the input connection point holds to a state
  which satisfies the assertion of the output connection point (this can be
  checked against the pre-condition, post-condition and modification rights
  of the procedure);

- for every branch node with branch condition B and with input labelled
  A, the *yes*-output must be labelled with A AND B and the *no*-output gets
  the label A AND NOT B.

As an example we shall consider a simple C program which operates on two
arrays called a and b and which is meant to investigate if the text strings stored
in a and b are anagrams, i.e. texts built-up from precisely the same characters,
taking the number of occurrences of each character into account. For example,
"parse" and "spear" are anagrams. We adopt the following macro definitions
and data structure declarations in C.

```
#define Char char
Char arrays[2][len];
#define a(N) arrays[0][N]
#define b(N) arrays[1][N]
#define Nat int
Nat i,j;
#define TRUE 1
#define FALSE 0
int fail;
```

We want to analyse the following C program, operating on these data structures. We give the C program immediately, omitting its COLD-1 version. The
main program uses a simple auxiliary operation to swap the contents of two
locations in the array b.

```
swap_b(n,m)
Nat n,m;
{    Char tmp;
     tmp=b(n);
     b(n)=b(m);
     b(m)=tmp;
}
```

The main program takes a and b as inputs. During its execution, the program will permute the contents of b, leaving a unaffected. This is the C program:

```
i=0;                                    /* C program to be verified */
fail=FALSE;
while (!fail && i < len)
        { j=i;
          while (b(j) != a(i) && j < len)
                {j++;}
          if (j == len)
             {fail=TRUE;}
          else
             {swap_b(i,j);}
          i++;
        }
```

The flow chart of this program is given in Figure 8.10. Before we can start

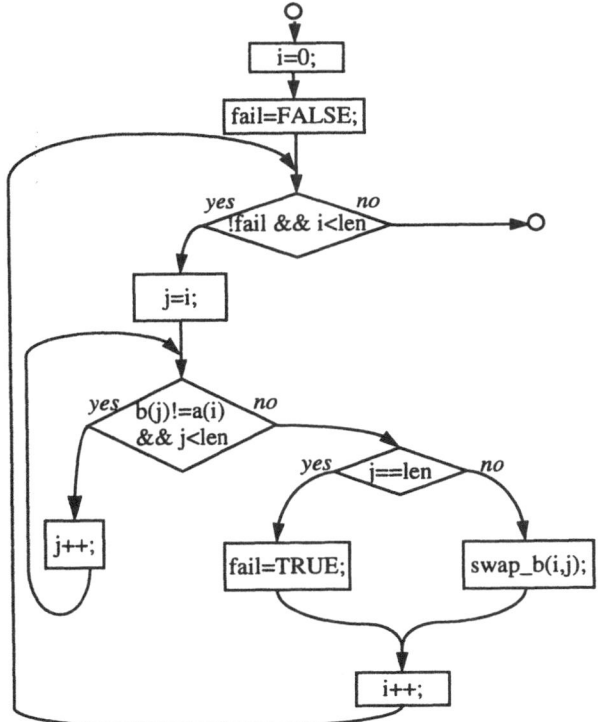

Figure 8.10: Flow chart for anagram program.

annotating this flow chart we must introduce several COLD-1 preliminaries. First, we should clarify how exactly the two arrays and the three simple variables are viewed as variable functions or predicates:

```
FUNC a : Nat -> Char
IN   p
PRE  p < len
VAR

FUNC b : Nat -> Char
IN   p
PRE  p < len
VAR


AXIOM len!

FUNC i :  -> Nat PRE TRUE VAR
FUNC j :  -> Nat PRE TRUE VAR
PRED fail : VAR
```

Moreover, before any correctness proof can be attempted, the specification of the program must be clear. We cast it into the form of a pre- and post-condition specification.

```
PROC anagram : ->
PRE  TRUE
SAT  MOD i,j,fail,b
POST NOT fail  <=>  abag'(len) = bbag'(len)
```

where the functions **abag** and **bbag** give bags of characters. The intuition is that **abag**(n) denotes the bag containing $a(0), \ldots, a(n-1)$. Similarly **bbag**(n) denotes the bag containing $b(0), \ldots b(n-1)$. These functions are useful because now we can describe the fact that the text strings stored in a and b are anagrams if **abag(len) = bbag(len)**. If we assume a context where NAT, CHAR and BAG[Char] have been imported, the following (recursive) definitions can be used:

```
FUNC abag : Nat -> Bag
IN   n
DEF  ( n = 0 ? ; empty
     | n > 0 ? ; ins(a(n - 1),abag(n - 1))
     )

FUNC bbag : Nat -> Bag
IN   n
DEF  ( n = 0 ? ; empty
     | n > 0 ? ; ins(b(n - 1),bbag(n - 1))
     )
```

It is also useful to abstract from the internal details of **swap_b**. It has the following specification.

```
PROC swap : Nat # Nat ->
IN   n,m
```

```
PRE   n < len AND m < len
SAT   MOD b(n),b(m)
POST  b(n) = b'(m) AND b(m) = b'(n)
```

Finally we employ an auxiliary predicate eqab(i) expressing that the arrays a and b are equal for all indices up to i. The predicate neqab is auxiliary too: neqab(i,j) means that the value of a(i) can not be found amongst b(i), ..., b($j - 1$).

```
PRED eqab : Nat
IN   n
DEF  FORALL m : Nat (m < n  =>  a(m) = b(m))


PRED neqab : Nat # Nat
IN   n,m
DEF  FORALL k : Nat (n <= k AND k < m  =>  a(n) /= b(k) )
```

We shall use the quote notation to refer to the value of variables upon entry of the program. Essentially, we have all the notational machinery for annotating the flow chart now. We make some further conventions to avoid complicating the drawing too much: first, when all connection points of a connection have the same label, this label is included just once. Secondly, we use ";" instead of AND because it is shorter. Thirdly, at an output of a node, we may write "... ; A" for some assertion A, where it is understood that the dots denote the assertion of the input of the node. Finally, one clause which holds at *all* connection points is therefore omitted: bbag(len) = bbag'(len) which says that b, when viewed as a bag, is not modified. Also the assertions i <= len and j <= len remain implicit; the former belongs to all connection points below the assignment that sets i to 0 and the latter holds for all connection points below the assignment that sets j to i. We refer to Figure 8.11. We conclude the example by showing a simple main program to test the anagram function and two test runs. The constant len was defined as 20, the C program was turned into a function called **anagram** and the following text was added:

```
gettext(s)
char s[];
{   int c,k=0;
    while ((c=getchar())!='\n') s[k++]=c;
}

main()
{   Nat k;
    for (k=0; k<len; k++) {a(k)=' '; b(k)=' ';}
    gettext(&a(0));
    gettext(&b(0));
    anagram();
    if (fail) printf("fail\n"); else printf("NOT fail\n");
}
```

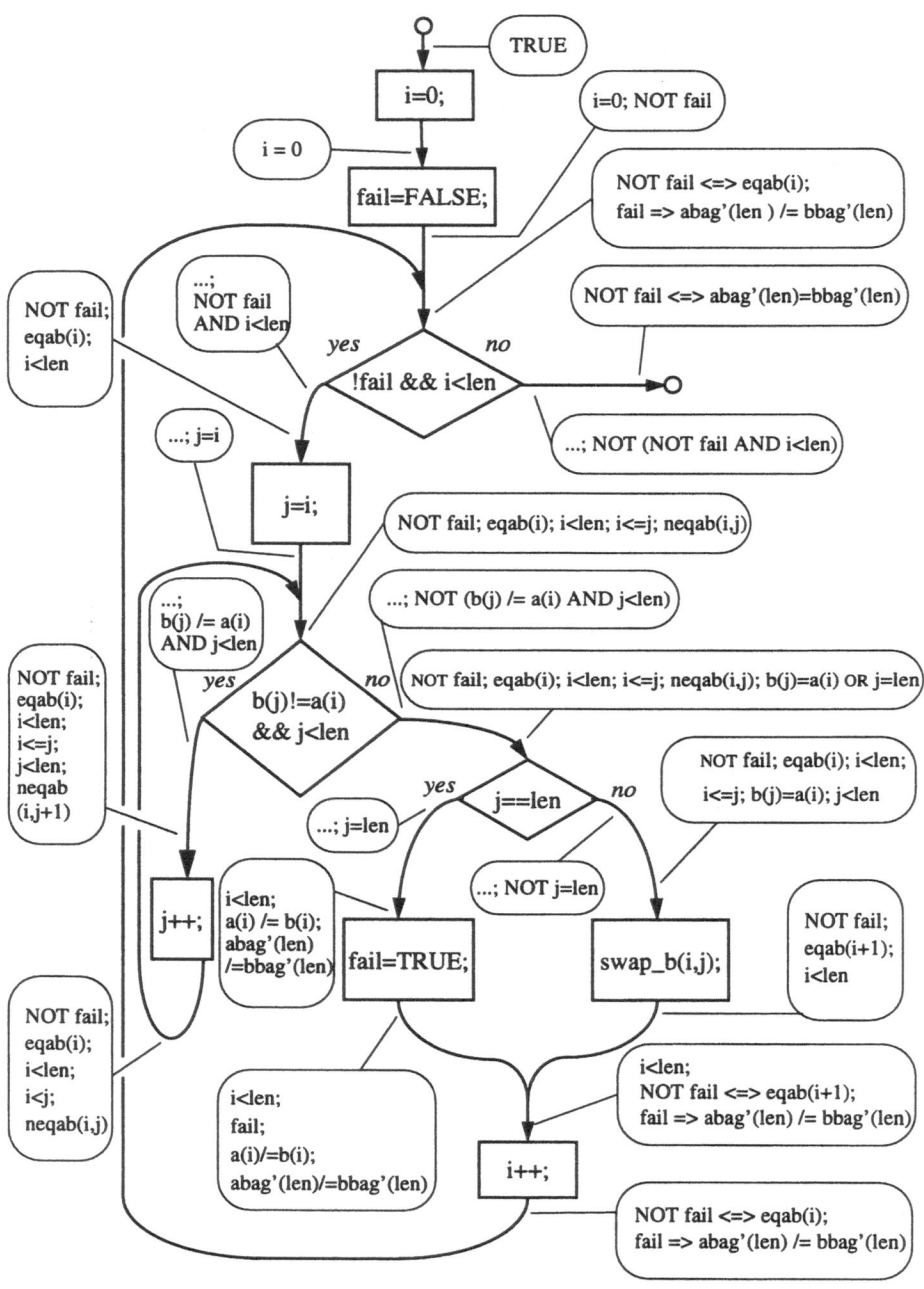

Figure 8.11: Annotated flow chart for anagram program.

After compilation with the standard compiler `cc` an executable file `a.out` is obtained. We show one sample test run:

```
% a.out
i paint modern
piet mondrian
NOT fail
```

8.5 Abstract Hardware Diagrams

An abstract hardware diagram is a network in which the nodes represent hardware devices and the connections describe how the outputs of certain hardware devices are inputs for other hardware devices. The diagrams can be nested by refining one or more of the nodes, revealing an internal structure which again takes the form of a hardware diagram. The external connection points of the node must match with the unbound ends of the connections of its internal hardware diagram.

In their simplest form, abstract hardware diagrams are similar to data flow diagrams, but the way we relate them to COLD-1 is different. Moreover, in Section 8.6 we shall discuss extended forms of abstract hardware diagrams which, are specifically geared towards certain hardware applications. The abstract hardware diagrams are also closely related to the Mascot diagrams described in [38].

In the following example there is a hardware device with three input connection points and two output connection points. Its diagram is given in Figure 8.12. The inputs are named `in1`, `in2` and `c_in` (for "carry" input).

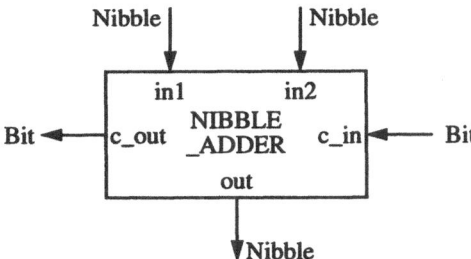

Figure 8.12: Abstract hardware diagram for nibble adder.

The outputs are named `out` and `c_out` (for "carry" output). The carry connection points transfer bits, modelled as elements of the data type `Bit`. The other connection points are of type `Nibble` (a nibble consists of four bits). `Bit` and `Nibble` are specified by the components `BIT` and `NIBBLE` respectively. It is characteristic for the description of hardware that there are special data types describing the "signals" that go in and come out of the devices.

`COMPONENT BIT SPECIFICATION`

```
EXPORT
   SORT Bit
   FUNC 0   : -> Bit,
        1   : -> Bit,
        nat : Bit -> Nat,
        bit : Nat -> Bit
IMPORT
  NAT,
  BOOL' RENAMING Bool TO Bit, false TO 0, true TO 1 END
CLASS
  FUNC nat : Bit -> Nat
  IND  nat(0) = 0; nat(1) = 1

  FUNC bit : Nat -> Bit
  IND  bit(0) = 0; bit(1) = 1
END

COMPONENT NIBBLE SPECIFICATION
EXPORT
   SORT Nibble
   FUNC nibble : Bit # Bit # Bit # Bit -> Nibble,
        b0     : Nibble -> Bit,
        b1     : Nibble -> Bit,
        b2     : Nibble -> Bit,
        b3     : Nibble -> Bit,
        nat    : Nibble -> Nat,
        nibble : Nat    -> Nibble
IMPORT
  BIT,
  NAT,
  TUP4'[Bit,Bit,Bit,Bit] RENAMING Tup4  TO Nibble,
                                  tup   TO nibble,
                                  proj1 TO b0,
                                  proj2 TO b1,
                                  proj3 TO b2,
                                  proj4 TO b3
                          END
CLASS
  FUNC nat : Nibble -> Nat
  IN   n
  DEF  8*nat(b3(n)) + 4*nat(b2(n)) + 2*nat(b1(n)) + nat(b0(n))

  FUNC nibble : Nat -> Nibble
  IN   i
  DEF  THAT n : Nibble (nat(n) = i)
END
```

The device of Figure 8.12 is called a *nibble adder* and its specification is given

as a component NIBBLE_ADDER. Note the function sum, which is not exported:
it is a hidden auxiliary function.

```
COMPONENT NIBBLE_ADDER SPECIFICATION
EXPORT
  FUNC in1   : -> Nibble,
       in2   : -> Nibble,
       c_in  : -> Bit,
       out   : -> Nibble,
       c_out : -> Bit
IMPORT
  NAT,
  BIT,
  NIBBLE
CLASS
  FUNC c_in : -> Bit     FREE
  FUNC in1  : -> Nibble FREE
  FUNC in2  : -> Nibble FREE

  FUNC sum : -> Nat
  DEF  nat(in1) + nat(in2) + nat(c_in)

  FUNC out : -> Nibble
  DEF  nibble(sum mod 16)

  FUNC c_out : -> Bit
  DEF  bit(sum / 16)
END
```

The operation mod must be declared as infix. Figure 8.12 shows a single node,
but abstract hardware diagrams only become interesting if we connect two or
more nodes to form a network. We shall do so below, aiming at a network
which can be viewed as an implementation of a *byte adder*. First we need an
additional device, which is very trivial. It is called *ground* and in practice it
is hardly a device at all: one just connects a wire to the low voltage power
supply line. Its diagram is given in Figure 8.13; its specification is given as a
component GND.

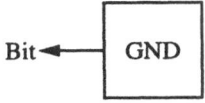

Figure 8.13: Abstract hardware diagram for "ground".

```
COMPONENT GND SPECIFICATION
EXPORT
  FUNC gnd_out : -> Bit
```

```
IMPORT
  BIT
CLASS
  FUNC gnd_out : -> Bit
  DEF  0
END
```

The *byte adder* is constructed using two nibble adders and one ground. Its diagram is given in Figure 8.14; its specification is given as BYTE_ADDER_IMPL.

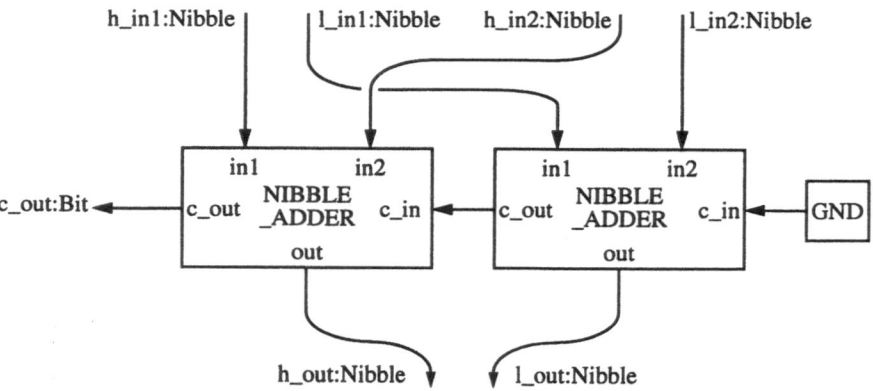

Figure 8.14: Abstract hardware diagram for byte adder implementation.

```
LET BYTE_ADDER_IMPL :=
IMPORT
  GND',
  NIBBLE_ADDER' RENAMING
                  in1 : -> Nibble TO l_in1,
                  in2 : -> Nibble TO l_in2,
                  c_in  : -> Bit  TO gnd_out,
                  out : -> Nibble TO l_out,
                  c_out : -> Bit  TO c_connect
                END,
  NIBBLE_ADDER' RENAMING
                  in1 : -> Nibble TO h_in1,
                  in2 : -> Nibble TO h_in2,
                  c_in  : -> Bit  TO c_connect,
                  out : -> Nibble TO h_out,
                  c_out : -> Bit  TO c_out
                END
END
```

Note how renamings are used to get desired name clashes, e.g. unifying the c_out of the first instance of NIBBLE_ADDER (the low-nibble adder) with the c_in of the second NIBBLE_ADDER (the high-nibble adder). This can be done because c_in was introduced as FREE, as is done for all inputs in the present approach.

The external view of the byte adder can be given as the one-node abstract hardware diagram of Figure 8.15; its specification is the SPECIFICATION part of the component BYTE_ADDER, which is given below. The IMPLEMENTATION part is BYTE_ADDER_IMPL as defined above.

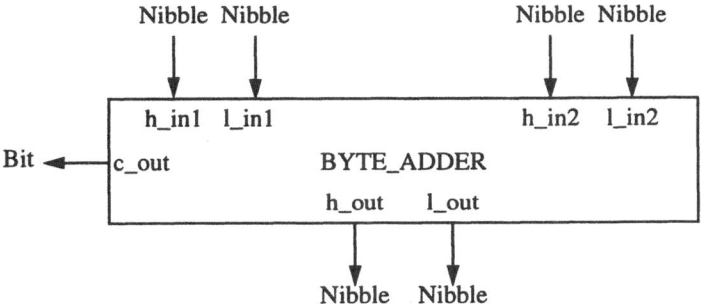

Figure 8.15: External view of byte adder.

```
COMPONENT BYTE_ADDER SPECIFICATION
EXPORT
  FUNC h_in1 : -> Nibble,
       h_in2 : -> Nibble,
       l_in1 : -> Nibble,
       l_in2 : -> Nibble,
       h_out : -> Nibble,
       l_out : -> Nibble,
       c_out : -> Bit
IMPORT
  NAT,
  BIT,
  NIBBLE
CLASS
  FUNC h_in1 : -> Nibble FREE
  FUNC l_in1 : -> Nibble FREE
  FUNC h_in2 : -> Nibble FREE
  FUNC l_in2 : -> Nibble FREE

  FUNC sum : -> Nat
  DEF  16 * nat(h_in1) + nat(l_in1) + 16 * nat(h_in2) + nat(l_in2)

  FUNC h_out : -> Nibble
  DEF  nibble((sum mod 256) / 16)
```

```
    FUNC l_out : -> Nibble
    DEF  nibble(sum mod 16)

    FUNC c_out : -> Bit
    DEF  bit(sum / 256)
END
```

IMPLEMENTATION BYTE_ADDER_IMPL

As already suggested by the term "byte adder", there is an abstract view
of BYTE_ADDER where the individual nibbles are not visible any more. Two
nibble-oriented connection points can be viewed as one byte-oriented connection point. This abstraction step is described in the specification BYTE_ADDER_.
We need a special component BYTE first, to specify the "signal" sort of *bytes*.
The diagram is given in Figure 8.16.

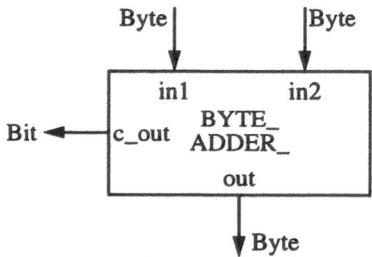

Figure 8.16: Abstract view of byte adder.

```
COMPONENT BYTE SPECIFICATION
EXPORT
  SORT Byte
  FUNC byte : Nibble # Nibble -> Byte,
       n0   : Byte -> Nibble,
       n1   : Byte -> Nibble,
       nat  : Byte -> Nat,
       byte : Nat  -> Byte
IMPORT
  NAT,
  NIBBLE,
  TUP2'[Nibble,Nibble] RENAMING Tup2  TO Byte,
                                tup   TO byte,
                                proj1 TO n0,
                                proj2 TO n1
                       END
CLASS
  FUNC nat : Byte -> Nat
  IN   b
```

```
    DEF  16*nat(n1(b)) + nat(n0(b))

    FUNC byte : Nat -> Byte
    IN   i
    DEF  THAT b : Byte (nat(b) = i)
END

COMPONENT BYTE_ADDER_ SPECIFICATION
EXPORT
    FUNC in1   : -> Byte,
         in2   : -> Byte,
         out   : -> Byte,
         c_out : -> Bit
IMPORT
    NAT,
    BIT,
    BYTE,
    NIBBLE,
    BYTE_ADDER
CLASS
    FUNC in1 : -> Byte FREE
    FUNC in2 : -> Byte FREE

    FUNC h_in1 : -> Nibble  DEF n1(in1)
    FUNC l_in1 : -> Nibble  DEF n0(in1)
    FUNC h_in2 : -> Nibble  DEF n1(in2)
    FUNC l_in2 : -> Nibble  DEF n0(in2)

    FUNC out : -> Byte
    DEF  byte(16 * nat(h_out) + nat(l_out))

    THEOREM out = byte((nat(in1) + nat(in2)) mod 256);
            c_out =  bit((nat(in1) + nat(in2)) / 256)
END
```

The axioms and the definitions relate the concrete representation of the ingoing
and the outgoing nibbles to the abstract view at the level of the ingoing and
the outgoing bytes. In particular, the first two DEF clauses explains how h_in1
and l_in1 together form one byte, viz. in1. Similarly, the next two definitions
relate the nibbles h_in2, l_in2 to the byte in2. The theorem states that, at
the level of the bytes, the byte adder works as expected: the values of in1 and
in2 are added and then out is the result modulo 256; the "carry out" is 1 iff
the result exceeds 255.

   To conclude this section we summarize the rules to draw abstract hardware diagrams for this type of COLD-1 specifications. We restrict ourselves
to components without sort definitions and without procedures. Sorts can be
imported from special components that specify the "signal" sorts needed. Pro-

cedures will be covered later in Section 8.6. Each node of an abstract hardware diagram is drawn by the following rules:

- the component is shown as a box with the component name inside it;
- every exported function which is introduced as FREE is shown as an input connection point of the component;
- every exported function which is variable (VAR), dependent (DEP) or defined (DEF) is shown as an output connection point of the component.

The connections between the nodes must be drawn as follows:

- if there is an output node out and a number of input nodes in$_i$ for $0 \leq i \leq n$, and by means of zero or more RENAMING clauses out and each of the in$_i$ is mapped to a common name (as e.g. gnd_out, or c_connect), then there is a connection from out to each of the connection points in$_i$;
- the remaining input and output connection points are shown as the inputs and the outputs of the resulting network.

Applying these rules we exploit the mechanism of free definitions as provided by COLD-1. A FREE definition has a variable (i.e. unknown) origin. When the name of a free definition (an input) clashes with the name of another definition, which is not FREE (an output), then this means that the former will have the same value (carry the same signal) as the latter. The signal "originates" at the output.

8.6   State-based Abstract Hardware Diagrams

So far, the hardware devices were memory-less, which is a severe limitation. The present section will extend the approach of Section 8.5 such that devices can have an internal state. The state is modelled by COLD-1 variables. A device can have actions or commands to modify its state. These commands are modelled by COLD-1 procedures.

Here we shall show an example concerned with signal switching. We shall use some terminology from the area of speech switching, as relevant to telephony [41], or [42]. The devices are called *switches*, in other applications also known as *source selectors*, or *multiplexers*.

We begin with the specification of an elementary switch with 3 inlets and 3 outlets. After that, we present several variations on this type of switch, such as concentrator switches with 6 inlets and 3 outlets, and expander switches with 3 inlets and 6 outlets. From these elementary switches we shall compose a switch with 18 inlets and 18 outlets, using multistage switching. Typical implementations of small switches contain a matrix with M inlets and N outlets and roughly speaking, the cost of a switch is $M \times N \times c$, where c is the cost of one basic switch, also called "crosspoint". To simplify the example, we focus on uni-directional speech traffic; it is not hard to add more details to get the

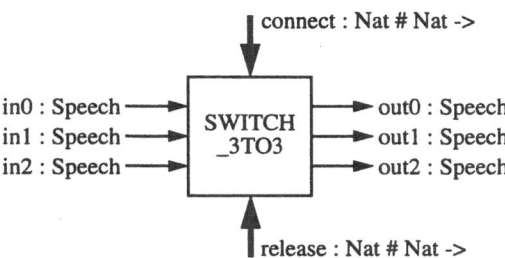

Figure 8.17: Abstract hardware diagram of switch.

two-way speech traffic as known from public telephony. Figure 8.17 shows a
switch with three inlets and three outlets.

Each inlet and outlet carries a speech signal; we assume a component
SPEECH, exporting a sort Speech, but we need not go into details such as
whether the speech signals are analogue, delta-modulated, or pulse-code mod-
ulated. The definition of SPEECH is not included here.

```
COMPONENT SWITCH_3TO3 SPECIFICATION
EXPORT
  PROC connect : Nat # Nat ->,
       release : Nat # Nat ->
  FUNC in0  : -> Speech,
       in1  : -> Speech,
       in2  : -> Speech
  FUNC out0 : -> Speech,
       out1 : -> Speech,
       out2 : -> Speech
IMPORT
  NAT,
  SPEECH
CLASS
  FUNC in0 : -> Speech FREE
  FUNC in1 : -> Speech FREE
  FUNC in2 : -> Speech FREE

  PRED link : Nat # Nat VAR

  AXIOM INIT => FORALL s,d : Nat (NOT link(s,d))

  PROC connect : Nat # Nat ->
  IN   s,d
  PRE  s < 3; d < 3; NOT EXISTS n : Nat (link(s,n) OR link(n,d))
  SAT  MOD link(s,d)
  POST link(s,d)
```

```
PROC release : Nat # Nat ->
IN   s,d
PRE  s < 3 AND d < 3 AND link(s,d)
SAT  MOD link(s,d)
POST NOT link(s,d)

FUNC in : Nat -> Speech
IN   n
DEF  ( n = 0 ?; in0
     | n = 1 ?; in1
     | n = 2 ?; in2
     )

DECL n : Nat

FUNC out0 : -> Speech
PRE  EXISTS n (link(n,0))
DEF  in(n)

FUNC out1 : -> Speech
PRE  EXISTS n (link(n,1))
DEF  in(n)

FUNC out2 : -> Speech
PRE  EXISTS n (link(n,2))
DEF  in(n)
END
```

The next elementary switch is called SWITCH_6TO3. Its diagram is given in
Figure 8.18. The diagrams 8.17 and 8.18 are obtained as in Section 8.5, but we
have added another kind of arrows (the thick arrows) to show the procedures.
This is a concentrator which has 6 inlets and 3 outlets. The specification is
similar to the specification of SWITCH_3TO3. We used a more compact layout
for the export list.

```
COMPONENT SWITCH_6TO3 SPECIFICATION
EXPORT
  connect, release, in0, in1, in2, in3, in4, in5, out0, out1, out2
IMPORT
  NAT, SPEECH
CLASS
  FUNC in0 : -> Speech FREE
  FUNC in1 : -> Speech FREE
  FUNC in2 : -> Speech FREE
  FUNC in3 : -> Speech FREE
  FUNC in4 : -> Speech FREE
  FUNC in5 : -> Speech FREE
```

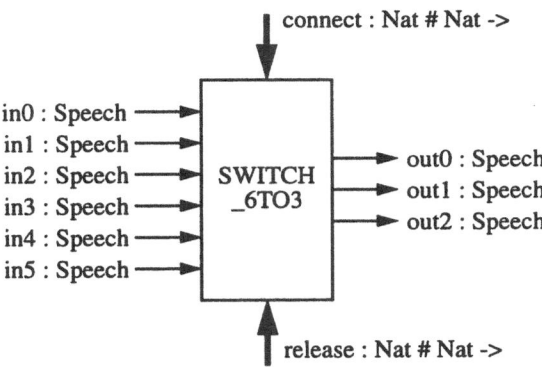

Figure 8.18: Abstract hardware diagram of concentrator switch.

```
PRED link : Nat # Nat VAR

AXIOM INIT => FORALL s,d : Nat (NOT link(s,d))

PROC connect : Nat # Nat ->
IN   s,d
PRE  s < 6; d < 3; NOT EXISTS n : Nat (link(s,n) OR link(n,d))
SAT  MOD link(s,d)
POST link(s,d)

PROC release : Nat # Nat ->
IN   s,d
PRE  s < 6 AND d < 3 AND link(s,d)
SAT  MOD link(s,d)
POST NOT link(s,d)

FUNC out0 : -> Speech
DEF  ( link(0,0) ?; in0 | link(1,0) ?; in1 | link(2,0) ?; in2
     | link(3,0) ?; in3 | link(4,0) ?; in4 | link(5,0) ?; in5
     )

FUNC out1 : -> Speech
DEF  ( link(0,1) ?; in0 | link(1,1) ?; in1 | link(2,1) ?; in2
     | link(3,1) ?; in3 | link(4,1) ?; in4 | link(5,1) ?; in5
     )

FUNC out2 : -> Speech
DEF  ( link(0,2) ?; in0 | link(1,2) ?; in1 | link(2,2) ?; in2
     | link(3,2) ?; in3 | link(4,2) ?; in4 | link(5,2) ?; in5
     )
END
```

Later we shall also employ an expander switch called SWITCH_3TO6. It is supposed to have 3 inlets and 6 outlets. Its specification is not included here. It is similar to the specification of SWITCH_3TO3 and SWITCH_6TO3. We refer to Figure 8.19.

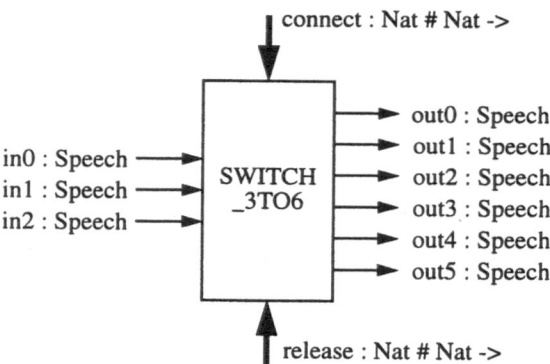

Figure 8.19: Abstract hardware diagram of expander switch.

Now assume that by way of example, we have to construct a switch with 18 inlets and 18 outlets. We shall use a technique called *multistage switching*, which has been used for about 100 years in the design of large telephony exchanges. Switching equipment is expensive and must be efficiently used. So, optimization of the network structure is an important aspect of telecommunication engineering. The number of crosspoints in a full-matrix type of switch with 18 inlets and 18 outlets is 324. In practice, when designing a switch with 1000 inlets and outlets, the quadratic cost-function demands other solutions. The usual solution is to accept the possibility of "blocking", or "congestion". Instead of assuming that *all* connect requests must succeed, one is satisfied if a great majority of connect requests is satisfied. After all, a telecommunication switching system has to cater for a fluctuating demand which is hard to predict anyhow. Below we construct a configuration of 9 switches, with a total of $3 \times 18 + 3 \times 9 + 3 \times 18 = 135$ crosspoints. Each link passes through 3 stages. The first stage performs a certain traffic concentration, because it reduces 18 inlets to 9. The second stage consist of three switches of the 3×3 type. Such an intermediate switch is called a "trunk", and for each connect requests there are 3 alternative routings, one through each trunk. The saving of $\frac{324-135}{324} \times 100\% = 58\%$ is achieved at the price of a non-zero chance of congestion. Only if the total number of requested links is 3 or less, the switch is free of blocking. At most 9 links can be set-up simultaneously (but not *any* 9 links). The detailed construction is given as SWITCH_18TO18 below. Figure 8.20 shows the abstract hardware diagram.

```
COMPONENT SWITCH_18TO18 SPECIFICATION
IMPORT
```

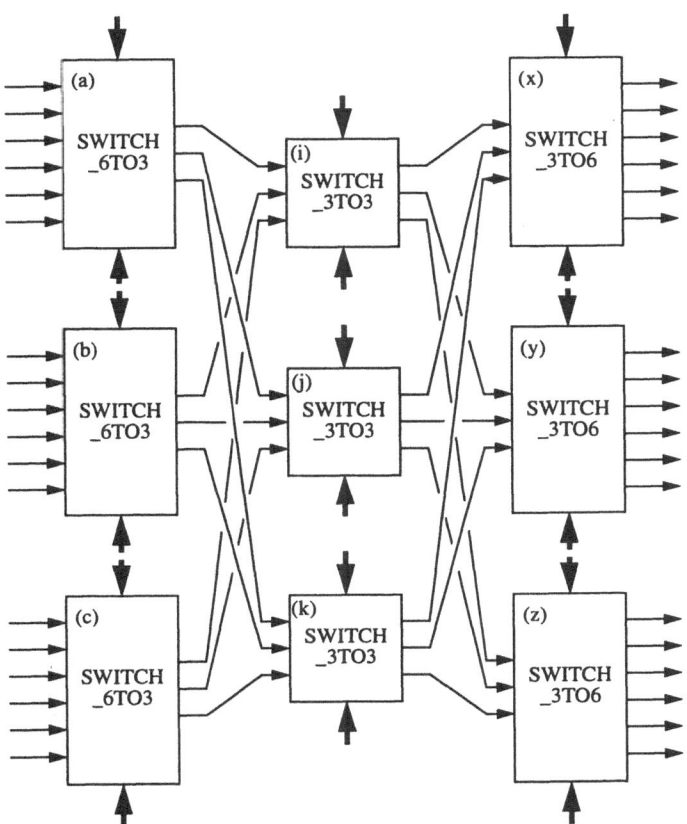

Figure 8.20: Three-stage switching network.

```
SWITCH_6TO3' QUALIFYING a END,
SWITCH_6TO3' QUALIFYING b END,
SWITCH_6TO3' QUALIFYING c END,

SWITCH_3TO6' QUALIFYING x END,
SWITCH_3TO6' QUALIFYING y END,
SWITCH_3TO6' QUALIFYING z END,

SWITCH_3TO3' RENAMING in0 TO a.out0,
                     in1 TO b.out0,
                     in2 TO c.out0,
                     out0 TO x.in0,
                     out1 TO y.in0,
                     out2 TO z.in0,
                     connect TO i.connect,
                     release TO i.release
             END,
```

```
    SWITCH_3TO3' RENAMING in0 TO a.out1,
                          in1 TO b.out1,
                          in2 TO c.out1,
                          out0 TO x.in1,
                          out1 TO y.in1,
                          out2 TO z.in1,
                          connect TO j.connect,
                          release TO j.release
              END,
    SWITCH_3TO3' RENAMING in0 TO a.out2,
                          in1 TO b.out2,
                          in2 TO c.out2,
                          out0 TO x.in2,
                          out1 TO y.in2,
                          out2 TO z.in2,
                          connect TO k.connect,
                          release TO k.release
              END,
  BOOL,
  NAT
CLASS
  PRED link : Nat # Nat # Nat VAR

  AXIOM INIT => FORALL s,t,d : Nat (NOT link(s,t,d))

  PROC set_link : Nat # Nat # Nat # Bool ->
  IN   s,t,d,b
  PRE  s < 18 AND t < 3 AND d < 18
  SAT  MOD link(s,t,d)
  POST link(s,t,d) <=> b = true

  PRED source_is_free : Nat
  IN   s
  DEF  s < 18 AND NOT EXISTS t,d : Nat (link(s,t,d))

  PRED destination_is_free : Nat
  IN   d
  DEF  d < 18 AND NOT EXISTS s,t : Nat (link(s,t,d))

  PROC connect : Nat # Nat ->
  IN   s,d
  DEF  ( LET t : Nat
       ; source_is_free(s) ?
       ; destination_is_free(d) ?
       ; ( i.connect(s/6,d/6); t := 0
         | j.connect(s/6,d/6); t := 1
         | k.connect(s/6,d/6); t := 2
```

```
                )
              ; connect_front(s,t)
              ; connect_back(t,d)
              ; set_link(s,t,d,true)
              )

      PROC connect_front : Nat # Nat ->
      IN   s,t
      DEF  ( s/6 = 0 ?; a.connect(s,t)
           | s/6 = 1 ?; b.connect(s - 6,t)
           | s/6 = 2 ?; c.connect(s - 12,t)
           )

      PROC connect_back : Nat # Nat ->
      IN   t,d
      DEF  ( d/6 = 0 ?; x.connect(t,d)
           | d/6 = 1 ?; y.connect(t,d - 6)
           | d/6 = 2 ?; z.connect(t,d - 12)
           )

      PROC release : Nat # Nat ->
      IN   s,d
      DEF  ( LET t : Nat
           ; ( link(s,0,d) ?; t := 0; i.release(s/6,d/6)
             | link(s,1,d) ?; t := 1; j.release(s/6,d/6)
             | link(s,2,d) ?; t := 2; k.release(s/6,d/6)
             )
           ; release_front(s,t)
           ; release_back(t,d)
           ; set_link(s,t,d,false)
           )

      PROC release_front : Nat # Nat ->
      IN   s,t
      DEF  ( s/6 = 0 ?; a.release(s,t)
           | s/6 = 1 ?; b.release(s - 6,t)
           | s/6 = 2 ?; c.release(s - 12,t)
           )

      PROC release_back : Nat # Nat ->
      IN   t,d
      DEF  ( d/6 = 0 ?; x.release(t,d)
           | d/6 = 1 ?; y.release(t,d - 6)
           | d/6 = 2 ?; z.release(t,d - 12)
           )
    END
```

Note how the new procedures connect and release have been implemented

using the procedures a.connect, a.release, b.connect, b.release, etc.,
which are the commands of the elementary building blocks. In a practical

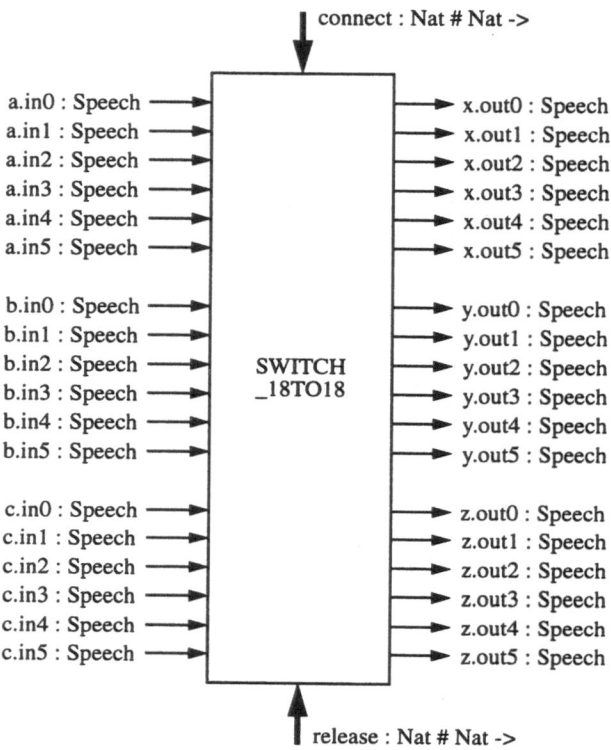

connect : Nat # Nat ->

a.in0 : Speech		x.out0 : Speech
a.in1 : Speech		x.out1 : Speech
a.in2 : Speech		x.out2 : Speech
a.in3 : Speech		x.out3 : Speech
a.in4 : Speech		x.out4 : Speech
a.in5 : Speech		x.out5 : Speech
b.in0 : Speech		y.out0 : Speech
b.in1 : Speech		y.out1 : Speech
b.in2 : Speech	SWITCH _18TO18	y.out2 : Speech
b.in3 : Speech		y.out3 : Speech
b.in4 : Speech		y.out4 : Speech
b.in5 : Speech		y.out5 : Speech
c.in0 : Speech		z.out0 : Speech
c.in1 : Speech		z.out1 : Speech
c.in2 : Speech		z.out2 : Speech
c.in3 : Speech		z.out3 : Speech
c.in4 : Speech		z.out4 : Speech
c.in5 : Speech		z.out5 : Speech

release : Nat # Nat ->

Figure 8.21: External view of three-stage switching network.

telephony exchange a switch may well consist of a combination of hardware
and software. The hardware is built-up from of switching circuitry, such as
Reed-relays in the Philips PRX programmable exchanges [43], or solid-state
switches in the later AT&T 5-ESS electronic switching systems. The software
takes the form of programs stored into, and executed by a computer which
controls the switching circuitry. Note that both the signal-processing aspects
(the "speech") and the link control aspects (the "connect" software) can be
described in COLD-1. The external view of the composed switch is given in
Figure 8.21.

The definitions of connect and release and the associated auxiliary operations connect_front, connect_back, release_front, and release_back
are written in a restricted style of COLD-1, which allows for code-generation
and automatic execution according to the PROTOCOLD 1.1 execution model
[19, 44, 45].

The definition of the full execution model is beyond the scope of this book,
but we can give an informal explanation of what happens when connect is

executed. First the tests `source_is_free(s)` and `destination_is_free(d)` are performed. If one of these fails, the `connect` fails, which means that it returns `"failed"`, without causing any side-effect. If the tests succeed, non-deterministically either `i.connect(s/3,d/3)`, `j.connect(s/3,d/3)`, or `k.connect(s/3,d/3)`is tried. If the first try fails (which implies that it did not cause any change in the hardware state), one of the other alternatives is chosen. Only if one of them succeeds, the front-end and the back-end parts of the link are connected. Note that once a trunk connection has been established, it is known that the subsequent calls of `connect_front` and `connect_back` will certainly succeed. Finally the `set_link(`s,d,t`,true)` expression serves to store the fact that there is a link from source s via trunk t to target d, in a kind of software administration of the composed switch. As a matter of fact, the PROTOCOLD 1.1 execution model is capable of some backtracking. It is not allowed to backtrack over side-effects, but it is possible to unbind object names introduced by the LET construct, and to try alternatives in a choice construct when previous paths failed. For example, the following version of connect could be executed too, with the same effect as the first version.

```
PROC connect : Nat # Nat ->
IN   s,d
DEF  ( LET t : Nat
     ; source_is_free(s) ?
     ; destination_is_free(d) ?
     ; ( t := 0; i.connect(s/6,d/6)
       | t := 1; j.connect(s/6,d/6)
       | t := 2; k.connect(s/6,d/6)
       )
     ; connect_front(s,t)
     ; connect_back(t,d)
     ; set_link(s,t,d,true)
     )
```

The COLD-1 based method SPRINT [40] employs an extended form of these hardware diagrams, called "box diagrams". We sketch one of the extensions used in box diagrams by means of Figure 8.22. There are two kinds of procedure arrows, related to the distinct methodological interpretations of procedures in SPRINT. An inward arrow is a command, requesting some action to be taken by the component. An outward arrow is an event-procedure: a procedure which succeeds if a certain event has happened, and fails otherwise. Calling the event-procedure then amounts to executing a "test-and-clear" action. `NEW_SWITCH_3TO3` is the component from which the diagram of Figure 8.22 can be derived. The example is about a switch which requires service (hardware maintenance) after 10.000 successful `connect`s. Furthermore there is a predicate called `blocked`; it holds if the maximal number of simultaneous calls is reached.

COMPONENT NEW_SWITCH_3TO3 SPECIFICATION

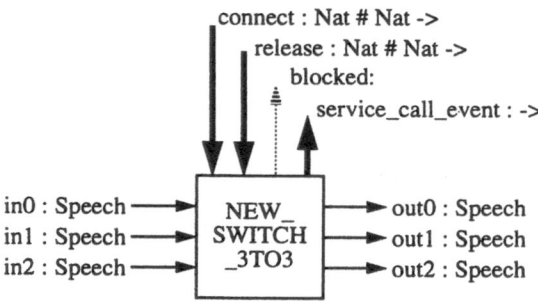

Figure 8.22: Abstract hardware diagram of switch.

```
EXPORT
  connect, release, service_call_event,
  blocked, in0, in1, in2, out0, out1, out2
IMPORT
  NAT,
  SPEECH
CLASS
  FUNC counter : -> Nat VAR

  PROC service_call_event : ->
  PRE   counter > 9999
  SAT   MOD counter
  POST  counter = 0

  PRED link : Nat # Nat VAR

  AXIOM INIT => counter = 0 AND FORALL s,d : Nat (NOT link(s,d))

  PRED blocked :
  DEF   FORALL d : Nat (d < 3 => EXISTS s : Nat (link(s,d)))

  PROC connect : Nat # Nat ->
  IN    s,d
  PRE   s < 3; d < 3; NOT EXISTS n : Nat (link(s,n) OR link(n,d))
  SAT   MOD counter, link(s,d)
  POST  counter = counter' + 1 AND link(s,d)

  % in0, in1, in2, release, out0, out1, and out2: as before
  END
```

The approach of this section has been used for the verification of very large-scale integration (VLSI) circuitry [39], and for the design of audio-video systems using SPRINT [40]. Each audio-video component is a combined hardware-software component with dedicated hardware for tuning, source-selection, amplification, etc. By means of buses, interrupt lines and I/O software, the commands are made available as COLD-1 procedures that can be called by the higher layers of control software written in PROTOCOLD.

8.7   Petri Nets

A Petri net has two kinds of nodes, called *places* and *transitions*. There are directed edges from places to transitions and from transitions to places. Places are shown as circles, whereas the transitions are shown as bars (some authors use boxes). If there is an arrow from place p to transition t, we say that p is an *input place* of t. If there is an arrow from transition t to place p, we say that p is an *output place* of t. Figure 8.23 shows a transition t_1 which has two input places p_1, p_2 and three output places p_3, p_4, and p_5. Petri nets are named

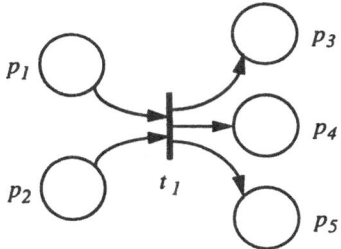

Figure 8.23: Petri net with one transition and five places.

after C.A. Petri who proposed them in 1962. Actually, the nets are much more than just another picture kind: they are part of a fundamental theory about concurrency and synchronization. Many variations of the formalism have been developed, such as *coloured* Petri nets [46] and *timed* Petri nets [47]. Here we shall show one of the many options for relating COLD-1 and Petri nets.

A net is a model of the dynamic behaviour of a system, which can be in many states. Each state is characterized by a *marking*, which is an assignment of tokens to the places: a place can contain zero, one, or more tokens. A token is shown as a dot. The precise nature of the tokens is considered irrelevant (except when considering coloured Petri nets). The state of the system can change by means of the *firing* of one or more transitions. A transition fires when *all* of its input places contain at least one token; if there are 2 (3,4,...) arrows from p to t, then p must have at least 2 (3,4,...) tokens to enable the firing of t. When a transition fires, one token is removed from each of its input places and a token is added to each of its output places (again: more arrows imply more tokens). Figure 8.24 (a) shows an initial marking of the simple net of Figure 8.23, whereas Figure 8.24 (b) shows the marking which results after firing transition t_1.

Next we present an example which is concerned with buffer synchronization

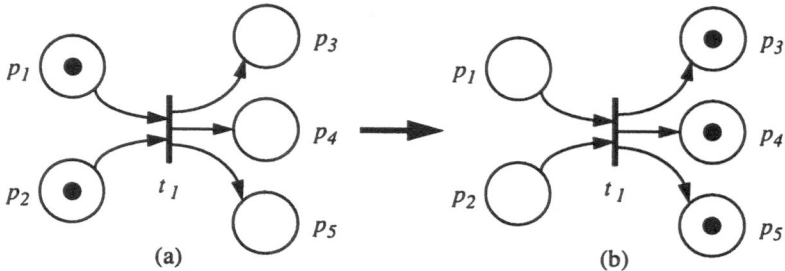

Figure 8.24: Firing of a transition.

in a packet-oriented radio receiver. The tasks to be performed inside the receiver are:

- *receiving packets* from the air and buffering the raw data;
- *decoding* the raw data, decompressing them and adapting the format to get plain text;
- *reproducing* the text from the buffer, using a speech-synthesizer and an acoustical device such as a loudspeaker.

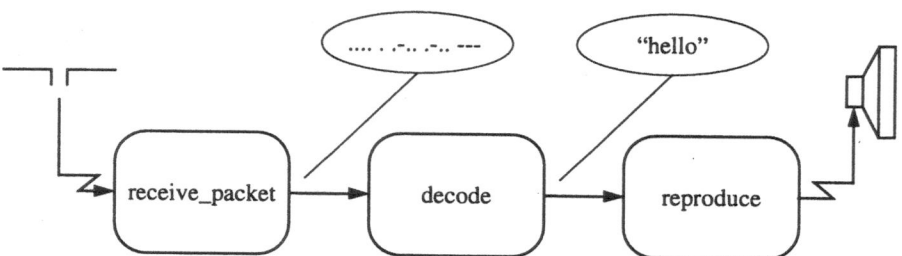

Figure 8.25: Packet-oriented radio receiver.

The picture of Figure 8.25 is meant to convey some intuition about the example. There are two buffers to store the raw data and the plain text. In the specification below, each buffer can contain zero, one or more raw packets, or texts. There are two auxiliary flags, modelled as counters, that play a rôle in the synchronization of the operations upon the buffers. The idea is that the `receive_packet` operation is enabled if `receive_test` is non-zero. Similarly, the `decode` operation is enabled if `decode_test` is non-zero. A function `f` is supposed to describe the functional transformation of raw data to text. The clause PRE TRUE which is attached to each of the four variable declarations below guarantees that all variables have a defined value in each state.

```
COMPONENT RECEIVER SPECIFICATION
EXPORT
  PROC receive_packet : ->,
```

```
          decode        : ->,
          reproduce     : ->
  FUNC raw_buffer  : -> Seq[Raw],
       text_buffer : -> Seq[Text]
IMPORT
  NAT,
  SEQ[Raw],
  SEQ[Text]
CLASS
  SORT Raw
  SORT Text
  FUNC f : Raw -> Text

  FUNC raw_buffer   : -> Seq[Raw]  PRE TRUE VAR
  FUNC text_buffer  : -> Seq[Text] PRE TRUE VAR
  FUNC receive_test : -> Nat       PRE TRUE VAR
  FUNC decode_test  : -> Nat       PRE TRUE VAR

  AXIOM INIT => ( raw_buffer  = empty
                ; text_buffer = empty
                ; receive_test = 1
                ; decode_test  = 1
                )

  PROC receive_packet : ->
  PRE  receive_test > 0
  SAT  MOD receive_test,
           raw_buffer
  POST receive_test = receive_test' - 1;
       raw_buffer = cons($,raw_buffer')

  PROC decode : ->
  PRE  decode_test > 0;
       len(raw_buffer) > 0
  SAT  MOD decode_test,
           receive_test,
           raw_buffer,
           text_buffer
  POST decode_test = decode_test' - 1;
       receive_test = receive_test' + 1;
       raw_buffer = tl(raw_buffer');
       text_buffer = cons(f(hd(raw_buffer')),text_buffer')

  PROC reproduce : ->
  PRE  len(text_buffer) > 0
  SAT  MOD decode_test,
           text_buffer
```

```
    POST decode_test = decode_test' + 1;
         text_buffer = tl(text_buffer')
END        •
```

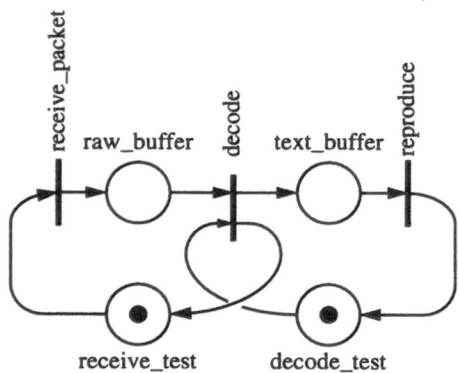

Figure 8.26: Petri net of RECEIVER with initial marking.

Normally we would have given an invariant for such a specification, but here it
has deliberately been omitted, because later the example will be used to show
a technique for calculating invariants.

In the diagram we abstracted from the fact that the raw_buffer and the
text_buffer contain sequences of raw data, or text data; only the length of
each sequence is shown by a corresponding number of tokens. The marking
shown in Figure 8.26 is the marking of the initial state of RECEIVER: since INIT
implies receive_test = decode_test = 1, the corresponding places have *one*
token each. Furthermore, since the length of the contents of the other buffers
is zero, their places contain *no* token.

The execution of the procedures of RECEIVER can be simulated by "playing
the token game": checking the presence of sufficient tokens in the input places
of a transition and then firing the transition by adapting the marking (lecturers
on Petri nets always bring drawing pins, except in the Netherlands where they
have extremely small 10-cent coins called "dubbeltjes"). Figure 8.27 shows an
execution sequence of receive_packet, decode, and reproduce, which starts
with the initial marking and which returns to the same marking in three steps.
Another execution sequence is shown in Figure 8.28, where it takes six firings
before reaching the initial marking again. From Figures 8.27 and 8.28 we see
that simulation is possible, in principle, and that it is quite intuitive. But it
is also clear that for large examples a state-space explosion occurs which is a
problem when aiming at exhaustive simulation.

But Petri nets can also be analysed by other techniques, such as the deriva-
tion of invariants. Here we shall show a kind of invariants called *place invariants*. The main tool is an incidence matrix W. For each place p_i and transition
t_j, the matrix element in the i-th row and the j-th column equals the number

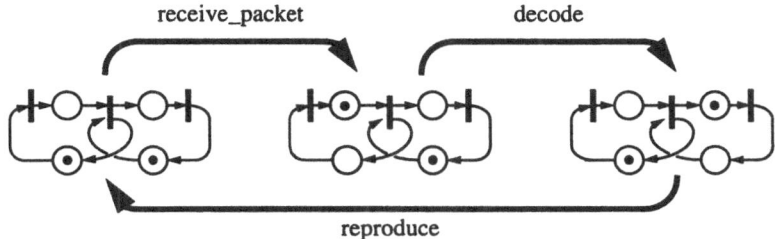

Figure 8.27: Petri net simulation of RECEIVER.

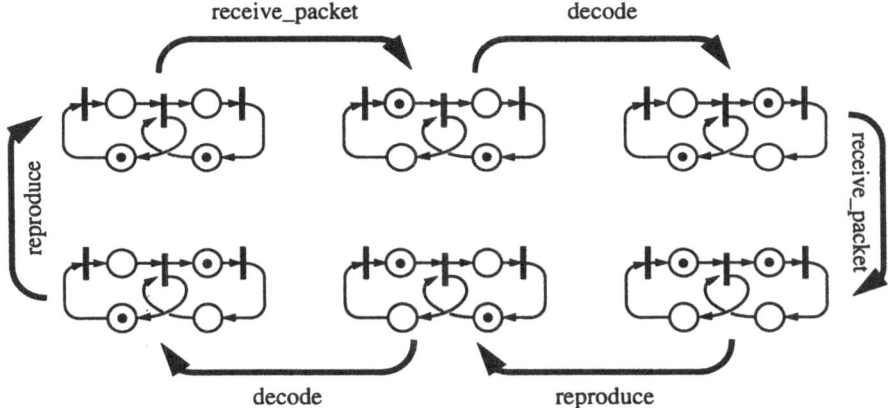

Figure 8.28: Petri net simulation of RECEIVER.

of arrows from t_j to p_i minus the number of arrows from p_i to t_j. For example, raw_buffer is an output place of receive_packet and therefore there is a 1 at $W_{1,1}$; here we define $t_1 = $ receive_packet, $t_2 = $ decode, and $t_3 = $ reproduce. We have ordered the places as follows: raw_buffer (rb), text_buffer (tb), receive_test (rt), and decode_test (dt). For the example we find the incidence matrix of Figure 8.29.

In [46] it is shown that solving the equation $\vec{v} * W = \vec{0}$ yields a set of weight factors (v_1, v_2, v_3, v_4) such that the weighted sum of the tokens in the various places is constant. So if m_{rb} is the number of tokens in raw_buffer, m_{tb} is the number of tokens in text_buffer etc., then $v_1 m_{\text{rb}} + v_2 m_{\text{tb}} + v_3 m_{\text{rt}} + v_4 m_{\text{dt}} = $ "constant". We must solve $\vec{v} * W = \vec{0}$, or

$$(v_1, v_2, v_3, v_4) \begin{pmatrix} 1 & -1 & 0 \\ 0 & 1 & -1 \\ -1 & 1 & 0 \\ 0 & -1 & 1 \end{pmatrix} = (0, 0, 0)$$

This vector equation splits into three equations $v_1 - v_3 = 0$, $-v_1 + v_2 + v_3 - v_4 = 0$, and $-v_2 + v_4 = 0$. Thus $v_1 = v_3$ and $v_2 = v_4$. Two independent solutions are

	t_1	t_2	t_3
rb	1	-1	
tb		1	-1
rt	-1	1	
dt		-1	1

Figure 8.29: Incidence matrix of RECEIVER.

$\vec{v} = (1, 0, 1, 0)$ and $\vec{v} = (0, 1, 0, 1)$, which means that $m_{rb} + m_{rt} = $ "constant", and $m_{tb} + m_{dt} = $ "constant". From the initial marking $m_{rb} = m_{tb} = 0$, and $m_{rt} = m_{dt} = 1$ we see that both constants are 1.

Interpreting the results in terms of RECEIVER we find that len(raw_buffer) + receive_test = 1, and that len(text_buffer) + decode_test = 1. This implies that for non-empty raw_buffer we find that receive_test = 0, or in other words: the procedure receive_packet can never change the raw_buffer when there is still data in it. The net turns out to be *safe*, by which we mean that no place ever contains more than one token. This analysis results allows us to transform RECEIVER into an equivalent but simpler RECEIVER_ where the multi-packet buffers are designed to contain one (raw or text) packet at a time. This was obvious from the original specification already if an invariant would have been defined.

```
COMPONENT RECEIVER_ SPECIFICATION
EXPORT
  PROC receive_packet : ->,
       decode          : ->,
       reproduce       : ->
  FUNC raw_buffer  : -> Raw,
       text_buffer : -> Text
IMPORT
  NAT
CLASS
  SORT Raw
  SORT Text
  FUNC f : Raw -> Text

  FUNC raw_buffer   : -> Raw  VAR
  FUNC text_buffer  : -> Text VAR
  PRED receive_test : VAR
  PRED decode_test  : VAR

  AXIOM INIT => raw_buffer^ AND text_buffer^
  AXIOM INIT => receive_test AND decode_test

  PROC receive_packet : ->
```

```
PRE  receive_test
SAT  MOD receive_test, raw_buffer
POST NOT receive_test AND raw_buffer!

PROC decode : ->
PRE  decode_test AND raw_buffer!
SAT  MOD decode_test, receive_test, raw_buffer, text_buffer
POST NOT decode_test AND receive_test;
     raw_buffer^ AND text_buffer = f(raw_buffer')

PROC reproduce : ->
PRE  text_buffer!
SAT  MOD decode_test, text_buffer
POST decode_test AND text_buffer^
END
```

When desired, this can be simplified further, noting that `receive_test` and `decode_test` can be defined as `raw_buffer^` and `text_buffer^` respectively.

After the example of `RECEIVER` and the nets derived from it, we present the rules for drawing Petri nets. In general, there are one or more variables, each of which will be represented as one "place" of the diagram, and one or more procedures, each of which will be presented as one "transition". To present the rules and their conditions of applicability we consider certain variables and procedures of a specification such that:

- each of the variables is a total nullary function of type **Nat** (the natural numbers), or otherwise of a type T, provided there is a function f that assigns a natural number $f(t)$ to every object t of type T;

- if p is one of the procedures, the success/failure behaviour of p depends on the value of some of the variables (v_1, v_2, etc.) and p has modification rights with respect to other variables (w_1, w_2, etc.).

The rules only apply under the following constraints:

- p fails if one of its v_i is zero (or if $f(v_i) = 0$) and succeeds if all $v_i > 0$ (or $f(v_i) > 0$ respectively);

- whenever p succeeds, each of the v_i is decremented by one (or $f(v_i)$ is decremented by one), whereas each of the w_j is *incremented* by one (or $f(w_j)$ is incremented by one).

Then we can draw a Petri net as follows:

- for each of the variables, the net has one place, and for each of the procedures, the net has one transition;

- for each procedure p and for each of the variables v_i upon which its success or failure depends, and which is decremented by it, the net has an arrow from the place of v_i to the transition of p;

- for each procedure p and for each of the variables w_j which is incremented by it, the net has an arrow from the transition of p to the place of w_j;

- for the initial marking, the number of tokens in a place is given by the value of its variable (or the f of that value) in the initial state.

Typical data types for the variables are Nat, Seq, Set, or Bag, where no f is needed for Nat, and where we can take $f = \text{len}$, $f = \text{card}$, or $f = \text{card}$ respectively, otherwise.

8.8 SDL-like Diagrams

An SDL-like diagram is a flow chart with two special symbols for elementary actions called "send" and "receive". Begin state and end states of transitions can be shown explicitly, as in a state transition diagram. Each SDL-like diagram can be viewed as a state machine, and by assuming a certain correspondence (communication channels) between send and receive actions, a collection of these state machines can be viewed as a system of communicating processes.

We shall present two variations of the SDL-like diagrams. The first variation is meant for asynchronous communication, which is when processes communicate indirectly, for example via queues. In that case process P_1 can send a message and proceed with its own actions; process P_2 can receive the message later. The second variation is meant for synchronous communication, by which we mean that whenever process P_1 communicates with process P_2, both processes take part in the communication *at the same time.*

For asynchronous communication, we shall use a subset of the original SDL notation, as proposed by the ITU (the former CCITT) for the specification and description of telecommunication systems [48]. This is the subject of Section 8.8.1. For synchronous communication, we shall use a notation which is inspired by SDL and which was proposed by Jacobson in the context of the Objectory method [49]. This is the subject of Section 8.8.2.

8.8.1 SDL-like Diagrams for Asynchronous Communication

In Figure 8.30 the nodes to represent a state, an action, a decision, a send action and a receive action for asynchronous communication are given.

Figure 8.30: Asynchronous SDL (state, action, decision, send, receive).

In COLD-1 there is no built-in queueing mechanism, but it is easy to model communication channels which can queue data. Each channel provides a send operation and a receive operation, as specified by the component CHANNEL below.

```
COMPONENT CHANNEL[Item] SPECIFICATION
ABSTRACT
  ITEM
EXPORT
 PROC send    : Item ->,
      receive : Item ->
IMPORT
  SEQ[Item]
CLASS
  FUNC queue : -> Seq[Item] PRE TRUE VAR

  AXIOM INIT => queue = empty

  PROC send : Item ->
  IN   i
  PRE  TRUE
  SAT  MOD queue
  POST queue = cat(queue',seq(i))

  PROC receive : Item ->
  IN   i
  PRE  NOT queue = empty
  SAT  MOD queue
  POST queue' = cons(i,queue)
END
```

We add some explanation to the definition of CHANNEL. The channel is modelled as a variable sequence of type Seq[Item], which is provided by the standard component SEQ. The relevant operations are empty, cat (concatenation), seq (one-element sequence construction), and cons (putting an element in front of a given sequence).

There may be certain variations; for example send is often called put, and receive is called get or message_event.

The reader might have expected PROC receive : -> Item instead of PROC receive : Item ->, which is more natural indeed. But here we want to illustrate that there is a significant freedom with respect to the interpretation of procedures. In the chosen approach, a call of receive(i) succeeds if there is an item in the queue, and at the same time i is bound to the item received. This idea is exploited in the SPRINT approach [40]. There is a similarity with the interpretation of parameters in Prolog. Consider the following program.

```
init :- asserta(queue([])).
```

```
send(X)  :- queue(Q),
            retract(queue(Q)),
            append(Q,[X],NEWQ),
            asserta(queue(NEWQ)).

receive(X)  :- queue([X|Q]),
               retract(queue([X|Q])),
               asserta(queue(Q)).
```

The definition of **append** is not included here. The style of the Prolog program is unusual, but that is because it serves to illustrate **CHANNEL**, which is a state-based component. The program gives rise to the dialogue given below. In COLD-1 terminology we say that the first call of **receive** *succeeds* for the value **batch77**, whereas the second call of **receive** fails because the queue is empty.

```
SB-Prolog Version 3.1
| ?- consult(channel).
yes
| ?- init.
yes
| ?- send(batch77).
yes
| ?- receive(X).

X = batch77
yes
| ?- receive(X).
no
| ?-
```

Of course there is also a similarity with the interpretation of **var** parameters in Pascal, where the header of receive would be **function receive(var i : Item) : Boolean;**. This concludes the explanation of **CHANNEL**.

We focus on the communication aspects, and do not address the question of how to model multiple instances of processes with the same process description here. If there is a collection of processes P_1, P_2, P_3, ..., these can be connected by a collection of communication channels. For example, one channel from P_1 to P_2, one channel from P_1 to P_3, etc. For each channel we need a distinct instantiation of **CHANNEL**, which gives rise to a number of distinct send and receive procedures; renamings can be used to keep them apart. Each process can be described by one COLD-1 component importing the channels whose send or receive actions are used. All procedures except the send and the receive operations work on variables which are strictly local to their processes (i.e no other process should have read or write access to the variables). We use the channels in a unidirectional way only.

Now we turn our attention to drawing the diagrams. The channels are *not* made explicit as processes in the diagram. Instead of that, one implicitly adopts the principles of queue-based asynchronous communication when interpreting the symbols of Figure 8.30.

We shall give an example of a printing system, which is adapted from [50]. In the example there are processes as follows:

- a spooler process called SPOOLER,
- a printer device, called PRINTER,
- a paper supply, called PAPER_SUPPLY.

In the context of the present section, the channels are not considered as processes – although they will turn out to be processes in a sense which will be worked out in Section 8.8.2. Figure 8.31 shows an overview in the form of an extended abstract hardware diagram, which was discussed in Section 8.6, and which is closely related to the "box diagrams" used in SPRINT [40]. It is also related to the so-called "SDL system diagrams" presented in [51]. Note the "line-printer queue" function lpq, which is an observer of SPOOLER. One can think of it as a physical display containing the number of unfinished print jobs.

We need a component DATA which describes the data to be manipulated by the spooler and the printer. A batch is a sequence of pages to be printed. Each page is a sequence of characters. Actually the internal structure of pages is not interesting. The sequence structure of a batch is relevant however, because the printer processes pages one at a time.

```
COMPONENT DATA SPECIFICATION
IMPORT
  CHAR,
  SEQ'[Char] RENAMING Seq TO Page END,
  SEQ'[Page] RENAMING Seq TO Batch END
END
```

We define the channels first. CHANNEL1 and CHANNEL2 queue data of sort Batch. CHANNEL3, CHANNEL4 and CHANNEL6 only need to convey confirmations or requests; they have been instantiated with a one-element sort Void. CHANNEL5 carries (amounts of) paper.

```
COMPONENT CHANNEL1 SPECIFICATION
EXPORT
 PROC lpr      : Batch ->,
      lpr_event : Batch ->
IMPORT
  DATA,
  CHANNEL'[Batch] RENAMING send TO lpr, receive TO lpr_event END
END

COMPONENT CHANNEL2 SPECIFICATION
EXPORT
 PROC spool    : Batch ->,
```

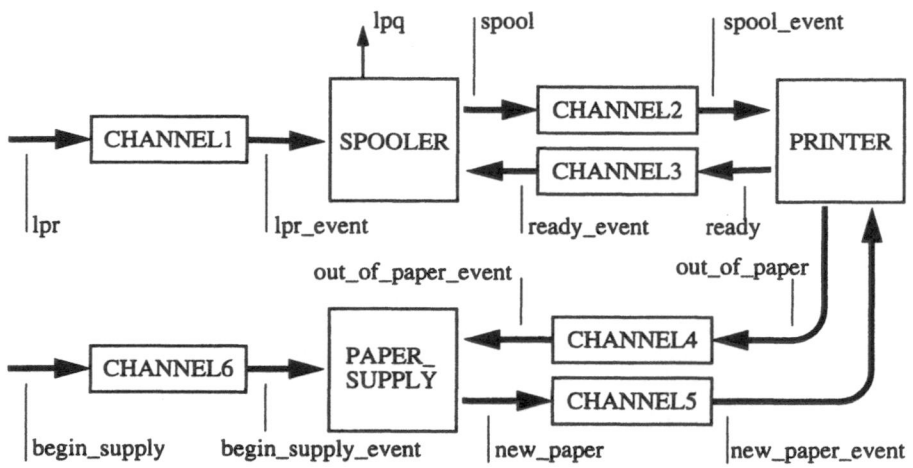

Figure 8.31: Printing system with queueing channels.

```
      spool_event : Batch ->
IMPORT
  DATA,
  CHANNEL'[Batch] RENAMING send TO spool, receive TO spool_event END
END

COMPONENT VOID SPECIFICATION
IMPORT
  ENUM1 RENAMING Enum1 TO Void, x0 TO void END
END

COMPONENT CHANNEL3 SPECIFICATION
EXPORT
 PROC ready       : Void ->,
      ready_event : Void ->
IMPORT
  VOID,
  CHANNEL'[Void] RENAMING send TO ready, receive TO ready_event END
END

COMPONENT CHANNEL4 SPECIFICATION
EXPORT
 PROC out_of_paper       : Void ->,
      out_of_paper_event : Void ->
IMPORT
  VOID,
  CHANNEL'[Void] RENAMING send TO out_of_paper,
                         receive TO out_of_paper_event
```

```
END               END

COMPONENT CHANNEL5 SPECIFICATION
EXPORT
 PROC new_paper       : Nat ->,
      new_paper_event : Nat ->
IMPORT
  NAT,
  CHANNEL'[Nat] RENAMING send TO new_paper,
                        receive TO new_paper_event
END               END

COMPONENT CHANNEL6 SPECIFICATION
EXPORT
 PROC begin_supply       : Void ->,
      begin_supply_event : Void ->
IMPORT
  VOID,
  CHANNEL'[Void] RENAMING send TO begin_supply,
                         receive TO begin_supply_event
END               END
```

The component SPOOLER is described below. Its diagram is given in Figure 8.32. The spooler process and the new printer process each only deal with one batch at a time; the queue of CHANNEL2 can be viewed as the "spool area" to store pending jobs. Also note that the Void values of CHANNEL3 are irrelevant; it is the success of the ready_event receive action which counts, not its data contents. The process can make a number of distinct transitions, which are described as the alternative clauses, separated by "|", in the body of spooler_step.

Note that each transition in Figure 8.32 is guarded by a receive action; it is customary in SDL [51] to adopt this restriction for all transitions, because it allows for the construction of particularly simple schedulers, which can be purely event-driven.

The original SDL has as a default rule that messages for which there is no input statement will be discarded; to escape from this default there is a construct called "save", preventing loss of messages. The example presented in the present section does not assume the default rule, and all messages not explicitly removed from their queue are saved.

The component STATE introduces two procedures named STATE and NEXT. They are useful for describing state tests and state transitions.

```
COMPONENT STATE[Item] SPECIFICATION
ABSTRACT
  ITEM
EXPORT
  FUNC state : -> Item
```

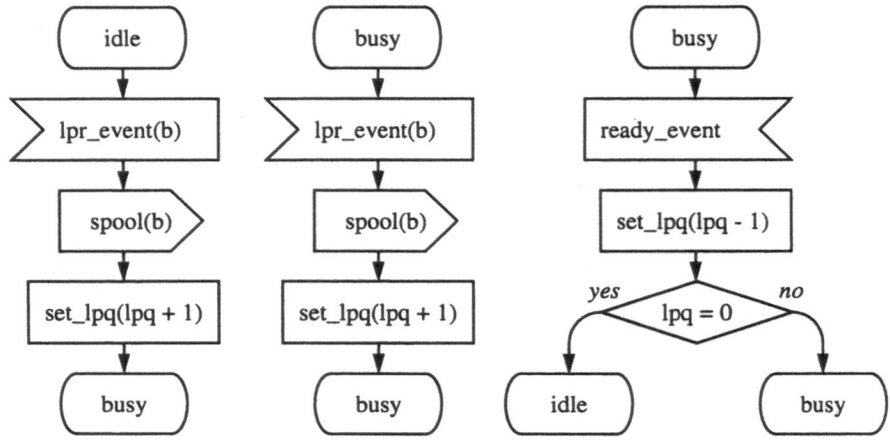

Figure 8.32: SDL-like diagram of SPOOLER.

```
    PROC STATE : Item ->,
         NEXT  : Item ->
CLASS
    FUNC state : -> Item PRE TRUE VAR

    PROC STATE : Item ->
    IN   s
    PRE  state = s
    SAT  SKIP
    POST TRUE

    PROC NEXT : Item ->
    IN   s
    PRE  TRUE
    SAT  MOD state
    POST state = s
END
```

In SPOOLER below, STATE will be instantiated as STATE[Enum2]. The expression
STATE(s) only succeeds if state = s. So STATE can be used to check for a
certain state and NEXT(s) makes the new state equal to s. We remark that
the brackets in STATE(s) can be omitted, which can be exploited to give the
COLD-1 text an SDL flavour at the syntactic level too.

```
    COMPONENT SPOOLER SPECIFICATION
    EXPORT
       FUNC lpq          : -> Nat
       PROC spooler_step : ->
    IMPORT
       NAT,
```

```
      DATA,
      CHANNEL1 EXPORTING lpr_event   END,
      CHANNEL2 EXPORTING spool       END,
      CHANNEL3 EXPORTING ready_event END,
      ENUM2    RENAMING  x0 TO idle, x1 TO busy END,
      STATE'[Enum2]
    CLASS
      FUNC lpq : -> Nat PRE TRUE VAR

      AXIOM INIT => state = idle AND lpq = 0

      PRED inv :
      DEF  state = idle <=> lpq = 0

      PROC set_lpq : Nat ->
      IN   n
      PRE  TRUE
      SAT  MOD lpq
      POST lpq = n

      PROC spooler_step : ->
      DEF  LET b : Batch,
               v : Void ;
           ( STATE idle ; lpr_event(b)
                        ; spool(b)
                        ; set_lpq(lpq + 1)
                        ; NEXT busy
           | STATE busy ; lpr_event(b)
                        ; spool(b)
                        ; set_lpq(lpq + 1)
                        ; NEXT busy
           | STATE busy ; ready_event(v)
                        ; set_lpq(lpq - 1)
                        ; ( lpq = 0 ? ; NEXT idle
                        |   lpq > 0 ? ; NEXT busy
           )              )

      THEOREM INIT => inv; inv => AFTER spooler_step THEN inv
    END
```

There is one main variable for each process, which is called state. In the state nodes of the diagrams we only mention the value of state (so instead of state = idle, we write idle). Other variables than state are not shown in the diagram, and for a complete understanding of the process behaviour one needs information about the other variables and also a specification of procedures such as set_lpq, or otherwise an implementation of procedures in terms of assignments.

The component **PRINTER** is described below. Its diagram is given in Figure 8.33. Note that the two transitions which start in state **printing** are guarded by assertions. This is allowed in SDL '88 as described in [51] too, except for the fact that in [51] the notation is $\langle$len(data) > 0$\rangle$ instead of $\boxed{\text{len(data) > 0 ?}}$. Also, in SDL '88 it is understood that there is a scheduling strategy where transitions which are guarded by assertions have a lower priority than transitions guarded by a receive action; in SDL terminology, the assertions are viewed as "continuous signals".

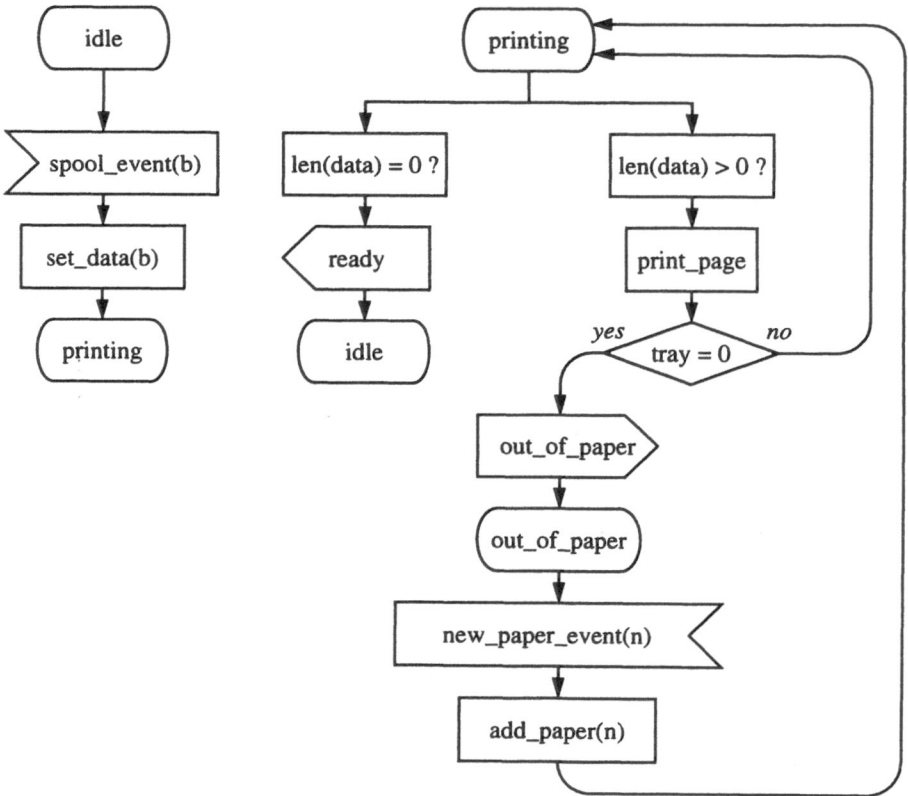

Figure 8.33: SDL-like diagram of **PRINTER**.

```
COMPONENT PRINTER SPECIFICATION
EXPORT
  PROC printer_step : ->
IMPORT
  NAT,
  VOID,
  DATA,
  ENUM3 RENAMING x0 TO idle, x1 TO printing, x2 TO out_of_paper
```

```
          END,
     STATE'[Enum3],
     CHANNEL2 EXPORTING spool_event     END,
     CHANNEL3 EXPORTING ready           END,
     CHANNEL4 EXPORTING out_of_paper    END,
     CHANNEL5 EXPORTING new_paper_event END
  CLASS
    FUNC tray  : -> Nat     PRE TRUE VAR
    FUNC data  : -> Batch  PRE TRUE VAR

    AXIOM INIT => state = idle AND tray = 100

    PRED inv :
    DEF  (state = idle OR state = printing) => tray > 0

    PROC set_data : Batch ->
    IN   b
    PRE  TRUE
    SAT  MOD data
    POST data = b

    PROC print_page : ->
    PRE  tray > 0 AND len(data) > 0
    SAT  MOD tray, data
    POST tray = tray' - 1;
         data = tl(data')

    PROC add_paper : Nat ->
    IN   n
    PRE  n > 0
    SAT  MOD tray
    POST tray = tray' + n

    PROC printer_step  : ->
    DEF  LET n : Nat,
             b : Batch;
         ( STATE idle          ; spool_event(b)
                                ; set_data(b)
                                ; NEXT printing
           | STATE printing     ; len(data) = 0 ?
                                ; ready(void)
                                ; NEXT idle
           | STATE printing     ; len(data) > 0 ?
                                ; print_page
                                ; ( tray = 0 ? ; out_of_paper(void)
                                            ; NEXT out_of_paper
                                    | tray > 0 ? ; NEXT printing
```

```
                                    )
        | STATE out_of_paper ; new_paper_event(n);
                              add_paper(n);
                              NEXT printing
      )


    THEOREM INIT => inv; inv => AFTER printer_step THEN inv
  END
```

The component PAPER_SUPPLY is described below. Its diagram is given in
Figure 8.34.

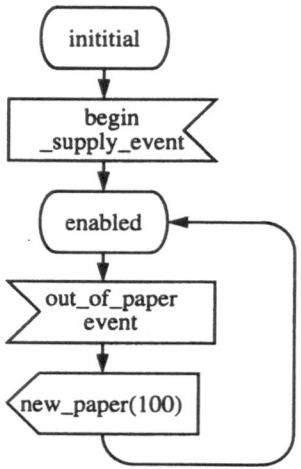

Figure 8.34: SDL-like diagram of PAPER_SUPPLY.

```
COMPONENT PAPER_SUPPLY SPECIFICATION
EXPORT
  PROC paper_supply_step  : ->
IMPORT
  NAT,
  VOID,
  ENUM2 RENAMING x0 TO initial, x1 TO enabled END,
  STATE'[Enum2],
  CHANNEL4 EXPORTING out_of_paper_event       END,
  CHANNEL5 EXPORTING new_paper                 END,
  CHANNEL6 EXPORTING begin_supply_event        END
CLASS
  AXIOM INIT => state = initial

  PROC paper_supply_step  : ->
  DEF  LET v : Void;
       ( STATE initial ; begin_supply_event(v)
```

```
                         ; NEXT enabled
        | STATE enabled ; out_of_paper_event(v)
                         ; new_paper(100)
                         ; NEXT enabled
        )
  END
```

It is an interesting exercise to simulate the system by playing a "token game" (this may be expensive, when using "dubbeltjes" as tokens, because the channels queue them).

The official SDL notation has much more features than shown here. For an overview we refer to [51] or [52]. Although SDL is based on queue-based communication, its queues are actually organized somewhat differently than shown in the example of the printing system: usually an SDL process has *one input queue* for each process; of course this could be modelled in COLD-1 too, using the same CHANNEL (but instantiated with a disjoint-union data type).

There is a formal standard, which is subject to regular revisions. Important versions are SDL '80 (1980) and SDL '88 (1988) [48]. A recent development of the language is known as object-oriented SDL [53]. Most European large telecommunication companies have their own tool development for SDL, see for example [54] and also specialised tool vendors offer graphical editors, simulators, and other tools.

8.8.2   SDL-like Diagrams for Synchronous Communication

In Figure 8.35 the nodes to represent a state, an action, a decision, a send action and a receive action for synchronous communication are given.

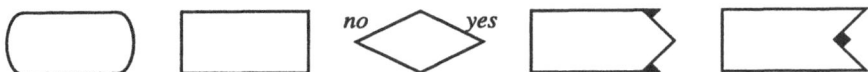

Figure 8.35: Synchronous SDL (state, action, decision, send, receive).

We assume a finite collection of processes $P_1, \ldots P_n$, each process with its own variables, which are strictly local. Furthermore each process has a number of procedures, which can be classified into procedures doing communication (send/receive) actions and procedures doing internal actions. Some of the procedures are common to two or more processes; notably the communication actions are shared. For example P_1 can offer a procedure p which succeeds always when called and which can be called by P_2 to pass an event to P_1 and/or to provide P_1 with certain data. Execution of this p is viewed as a "send" action of P_2, and at the same time as a "receive" action of P_1.

But for certain shared procedures the interpretation as a "send" action or a "receive" action is the other way around. For example P_1 can offer a procedure q whose success or failure depends on the internal state of P_1, and which returns a value, again depending on the internal state of P_1. Execution of this q is viewed as a "send" action of P_1, and at the same time as a "receive" action of P_2 – even when P_2 must poll or ask P_1.

In the example, there are three processes:

- a command module,
- a printer,
- a paper-supply.

Figure 8.36 shows an overview in the form of an extended abstract hardware diagram.

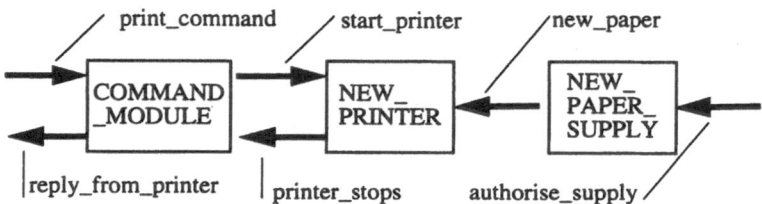

Figure 8.36: Three communicating processes.

The component `COMMAND_MODULE` is described below. Its diagram is given in Figure 8.37. The diagram is organized into two subdiagrams, but one could equally well attach the right-hand side subdiagram below the left-hand side subdiagram, unifying the two occurrences of the node labelled busy.

The main difference between the printing system presented here, and the printing system presented in Section 8.8.1 is that here print jobs are not queued. When the printer is printing, the `start_printer` action is blocked, and the command module process is unable to send a job to the printer.

Another difference is that we have added a decision to the command-module process, which deals with empty print jobs without sending them to the printer process. This feature is independent of the communication mechanism used; if desired, it could be added in Section 8.8.1.

```
COMPONENT COMMAND_MODULE SPECIFICATION
EXPORT
   PROC print_command       : Batch ->,
        reply_from_printer   :       ->,
        start_printer        : Batch ->,
        printer_stops        :       ->,
        command_module_step  :       ->
IMPORT
   NAT,
   DATA,
   ENUM4 RENAMING x0 TO idle,
```

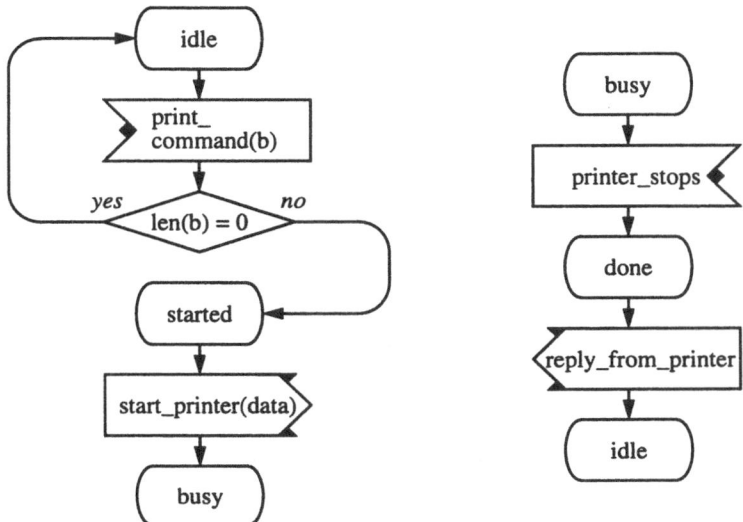

Figure 8.37: SDL-like diagram of COMMAND_MODULE.

```
                   x1 TO started,
                   x2 TO busy,
                   x3 TO done
         END,
   STATE'[Enum4]
CLASS
   FUNC data : -> Batch PRE TRUE VAR

   AXIOM INIT => state = idle

   PRED inv :
   DEF   state = started => len(data) > 0

   PROC print_command : Batch   ->
   IN    b
   PRE   state = idle
   SAT   NEXT($); MOD data
   POST len(b) = 0 => state = idle      AND data = empty;
        len(b) > 0 => state = started AND data = b

   PROC reply_from_printer  : ->
   PRE   state = done
   SAT   NEXT($)
   POST state = idle

   PROC command_module_step : ->
```

```
DEF  ( STATE started ; start_printer(data) ; NEXT busy
     | STATE busy    ; printer_stops       ; NEXT done
     )

THEOREM INIT => inv;
        inv => AFTER ( print_command($)
                     | reply_from_printer
                     | command_module_step
                     ) THEN inv

PROC start_printer : Batch -> FREE
PROC printer_stops : ->      FREE
END
```

The export list of COMMAND_MODULE includes all communication actions. If
we view COMMAND_MODULE as a process, then print_command is a receive action of this process; reply_from_printer is a send action. For this process,
start_printer and printer_stops are a send action and a receive action
respectively, which are defined elsewhere, viz. in the printer component below. The procedure command_module_step can be viewed as the autonomous
step, or the internal scheduler of COMMAND_MODULE. Of course the latter step
need not succeed always. It requires special operating system techniques to
avoid wasting processor time and to find the right moments for executing
command_module_step – but such techniques are outside the scope of the
present book. In command_module_step there are no clauses for STATE idle
and for STATE done; this is related to the fact that the transitions to leave
these states are triggered by the communication actions print_command and
reply_from_printer.

The invariance theorem only holds under the assumption that the send
and receiver procedures which are defined elsewhere have no access to the
local variables state and data (except via the procedures). If start_printer
and printer_stops are the procedures exported by the printer below, there
is no problem.

To avoid confusion with the asynchronous version of the printer process,
we prefix certain component names by "NEW_", writing NEW_PRINTER and similarly NEW_PAPER_SUPPLY. The component NEW_PRINTER is described below. Its
diagram is given in Figure 8.38.

```
COMPONENT NEW_PRINTER SPECIFICATION
EXPORT
  PROC start_printer : Batch ->,
       printer_stops :       ->,
       new_paper     : Nat   ->,
       printer_step  :       ->
IMPORT
  NAT,
  DATA,
```

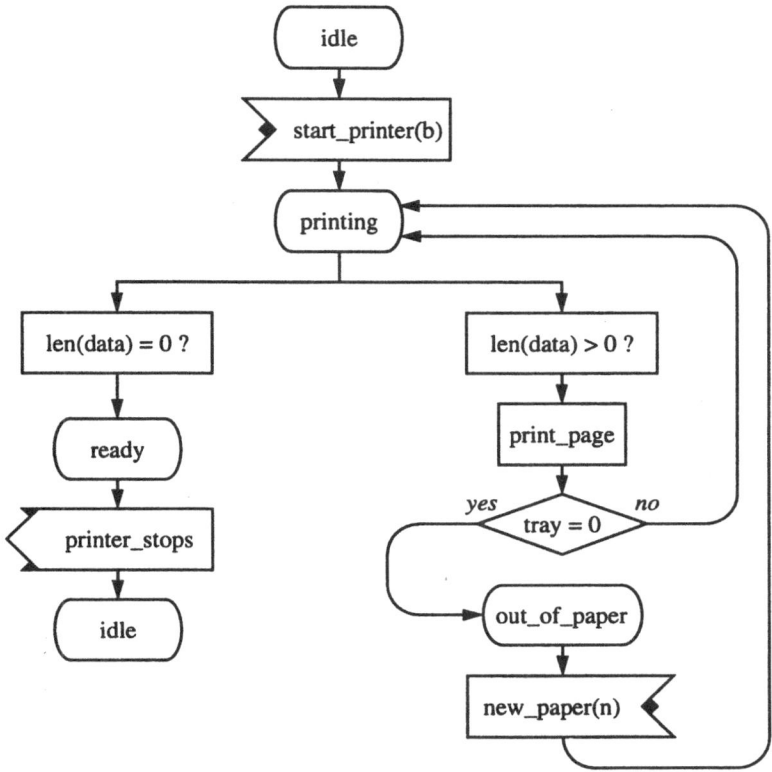

Figure 8.38: SDL-like diagram of NEW_PRINTER.

```
   ENUM4 RENAMING x0 TO idle,
                  x1 TO printing,
                  x2 TO out_of_paper,
                  x3 TO ready
         END,
   STATE'[Enum4]
CLASS
  FUNC tray  : -> Nat    PRE TRUE VAR
  FUNC data  : -> Batch  PRE TRUE VAR

  AXIOM INIT => state = idle AND tray = 100

  PRED inv :
  DEF  state /= out_of_paper => tray > 0

  PROC start_printer : Batch ->
  IN   b
  PRE  state = idle
```

```
      SAT   NEXT(printing);
            MOD data
      POST data = b

      PROC print_page : ->
      PRE   state = printing AND len(data) > 0
      SAT   MOD tray, data
      POST tray = tray' - 1;
            data = tl(data')

      PROC new_paper : Nat ->
      IN    n
      PRE   state = out_of_paper AND n > 0
      SAT   NEXT(printing);
            MOD tray
      POST tray = tray' + n

      PROC printer_stops : ->
      PRE   state = ready
      SAT   NEXT(idle)
      POST TRUE

      PROC printer_step : ->
      DEF   ( STATE printing ; len(data) > 0 ?
                            ; print_page
                            ; ( tray = 0 ? ; NEXT out_of_paper
                              | tray > 0 ? ; NEXT printing
                              )
            | STATE printing ; len(data) = 0 ? ; NEXT ready
            )

      THEOREM INIT => inv;
              inv => AFTER ( start_printer($)
                          | printer_stops
                          | new_paper($)
                          | printer_step
                          ) THEN inv
    END
```

In the above printer component, the variable tray models the number of blank pages in the printer tray. Clearly, if tray = 0, printing must be suspended; therefore the printer maintains the invariant that tray > 0, except of course in the state out_of_paper. In the latter state, there is only one way out: receiving new paper.

The component NEW_PAPER_SUPPLY is described below. Its diagram is given in Figure 8.39. We must assume that there is some "paper supply master" which calls the procedure begin_supply to enable the paper supply process.

The "paper supply master" could be another process, but is not described
here.

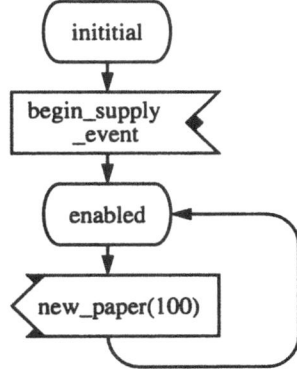

Figure 8.39: SDL-like diagram of NEW_PAPER_SUPPLY.

```
COMPONENT NEW_PAPER_SUPPLY SPECIFICATION
EXPORT
  PROC begin_supply      :     ->,
       paper_supply_step :     ->,
       new_paper         : Nat ->
IMPORT
  NAT,
  ENUM2 RENAMING x0 TO initial, x1 TO enabled END
CLASS
  FUNC state : -> Enum2  PRE TRUE VAR

  AXIOM INIT => state = initial

  PROC begin_supply : ->
  PRE  state = initial
  SAT  MOD state
  POST state = enabled

  PROC paper_supply_step : ->
  DEF  state = enabled ? ; new_paper(100)

  PROC new_paper : Nat -> FREE
END
```

Again it is an interesting exercise to simulate the system by playing a "token
game" (use three "dubbeltjes", one for each process). Whenever a shared
action is executed, the tokens in the corresponding state nodes most be moved
simultaneously. For example, if the command module is in state started
and the printer is in state idle, the shared action start_printer(data) can

occur. In the resulting system state we find that the command module is in state busy and the printer is in state printing.

It is interesting to note how the concepts of SDL deal with the problem of state transition diagrams becoming too large and too complex. When using SDL, or SDL-like notations, there are three mechanisms at work which help:

- decomposition into processes; although the composition of two processes with m and n states each, can have up to $m \times n$ states, the diagrams contain only $m + n$ states;
- focus of the state transition diagram on one main variable only; other variables (counters, data stores etc.) are added to the state space of the diagrams;
- implicit queueing; each of the channels has a large state space without contributing to the complexity of the diagram (it contributes to the semantic complexity, which counts when simulating however).

The first two mechanisms are at work when adopting either the synchronous or the asynchronous form of the SDL-like notatation. The third mechanism only applies to the asynchronous form presented in the previous section.

8.9   Sequence Charts: General

A sequence chart, or interaction diagram is a system of vertical lines and arrows between them. The vertical lines are labelled with the names of processes, and the arrows are labelled with the names of communication actions. The arrows are horizontal, or have a downward inclination. Each process line models a time axis, which runs from top to bottom. Along each axis, the collection of arrows must be linearly ordered, so for example ⌐⌐⌐ is in order, but ⊢⊬⊣ is not. The communication actions can be either synchronization actions or send/receive action pairs.

The diagrams give a compact and highly intuitive view of possible interaction scenarios or use-cases of a multi-process system. Because the diagrams show nothing about the internals of the processes, they are useful for purposes of requirements engineering and testing.

There are two main types of sequence charts:

- Asynchronous sequence charts; the most important variation is called MSCs (Message Sequence Charts), and they are being standardised by the ITU-T (the former CCITT), initiated by Rudolph et.al. [9], [10], [11], [12].
- Synchronous sequence charts, or interworking diagrams, as studied by Mauw et al. in [55].

Section 8.10 is devoted to asynchronous sequence charts and Section 8.11 to synchronous sequence charts.

8.10 Asynchronous Sequence Charts

An asynchronous sequence chart is a sequence chart where the arrows need not be strictly horizontal, but can have a downward inclination. It can be used to describe *asynchronous* communication behaviour. The begin point of an arrow is interpreted as a send action and the end point (the arrowhead) is interpreted as the corresponding receive action. The combined occurrence of a send action followed by the corresponding receive action is called a "message".

The diagrams essentially describe partial orders. In particular, we consider two specific asynchronous sequence charts equivalent if the same processes and the same send and receive actions are shown and if furthermore the order of these actions for each process is the same in both diagrams. So the first two diagrams of Figure 8.40 are equivalent, because both diagrams only express the following ordering requirements: for P_1 that $\text{send}(c_1) < \text{receive}(c_4)$, for P_2 that $\text{receive}(c_1) < \text{receive}(c_3) < \text{send}(c_4)$, and for P_3 that $\text{receive}(c_2) < \text{send}(c_3)$, where "$<$" denotes "occurs before". Furthermore there is of course the implicit constraint that $\text{send}(c_i) < \text{receive}(c_i)$ for all messages c_i. The third and the fourth diagram of Figure 8.40 are equivalent because both diagrams express: for P_1 that $\text{send}(c_1) < \text{receive}(c_3)$, for P_2 that $\text{receive}(c_1) < \text{send}(c_2)$, and for P_3 that $\text{send}(c_3) < \text{receive}(c_2)$. Figure 8.41 shows several diagrams which can not be identified.

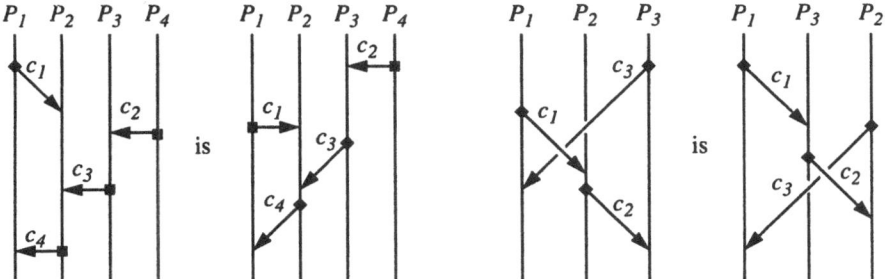

Figure 8.40: Equivalence of asynchronous sequence charts.

To discuss the relation between COLD-1 and the diagrams we assume a collection of processes, each with its local state space and a main step (like `spooler_step`, `printer_step`, etc. of Section 8.8.1). We also assume a collection of communication channels, which are queues of the "first-in first-out" type, like `CHANNEL` of Section 8.8.1. The processes can invoke the send and receive procedures of the channels. Each channel is shared between two processes: its sender and its receiver.

Suppose that we have a COLD-1 specification of the processes. A model of this specification can be executed, or simulated. An execution is a sequence of states and procedure calls, which begins in the initial state, and such that each step from one state to the next state is the effect of one of the procedures of

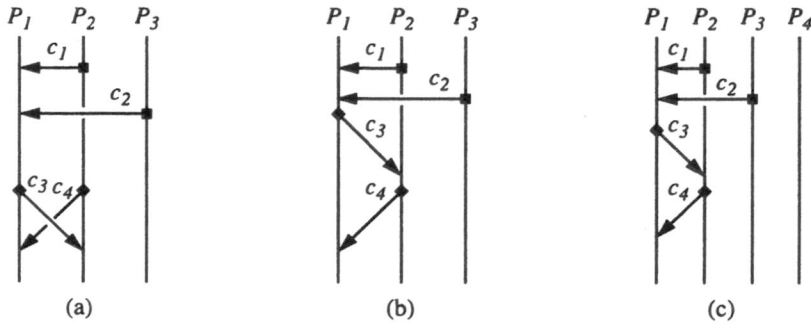

Figure 8.41: Three mutually distinct asynchronous sequence charts.

the COLD-1 specification. There may be many ways to execute a model of a given specification, and each execution gives rise to an asynchronous sequence chart. The diagram shows the send actions and the receive actions that play a rôle in the execution, but does not show the other actions, like assignments to internal variables. Moreover, the diagram expresses the partial ordering constraints which are satisfied by the execution. Each send action is shown as the begin point of an arrow labelled with the name and the actual parameters of the send procedure. Each receive action is shown as an arrowhead. There must be a one-one correspondence between matching send/receive action pairs in the execution, and arrows in the diagram.

By way of example, we give two asynchronous sequence charts of the processes described in Section 8.8.1 (asynchronous SDL). The processes are the spooler, the printer, and the paper supply, to which we added an environment process "env". The scheduling strategy is to choose from four main step procedures repeatedly, namely: `spooler_step`, `printer_step`, `paper_supply_step`, and `env_step`, where the latter is given as:

```
PROC env_step : ->
DEF  ( begin_supply
     | lpr($)
     )
```

We assume that "empty" is a batch with no pages, that "b1" is a batch with one page, "b2" with two pages and so on. Figures 8.42 and 8.43 each give one asynchronous sequence chart.

We must add one remark about the concrete syntax used for the messages in this section. The begin point of each arrow (representing the send action) is shown as a black square. This syntax has been used here to distinguish the asynchronous sequence charts of this section clearly from the diagrams of Section 8.11. The ITU-T MSCs formally do not have the black squares.

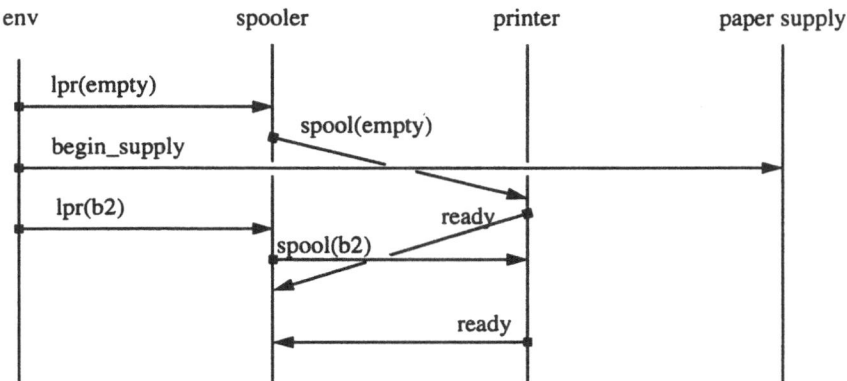

Figure 8.42: Sequence chart of asynchronous printing system.

8.11   Synchronous Sequence Charts

A synchronous sequence chart is a sequence chart where the arrows are strictly horizontal. The arrows are interpreted as *synchronous* communication actions.

Like asynchronous sequence charts, the diagrams represent partial orders. In particular, we consider two specific synchronous sequence charts equivalent if the same processes and the same communication actions are shown and if furthermore the order of these actions for each process is the same in both diagrams. So the first two diagrams of Figure 8.44 are equivalent, because both diagrams only express the following ordering requirements: for P_1 that $c_1 < c_4$, for P_2 that $c_1 < c_3 < c_4$, and for P_3 that $c_2 < c_3$. Here we use "<" to denote "occurs before". Also, the structure of the diagrams with respect to the left-right ordering of the processes is considered irrelevant. Therefore the third and the fourth diagram of Figure 8.44 are equivalent too.

Figure 8.45 shows several diagrams which can not be identified. Note that in Figure 8.45 (a) there are communication actions c_1 and c_2, whereas in (b) we find that c_1 occurs twice. In (c) there are four processes instead of three.

To discuss the relation between COLD-1 and the diagrams we assume a collection of processes, each with its local state space and a P_step. Suppose that we have a COLD-1 description of all communication procedures and all internal procedures of the given collection of processes. We must assume that the procedures are classified into procedures doing *communication* actions and procedures doing *internal* actions. A communication procedure can be shared between two processes: its sender and its receiver. The synchronous sequence chart shows the communication actions that play a rôle in an execution, but does not show the other actions, like assignments to internal variables. Each communication action is shown as a labelled arrow from the line of the sender of this procedure to the line of its receiver. And of course, the diagram expresses the partial ordering constraints which are satisfied by the execution.

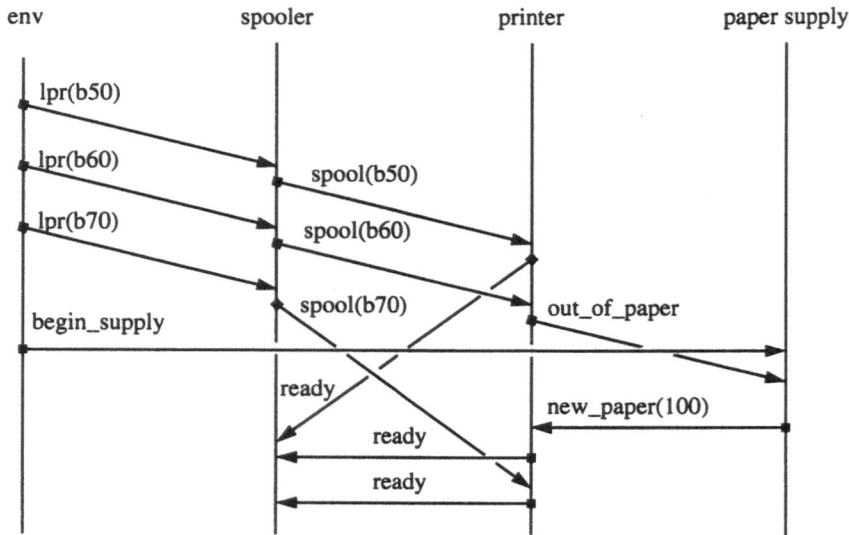

Figure 8.43: Sequence chart of asynchronous printing system.

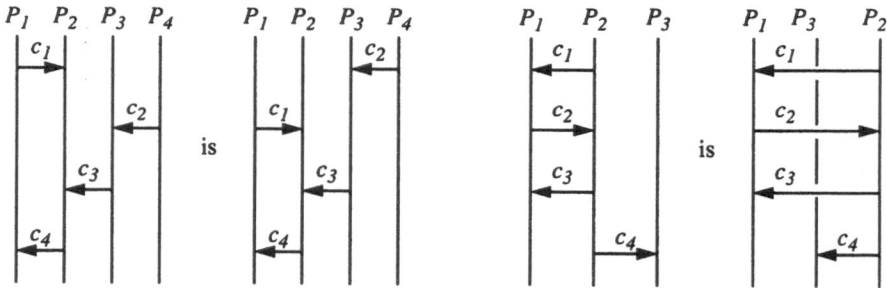

Figure 8.44: Equivalence of synchronous sequence charts.

By way of example we give two synchronous sequence charts of the processes described in Section 8.8.2 (synchronous SDL). The processes are the command module (COMMAND_MODULE), the printer (NEW_PRINTER), and the paper supply (NEW_PAPER_SUPPLY), to which we added an environment process "env". We adopt a classification of the procedures as given in Figure 8.46.

The scheduling strategy is to choose from four "step" procedures repeatedly, namely: command_module_step, printer_step, paper_supply_step, and env_step, where the latter is given as:

```
PROC env_step : ->
DEF  ( begin_supply
     | print_command($)
     )
```

The first diagram is given in Figure 8.47. Again, we assume that "empty"

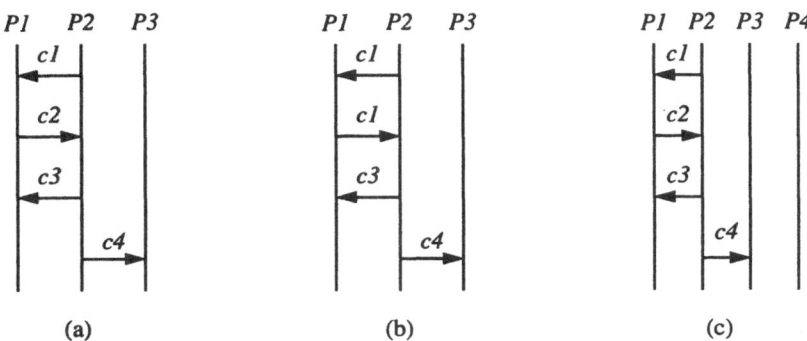

Figure 8.45: Three mutually distinct synchronous sequence charts.

action	sender	receiver	internal of
print_command	env	cm	
reply_from_printer	cm	env	
start_printer	cm	printer	
printer_stops	printer	cm	
NEXT			cm
new_paper	paper supply	printer	
NEXT			printer
print_page			printer
begin_supply	env	paper supply	
new_paper	paper supply	printer	

Figure 8.46: Classification of procedures.

is a batch with no pages, that "b1" is a batch with one page, "b2" with two pages and so on. To see that Figure 8.47 can be drawn for the COLD-1 specification of Section 8.8.2, one must find a complete action sequence in which the communication actions of the diagram occur, mixed with other actions:

```
print_command(empty)
begin_supply
print_command(b2)
start_printer(b2)
NEXT(busy)                                          (internal action)
print_page                                          (internal action)
NEXT(printing)                                       (internal action)
print_page                                          (internal action)
NEXT(printing)                                       (internal action)
NEXT(ready)                                          (internal action)
printer_stops
NEXT(done)                                           (internal action)
```

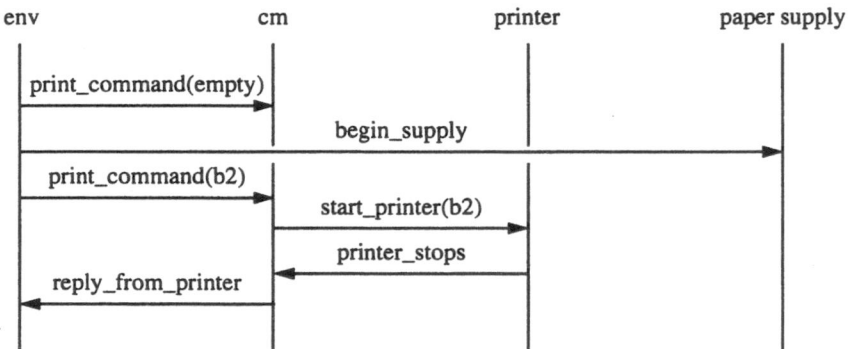

Figure 8.47: Sequence chart of synchronous printing system.

`reply_from_printer`

Here the internal actions NEXT(busy) and NEXT(done) are done by the command module, whereas print_page, NEXT(printing) and NEXT(ready) are done by the printer.

Another diagram given in Figure 8.48. It shows a possible sequence of synchronization actions that occur when processing "b250", which is batch of 250 pages.

8.12   Concluding Remarks

We can classify the picture kinds addressed in the present chapter according to the nature of their interpretation. This is done in Figure 8.49, which is based on the classification scheme discussed in Section 7.1.

We can mention a number of other picture kinds, which are not worked out in detail. They are useful, and can be related to COLD-1 too, but their scope is much wider than software design. *Images* are two-dimensional representations of a state of affairs in the three-dimensional space. *Plot diagrams* (bar charts, pie charts, continuous plots) represent functions of one argument. *Matrix-like diagrams* (function tables, transition tables) represent functions of two arguments. Finally we mention the *commuting diagrams*: systems of objects and morphisms (structure preserving mappings); the objects are drawn as points, bullets or mathematical symbols whereas the morphisms are drawn as arrows from one object to another. They arise often in connection with the notion of abstraction functions.

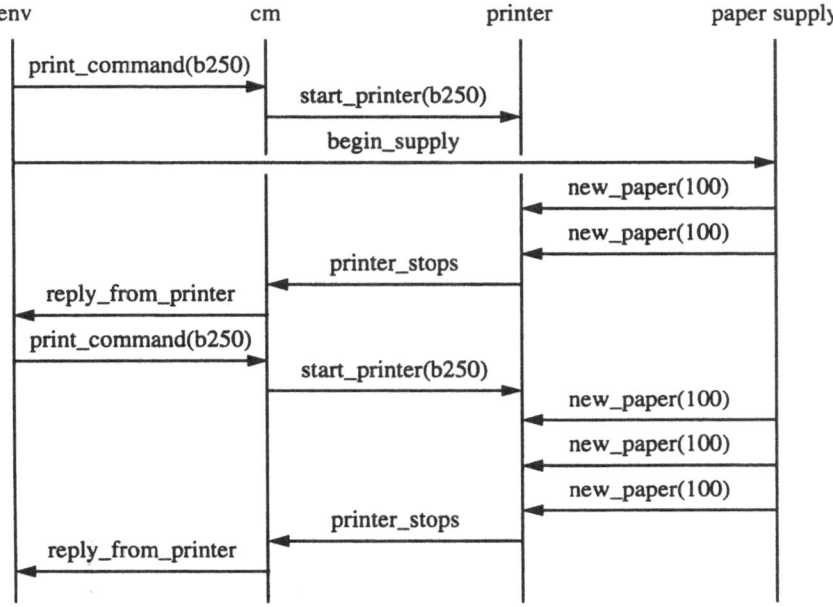

Figure 8.48: Sequence chart of synchronous printing system.

picture kind	form	interpretation
restricted data flow diagram	network	behaviour (static)
data flow diagram with stores	network	structure (1)
flow chart	network	behaviour (dynamic)
abstract hardware diagram	network	structure (2)
state-based abstract hardware diagram	network	structure (2)
Petri net	network	behaviour (dynamic)
SDL-like diagram	network	behaviour (dynamic)
sequence chart	special	behaviour (dynamic)

Figure 8.49: Picture kinds presented in this chapter.

Chapter 9

Advanced Topics

"But everybody needs a little proof," said Owen Meany. (John Irving)

9.1 Introduction and Motivation

In COLD-1, property-oriented, algebraic specification can be combined with model-oriented, state-based specification. Many existing styles of specification are supported: specification in equational style, specification in pre- and post-condition style, inductive definitions, algorithmic definitions in functional as well as imperative style, etc. Furthermore, there are facilities for modular structuring of specifications. These virtues of the language do not guarantee good specifications and designs. This chapter treats some principles of specification and design whose usefulness in practice has been established. Guidelines and techniques concerning these principles are included as well. The topics concerned are primarily of a stylistic nature. Some topics concerning established scientific results are treated as well.

The principles, guidelines and techniques concerning modular structuring are related to the facilities for modular structuring provided by COLD-1. These facilities are first reviewed and some attention is paid to setting up modules about basic state-based units of the system to be specified and modules about data types relevant to the application domain concerned. The issue of state space sharing between modules will also be treated. Some further advanced topics – mirroring, object-orientedness, conservativity, visibility consistency, black box correctness, invariants and memoization – are treated later on.

9.2 Review of Modular Structuring

Specification languages have been developed, and are being developed, which provide facilities for the modular structuring of specifications. Supporting modularity is obviously considered important. The following goals of the modular structuring of a formal specification are generally recognized (see e.g. [56]):

1. to enhance the comprehensibility of the specification;

2. to make reasoning about the specification easier;
3. to improve the adaptability of the specification;
4. to make reuse of the specification, in part, possible.

These goals are directly connected with reliability, extendibility and reusability. These quality factors of software products reflect main issues in software development practice at present: software products often do not do what they should do, they are too hard to modify and their construction does not rely enough on efforts made before.

As the size or complexity of the system being specified increases, it becomes more difficult to achieve the above-mentioned goals without facilities for the modular structuring of the specification in the language concerned. Modular structuring facilities especially supply a need in case of large and complex systems.

The goals of modular structuring lead to the use of the following main criteria for the judgement of specifications with respect to their modular structure:

1. the intuitive clarity of the modular structure;
2. the simplicity of the separate modules;
3. the ability to reason about the separate modules in isolation;
4. the suitability of the separate modules for reuse.

Criterion 1 stems in particular from goal 1, criterion 2 from goals 1 and 3, criterion 3 not only from goal 2 but also from goals 3 and 4, and criterion 4 directly from goal 4. Consequently, the criteria are not independent from each other. For example, consider a module about which can be reasoned in isolation. Such a module is necessarily a self-contained unit, which is a prerequisite for reusability.

The modular structuring facilities of COLD-1 make it easy to meet the above-mentioned criteria. Their main virtue is separation of concerns. Modules are possibly parametrized units containing definitions, axioms and theorems, importing other modules and hiding names of sorts and operations intended to remain local. Non-parametrized modules can be explained in terms of

1. *visible names*: a collection of (complete) names for sorts and operations which are made available;
2. *formulae:* a collection of formulae characterizing these sorts and operations.

Names other than visible names may occur in the collection of formulae as well. Such names are called hidden names.

In component definitions modules are given a name. Non-parametrized modules are of the following general form:

EXPORT S

```
IMPORT C₁ , ... ,Cₘ
CLASS D₁ ... Dₙ
END
```

The IMPORT section combines the modules referred to by $C_1, \ldots, C_m$ and the CLASS section extends the combination with the definitions and axioms $D_1, \ldots, D_n$. The EXPORT section restricts the visible names to the names in the signature S – all names in S should come from the visible names of the modules referred to by $C_1, \ldots, C_m$ or the names introduced by the definitions and axioms $D_1, \ldots, D_n$. The set of formulae of the module concerned are combined accordingly.

Consider for example the component BYTE_ of which a complete specification is given in Section 5.6.[1] The CLASS section of the component BYTE_ extends the component NAT by definitions and axioms about the sort Byte and the functions byte and nat. This is accomplished by using the following IMPORT section:

```
IMPORT
    NAT
```

The intended restriction of the visible names is accomplished by the following EXPORT section:

```
EXPORT
    SORT Byte
    FUNC byte : Nat  -> Byte,
         nat  : Byte -> Nat
```

As explained before, e.g. in Section 5.4, a given signature is automatically complemented by the unmentioned sort names appearing in domain and range types. This means that the set of visible names of BYTE_ consists of SORT Nat, which belongs to the visible names of NAT, and all names introduced in BYTE_: SORT Byte, FUNC byte : Nat -> Byte and FUNC nat : Byte -> Nat. The set of formulae of BYTE_ is the set of formulae of NAT extended with the formulae corresponding to the definitions and axioms in BYTE_ – i.e. the formulae which characterize Byte, byte and nat. So the set of formulae of BYTE_ includes the set of formulae of NAT, although none of the names of the arithmetic functions made available by NAT is visible. Some of these hidden names are needed to characterize the sort Nat introduced in NAT, some of them are needed to characterize the functions byte and nat introduced in BYTE_ and others are not needed at all.

In case of parametrized modules, the EXPORT section must be preceded by an ABSTRACT section of the form:

```
ABSTRACT B₁ , ... ,Bₗ
```

---

[1] The specification of BYTE, given in Section 8.5, differs slightly from the specification of BYTE_, given in Section 5.6.

All modules referred to in the ABSTRACT section and the IMPORT section are combined in this case. Furthermore, the combination of $B_1, \ldots, B_l$ restricts the actual parameters: the combination of the components from which the actual parameters come, must have at least the visible names and properties of the combination of $B_1, \ldots, B_l$.

The non-parametrized component references in the IMPORT and ABSTRACT sections of component definitions are of the following general form:

```
C EXPORTING S
  RENAMING ρ
  QUALIFYING a
  END
```

The EXPORTING section restricts the visible names of the module C as above and the RENAMING section changes the names according to the renaming ρ in both the restricted collection of visible names and the collection of formulae. As explained in Section 4.3, the QUALIFYING section provides yet another way of renaming. The EXPORTING section is meant for *selective import*, which is closely related to the principle of weak coupling being explained in Section 9.5.

For example, in a component where Boolean values are used to model bits, one could have the following component reference:

```
BOOL
  EXPORTING
    SORT Bool
    FUNC false :        -> Bool,
         true  :        -> Bool,
         not   : Bool -> Bool
  RENAMING
    SORT Bool  TO Bit
    FUNC false TO 0,
         true  TO 1,
         not   TO invert
  END
```

The EXPORTING section restricts the visible names of BOOL to SORT Bool, FUNC false : -> Bool, FUNC true : -> Bool, FUNC not : Bool -> Bool. These names are changed to SORT Bit, FUNC 0 : -> Bit, FUNC 1 : -> Bit, FUNC invert : Bit -> Bit by the RENAMING section. The names in the formulae of BOOL are changed accordingly.

In the case that name clashes occur by importing modules, the union of the formulae concerned may lead to undesirable changes in the properties represented by the formulae. Therefore, a restriction applies to visible names. Visible names are allowed to clash, provided that the name can always be traced back to at most one definition that is not a forward declaration. Name clashes of hidden names can be regarded as being avoided by automatic renamings, in case the name can be traced back to more than one definition that is not a forward declaration. Otherwise they are not avoided.

In the example above, `Bit` becomes just an alias for `Bool`. Either is traced back to the definition of `Bool` in the component BOOL. By applying the copy operator " ' " to BOOL one accomplishes that `Bit` gets its own definition (and 0, 1 and `invert` as well). This means that if `Bit` is renamed to `Bool` again by accident, a clash with `Bool` from BOOL is considered to be an erroneous situation.

The copy operator may be added in any component reference. Actual parameters must be added in case of parameterized modules to mark the intended instantiation. The following is a reference to a particular instantiation of the component TUP2:

```
TUP2'[Byte] RENAMING Tup2 TO MachineWord END
```

9.3   How to Set up Basic Components

A basic component is about a (static) data type relevant to the application domain concerned or about a basic state-based unit of the system. For example, in a specification of a display-oriented text editor, a basic component that is about a data type relevant to the application domain could be a component about texts. Furthermore, basic components that are about a state-based unit of the text editor could be components corresponding to the keyboard from which the editing commands are given, the window on the screen in which part of the edited text is displayed, etc.

The following are some guidelines for setting up a basic component corresponding to a data type relevant to the application domain concerned:

1. choose the name for the sort of objects in the data type to be specified as well as the names, domain types and result types of the functions characterizing the data type;
2. choose a minimal set of functions sufficient for generating all objects in the data type, these functions are called the constructors of the data type;
3. formulate axioms uniquely characterizing the definedness predicate "!" and the equality predicate "=" for the sort;
4. add an inductively defined auxiliary predicate holding exactly for the objects in the data type that can be generated by the constructors of the data type;
5. add an axiom expressing that this predicate holds for all objects in the data type;
6. characterize the functions that are not constructors of the data type by means of inductive definitions or axioms.

For example, the following very simple component has been set up according to these guidelines:

```
COMPONENT BOOL SPECIFICATION
EXPORT
  SORT Bool                          % names of sort and
  FUNC false :              -> Bool, % functions              (1)
       true  :              -> Bool,
       not   : Bool         -> Bool,
       and   : Bool # Bool -> Bool
CLASS
  SORT Bool
  FUNC false : -> Bool               % the constructors of Bool (2)
  FUNC true  : -> Bool               %

  DECL b,c : Bool

  PRED is_gen : Bool                 % inductive definition of
  IND  is_gen(false);                % is-generated predicate   (4)
       is_gen(true)

  AXIOM false! AND true!;            % axiom characterizing
        NOT false = true;            % ``!'' , ``='' and        (3)
        is_gen(b)                    % ``Bool''                 (5)

  FUNC not : Bool -> Bool            % inductive definitions of
  IND  not(false) = true;            % negation and conjunction (6)
       not(true)  = false

  FUNC and : Bool # Bool -> Bool
  IND  and(false,false) = false;
       and(false,true)  = false;
       and(true,false)  = false;
       and(true,true)   = true

  THEOREM not(b)! AND and(b,c)!      % theorem about definedness
END
```

The components in the IGLOO library correspond to more complex data types. They have been set up according to these guidelines as well.

The use of a library of reusable components corresponding to data types can be increased by the technique of abstract representation. This is obtained by specializing step 2 and 6 as follows:

2'. choose one constructor, which is called the abstraction function, mapping the objects in a "concrete" data type – available from the library – to the "abstract" data type to be specified;

6'. define the remaining functions of the abstract data type in terms of functions of the concrete data type.

Logical variables could, for example, be represented by natural numbers as in the following component:

```
COMPONENT VARIABLE SPECIFICATION
EXPORT
  SORT Var
  FUNC '    : Nat -> Var,
  FUNC x0   :      -> Var,
  FUNC succ : Var -> Var
IMPORT
  NAT
CLASS
  SORT Var
  FUNC ' : Nat -> Var                  % abstraction function (2')

  DECL v   : Var,
       m,n : Nat

  PRED is_gen : Var
  IND  v = 'n => is_gen(v)

  AXIOM 'n!;
        'm = 'n => m = n;
        is_gen(v)

  FUNC x0 : -> Var                     % remaining functions  (6')
  IND  x0 = '0

  FUNC succ : Var -> Var
  IND  succ('n) = 'succ(n)

  THEOREM succ(v)!
END
```

The function nat is an auxiliary function used in the definition of succ for variables. Note that this function is not exported.

The following are some guidelines for setting up a basic component corresponding to a state-based unit of the system to be described:

1. choose the names for the sorts, functions and predicates corresponding to the state components for the system unit to be specified as well as the names for the procedures which capture the essential mechanisms of state change for the system unit, and – as a matter of course – also their domain types and result types in so far as appropriate;

2. import components corresponding to the data types relevant to the system unit;

3. choose the set of state components which may vary from state to state and assign modification rights to the procedures;

4. formulate axioms characterizing the states wherein the system unit may

be and its initial state (add, where appropriate, auxiliary dependent variable functions and predicates to simplify the formulation of these axioms);

5. characterize the procedures by adding pre- and post-conditions to the modification rights.

In the following example, a component corresponding to a line editor has been set up according to these guidelines. The line editor offers editing facilities that are available under almost any operating system while entering a command line.

```
COMPONENT LINE_EDITOR SPECIFICATION
EXPORT
    PROC erase_line    :        ->,    % names of procedures       (1)
         forward_char  :        ->,
         backward_char :        ->,
         insert_char   : Char ->,
         delete_char   :        ->
IMPORT                                 % import of
    NAT,                               % relevant data types        (2)
    CHAR,
    STRING
CLASS
    FUNC buffer : -> String  VAR       % the variable state components
    FUNC index  : -> Nat     VAR       % of the line editor          (3)

    DECL i : Nat
                                       % axiom characterizing
    AXIOM index <= len(buffer);        % possible states and
          INIT => buffer = empty       % the initial state           (4)

    PROC erase_line : ->               % pre- and post-condition style
    PRE  TRUE                          % definitions of procedures
    SAT  MOD buffer,index              % including modification rights
    POST buffer = empty;               %                             (5)
         index = 0

    PROC forward_char : ->
    PRE  TRUE
    SAT  MOD index
    POST index' = len(buffer') => index = index';
         index' < len(buffer') => index = index' + 1

    PROC backward_char : ->
    PRE  TRUE
    SAT  MOD index
    POST index' = 0 => index = index';
         index' > 0 => index = index' - 1
```

```
PROC insert_char : Char ->
IN   c
PRE  TRUE
SAT  MOD buffer,index
POST sel(buffer,index') = c;
     index = index' + 1;
     FORALL i
     ( i <  index' => sel(buffer,i) = sel(buffer',i)
     ; i >= index' => sel(buffer,i + 1) == sel(buffer',i)
     )

PROC delete_char : ->
PRE  TRUE
SAT  MOD buffer
POST index' = len(buffer') => buffer = buffer';
     index' < len(buffer') =>
      FORALL i
     ( i <  index' => sel(buffer,i) = sel(buffer',i)
     ; i >= index' => sel(buffer,i) == sel(buffer',i + 1)
     )

THEOREM INIT => buffer! AND index!
END
```

The variable state components buffer and index are hidden, as generally recommended for variable state components. Because they do not originate from imported components, buffer and index are not in common with any other component.

9.4   Sharing a State Space

The treatment of name clashes of hidden names in COLD-1 makes it possible for two or more modules to have hidden variable state components in common. This is considered important. Effective separation of concerns often motivates the hiding of variable state components from a module. In case a suitable modular structuring requires that the same variable state components are accessed from several modules, it is indispensable for the adequacy of a modularization mechanism that it permits two or more modules to have hidden variable state components in common. It is usually wanted if loosely connected operations interrogate and/or modify the same variable state component(s). This occurs in many large software systems.

For example, operations for querying and updating a database are not specified in the same module as operations for changing the schema of the database; only operations are exported from the modules concerned, but the operations of both kinds interrogate or modify the current database as well as the current database schema. Such a modular structure allows separate reasoning about data manipulation and data definition – which are not fully independent – to the highest possible degree.

The modules concerned are as follows. The module MANIPULATION contains the definitions of the data manipulation operations which can be performed by a database management system (DBMS). Only these operations are exported. The variable functions curr_dbschema (the current database schema) and curr_database (the current database), which were exported from the imported module DBMSSTATE, are hidden. Interrogating or modifying them for data manipulation can only be done by means of the operations made available.[2]

```
COMPONENT MANIPULATION SPECIFICATION
EXPORT
  PROC select  : Query                    -> Relation,
       insert  : RelNm # Query            ->,
       delete  : RelNm # Query            ->,
       replace : RelNm # Query # Query -> 
  SIG  QUERY_SYNTAX
IMPORT
  DATABASE,
  DBSCHEMA,
  QUERY,
  DBMSSTATE
CLASS
  % details omitted here
END
```

The module DEFINITION contains the definitions of the data definition operations which can be performed by a database management system. The variable functions curr_dbschema and curr_database are again hidden. Interrogating or modifying them for data definition can only be done by means of the operations made available.

```
COMPONENT DEFINITION SPECIFICATION
EXPORT
  PROC create    : RelNm # RelDescr ->,
       destroy   : RelNm            ->,
       constrain : InclDescr        -> 
  SIG  DESCR_SYNTAX
IMPORT
  DATABASE,
  DBSCHEMA,
  DESCR,
  DBMSSTATE
CLASS
```

---

[2]In Section 5.7, some components of a COLD-1 specification of a database management system are outlined. Amongst them are DATABASE and DBSCHEMA.

```
% details omitted here
END
```

The former modules combined cover all things relevant to an external DBMS interface. Therefore, the module DBMS contains no definitions. Instead the relevant definitions from other modules are combined and it is specified what, from the defined concepts, constitutes the external DBMS interface by making only the names of these concepts visible.

```
COMPONENT DBMS SPECIFICATION
EXPORT
  SIG MANIPULATION,
      DEFINITION
IMPORT
  MANIPULATION,
  DEFINITION
END
```

The import structure is shown in Figure 9.1. Notice that the EXPORT section

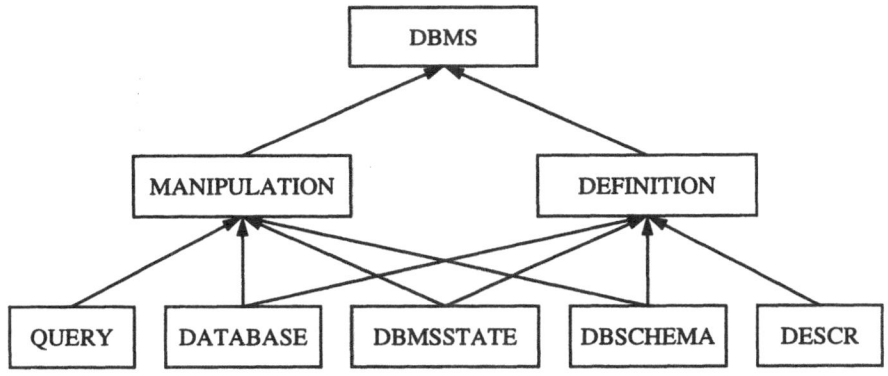

Figure 9.1: Import structure of database management system.

of the module DBMS could be omitted completely. The modules MANIPULATION and DEFINITION, which are combined in this module, have the two hidden variable state components curr_dbschema and curr_database in common. Although data manipulation operations and data definition operations are only loosely connected, operations of both kinds interrogate or modify both of these state components. If name clashes of hidden names would have been avoided by automatic renamings in all cases, the modules would have their own separate copies of these variable state components.

It is clear that in the above example, the emphasis is on the ability to reason about data manipulation and data definition in isolation. Other criteria are met as well, but the modules MANIPULATION and DEFINITION are only suitable for reuse if combined.

Although sharing a state space might be a useful technique for structuring the specification of a large and complex system, it should be used with care. It is important to keep constantly in mind the principles of modular structuring given in the next section.

9.5   Principles of Modular Structuring

For COLD-1, the following principles of modular structuring follow from the criteria for the judgement of specifications with respect to their modular structure given in Section 9.2:

1. *few connections*: the number of connections made between components by means of importing should remain as close to the minimum as possible;
2. *weak coupling*: if two components are coupled by importing, the number of sorts and operations from the imported component that are made available in the importing component should be kept as small as possible;
3. *encapsulation*: if some sorts and operations of a component are not relevant to the component's intended functionality, they should be hidden by means of exporting (recall that, despite its name, the purpose of exporting is hiding).

Figure 9.2 pictures the opposites of these three principles. The principles of

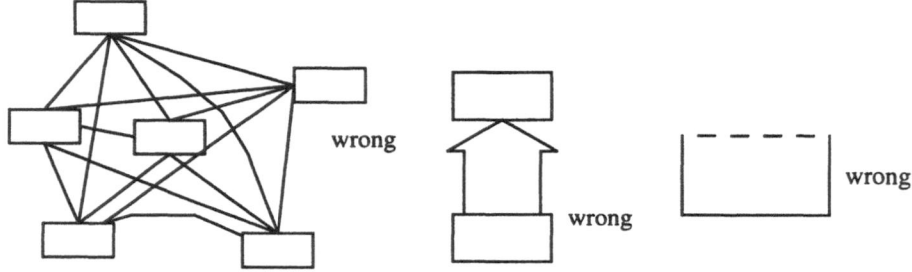

Figure 9.2: Examples of poor modular structuring.

few connections and weak coupling are connected with all criteria concerned; application of these principles is needed to meet any of the criteria. The main reasons behind the encapsulation principle are the criteria stemming from the goal of improving the adaptability.

Modular structuring of programs and software systems has long been regarded as being important for coping with their size and complexity. The goals of modular structuring in that context can roughly be viewed as more concrete counterparts of the goals in the current context. So it is not surprising that the principles given above have much in common with those described by pioneers in this area such as Parnas [57] and Yourdon [58].

The COLD-1 specification of a relational database management system considered in Sections 5.7 and 9.4 could have the following component concerning
relations:

```
COMPONENT RELATION SPECIFICATION
EXPORT
  SORT Relation
  FUNC emptyrel   :                               -> Relation,
       singleton  : Tuple                         -> Relation,
       union      : Relation # Relation           -> Relation,
       difference : Relation # Relation           -> Relation,
       product    : Relation # Relation           -> Relation,
       projection : Relation # Set[Attr]          -> Relation,
       selection  : Relation # Set[Tuple]         -> Relation,
       rename     : Relation # Map[Attr,Attr]     -> Relation,
       attributes : Relation                      -> Set[Attr],
       values     : Relation # Attr               -> Set[Val]
  PRED is_in      : Tuple     # Relation
IMPORT
  TUPLE,
  SET'[Tuple] RENAMING Set TO Relation END,
  SET[Attr],
  SET[Tuple],
  MAP[Attr,Attr],
  SET[Val]
CLASS
  % details omitted here
END
```

It is assumed that the sorts Attr and Val are made available by TUPLE. The
number of connections between RELATION and other components is kept as
small as possible. It is connected with the components TUPLE, DATABASE,
RELSCHEMA and some general purpose reusable library components. These
connections are necessary ones, although one might wonder why there is a
separate component TUPLE. That will be explained below. The number of
sorts and operations that are made available by RELATION are also kept as small
as possible. There are eight functions for combining and adapting relations.
Additional functions, e.g. intersection, equi_join and division, are not
provided because they can be defined in terms of the others. The remaining
two functions and the predicate are needed in RELSCHEMA to define what a valid
instance of a relation schema is. All sorts and operations that are not relevant
to RELATION's intended functionality are hidden. For example, the functions
on the sets that are used to represent relations are not made available.

Each function for combining and adapting relations corresponds to queries
of a different form, i.e. to a different function for constructing queries. In particular, selection : Relation # Set[Tuple] -> Relation corresponds to
mk_selection : Query # SelWff -> Query. The evaluation of objects of

sort `Query` (queries) is database dependent and yields relations. The evaluation of objects of sort `SelWff` (selection formulae) is database independent and yields predicates on tuples, i.e. sets of tuples. These differences suggest separate components for selection formulae and queries. The following could be the component concerning selection formulae:

```
COMPONENT SELWFF SPECIFICATION
EXPORT
  SORT SelWff
  FUNC mk_Eq          : Attr   # Expr        -> SelWff,
       mk_Less        : Attr   # Expr        -> SelWff,
       mk_Greater     : Attr   # Expr        -> SelWff,
       mk_Negation    : SelWff                -> SelWff,
       mk_Disjunction : SelWff # SelWff       -> SelWff,
       eval           : SelWff # TupleStruct -> Set[Tuple]
  PRED is_wf          : SelWff # TupleStruct
IMPORT
  EXPR,
  TUPLE,
  TUPLESTRUCT,
  SET[Tuple]
CLASS
  % details omitted here
END
```

Again all three above-mentioned principles of modular structuring have been applied. `TUPLE` is imported because tuples and some functions on them are needed to define the function `eval`. Without a separate component concerning tuples, `RELATION` had to be imported. However, in that case functions on tuples had to be made available by `RELATION` as well. So a separate component `TUPLE` improves the specification from the view-point of the principles of modular structuring. It leads to a better judgement under the criteria mentioned in Section 9.2. Figure 9.3 pictures the alternatives. For similar reasons there is

Figure 9.3: Separating a component about tuples.

a separate component `TUPLESTRUCT`.

This section was about principles of modular structuring. In order to get a modular structure that is in accordance with these principles, guidelines to follow and techniques to use are needed.

9.6   Guidelines and Techniques

It may be useful to use the following guidelines and techniques for finding a decomposition into components that is in accordance with the criteria and principles concerning modular structuring given in Sections 9.2 and 9.5, respectively:

1. each component should be a self-contained unit;
2. the functionality provided by each component must constitute a coherent whole;
3. each component should be generally applicable in the sense that it can easily be extended without having to change the existing functionality;
4. decompose into components on the basis of the sorts of objects that are most relevant to the purpose of the system being specified;
5. check whether each component makes the essential operations available that may be applied to objects of the component's sort of interest;
6. explore the commonalities between the functionalities of candidate components to find more general components.

The guidelines 1 and 2 reflect the principles of few connections and weak coupling, which have to be applied to meet any of the criteria concerning the modular structure of specifications. These guidelines as well as guideline 3 must be pursued to the utmost when customizing a component for reusability. How to comply with these guidelines with the facilities offered by COLD-1, is explained below by means of an example. The techniques 4 and 5 are appropriate techniques for minimizing the danger that a large number of components are impacted by a small change of the system. A basic idea underlying these techniques is that a sort of objects is characterized by its operations. The techniques 5 and 6 are geared to extendibility and reusability by specialization through inheritance.

Guidelines 1 and 2 have been followed to single out the components for the specification of a database management system outlined in previous sections. Techniques 4 and 5 have been used as well. Guideline 3 is essentially the subject of Section 9.7.

An example (adapted from [59]) of the result of technique 6 is now given. It is about a computer animation system which has, amongst other things, to control the position and orientation of actors, cameras and lights by translation, rotation around different axes, etc. Actors are the participants in the animation; for example, gears, cams, etc. are the actors in animation of mechanical construction. All animation is viewed through cameras and lights can be used to illuminate the animation. So one could single out a general component about "mobile objects":

```
COMPONENT MOBJECT SPECIFICATION
EXPORT
   PROC create    : Real # Real # Real        -> MObject,
```

```
          translate : MObject # Real # Real # Real ->,
          rotate_x  : MObject # Real                ->,
          rotate_y  : MObject # Real                ->,
          rotate_z  : MObject # Real                ->
  IMPORT
    REAL
  CLASS
    SORT MObject                                            VAR
    FUNC position   : MObject -> Real # Real # Real  VAR
    FUNC orientation : MObject -> Real # Real # Real  VAR

    % further details omitted here
  END
```

It is mentioned above that generalization by abstracting from similarities between candidate components is relevant to extendibility and reusability. The common mechanism for adapting the general components to specific needs is now sketched. This mechanism is an inheritance mechanism. It can be used for extension with new operations as well as for restriction. The following component about actors explains how one inherits in COLD-1. For actors, the animation system has to control – in addition to their position and orientation – their scale, tone and visibility.

```
  COMPONENT ACTOR SPECIFICATION
  EXPORT
    PROC create     : Real # Real # Real            -> Actor,
         translate : Actor # Real # Real # Real ->,
         rotate_x  : Actor # Real                ->,
         rotate_y  : Actor # Real                ->,
         rotate_z  : Actor # Real                ->,
         scale     : Actor # Real # Real # Real ->,
         tone      : Actor # Colour              ->,
         turn_on   : Actor                       ->,
         turn_off  : Actor                       ->
  IMPORT
    REAL,
    COLOUR,
    MOBJECT' RENAMING MObject TO Actor END
  CLASS
    FUNC scaling    : Actor -> Real # Real # Real  VAR
    FUNC colour     : Actor -> Colour              VAR
    PRED visibility : Actor                        VAR

    % further details omitted here
  END
```

The component ACTOR inherits the component MOBJECT by importing a copy of it with the sort MObject renamed to Actor. Some operations could have been renamed as well and even some other operations could have been hidden, but in this case neither is needed. In the CLASS section of ACTOR, MOBJECT is extended with some operations (variable functions and predicates as well as procedures) related to scale, tone and visibility.

9.7   Mirroring

In Chapter 6, a case study concerned with a computer-controlled railway system was worked out. In the resulting design of the controller, the data needed to control the train movement via stoppers and selectors, is organized for the intended control. The data concerned represent concrete and abstract entities from the railway system. In this section, the data is organized such that it mirrors the external reality that is relevant to the controller. This leads to components which together serve the same purpose as the original components STATIC_DATA and DYNAMIC_DATA. As a matter of course, the new data organization brings on a new invariant and new algorithms. So the components about these aspects of the controller software need adaptation of some kind. But the components about the hardware involved in the computer-controlled railway system (which are also given in Chapter 6), i.e. the components about the environment of the controller, do not need any adaptation.

The goal of mirroring the external reality is to make it easier to adapt the software concerned to changes in that reality. It is in line with the principles of object-oriented design (see Section 9.8).

In the external reality relevant to the controller software for the railway system there are, first of all, trains. The aspects of a train that are relevant to the control of the train movement on a railway are the detector where the train has been observed most recently – roughly speaking: its location – and its stopper state (a train can be stopped in forward direction, in backward direction or in both directions). So one could have the following component about trains:

```
COMPONENT TRAIN_ SPECIFICATION
IMPORT
  TRAIN_SORTS
    EXPORTING
      SORT StopperState
      FUNC full_stop     : -> StopperState,
           non_stop      : -> StopperState,
           forward_stop  : -> StopperState,
           backward_stop : -> StopperState
    END
CLASS
  SORT Detector_                    FREE

  SORT Train_                       VAR
```

```
FUNC loc : Train_ -> Detector_      VAR
FUNC stp : Train_ -> StopperState  VAR

PROC new_train : -> Train_
OUT  t
PRE  TRUE
SAT  NEW Train_
POST loc(t)^ AND stp(t)^

PROC upd_loc : Train_ # Detector_ ->
IN   t,d
SAT  MOD loc(t)
POST loc(t) = d

PROC upd_stp : Train_ # StopperState ->
IN   t,ss
SAT  MOD stp(t)
POST stp(t) = ss
END
```

Note the forward declaration of Detector_. The component TRAIN_ differs
from the component TRAIN from Chapter 6 as follows: TRAIN_ is about aspects
of a train relevant to the control of its movement on a railway, while TRAIN is
about the movement itself (position, speed, etc.).

Secondly, there are sections. The most relevant aspect of a section is the
train that is in the section. This gives rise to the following component:

```
COMPONENT SECTION_ SPECIFICATION
CLASS
  SORT Train_                       FREE

  SORT Section_                     VAR
  FUNC sel : Section_ -> Train_   VAR

  PROC new_sect : -> Section_
  OUT  s
  PRE  TRUE
  SAT  NEW Section_
  POST sel(s)^

  PROC upd_sel : Section_ # Train_ ->
  IN   s,t
  SAT  MOD sel(s)
  POST sel(s) = t
END
```

This component has the same pattern as the previous one (instead of the
forward declaration of Train_, a selective import of this sort could have been

used). The next component deviates only slightly from that pattern.

Very important for the control of the train movement are the detectors. There are various aspects of a detector that are relevant to the intended control. The section on which the detector is situated as well as the section that is most near by, are relevant and so is the position of the detector within the section (entry, middle or exit). These aspects are static: they do not change after the placement of a new detector. The most relevant dynamic aspect of a detector is the most recently communicated state of the detector. A detector is in one of two states. One state indicates that there is a train above the detector and the other state indicates that this is not the case. Reflecting the static nature of some aspects necessitates a slight deviation from the pattern of the previous two components:

```
COMPONENT DETECTOR_ SPECIFICATION
IMPORT
  ENUM3'
    RENAMING
      Enum3 TO DetectorKind,
      x0 TO entry,
      x1 TO exit,
      x2 TO mid
    END,
  BOOL
CLASS
  SORT Section_                                     FREE

  SORT Detector_                                    VAR
  FUNC sect : Detector_ -> Section_        PRE TRUE
  FUNC next : Detector_ -> Section_        PRE TRUE
  FUNC kind : Detector_ -> DetectorKind    PRE TRUE
  PRED det  : Detector_                             VAR

  PROC new_det : Section_ # Section_ # DetectorKind -> Detector_
  IN   s1,s2,k
  OUT  d
  PRE  TRUE
  SAT  NEW Detector_
  POST sect(d) = s1 AND next(d) = s2 AND kind(d) = k ;
       NOT det(d)

  PROC upd_det : Detector_ # Bool ->
  IN   d,b
  SAT  MOD det(d)
  POST det(d) <=> b = true
END
```

The difference is that some functions are not variable: sect, next and kind

are defined as (total) constant functions. Recall that a constant function may
only vary when its domain changes due to object creation. When this happens,
it is allowed to add the values of the function for the new argument tuples.
However, it is not allowed to modify its value for any other argument tuple.
So each of the functions sect, next and kind may only be changed by adding
its value for each newly created object of the sort Detector_ in the state in
which the object concerned is created. This reflects the intuition that the
section on which the detector is situated, the section that is most near by
and the position of the detector within the section do not change after the
placement of a detector.

The components SECTION_ and DETECTOR_ differ from the components
SECTION and DETECTOR from Chapter 6 like TRAIN_ differs from TRAIN.

The following component, which imports the previous three components,
is about the data needed to control the specific railway system treated in
Chapter 6. It includes an initialization procedure for the data concerned.

```
COMPONENT DATA SPECIFICATION
EXPORT
   FUNC train : Train     -> Train_,
        sect  : Section    -> Section_,
        det   : Detector   -> Detector_
   PROC init : ->
   SIG  TRAIN_,
        SECTION_,
        DETECTOR_
IMPORT
   TRAIN_,
   SECTION_,
   DETECTOR_,
   TRAIN_SORTS,
   ARRAY1'[Train,Train_] RENAMING var TO train END,
   ARRAY1'[Section,Section_] RENAMING var TO sect END,
   ARRAY1'[Detector,Detector_] RENAMING var TO det END
CLASS
   PROC init : ->
   PRE  TRUE
   DEF  set(nil,new_train) ;
        set(t1,new_train) ;
        set(t2,new_train) ;
        set(t3,new_train) ;

        set(nil,new_sect) ;
        set(s1,new_sect) ;
        set(s2,new_sect) ;
        % etc.

        set(d1,new_det(sect(s1),sect(s8),entry)) ;
```

```
          set(d2,new_det(sect(s1),sect(s2),exit)) ;
          set(d3,new_det(sect(s2),sect(s1),entry)) ;
          % etc.
END
```

The data is organized as three one-dimensional arrays – one for each kind
of entities that is relevant to the controller. These arrays are obtained by
instantiating the component ARRAY1 given in Section 6.9.

In Section 9.6, it was said that a component should be easily extendible
without having to change its existing functionality. Mirroring the external
reality that is relevant to the software system concerned seems a useful technique to obtain such components. For example if the controller software for
the railway system requires adaptation, it is most likely that this requires just
additions to TRAIN_, SECTION_ and DETECTOR_ which correspond to additional
aspects of trains, sections and detectors that become relevant.

9.8   Object-orientedness

Section 9.6 suggests some techniques for finding a decomposition into components that is in accordance with the criteria and principles concerning modular
structuring given earlier:

- decompose into components on the basis of the sorts of objects that are
  most relevant to the purpose of the system being specified;
- check whether each component makes the essential operations available
  that may be applied to objects of the component's sort of interest;
- explore the commonalities between the functionalities of candidate components to find more general components.

These techniques are roughly the principles of object-oriented design. Other
principles of object-oriented design, such as abstraction and encapsulation,
are in common with almost any approach of design (and as a matter of course
also supported by COLD-1). Object-oriented concepts of design are described
by, for example, Meyer [60] and Rumbaugh [59]. Programming languages
supporting object-orientedness include Smalltalk [61], C++ [62] and Eiffel [60].
This section outlines one way to exploit COLD-1 more fully as a language for
object-oriented design.

In the terminology of object-oriented design, objects have a distinguishable
identity and an internal state which is characterized by attributes, operations
and relationships to other objects. Similar objects are furthermore grouped
into classes. All objects in a class share the same attributes and operations.
The attributes of objects have ordinary values – such as natural numbers or
strings – which, unlike objects, can only be distinguished by properties that
they may have. Different objects in a class may have the same or different
values for a given attribute. The operations may change the state of objects

and/or compute values which depend upon the values of their attributes. Both attributes and operations of the objects in a class are called features.

A component can be viewed as a class if it is about a certain sort of objects: the features of the objects in the class are the COLD-1 operations that may be applied to the objects of the sort concerned (attributes are functions and operations are functions, predicates and procedures – just as in COLD-1).

A component describes the part of the state space concerning one object class, including its dynamic aspects. For example, the windows managed by a windowing system could be described by:

```
COMPONENT WINDOW SPECIFICATION
EXPORT
   PROC create : Nat # Nat # Nat # Nat -> Window,
        move   : Window # Nat # Nat       ->,
        resize : Window # Nat # Nat       ->,
        open   : Icon                     ->,
        close  : Window                   ->
IMPORT
   NAT,
   ICON
CLASS
   SORT Window                      VAR
% attributes
   FUNC x0     : Window -> Nat   VAR
   FUNC y0     : Window -> Nat   VAR
   FUNC width  : Window -> Nat   VAR
   FUNC height : Window -> Nat   VAR
   PRED opened : Window          VAR
% relationships
   FUNC icon   : Window -> Icon  VAR
% operations
   % details omitted here
END
```

When closing a window w, it becomes an icon and its attribute **opened** becomes false to indicate that it is closed. The window can be returned by opening the icon, which of course causes **opened**(w) to hold again. At first sight it may seem strange to have an operation **open** without argument or result of sort Window in the EXPORT section of WINDOW – that is to have the opening of icons made available by the component WINDOW. However, as explained above, opening an icon i means changing the internal state of a window, viz. the window w such that `icon(w) = i`.

An important mechanism provided by object-oriented languages is inheritance (in the sense of object-oriented technology). Section 9.6 shows that this mechanism is supported by COLD-1 in a rather direct way, but does not treat inheritance in the context of object-orientedness. Here an object-oriented treatment is given. Consider the objects in the class SCROLLING_WINDOW described below in COLD-1.

```
COMPONENT SCROLLING_WINDOW SPECIFICATION
EXPORT
  PROC create  : Nat # Nat # Nat # Nat      -> ScrollingWindow,
       move    : ScrollingWindow # Nat # Nat ->,
       resize  : ScrollingWindow # Nat # Nat ->,
       open    : Icon                        ->,
       close   : ScrollingWindow             ->,
       hscroll : ScrollingWindow # Nat       ->,
       vscroll : ScrollingWindow # Nat       ->
IMPORT
  NAT,
  WINDOW' RENAMING Window TO ScrollingWindow END
CLASS
% attributes
  FUNC hoffset : ScrollingWindow -> Nat  VAR
  FUNC voffset : ScrollingWindow -> Nat  VAR
% operations
  % further details omitted here
END
```

They inherit all operations of the objects in the class WINDOW and have in addition hscroll and vscroll for scrolling horizontally and vertically, respectively.

Both text windows and canvas windows inherit all features of scrolling windows. As a matter of course, they have different additional features. For example, text windows have features for deleting and inserting strings of characters:

```
COMPONENT TEXT_WINDOW SPECIFICATION
EXPORT
  PROC create  : Nat # Nat # Nat # Nat     -> TextWindow,
       move    : TextWindow # Nat # Nat    ->,
       resize  : TextWindow # Nat # Nat    ->,
       open    : Icon                      ->,
       close   : TextWindow                ->,
       hscroll : TextWindow # Nat          ->,
       vscroll : TextWindow # Nat          ->,
       cut     : TextWindow # Nat # Nat    ->,
       paste   : TextWindow # String # Nat ->
IMPORT
  NAT,
  STRING,
  SCROLLING_WINDOW' RENAMING ScrollingWindow TO TextWindow END
CLASS
% attributes
  FUNC contents : TextWindow -> String  VAR
% operations
  % further details omitted here
```

```
END
```

Suppose that menus have been described in MENU and there arises a need for a variety of windows – without scrolling features – for menus. It means that the features of both windows and menus have to be inherited. This is known as multiple inheritance. The simple-minded solution causes a problem:

```
COMPONENT MENU_WINDOW SPECIFICATION
IMPORT
  WINDOW' RENAMING Window TO MenuWindow END,
  MENU'   RENAMING Menu   TO MenuWindow END
END
```

The problem is that the clash of the name MenuWindow is an erroneous situation. This can be solved as follows:[3]

```
COMPONENT MENU_WINDOW SPECIFICATION
EXPORT
  PROC create : Nat # Nat # Nat # Nat # Seq[Choice] -> MenuWindow,
       move   : MenuWindow # Nat # Nat                ->,
       resize : MenuWindow # Nat # Nat                ->,
       open   : Icon                                  ->,
       close  : MenuWindow                            ->,
       select : MenuWindow # Nat                      ->
IMPORT
  NAT,
  SEQ[Choice FROM MENU],
  WINDOW,
  MENU,
  TUP2'[Window,Menu] RENAMING Tup2 TO MenuWindow END
CLASS
  PROC create : Nat # Nat # Nat # Nat # Seq[Choice] -> MenuWindow
  IN   x,y,w,h,cs
  DEF  tup(create(x,y,w,h),create(cs))

  PROC move : MenuWindow # Nat # Nat ->
  IN   mw,x,y
  DEF  move(proj1(mw),x,y)

  PROC resize : MenuWindow # Nat # Nat ->
  IN   mw,w,h
  DEF  resize(proj1(mw),w,h)

  % details of remaining operations originating from WINDOW
  % omitted here

  PROC select : MenuWindow # Nat ->
```

---

[3]This solution was first suggested by Frank van der Linden from Philips Research Laboratories Eindhoven.

```
IN   mw,i
DEF  select(proj2(mw),i)
END
```

So multiple inheritance is supported, but not in such a direct way as single inheritance. Note that the object creation procedure has to be redefined anyhow: the arguments of both original object creation procedures are needed.

Inheritance pre-supposes generalization. This should not be confused with aggregation: introducing a class in which every object is made of objects in other classes. The latter objects are part of the compound object; there is no inheritance of features involved.

9.9   Conservativity and Visibility Consistency

The topics treated in the remainder of this chapter are less of a stylistic nature than the topics treated in the previous sections. They relate to established theoretical results, but for most of them the usefulness in practice can still be questioned because there is not yet much experience gained.

When components are combined, extended and restricted in their visible names, undesirable changes in the properties represented by their formulae may occur. The consequences of name clashes where the name concerned is used for different things are precluded by COLD-1 (such name clashes are considered to be erroneous situations), but not all undesirable changes are caused by these name clashes. The following two anomalies are considered to be the most serious ones:

1. the combined properties become inconsistent,
2. hidden properties become visible.

This section explains the principles of *conservativity* and *visibility consistency*, which are meant to avoid these anomalies.

In the following example, the component BYTE_ from Section 5.6 is extended with an axiom about the function **nat**. The intention is to forget about the most significant bit of a byte.

```
COMPONENT SBYTE_ SPECIFICATION
IMPORT
  BYTE_
CLASS
  DECL n : Nat

  AXIOM n > 127 => nat(byte(n)) = n - 128
END
```

The following theorem can now be derived:

```
THEOREM n > 127 AND n < 256 => n = n - 128
```

From this it follows that $0 = 1$. All this means that the additional axiom
has introduced an inconsistency. This was to be expected because that axiom
changes the definition of **nat** which is generally dangerous. It is a special kind
of non-conservative extension.

A module of the form

```
EXPORT S
IMPORT C₁, ... ,Cₘ
CLASS D₁ ... Dₙ
END
```

is a conservative extension if $C_1, \ldots, C_m$ are conservative extensions and, for
$i = 1, \ldots, m$, the properties represented by the formulae of C_i and the properties represented by the formulae of the new module are the same as far as
the visible names of C_i are concerned. $C_1, \ldots, C_m$ are component references.
A component reference of the form

```
C EXPORTING S
  RENAMING ρ
  QUALIFYING a
  END
```

is a conservative extension if the properties represented by the formulae of C do
not change under the renaming ρ (if present).[4] With conservative extensions,
inconsistencies can not occur. Sometimes it is very convenient in practice to
introduce a non-conservative extension. Should the occasion arise, they are
not considered to be erroneous situations *per se*, but extensive checking for
unexpected properties (including inconsistencies) is recommended.

The following example is used to explain another serious anomaly. The
example is about a very simple seat reservation system.

```
COMPONENT SEAT_RESERVATION SPECIFICATION
EXPORT
  PRED is_free : Seat
  PROC free    : Seat ->,
  PROC lock    : Seat ->
IMPORT
  SEAT
CLASS
  PRED is_free : Seat   VAR

  PROC free : Seat ->
  IN   s
  PRE  TRUE
  SAT  MOD is_free(s)
```

---

[4]A renaming does not have to be injective, i.e. it may map different old names to the
same new name.

```
        POST is_free(s)

        PROC lock : Seat ->
        IN    s
        PRE   TRUE
        SAT   MOD is_free(s)
        POST NOT is_free(s)
     END
```

The following component differs from SEAT_RESERVATION in its visible names: only the variable predicate name is_free and the procedure name lock are visible.

```
     COMPONENT SEAT_LOCKING SPECIFICATION
     EXPORT
       PRED is_free : Seat
       PROC lock    : Seat ->
     IMPORT
       SEAT_RESERVATION
     END
```

The following component differs from SEAT_RESERVATION in its visible names as well, but in this case only the procedure name free is visible.

```
     COMPONENT SEAT_FREEING SPECIFICATION
     EXPORT
       PROC free : Seat ->
     IMPORT
       SEAT_RESERVATION
     END
```

The components SEAT_LOCKING and SEAT_FREEING can again be combined:

```
     COMPONENT SEAT_COMP_COMB SPECIFICATION
     IMPORT
       SEAT_LOCKING,
       SEAT_FREEING
     END
```

Note that SEAT_RESERVATION and SEAT_COMP_COMB are equivalent in the sense that the properties represented by the formulae of SEAT_RESERVATION and the properties represented by the formulae of SEAT_COMP_COMB are the same as far as the visible names are concerned. Now consider the following alternative to SEAT_FREEING:

```
     COMPONENT SEAT_FREEING_ALT SPECIFICATION
     EXPORT
       PROC free : Seat ->
     IMPORT
       SEAT
     CLASS
```

```
PRED available : Seat   VAR

PROC free : Seat ->
IN   s
PRE  TRUE
SAT  MOD available(s)
POST available(s)
END
```

The components SEAT_FREEING and SEAT_FREEING_ALT are equivalent, but in spite of that the component SEAT_COMP_COMB given above and the component SEAT_COMP_COMB_ALT given below are not equivalent!

```
COMPONENT SEAT_COMP_COMB_ALT SPECIFICATION
IMPORT
  SEAT_LOCKING,
  SEAT_FREEING_ALT
END
```

This problem is caused by the fact that SEAT_LOCKING exports the predicate is_free which is modified by the procedure free exported by SEAT_FREEING while SEAT_FREEING does not export is_free. Combining these components makes properties about both free and is_free visible that are hidden in SEAT_FREEING – against non-existent in SEAT_FREEING_ALT. In other words, the anomaly occurs because the components SEAT_LOCKING and SEAT_FREEING are inconsistent with respect to visibility. Because the example had to be kept simple for a comprehesible explanation of the anomaly, the problem appears to be contrived. However, especially in case large and complex systems are modularly structured, one has to be very careful not to introduce visibility inconsistencies.

A module of the form

```
EXPORT S
IMPORT C_1, ... ,C_m
CLASS D_1 ... D_n
END
```

is visibility consistent if $C_1, \ldots, C_m$ are visibility consistent and, for $i = 1, \ldots,$ m, each name of a variable sort, function or predicate that is exported by a component other than C_i, is exported by C_i as well if it may be modified by a procedure whose name is exported by C_i. A component reference of the form

```
C EXPORTING S
  RENAMING ρ
  QUALIFYING a
END
```

is visibility consistent if the module with name C is visibility consistent. With visibility consistency, hidden properties can not become visible.

Conservativity and visibility consistency are recommended to avoid undesirable effects of combining and adapting components. It should be understood that not all effects that might be considered to be anomalous are avoided by these conditions.

9.10   Black Box Correctness

In addition to a specification of a component, a component definition can give an implementation of the component. A number of such component definitions together with a system description in terms of the components concerned constitute a design in COLD-1. The implementation of each component has to be proven correct with respect to its specification on the basis of the preceding component definitions. If the proofs do not rely on the chosen implementations, replacement of a correct implementation of one component by another correct implementation will not disturb the correctness of other components. That makes this notion of correctness, called black box correctness, a very useful one. It will be explained in more detail in this section.

The word description is used for any design-like COLD-1 text. A description consists of

1. an optional operator clause,
2. an optional list of component definitions (ended with SYSTEM),
3. a system description.

System descriptions are just modules and component references of the forms described before. There are two kinds of component definitions, which are of the following general forms:

LET C := P

COMPONENT C SPECIFICATION P
         IMPLEMENTATION Q

where P and Q are also descriptions – usually without the optional operator clause and component list. The IMPLEMENTATION section is optional in the component definitions of the second form. For example, all preceding component definitions in this chapter are without an IMPLEMENTATION section.

In the following example about paths (as in use in file systems), a component definition with an IMPLEMENTATION section is given. The example also shows the use of abbreviations, i.e. component definitions of the first form.

```
LET PATH_SPEC :=
EXPORT
  SORT Path
  FUNC root   :                   -> Path,
       append : Path # Name -> Path,
```

```
          prefix : Path         -> Path,
          name   : Path         -> Name
   IMPORT
     NAME
   CLASS
     SORT Path

     FUNC root   :              -> Path
     FUNC append : Path # Name -> Path

     DECL p,q : Path,
          n,m : Name

     PRED is_gen : Path
     IND  is_gen(root);
          is_gen(p) => is_gen(append(p,n))

     AXIOM root! AND append(p,n)!;
           NOT append(p,n) = root;
           append(p,n) = append(q,m) => p = q AND n = m;
           is_gen(p)

     FUNC prefix : Path -> Path
     IND  p = append(q,m) => prefix(p) = q

     FUNC name : Path -> Name
     IND  p = append(q,m) => name(p) = m
   END

   LET PATH_IMPL :=
   EXPORT
     SORT Path
     FUNC root   :              -> Path,
          append : Path # Name -> Path,
          prefix : Path         -> Path,
          name   : Path         -> Name
   IMPORT
     NAME,
     SEQ[Name] RENAMING Seq TO Path, empty TO root END
   CLASS
     FUNC append : Path # Name -> Path
     IN   p,n
     DEF  cat(p,seq(n))

     FUNC prefix : Path -> Path
     IN   p
     DEF  ( len(p) = 1 ?; root
```

```
              | len(p) > 1 ?; cat(seq(head(p)),prefix(tail(p)))
              )

       FUNC name : Path -> Name
       IN   p
       DEF  ( len(p) = 1 ?; head(p)
              | len(p) > 1 ?; name(tail(p))
              )
   END


       COMPONENT PATH SPECIFICATION   PATH_SPEC
                     IMPLEMENTATION PATH_IMPL
```

Because well-formedness requires "define before use" for component names, it is assumed that NAME is introduced in a preceding component definition.

The following well-formedness conditions apply to any description:

1. all components have distinct names,
2. in each component definition only component names introduced in preceding component definitions may occur,
3. in the system description only component names introduced in the component definitions may occur.

The example about paths raises the question whether PATH stands for PATH_SPEC or PATH_IMPL. The SPECIFICATION and IMPLEMENTATION sections of a component definition correspond to different interpretations of the component name concerned. The component name is interpreted differently dependent on whether it occurs in a specification context or in an implementation context. An occurrence in a specification context is interpreted according to the SPECIFICATION section of the component definition. An occurrence in an implementation context is interpreted according to the IMPLEMENTATION section if present and according to the SPECIFICATION section otherwise. SPECIFICATION sections are specification contexts. IMPLEMENTATION sections are implementation contexts with the exception of their ABSTRACT sections, in so far as present. ABSTRACT sections are always specification contexts.

In the example given above names were introduced for the specification and implementation descriptions of the component PATH of a file system. This practice is mainly for convenience; it is seldom needed. If no names are introduced for the specification and implementation descriptions of the various components, the description of the file system could look like:

```
COMPONENT NAME SPECIFICATION ... IMPLEMENTATION ...
COMPONENT PATH SPECIFICATION ... IMPLEMENTATION ...
COMPONENT BYTE SPECIFICATION ... IMPLEMENTATION ...
COMPONENT FILE SPECIFICATION ... IMPLEMENTATION ...
COMPONENT DIR  SPECIFICATION ... IMPLEMENTATION ...
COMPONENT FILESYS SPECIFICATION ... IMPLEMENTATION ...
```

SYSTEM FILESYS

PATH uses only NAME and is used by FILESYS only. So its definition could have been preceded by the definitions of BYTE, FILE and DIR as well. NAME occurs in both the SPECIFICATION section and the IMPLEMENTATION section of the definition of PATH. In the former section NAME stands for its interpretation as specification and in the latter section for its interpretation as implementation.

A description is *black box correct* if for each component it can be proved that the implementation correctly implements the specification under the assumption that the names of the preceding components are arbitrary implementations of their specifications.

For example, whether the implementation of FILESYS correctly implements its specification should be proved without taking into account that paths are implemented as sequences of names. Below black box correctness will be explained in more detail using an extremely simple but complete description of bits. Black box correctness of a description is very useful because replacement of the current implementation of one component by a new one that still correctly implements the specification concerned (in the black box sense) preserves black box correctness of the whole description.

The following example is kept very simple in order to be able to give a comprehensible explanation of black box correctness using a complete description. Two components are defined: SWITCH and BIT_.[5] A specification as well as an implementation is given for both components. A switch is either on or off and can be switched from off to on and vice versa. An enumerated type consisting of two values is used to implement switches in the obvious way. A bit is essentially a Boolean value that can only be negated. Switches are used to implement bits.

```
LET SWITCH_SPEC :=
EXPORT
  SORT Switch
  FUNC off    :              -> Switch,
       on     :              -> Switch,
       switch : Switch -> Switch
CLASS
  SORT Switch
  FUNC off    :              -> Switch
  FUNC on     :              -> Switch
  FUNC switch : Switch -> Switch

  AXIOM off! AND on!;
        NOT off = on;
        switch(off) = on AND switch(on) = off
END
```

---

[5]The specification of BIT, given in Section 8.5, differs slightly from the specification description of the component BIT_ defined here.

```
LET SWITCH_IMPL :=
EXPORT
  SORT Switch
  FUNC off    :           -> Switch,
       on     :           -> Switch,
       switch : Switch -> Switch
IMPORT
  ENUM2
    RENAMING
      SORT Enum2 TO Switch
      FUNC x0    TO off,
           x1    TO on
    END
CLASS
  FUNC switch : Switch -> Switch
  IN   s
  DEF  ( s = off ?; on
       | s = on  ?; off
       )
END

COMPONENT SWITCH SPECIFICATION  SWITCH_SPEC
                 IMPLEMENTATION SWITCH_IMPL

LET BIT_SPEC :=
BOOL'
  EXPORTING
    SORT Bool
    FUNC false :      -> Bool,
         true  :      -> Bool,
         not   : Bool -> Bool
  RENAMING
    SORT Bool  TO Bit
    FUNC false TO 0,
         true  TO 1,
         not   TO invert
  END

LET BIT_IMPL :=
SWITCH
  RENAMING
    SORT Switch TO Bit
    FUNC off    TO 0,
         on     TO 1,
         switch TO invert
  END
```

```
COMPONENT BIT_ SPECIFICATION  BIT_SPEC
             IMPLEMENTATION BIT_IMPL
```

```
SYSTEM BIT_                                  % not black-box correct
```

This description is not black box correct. The specification of BIT_ requires
that invert is a total function (see the definedness theorem in the specification
of BOOL given in Section 9.3). The implementation uses switch to model
invert. But it can not be proved on the basis of the specification of SWITCH
that switch is a total function because it is not required that off and on are
the only values of the sort Switch.

Note that it could be proved that switch is a total function in the current implementation of SWITCH. Using this knowledge would lead to glass box
correctness which is not preserved by replacement of implementations as described above. For example, the following is also a correct implementation of
SWITCH:

```
LET SWITCH_IMPL_ALT :=
EXPORT
  SORT Switch
  FUNC off   :          -> Switch,
       on    :          -> Switch,
       switch : Switch -> Switch
IMPORT
  NAT
    RENAMING
      SORT Nat TO Switch
      FUNC 0   TO off,
           1   TO on
    END
CLASS
  FUNC switch : Switch -> Switch
  IN   s
  DEF  ( s = off ?; on
       | s = on  ?; off
       )
END
```

In this alternative implementation, switch is not a total function. Therefore,
if SWITCH_IMPL is replaced by SWITCH_IMPL_ALT, then BIT_IMPL is not even a
correct implementation of BIT_ in the glass box sense.

9.11   Component Invariants

The states of a computer-based system do not always fit a neat mathematical
abstraction, in particular if the abstraction has to reflect design decisions.

Due to irregularities, not all states may really arise. An invariant is a property that is common to a designated initial state and the states before and after designated state transformations. It generally does not exclude all states that can not arise – this means that it may be "loose" – and it forgets about the intermediate states arising during the state transformations concerned. Note that whether a state is forgotten about – for being an intermediate one – depends upon the state transformations being considered. In this section we focus on invariants that are common to the initial state of a system unit and the states before and after the execution of any of the procedures thereof. There are various reasons to record such invariants:

1. to check consistency of specifications;
2. to check whether specifications implement other more abstract ones;
3. to guide the development and revisions of specifications;

All this is illustrated below by means of examples, but first we expand somewhat on the given list.

Formulating and proving theorems that should follow from a specification increase the chance that unexpected properties are discovered. In case of theorems about invariants, it may in particular increase the confidence in the consistency of the specification. It is usually very difficult to prove that a (state-based) specification implements another one unless invariants are used. If the invariants are not too loose, they make it possible to prove it in a systematic and relatively easy way (otherwise, the best approach might be to tighten them first). Recording an invariant may be viewed as recording a global restriction on the procedures concerned which would otherwise remain implicit – it has to be preserved by each of them. Moreover, because this restriction has to be met initially as well, the definitions of the procedures may even rely on it. So if someone is making a revision to one of the procedures without being alerted by the invariant, the chances are that the other procedures will no longer behave as expected.

Formulating the relevant theorems about invariants in the specifications concerned, as suggested above, is one way to deal with them. In this way, the theorems themselves are the proof obligations to be discharged. Alternatively, axioms may be used. In that case, there is an obligation to prove that the definitions of the procedures concerned are consistent with these axioms. Because such proof obligations can not be expressed as theorems in COLD-1, we adopt the former way.

The following example (adapted from [63]) illustrates various reasons to record invariants. Suppose that there is a need to record for each student enrolled on a course whether he or she has handed in adequate anwers to the set of exercises for the course or not. At the beginning of the course no students are enrolled. The students who enroll are not expected to have done the exercises before. One should be able to extract the students who have completed the exercises successfully. This could be described by:

```
LET STUDX_SPEC :=
EXPORT
  PROC enroll : Student ->,
       compl  : Student ->,
       result :              -> Set[Student]
IMPORT
  STUDENT,
  SET[Student],
  ENUM2
    RENAMING
      Enum2 TO StudxState,
      x0    TO not_done,
      x1    TO done
    END,
  MAP[Student,StudxState]
CLASS
  FUNC studx : -> Map[Student,StudxState]  VAR

  PRED inv :
  DEF  studx!

  DECL s  : Student,
       ss : Set[Student]

  AXIOM INIT => studx = empty

  PROC enroll : Student ->
  IN   s
  PRE  studx! AND NOT is_in(s,dom(studx))
  SAT  MOD studx
  POST studx = add(studx',s,not_done)

  PROC compl : Student ->
  IN   s
  PRE  app(studx,s) = not_done
  SAT  MOD studx
  POST studx = add(studx',s,done)

  PROC result : -> Set[Student]
  OUT  ss
  PRE  studx!
  POST FORALL s ( is_in(s,ss) <=> app(studx,s) = done )

  % proof obligation: invariant preservation
  THEOREM
    INIT => inv ;
    inv => AFTER ( enroll($) | compl($) | FLUSH result ) THEN inv
```

END

The variable function **studx** is used to record, by means of a map, for each student enrolled on the course whether he or she has done the set of exercises or not. The state invariant **inv** holds in states in which this variable function is defined. The theorem states that this property holds in the initial state and that it is preserved by the procedures **enroll**, **compl** and **result**. It is a proof obligation which can be discharged with little work. However, one might wonder why there is no PRE section PRE TRUE present in the definition of **studx** instead. Although this is largely a matter of taste, the approach followed in this example, i.e. to make the definedness of variable functions part of the invariant, is more consistent with the way to deal with invariants pursued here. The other approach gives rise to an obligation to prove that the definitions of the procedures **enroll**, **compl** and **result** are consistent with the definition of the variable function **studx** which is affected by and affects these procedures. Just as the consistency proof obligations mentioned before, this one can not be expressed as a theorem in COLD-1.

The following specification describes an implementation of the previous one wherein the mutable map **studx** is represented by two "programming variables" **not_done_set** and **done_set** whose values are sets of students. These programming variables are obtained by instantiating the component SVAR given in Section 2.3. The intention is that **not_done_set** contains the students who are enrolled but have not done the set of exercises until now and **done_set** contains the students who are enrolled and have done the set of exercises. How the concrete states consisting of **not_done_set** and **done_set** correspond to the abstract states consisting of **studx** is given by defining **studx** in terms of **not_done_set** and **done_set**. The intention is pictured by means of an example in Figure 9.4.

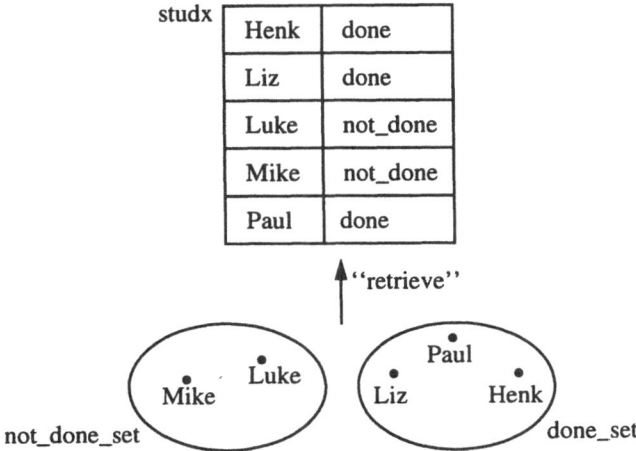

Figure 9.4: Retrieving **studx** from a concrete state.

```
LET STUDX_IMPL :=
EXPORT
  PROC enroll : Student ->,
       compl  : Student ->,
       result :            -> Set[Student]
IMPORT
  STUDENT,
  SET[Student],
  ENUM2
    RENAMING
      Enum2 TO StudxState,
      x0    TO not_done,
      x1    TO done
    END,
  MAP[Student,StudxState],
  SVAR'[Set[Student]]
    RENAMING var TO not_done_set, set TO set_not_done_set END,
  SVAR'[Set[Student]]
    RENAMING var TO done_set, set TO set_done_set END
CLASS
  PRED inv :
  DEF  isect(not_done_set,done_set) = empty

  FUNC studx : -> Map[Student,StudxState]
  PRE  inv
  DEF  THAT m : Map[Student,StudxState]
       ( FORALL s : Student
         ( app(m,s) = not_done <=> is_in(s,not_done_set)
         ; app(m,s) = done     <=> is_in(s,done_set)
         )
       )

  DECL s  : Student,
       ss : Set[Student]

  AXIOM INIT => not_done_set = empty AND done_set = empty

  PROC enroll : Student ->
  IN   s
  DEF  NOT is_in(s,union(not_done_set,done_set)) ?;
       set_not_done_set(ins(s,not_done_set))

  PROC compl : Student ->
  IN   s
  DEF  is_in(s,not_done_set) ?;
       set_not_done_set(rem(s,not_done_set)) ;
       set_done_set(ins(s,done_set))
```

```
PROC result : -> Set[Student]
DEF  done_set

% proof obligation: invariant preservation
THEOREM
  INIT => inv ;
  inv => AFTER ( enroll($) | compl($) | FLUSH result ) THEN inv

% proof obligations for implementation of STUDX_SPEC

% proof obligation: invariant reflection
THEOREM
  inv => studx!

% proof obligation: state initialization
THEOREM
  INIT => studx = empty ;

% proof obligation: termination of procedures
THEOREM
  inv =>
  ( studx! AND NOT is_in(s,dom(studx)) <=> FIN enroll(s)
  ; app(studx,s) = not_done <=> FIN compl(s)
  ; studx! <=> FIN result
  )

% proof obligation: effects of procedures
THEOREM
  inv =>
  ( AFTER enroll(s) THEN studx = add(studx',s,not_done)
  ; AFTER compl(s)  THEN studx = add(studx',s,done)
  ; AFTER LET ss := result
      THEN FORALL s ( is_in(s,ss) <=> app(studx,s) = done )
  )
END
```

Note the pre-condition PRE inv in the definition of studx. It enforces studx to be defined for exactly the concrete states wherein the invariant inv from STUDX_IMPL holds. If in addition the proof obligation for invariant reflection (which is explained below) can be discharged, studx will furthermore relate these states to the abstract states wherein the invariant inv from STUDX_SPEC holds. Thus studx turns out to be restricted to the concrete and abstract states that may arise according to the invariants.

The proof obligations following the proof obligation for invariant preservation relate this specification to the previous one. They all use the "retrieved" studx. The proof obligation for *invariant reflection* requires that the invariant to be preserved by the concrete procedures reflects the invariant to be preserved by the abstract procedures. The proof obligation for *state initialization* requires that the abstract initial state corresponding to the concrete initial state satisfies the constraints postulated for it. The proof obligation for *termination of procedures* requires that each of the concrete procedures succeeds in a concrete state if and only if its abstract counterpart must do so in the corresponding abstract state according to the pre-condition specified for it, but only in case that the invariant to be preserved by the concrete procedures holds in the starting state. The proof obligation for *effects of procedures* requires that each of the concrete procedures can transform a concrete state to another one and yield some tuple of results only if its abstract counterpart may do so for the corresponding abstract states according to the post-condition specified for it, but only in case that the invariant to be preserved by the concrete procedures holds in the state to be transformed.

The proof obligations concerning procedures appear to be rather weak because the obvious requirements are relaxed by "but only in case that the invariant ...". This relaxation expresses that the constraints on the behaviour of an abstract procedure do not have to be met by its concrete counterpart in starting states that are unreachable from the concrete initial state via the concrete procedures. This gives considerable implementation freedom. For example, the concrete procedure `enroll` is defined such that `enroll(s)` would succeed in all unreachable states in which `NOT is_in(s,dom(studx))`. In these states it is not required that `studx!` holds as well.

Note that these proof obligations in addition allow the concrete procedures to be more deterministic than their abstract counterparts. This means that there are abstract states for which there do not have to be corresponding concrete states because they are unreachable by means of the concrete procedures. Therefore only a weak kind of "adequacy" of the representation is required, namely adequacy as far as needed for the non-determinism remaining in the implementation. This kind of adequacy is however implied by the proof obligation for state initialization and the proof obligations concerning procedures. This gives considerable implementation freedom as well, but no use is made of this freedom in the example above (i.e., there is a representation for each abstract state).

If all the proof obligations occurring as theorems in the specifications STUDX_SPEC and STUDX_IMPL have been discharged, it has been proved that STUDX_IMPL implements STUDX_SPEC. This does not work in general; the sufficient (but not necessary) condition met here is that the specifications do not export variable sorts, functions and predicates, thus hiding the internals of the states. The rôle of the invariants `inv` from STUDX_SPEC and STUDX_IMPL is important to make it easier to prove that STUDX_IMPL implements STUDX_SPEC. Without these invariants, it would have been much more difficult to show that, for example, the concrete procedure `enroll` sufficiently models its abstract counterpart in the context of the other concrete procedures.

The way to check whether STUDX_IMPL implements STUDX_SPEC outlined above is of course not restricted to this specific case. It also works for the general case where there is more than one variable state component. Many ideas concerning proof obligations applied here, such as using state invariants and distinguishing pre-conditions in operation specifications in order to simplify the proof obligations to be discharged, originate from Jones' VDM (described in [64]).

9.12 Loop Invariants

In the previous section we focussed on component invariants, i.e. invariants that are common to the initial state of a system unit and the states before and after the execution of any of the procedures thereof. In this section we give an example of another kind of invariants: loop invariants. A loop invariant rules out certain states that can not arise before or after iterations of the loop concerned. This means that the loop invariant permits to ignore irrelevant states when reasoning about the loop.

The example is about computing the maximum of a set of integers. Below a procedure max is defined for this purpose. The set of integers concerned is passed to max in s : -> Set[Int] and its maximum is returned by max in r : -> Int. These variable functions are modified by procedures set_s : Set[Int] -> and set_r : Int ->.

The procedure max can be specified in pre- and post-condition style as follows:

```
PROC max : ->
PRE  card(s) > 0
SAT  MOD s,r
POST is_in(r,s') AND FORALL i : Int ( is_in(i,s') => i <= r )
```

Note that the specification allows max to modify the value of s.

In the following algorithmic definition, max is decomposed into an initialization max_init and a loop max_loop:

```
PROC max : ->
DEF  max_init ; max_loop
```

The intention is that max_loop iterates over the elements of the set s to compute its maximum in r after r has been initialized by max_init. Because the maximum must be an element of s, it is an obvious choice if r gets an arbitrary element of s as its initial value.

It is not difficult to see that the algorithmic definition of max satisfies its specification if the definitions of max_init and max_loop satisfy the following specifications:

```
PROC max_init : ->
PRE  card(s) > 0
```

```
SAT   MOD r
POST is_in(r,s)

PROC max_loop : ->
PRE   card(s) > 0 => r!
SAT   MOD s,r
POST FORALL i : Int ( is_in(i,s') => r = max(i,r') )
```

The pre-condition of **max** and **max_init** are the very same and the post-condition of **max_init** implies the pre-condition of **max_loop**. This means that the states for which the pre-condition of **max** holds are exactly the states in which it is the case that **max_init** ; **max_loop** succeeds. The composition of the post-conditions of **max_init** and **max_loop** yields:[6]

```
EXISTS ir : Int
( is_in(ir,s') ; FORALL i : Int ( is_in(i,s') => r = max(i,ir) ) )
```

Using the well-known equivalence

```
r = max(i1,i2) <=> ( r = i1 OR r = i2 ) AND i1 <= r AND i2 <= r
```

it is easy to prove that this condition implies the post-condition of **max**. In other words, if **max_init** ; **max_loop** can transform a state to another state, the post-condition of **max** holds between those states.

The post-condition of **max_loop** has been formulated in such a way that it reflects an iterative computation of the maximum in r. Below it will be explained how to check whether the intended algorithmic definition of the loop satisfies its specification.

One might wonder why the parts of the decomposition are given names. It turns out to be more useful in practice to name the parts of a decomposition as the size of the procedure concerned increases. For small procedures, such as **max**, one could easily proceed without naming the parts; however this example is meant to illustrate a general approach to develop algorithmic definitions from specifications in pre- and post-condition style. It is recommended to follow the approach with a light touch whenever that does not give rise to loss of rigour.

It is intuitively clear that the following algorithmic definitions of **max_init** and **max_loop** satisfy their specifications:

```
PROC max_init : ->
DEF  set_r(select(s))

PROC max_loop : ->
DEF  ( ( card(s) > 0 ?;
           ( LET i : Int := select(s)
         ; set_r(max(i,r))
         ; set_s(rem(i,s))
         )
```

---

[6]The name ir refers to the value of r in the intermediate state after the initialization.

```
      ) *
    ; NOT card(s) > 0 ?
    )
```

The body of `max_loop` is a statement of the form (*A* ?; *X*) * ; NOT *A* ?, which is written `while` *A* `do` *X* or something similar to that in most programming languages. Prior to each iteration, r contains the maximum of the elements of the original value of s iterated over hitherto (except prior to the first iteration) and s contains the set of elements left to iterate over. The number of elements left decreases by one at each iteration and eventually there will be no elements left – which stipulates the termination of the iterative computation of the maximum.

Because the statement that is repeated in `max_loop` occurs several times in the remainder of this section, we introduce the name `max_step` for it:

```
PROC max_step : ->
DEF  card(s) > 0 ?;
     ( LET i : Int := select(s)
     ; set_r(max(i,r))
     ; set_s(rem(i,s))
     )
```

A loop invariant is used below to check whether the algorithmic definition of `max_loop` satisfies its specification. A loop invariant is a property common to the state prior to the first iteration of the loop and the states before and after each of its iterations. For `max_loop`, this is expressed by the following proof obligation for loop invariant preservation, where `inv` stands for the loop invariant:

```
THEOREM ( ( card(s) > 0 => r! ) AND card(s) > 0 => inv
        ; inv => AFTER max_step THEN inv
        )
```

The state prior to the first iteration is characterized by the conjunction of the pre-condition and the test of the loop. In order to check whether the algorithmic definition of `max_loop` satisfies its specification, the loop invariant must also assure the termination of each iteration if the test succeeds. This is expressed by the following additional proof obligation concerning `inv`:

```
THEOREM inv AND card(s) > 0 => FIN max_step
```

The condition `card(s) >= 0 AND r!` is appropriate in this case:

```
PRED inv :
DEF  card(s) >= 0 AND r!
```

The condition `card(s) >= 0` is implied by the test `card(s) > 0` which must hold in the state prior to each iteration. But if `card(s) > 0` holds in the state prior to an iteration, `card(s) >= 0` holds in the state after that iteration because `card(s)` decreases only by one at each iteration. The loop terminates when `card(s) = 0` holds in the state after the iteration. The additional condition **r!** is needed to assure the termination of all iterations. It is not difficult to see that this additional condition is also preserved by the iterations.

Showing that the algorithmic definition of **max_loop** satisfies its specification is facilitated by this loop invariant, because it enables us to forget further about states that can not arise during the execution of the loop.

Forgetting about state transformations that can not arise is generally even more rewarding. Therefore a loop variant is used, in addition to the loop invariant, to check whether the algorithmic definition of **max_loop** satisfies its specification. A loop variant is a property that is common to the state transformations resulting from each of the iterations of the loop and is preserved when such state transformations are composed. The latter means that it is a transitive property, i.e. it also holds for any number of successive iterations. For the current purpose, we are almost done if the loop variant is such that the post-condition is implied by it in case the invariant and the negation of the test of the loop hold. For **max_loop**, all this is expressed by the following two proof obligations where **var** stands for the loop variant:[7]

```
THEOREM ( inv => AFTER max_step THEN var(s',r',s,r)
        ; AFTER MOD s,r
          THEN  EXISTS is : Set[Int], ir : Int
                ( var(s',r',is,ir) AND var(is,ir,s,r) ) =>
                var(s',r',s,r)
        )
```

and

```
THEOREM AFTER MOD s,r
        THEN  inv AND NOT card(s) > 0 AND var(s',r',s,r) =>
              FORALL i : Int ( is_in(i,s') => r = max(i,r') )
```

In order to establish termination of the loop, the loop variant is further required to be well-founded, i.e. there must be no infinite descending paths of states related by the loop variant. This can not be expressed in COLD-1. The following loop variant is appropriate in this case:

```
PRED var : Set[Int] # Int # Set[Int] # Int
IN   ps,pr,cs,cr
DEF  ( FORALL i : Int ( is_in(i,diff(ps,cs)) => cr = max(i,pr) )
     ; subset(cs,ps) AND cs /= ps
     )
```

It is easy to check that this variant holds for each iteration. In the state after each iteration **s** contains one element less than before, viz. the (non-deterministically) selected element, and **r** is set to the maximum of this element and the value of **r** in the state prior to the iteration concerned. That **var** is furthermore transitive follows from two lemmas, which are easily proved. One lemma is about a property of the function **max**:

---

[7]The values of **s** and **r** in the previous state as well as the current state are explicitly passed as arguments to **var** to be able to express that it is transitive.

```
r = max(i,r') <=> r = max(i,ir) AND ir = max(i,r')
```

The other one is about two general properties about sets:

```
subset(s,is) AND s /= is AND subset(is,s') AND is /= s' =>
( is_in(i,diff(s',s)) <=>
  is_in(i,diff(s',is)) OR is_in(i,diff(is,s))
; NOT ( is_in(i,diff(s',is)) AND is_in(i,diff(is,s)) )
)
```

It is trivial to discharge the second of the above-mentioned proof obligations concerning **var** because s is empty if both the invariant and the negation of the test of the loop hold.

Summarizing, we have checked the following proof obligations concerning inv and **var**:

1. **inv** is implied by the pre-condition and the test of the loop and it is furthermore preserved by each iteration of the loop;
2. **inv** implies termination of each iteration if the test succeeds;
3. **var** is established at each iteration and it is furthermore transitive;
4. **inv**, **var** and the negation of the test of the loop imply the post-condition.

When these proof obligations have been discharged and it has also been ensured that **var** is well-founded, it has been shown that, if its pre-condition holds in the state wherein the execution of **max_loop** starts, it terminates and it does so in a state in which its post-condition holds. The outlined way to check this is of course not restricted to this specific case.

To see that **var** is also well-founded is easy: a state where s is empty is not related to another state by **var** and, because s is always a finite set, such a state is encountered after finitely many steps.

It has not yet been proved that **max_loop** terminates if and only if its pre-condition holds in the state wherein the execution starts; only the if part has been proved (and it can be argued that this is sufficient for the current purpose). In order to prove that the algorithmic definition of **max_loop** satisfies its specification with respect to its termination as well, the following proof obligation remains to be discharged:

```
THEOREM card(s) > 0 => r! <=> FIN max_loop
```

If the second proof obligation concerning inv has been discharged, it is sufficient to prove that

```
( NOT card(s) > 0        => FIN max_loop
; card(s) > 0 AND NOT r! => NOT FIN max_loop
)
```

holds, which follows immediately from the algorithmic definition of **max_loop**.

In the following algorithmic definition of **max_loop**, the loop is replaced by a conditional "unfolding":

```
PROC max_loop : ->
```

```
DEF  ( ( card(s) > 0 ?;     ( LET i : Int := select(s)
                            ; set_r(max(i,r))
                            ; set_s(rem(i,s))
                            ; max_loop
                            )    )
     | ( NOT card(s) > 0 ?; SKIP )
     )
```

This unfolding strongly suggests an inductive proof to check whether, if its
pre-condition holds in the state wherein the execution of max_loop starts, it
terminates and it does so in a state in which its post-condition holds. Such an
inductive proof would consist of a proof of

```
inv =>
  AFTER NOT card(s) > 0 ?
  THEN  FORALL i : Int ( is_in(i,s') => r = max(i,r') )
```

and a proof of

```
inv =>
  AFTER card(s) > 0 ?;
        ( LET i : Int := select(s)
        ; set_r(max(i,r))
        ; set_s(rem(i,s))
        ; max_loop
        )
  THEN  FORALL i : Int ( is_in(i,s') => r = max(i,r') )
```

under the assumption that

```
inv =>
  AFTER max_loop
  THEN  FORALL i : Int ( is_in(i,s') => r = max(i,r') )
```

has been proved. By using a loop variant, we could get round such a proof.

The conditional unfolding of max_loop suggests also a way to remove "tail"
recursion from algorithms. The reason to do so is that recursion leads usually
to less efficient programs than iteration. Another way to improve the efficiency
of recursive programs is treated in the next section.

9.13   Memoization

Memoization is a simple and powerful technique to improve the efficiency of
programs by storing results such that they can be reused in subsequent calls
of the same function. The idea of memoization can be applied to programs
in almost every programming language. In this section we give an example
of memoization. COLD-1 offers the appropriate language constructs needed
to explain the idea. In particular, the language does not distinguish between
function application and array lookup. Traditional imperative languages hide

the common nature of these concepts by insisting on different notations: "("
and ")" for functions but "[" and "]" for arrays.

The example is about computing binomial coefficients.[8] If n and k are natural numbers, then the binomial coefficient $\binom{n}{k}$, read "n choose k", is defined
by $n(n-1)\ldots(n-k+1)/k(k-1)\ldots(1)$. It is the number of combinations of n
things, k at a time. These coefficients satisfy the addition formula given below,
which together with the equations for the case of $n = 0$ or $k = 0$ determine
the concept of binomial coefficient completely.

$$\binom{n}{k} = \binom{n-1}{k-1} + \binom{n-1}{k} \qquad\qquad (n > 0, k > 0)$$

$$\binom{n}{0} = 1, \quad \binom{0}{k} = 0 \qquad\qquad (k > 0)$$

The equations give rise to a recursive function definition in COLD-1.

```
FUNC bino : Nat # Nat -> Nat
IN   n,k
DEF  ( k = 0 ?; 1
     | k > 0 ?; ( n = 0 ?; 0
                | n > 0 ?; bino(n - 1,k - 1) + bino(n - 1,k)
                )
     )
```

According to the functional programming paradigm, a recursive definition can
be interpreted as a program to calculate the coefficients. We follow a transfor-
mational approach, and the first procedure called bino1 has the same definition
as bino, except that it is a procedure.

```
PROC bino1 : Nat # Nat -> Nat
IN   n,k
DEF  ( k = 0 ?; 1
     | k > 0 ?; ( n = 0 ?;
                  0
                | n > 0 ?;
                  bino1(n - 1,k - 1) + bino1(n - 1,k)
                )
     )
```

For small numbers there is no problem, but soon this implementation turns
out very inefficient. One call of the procedure bino1 can give rise to two
recursive calls, which at their turn give rise to 4 recursive calls and although
eventually some of the calls can be answered with either 1 or 0, the whole
process is a waste of resources; the same intermediate results are calculated
over and over again. One could calculate and store a sufficient number of
binomial coefficients, but often it is not clear what is sufficient, and one could

---

[8]Binomial coefficients have many useful applications, for example in combinatorics and
in the analysis of algorithms.

also exploit certain further properties of binomial coefficients (e.g. the top ten binomial coefficient identities in [65]).

Memoization however offers an easy option for improvement which avoids some of the choices; and which also does not depend on the mathematics of binomial coefficients. We need a sufficiently large memory for storing results already calculated.

```
FUNC memo : Nat # Nat -> Nat VAR

DECL n,k : Nat

AXIOM INIT => memo(n,k)^

PROC set_memo : Nat # Nat # Nat ->
IN   n,k,b
PRE  TRUE
SAT  MOD memo(n,k)
POST memo(n,k) = b
```

The recursive procedure bino2 defined below is obtained as follows: when asked for bino2(n,k), it is checked first if the value is already stored in the memory. In that case it can be retrieved from memory, otherwise it is calculated. Whenever a non-trivial value is calculated, it is stored by means of set_memo for possible re-use.

```
PROC bino2 : Nat # Nat -> Nat
IN   n,k
DEF  ( memo(n,k)! ?;
         memo(n,k)
     | memo(n,k)^ ?;
       ( k = 0 ?; 1
       | k > 0 ?; ( n = 0 ?;
                      0
                   | n > 0 ?;
                     LET out :=
                           bino2(n - 1,k - 1) + bino2(n - 1,k);
                     set_memo(n,k,out);
                     out
                   )
       )
     )
```

The approach is correct in the sense that bino2(n,k) = bino(n,k) because an invariant memo_inv is maintained.

```
PRED memo_inv :
DEF  FORALL n,k ( memo(n,k)!  =>  memo(n,k) = bino(n,k) )

THEOREM INIT => memo_inv;
```

```
memo_inv => AFTER FLUSH bino2(n,k) THEN memo_inv
```

In practice one does not have an infinite memory, but probably something which only works for a limited set of address values, like the following memory, where **max** denotes a constant:

```
FUNC memo : Nat # Nat -> Nat VAR

FUNC max : -> Nat
PRE  TRUE
POST max > 0

DECL n,k : Nat

AXIOM INIT AND n < max AND k < max  =>  memo(n,k)^

PROC set_memo : Nat # Nat # Nat ->
IN   n,k,b
PRE  n < max AND k < max
SAT  MOD memo(n,k)
POST memo(n,k) = b
```

Again there is a simple transformation which can be applied to bino2. The result is bino3. The memory may only be used for $n <$ **max** and for $k <$ **max**, so another case analysis must be made.

```
PROC bino3 : Nat # Nat -> Nat
IN   n,k
PRE  TRUE
DEF  ( n < max AND k < max AND memo(n,k)! ?;
       memo(n,k)
     | n >= max OR k >= max OR memo(n,k)^ ?;
       ( k = 0 ?; 1
       | k > 0 ?; ( n = 0 ?;
                    0
                  | n > 0 ?;
                    LET out :=
                        bino3(n - 1,k - 1) + bino3(n - 1,k);
                    ( n < max AND k <  max ?; set_memo(n,k,out)
                    | n >= max OR k >= max ?; SKIP
                    ) ;
                    out
                  )
       )
     )
```

The transformation process is independent of the function being calculated. The case analysis guards and the memory update statements are the same for any recursive procedure to which memoization is applied. But of course, insight in the calculation is important, particularly when really efficient solutions are demanded.

Below we show how the outcome of the above transformation process is mapped to C, using Kernighan and Ritchie C [66]. Because binomial coefficients can become large, even for small values of n and k, the natural numbers are represented as long integers. The value of -1 is used to represent "undefined". If we invoke the program with arguments 20 and 10, it immediately writes the result 184756. But if we remove the assignment memo[n][k]=out;, we find that this takes already 40 sec. on a 80386 computer.

```
#define MAX 100
long memo[MAX][MAX];
#define set_memo(N,K,X) memo[N][K]=(X)
#define UNDEFINED  -1
#define DEFINED(N) (N) >= 0

void INIT()
{ int i,j;
  for (i=0; i<MAX; i++)
      for (j=0; j<MAX; j++)
          memo[i][j]=UNDEFINED;
}


long int bino3(n,k)
long int n;
long int k;
{ if (n<MAX && k<MAX && DEFINED(memo[n][k]))
      return(memo[n][k]);
  else { if (k==0)
              return(1);
          else if (n==0)
                  return(0);
              else { long int out;
                     out=bino3(n - 1,k - 1) + bino3(n - 1,k);
                     if (n<MAX && k<MAX) set_memo(n,k,out);
                     return(out);
                   }
       }
}

main(argc,argv)
int argc;
char *argv[];
{ long int n,k;
  INIT();
  if (argc == 3)
    { sscanf(argv[1],"%ld",&n);
```

```
        sscanf(argv[2],"%ld",&k);
        printf("%ld",bino3(n,k));
    }
}
```

Further optimizations on bino3 can be made, for example using the facts that bino$(n,n) = 1$ and that for $n < k$ always bino$(n,k) = 0$. We leave these optimizations here, because the only point of the example is to explain the basic principle of memoization.

In languages for pure logic programming or pure functional programming there is no global storage facility and, most often, naive programs suffer from gross inefficiencies. Experienced programmers know how to transform such programs into more efficient ones, usually at the expense of introducing auxiliary functions which have extra arguments for moving around the intermediate results which are to be re-used.

In an imperative language the situation is just the other way around. Many imperative programs have lots of variables, and the storage of all kinds of intermediate results is taking place anyhow – even if there is no clear view on the options for later use of the values.

The imperative programming languages have already provided the technical means to exploit memoization for decades, but logic programming and functional programming have catalysed the awareness with respect to the concept.

In the context of functional programming, the idea of an implementation supporting "memo functions" has been explained in [67]. It can fruitfully be combined with the concepts of lazy evaluation and cyclic data structures.

In the context of logic programming, the idea can be exploited too. In [68] it is explained that a useful application of the impure **assert** and **asserta** predicates built in to Prolog is to store already computed answers to questions (these predicates change a kind of global state).[9] Below we show how bino2 is mapped to Prolog, using the SB-Prolog system (version 3.1) described in [73]. If we "consult" this program on a SUN SPARC station1 by entering the goal bino2(20,10,X)., the system immediately returns **yes** and the solution X = 184756. But if we remove the clause set_memo(N,K,OUT), a heap overflow may result.

```
set_memo(N,K,X) :- asserta(bino2(N,K,X)).

bino2(N,0,1).
bino2(0,K,0) :- K > 0.
bino2(N,K,OUT) :- N > 0,
                  K > 0,
                  N1 is N - 1,
                  K1 is K - 1,
```

---

[9]This use of asserts was criticized (e.g. in [70]) and special table structures to support storage of intermediate results has been introduced (e.g. in [71] and [72]) as an alternative.

```
bino2(N1,K1,OUT1),
bino2(N1,K ,OUT2),
OUT is OUT1 + OUT2,
set_memo(N,K,OUT).
```

Memoization can be helpful in many ways. For example, when used in theorem proving programs, it can be useful to memoize negative results: if a lemma L was not provable for a search-depth of n say, then a later question if L is provable for depth $m < n$ can be answered negatively immediately. In that case the memoization technique helps pruning the search tree. More generally, it is often possible to make a trade-off between memory usage and execution time. It is often the motivation for using state-based programming paradigms. Memoization is a special case of this trade-off, but it is a particularly clear one. There are many variations upon the basic idea, some of which can be found in the references given.

9.14   Concluding Remarks

All topics concerning specification and design treated in this chapter put forward ideas to profit by facilities offered by COLD-1. The accent is on principles, guidelines and techniques concerning modular structuring of specifications. Most of them are relatively unknown and not extensively treated elsewhere. They explain useful ways of exploiting the powerful facilities for modular structuring of specifications offered by COLD-1.

Because it is a wide-spectrum language and it supports many existing styles of specification, many ideas originating from various approaches to specification, design and implementation of computer-based systems – including ideas from logic programming and functional programming – are applicable (see e.g. [74, 75, 76, 64, 60]). Consequently, there is a wide variety of established principles, guidelines and techniques that can be followed and used in conjunction with COLD-1, but which are not treated in this chapter.

Bibliography

[1] Berzins V.A., Luqi. *Software engineering with abstractions*. Addison-Wesley, 1991.

[2] Popper K.R. *Objective knowledge, and evolutionary approach*. Oxford University Press, 1972.

[3] Feijs L.M.G., Jonkers H.B.M. *Formal specification and design*. Cambridge University Press, Cambridge tracts in theoretical computer science 35, 1992.

[4] Feijs L.M.G., Jonkers H.B.M., Koymans C.P.J., Renardel de Lavalette G.R. *Formal definition of the design language COLD-K*. revised edition, ESPRIT document METEOR/t7/PRLE/7, 1987.

[5] Hagelstein J., Ponsaert F. *Introducing formal requirements into industry*. In: Bergstra J.A., Feijs L.M.G. (Eds.), Algebraic methods: theory, tools and applications part II, Springer-Verlag LNCS 490, pp. 129–141, 1991.

[6] Lamport L. *A simple approach to specifying concurrent systems*. Communications of the ACM, 32(1):32–45, 1989.

[7] Hatley D.J., Pirbhai I.A. *Strategies for real-time system specification*. Dorset House Publishing, 1987.

[8] Hasse H. *Über die Klassenzahl abelschen Zahlkörper*. Berlin: Akademie Verlag, 1952.

[9] Rudolph E., Graubmann P., Grabowski J. *Towards an SDL design methodology using sequence chart segments*. In: SDL '91, evolving methods, Faergemand O. and Reed R. (Eds.), Elsevier Science Publishers, pp. 237-252, 1991.

[10] Kristoffersen T. *Message sequence chart and SDL specification consistency check*. In: SDL '91, evolving methods, Faergemand O. and Reed R. (Eds.), Elsevier Science Publishers, pp. 253-259, 1991.

[11] Tilanus P.A.J. *A formalization of message sequence charts*. In: SDL '91, evolving methods, Faergemand O. and Reed R. (Eds.), Elsevier Science Publishers, pp. 273-288, 1991.

[12] Mauw S., Reniers M.A. *An algebraic semantics of basic message sequence charts*. The Computer Journal 37(4) (to appear), 1994.

[13] Welsh J. and Elder J. *Introduction to Pascal*. Prentice-Hall, Series in computer science, 1988.

[14] Kalicharan N. *C by example*. Cambridge University Press, Cambridge computer science texts 29, 1993.

[15] Bird R. and Wadler P. *Introduction to functional programming*. Prentice-Hall, series in computer science, 1988.

[16] Paulson L.C. *ML for the working programmer*. Cambridge University Press, 1991.

[17] Davie A.J.T. *An Introduction to functional programming systems using Haskell*. Cambridge University Press, Cambridge computer science texts 27, 1992.

[18] Crookes D. *Introduction to programming in Prolog*. Prentice-Hall, series in computer science, 1988.

[19] Jonkers H.B.M. *PROTOCOLD 1.1 user manual*. IST Report RWR-513-hj-91080-hj, Philips research, Information and Software Technology, 1991.

[20] Gallier J.H. *Logic for computer science*. John Wiley & Sons, 1987.

[21] Harel D. *First-order dynamic logic*. Springer-Verlag, LNCS 68, 1979.

[22] Lichtenstein O., Pnueli A., and Zuck L. *The glory of the past*. In: Parikh R. (Ed.), *Proceedings logics of programs 1985*, pp. 196–218. Springer-Verlag, LNCS 193, 1985.

[23] Bril R.J. *COLD-1 IGLOO library, abstract COLD-1 specifications*. IST Report RWB-508-RE92255, Philips research, Information and Software Technology, 1992.

[24] Middelburg C.A. *Logic and specification – extending VDM-SL for advanced formal specification*. Chapman & Hall, Computer science: research and practice 1, 1993.

[25] Ullman J.D. *Principles of database and knowledge-base systems, Volume I*. Computer Science Press, 1988.

[26] Feijs L.M.G. *Modelbaan met ATB, Overzicht van een project*. Radio Bulletin 53(8):321–324, 1994.

[27] Wirth N. *Algorithms + data structures = programs*. Prentice-Hall, 1976.

[28] Harel D. *Statecharts, a visual formalism for complex systems.* Science of Computer Programming 8(3):231–274, 1987.

[29] Nassi I., Shneidermann B. *Flowchart techniques for structured programming.* ACM SIGPLAN Not. 8(8):12–16, 1973.

[30] Van den Bos R.D., Feijs L.M.G., van Ommering R.C. *POLAR, a picture-oriented language for abstract representations.* In: Bergstra J.A., Feijs L.M.G. (Eds.), Algebraic methods: theory, tools and applications part II Springer-Verlag LNCS 490, pp. 233–276, 1991.

[31] Baeten J.C.M., Weijland W.P. *Process algebra.* Cambridge Universtity Press, Cambridge tracts in theoretical computer science 18, 1990.

[32] Van Ommering R.C. *TEDDY user's manual.* Technical report 12NC 4322 2730176 1, Philips Research, Dept. for Information and Software Technology, 1993.

[33] Robinson P.J. *Hierarchical object-oriented design.* Prentice-Hall, 1992.

[34] DeMarco T. *Structured analysis and system specification.* Prentice-Hall, 1978.

[35] Yourdon E. *Modern structured analysis.* Prentice-Hall, 1989.

[36] Semmens L.T., France R.B., Docker T.W.G. *Integrated structured analysis and formal specification techniques.* The Computer Journal, 35(6):600–610, 1992

[37] Floyd R. *Assigning meaning to programs.* In: Mathematical Aspects of Computer Science, XIX American Mathematical Society, pp. 19–32, 1967.

[38] Bate G. *Mascot 3: an informal introductory example.* Software Engineering Journal, pp. 95–102, 1986.

[39] Gorissen P.M.H., Koymans R.L.C., F.C.J.P Stevers. *Formal specification and design of a CD-I full motion decoder IC.* Philips internal report RWR-113-rk-90216-rk, 1990.

[40] Jonkers H.B.M. *An overview of the SPRINT method,* In: Woodcock J.C.P., Larsen P.G. (Eds.). FME'93: industrial-strength formal methods, Springer-Verlag LNCS 670, pp. 403–427, 1993.

[41] Bear D. *Principles of telecommunication traffic engineering.* Peter Peregrinus, 1976.

[42] Joel A.E. Jr., *Electronic switching: central office systems of the world.* IEEE Int. switching Symp. Rec., IEEE Press, 1976.

[43] Schramel F.J., Van't Slot I.A.W. *General introduction to PRX 205*. In: [42] pp. 232–243, 1972.

[44] Bergstra J.A., Ponse A., Van Wamel J.J. *Process algebra with backtracking*. University of Amsterdam report P9306, 1993.

[45] Van S.F.M. Vlijmen, Van Wamel J.J. *A semantic approach to Protocold using process algebra*. University of Amsterdam report P9317, 1993.

[46] Jensen K. *Coloured Petri nets and the invariant method*. Theoretical Computer Science 14, pp. 317–336, 1981.

[47] Van der Aalst W.M.P. *Timed coloured Petri nets and their application to logistics*. Ph. D. thesis, Technical University Eindhoven, 1992.

[48] CCITT. *Recommendation Z100, Specification and description language (SDL)*. document AP IX-35-E, International Telegraph and Telephone Consultative Committee, Geneva, 1988.

[49] Jacobson I. *Object-oriented software engineering*. Addison-Wesley, 1992.

[50] Bergstra J.A., Klop J.W., Tucker J.V. *Process algebra with asynchronous communication mechanisms*, Report CS-R8410, Centre for Mathematics and Computer Science, Amsterdam, 1994.

[51] Saracco R., Smith J.R.W., Reed R. *Telecommunications systems engineering using SDL*. Elsevier Science Publishers, 1989.

[52] Saracco R., Tilanus P.A.J. *CCITT SDL: overview of the language and its applications*. In: Computer networks and ISDN systems, special issue on CCITT SDL, 13(2):65–74, Elsevier Science Publishers, 1987 .

[53] Møller-Pedersen B., Belsnes D., Dahle H.P. *Rationale and tutorial on OSDL: an object-oriented extension of SDL*. In: Computer networks and ISDN systems, special issue on CCITT SDL, 13(2):97–117. Elsevier Science Publishers, 1987.

[54] Kossmann H. *A graphic SDL support environment.* In: Computer networks and ISDN systems, special issue on CCITT SDL, 13(2):91–96 Elsevier Science Publishers, 1987.

[55] Mauw S., Van Wijk M., Winter T. *A formal semantics of synchronous interworkings*. In: O. Færgemand and Sarma A., (Eds.), SDL'93 using objects, Proceedings of the sixth SDL forum, Darmstadt, Elsevier Science Publishers, 1993.

[56] Fitzgerald J.S. *Modularity in model-oriented formal specification and its interaction with formal reasoning*. Technical Report UMCS-91-11-2, University of Manchester, Department of computer science, 1991.

[57] Parnas D.L. *On the criteria to be used in decomposing systems into modules.* Communications of the ACM, 5(12):1053–1058, 1972.

[58] Yourdon E.N. and Constantine L.L. *Structured design: fundamentals of a discipline of computer program and systems design.* Prentice-Hall, 1979.

[59] Rumbaugh J. et al. *Object-oriented modeling and design.* Prentice-Hall, 1991.

[60] Meyer B. *Object-oriented software construction.* Prentice-Hall, 1988.

[61] Goldberg A. and Robson D. *Smalltalk-80: the language and its implementation.* Addison-Wesley, 1983.

[62] Stroustrup B. *The C++ programming language.* Addison-Wesley, 1986.

[63] Jones C.B. *Software development: a rigorous approach.* Prentice-Hall, 1980.

[64] Jones C.B. *Systematic software development using VDM.* Prentice-Hall, second edition, 1990.

[65] Graham R.L., Knuth D.E., Patashnik O. *Concrete mathematics.* Addison-Wesley, 1990.

[66] Kernighan B.W., Ritchie D.M. *The C programming language.* Prentice-Hall, 1978.

[67] Hughes R.J.M. *Lazy memo functions.* In: Jouannaud (Ed.), proceedings of the IFIP conference on functional programming languages and computer architecture, Nancy, pp. 129–46, LNCS 201, Springer-Verlag, 1985.

[68] Bratko I. *Prolog programming for artificial intelligence.* Addison-Wesley, 1986.

[69] Hall M., Mayfield J. *Improving the performance of AI software: payoffs and pitfalls in automatic memoization.* In: Sixth international symposium on AI, Monterrey, Mexico, 1993.

[70] Knuutila T. *Efficient Prolog programming.* Software – Practice and Experience, 22(3):209–221, 1992.

[71] Fan C., Dietrich S.W. *Extension table built-ins for Prolog.* Software – Practice and Experience, 22(7):573–597, 1992.

[72] Asakawa Y., et al. *Zephyr: toward true compiler-based programming in Prolog.* IBM Journal of research and development, 36(3):391–408, 1992.

[73] Debray S.K. *The SB-Prolog System, Version 3.1, a user manual.* from material by D.S. Warren, S. Dietrich, F. Pereira, Report department of computer science, University of Arizona, Tucson (1989).

[74] Guttag J.V. and Horning J.J. *Report on the Larch shared language.* Science of Computer Programming, 6(2):103–134, 1986.

[75] Wing J.M. *Writing Larch interface language specifications.* ACM Transactions on Programming Languages and Systems, 9(1):1–24, 1987.

[76] Bergstra J.A., Heering J., and Klint P. *Algebraic specification.* ACM Press, Addison-Wesley, 1989.

Appendix A
Syntax of COLD-1

A.1 Introduction

In this appendix we define the concrete syntax of COLD-1 by means of a context free grammar and priority and associativity rules for the built-in and user-defined operators. In Section A.2 we define the lexical units. In Section A.3 we give the context free syntax of the language using extended BNF notation. The priorities and associativities of the built-in operators are defined in Section A.4.

We shall use typewriter face to denote concrete representations of COLD-1 constructs. The characters of this type face are listed below:

```
  !  "  #  $  %  &  '  (  )  *  +  ,  -  .  /  0  1  2  3  4  5  6  7  8  9  :  ;  <  =  >  ?
  @  A  B  C  D  E  F  G  H  I  J  K  L  M  N  O  P  Q  R  S  T  U  V  W  X  Y  Z  [  \  ]  ^  _
  '  a  b  c  d  e  f  g  h  i  j  k  l  m  n  o  p  q  r  s  t  u  v  w  x  y  z  {  |  }  ~
```

A.2 Lexical Units

A terminal production of the concrete syntax of COLD-1 is a sequence of lexical units, where each lexical unit is a sequence of ASCII characters. The lexical units are subdivided into keywords, symbols and comments, to be discussed in the following subsections. In a given string of ASCII characters, the lexical units are recognized on the basis of left to right reading, taking the longest possible match. The only exceptions are string tokens and comments between brackets, for which the shortest possible match is taken. Spaces and new lines act as separators.

A.2.1 Keywords

A keyword is one of the following sequences of characters:

ABSTRACT	IMPORT	RENAMING	)
AFTER	IN	RIGHT	,
AND	IND	SAT	->
AXIOM	INFIX	SIG	.
BEGIN	INIT	SKIP	/=
CLASS	ISNEW	SOME	:
COMPONENT	LEFT	SORT	::
DECL	LET	SPECIFICATION	:=
DEF	MOD	STOP	;
DEP	NEW	SYSTEM	<=>
END	NOT	THAT	=
EXISTS	OPERATORS	THEN	=/=
EXPORT	OR	THEOREM	==
EXPORTING	OUT	TO	=>
FALSE	POST	TRUE	?
FIN	POSTFIX	VAR	[
FLUSH	PRE	XOR	]
FORALL	PRED	!	^
FREE	PREFIX	#	|
FROM	PREV	$	
FUNC	PROC	'	
IMPLEMENTATION	QUALIFYING	(	

A.2.2 Symbols

A symbol is an arbitrary non-empty sequence of *tokens* separated by periods. Tokens are sequences of characters that are not keywords, and are divided into four classes:

1. *alphanumeric tokens*: non-empty sequences of letters, digits and underscores, excluding those sequences that are keywords or number tokens (see below);

2. *operator tokens*: non-empty sequences of the following characters:

    ! # $ & * + - / : < = > ? @ \ ^ ' | ~

    excluding those sequences that are keywords;

3. *number tokens*: non-empty sequences of digits;

4. *string tokens*: sequences of characters enclosed by double quotes, where special characters and the double quote character itself are denoted by using \ as an escape character.

A.2.3 Comments

Two comment facilities are provided. The first is the use of the comment
brackets { and }, which turn the enclosed text (not containing a }) into a
comment:

    { This is comment }

The comment brackets can not be nested. The second is the use of a %-sign,
which turns the rest of the line into a comment:

    % This is comment

Comments may be inserted anywhere between two lexical units and have no
meaning in terms of the abstract syntax, hence they are ignored in the grammar
in Section A.3.

A.3 Grammar

In this section we present the concrete syntax of COLD-1 by means of a context
free grammar. The notation used is extended Backus-Naur form (BNF) with
the following conventions:

1. All characters in typewriter face are terminal symbols.

2. [X] in a production rule denotes X or the empty string.

3. {X} in a production rule denotes an arbitary sequence of X's, including
   the empty sequence.

The start symbol of the grammar is the nonterminal <description>. The
nonterminal <token> has no production rule in the grammar and denotes an
arbitrary token (see A.2.2).

<description> ::= [[OPERATORS { <priority level> }]
    { <component definition> } SYSTEM] <system description>
<priority level> ::= PREFIX [<token> { , <token> }]
    | POSTFIX [<token> { , <token> }]
    | INFIX [<associativity>] [<token> { , <token> }]
<associativity> ::= LEFT
    | RIGHT
<component definition> ::= COMPONENT <identifier>
    SPECIFICATION <description> [IMPLEMENTATION <description>]
    | LET <identifier> := <description>
<identifier> ::= <symbol> [[{ <item section> }]]
<symbol> ::= <token> { . <token> }
<item section> ::= <item> { , <item> }
    | SORT [<sort item> { , <sort item> }]

```
      | PRED [ <predicate item> { , <predicate item> } ]
      | FUNC [ <function item> { , <function item> } ]
      | PROC [ <procedure item> { , <procedure item> } ]
<item> ::= <identifier> [ : <type> [ -> <type> ] ]
      | ( [ <item> { , <item> } ] )
<type> ::= [ <identifier> { # <identifier> } ]
<sort item> ::= <identifier>
      | ( [ <sort item> { , <sort item> } ] )
<predicate item> ::= <identifier> [ : <type> ]
      | ( [ <predicate item> { , <predicate item> } ] )
<function item> ::= <identifier> [ : <type> -> <type> ]
      | ( [ <function item> { , <function item> } ] )
<procedure item> ::= <identifier> [ : <type> -> <type> ]
      | ( [ <procedure item> { , <procedure item> } ] )
<system description> ::= <component>
      | [ ABSTRACT [ <component> { , <component> } ] ]
      [ EXPORT { <signature section> } ]
      [ IMPORT [ <component> { , <component> } ] ]
      [ CLASS { <definition> } ] END
<component> ::= <component name>
      [ [ EXPORTING { <signature section> } ]
       [ RENAMING { <renaming section> } ]
       [ QUALIFYING <symbol> ] END ]
<component name> ::=
      <symbol> [ ' ] [ [ { <parameter section> } ] ]
<parameter section> ::= <parameter> { , <parameter> }
      | SORT [ <sort parameter> { , <sort parameter> } ]
      | PRED [ <predicate parameter> { , <predicate parameter> } ]
      | FUNC [ <function parameter> { , <function parameter> } ]
      | PROC [ <procedure parameter> { , <procedure parameter> } ]
<parameter> ::= <identifier> [ : <type> [ -> <type> ] ]
      [ FROM <component name> ]
      | ( [ <parameter> { , <parameter> } ] )
      [ FROM <component name> ]
<sort parameter> ::= <identifier> [ FROM <component name> ]
      | ( [ <sort parameter> { , <sort parameter> } ] )
      [ FROM <component name> ]
<predicate parameter> ::= <identifier> [ : <type> ]
      [ FROM <component name> ]
      | ( [ <predicate parameter> { , <predicate parameter> } ] )
      [ FROM <component name> ]
<function parameter> ::= <identifier> [ : <type> -> <type> ]
      [ FROM <component name> ]
      | ( [ <function parameter> { , <function parameter> } ] )
```

      [FROM <component name>]
<procedure parameter> ::= <identifier> [: <type> -> <type>]
      [FROM <component name>]
    | ([<procedure parameter> { , <procedure parameter> }])
      [FROM <component name>]
<signature section> ::= <item section>
    | SIG [<component name> { , <component name> }]
<renaming section> ::= <pair> { , <pair> }
    | SORT [<sort pair> { , <sort pair> }]
    | PRED [<predicate pair> { , <predicate pair> }]
    | FUNC [<function pair> { , <function pair> }]
    | PROC [<procedure pair> { , <procedure pair> }]
<pair> ::= [<item> { , <item> }] TO <symbol>
<sort pair> ::= [<sort item> { , <sort item> }] TO <symbol>
<predicate pair> ::=
    [<predicate item> { , <predicate item> }] TO <symbol>
<function pair> ::=
    [<function item> { , <function item> }] TO <symbol>
<procedure pair> ::=
    [<procedure item> { , <procedure item> }] TO <symbol>
<definition> ::= SORT <symbol> [<sort body>]
    | PRED <symbol> : <type>
      [IN [<object list>]]
      [<predicate body>]
    | FUNC <symbol> : <type> -> <type>
      [IN [<object list>]] [OUT [<object list>]]
      [PRE [<assertion>]] [<function body>]
      [POST [<assertion>]]
    | PROC <symbol> : <type> -> <type>
      [IN [<object list>]] [OUT [<object list>]]
      [PRE [<assertion>]] [<procedure body>]
      [POST [<assertion>]]
    | DECL [<object list>]
    | AXIOM [<assertion>]
    | THEOREM [<assertion>]
<sort body> ::= FREE
    | VAR
    | DEP [<entity list>]
<predicate body> ::= FREE
    | VAR
    | DEP [<entity list>]
    | IND [<assertion>]
    | DEF [<assertion>]
<function body> ::= FREE

```
        | VAR
        | DEP [ <entity list> ]
        | IND [ <assertion> ]
        | DEF [ <expression> ]
<procedure body> ::= FREE
        | SAT [ <expression> ]
        | DEF [ <expression> ]
<object list> ::= <object> { , <object> }
<object> ::= <symbol> [ : <type> ]
        | ( [ <object list> ] )
<entity list> ::= <entity> { , <entity> }
<entity> ::= [ <expression> ] <operator> [ <expression> ]
<operator> ::= <symbol> [ [ { <item section> } ] ]
        [ : <type> [ -> <type> ] ]
<assertion> ::= <expression> !
        | <expression> ^
        | <expression> = <expression>
        | <expression> /= <expression>
        | <expression> == <expression>
        | <expression> =/= <expression>
        | [ <expression> ] <assertion operator> [ <expression> ]
        | TRUE
        | FALSE
        | NOT <assertion>
        | <assertion> AND <assertion>
        | <assertion> OR <assertion>
        | <assertion> XOR <assertion>
        | <assertion> => <assertion>
        | <assertion> <=> <assertion>
        | FORALL <object list> <assertion>
        | EXISTS <object list> <assertion>
        | INIT
        | AFTER <expression> THEN <assertion>
        | FIN <expression>
        | PREV <assertion>
        | ISNEW <expression>
        | LET <object list> [ := <expression> ]
        | <object list> := <expression>
        | <assertion> ; <assertion>
        | BEGIN [ <assertion> ] END
        | ( [ <assertion> ] )
<assertion operator> ::=
        <symbol> { ' } [ [ { <item section> } ] ] [ : <type> ]
<expression> ::= $
```

```
            | SOME <object list> <assertion>
            | THAT <object list> <assertion>
            | SKIP
            | STOP
            | <assertion> ?
            | [ <expression> ] <expression operator> [ <expression> ]
            | <expression> | <expression>
            | <expression> *
            | MOD <entity list>
            | FLUSH <expression>
            | PREV <expression>
            | NEW <type>
            | LET <object list> [ := <expression> ]
            | <object list> := <expression>
            | <expression> ; <expression>
            | <expression> , <expression>
            | BEGIN [ <expression> ] END
            | <expression> :: <type>
            | ( [ <expression> ] )
<expression operator> ::= <symbol> { ' }
      [ [ { <item section> } ] ] [ : <type> -> <type> ]
```

A.4 Operator Priorities and Associativities

Assertions and expressions in COLD-1 are meant for being parsed by means of operator precedence techniques, taking the priorities and associativities of the built-in and user-defined operators into account. In this section we define the priorities and associativities of the built-in operators. The priorities and associativities of the user-defined operators are defined by the user in operator clauses (see Section 4.7). The tables below define the priorities and associativities of the various built-in operators.

We distinguish nullary, unary and binary operators, where operators may consist of more than one token (as indicated by the tables). Unary operators can be prefix or postfix, while binary operators are always infix. The holes for the arguments of the operators are indicated by bullets ($\bullet$). The priority levels are listed in decreasing order of binding strength of the associated operators. The operators at a given priority level are either all nullary, unary or binary. As indicated in the table, the user-defined operators have priorities higher than all non-nullary built-in operators.

The priorities and associativities (L for left and R for right) are used to associate a unique parse tree with each assertion and expression produced by the ambiguous grammar presented in A.3. The parse tree associated with a construct is defined as the tree obtained by parsing the construct in accordance with the strict priority and associativity rules. The tree obtained this way

Operator	Pri	Ass	Description
TRUE	0	-	true
FALSE	0	-	false
INIT	0	-	initially
$	0	-	any
SKIP	0	-	skip
STOP	0	-	stop
NEW ...	0	-	new
LET ...	0	-	declaration
BEGIN ... END	0	-	block
(...)	0	-	parentheses
x	0	-	nullary non-user-defined operator

Table A.1: Operator priorities and associativities.

need not be a legal parse tree of the grammar defined in A.3, in which case the construct is considered syntactically incorrect. Hence the set of syntactically correct COLD-1 constructs is the set of terminal productions of grammar A.3 which have a legal parse tree (as defined above) associated with them.

As an example, consider the following assertion, which is a terminal production of the nonterminal <assertion>:

```
FORALL x:T x = x
```

This assertion is not syntactically correct since it would be parsed as: (FORALL x:T x) = x which is not a legal assertion. Problems such as this are a consequence of the operator precedence technique used. They can generally be avoided in a simple way by the use of parentheses, e.g., in the case above:
FORALL x:T (x = x)

f •	1	-	unary non-user-defined operator
...	2	...	user-defined operators
• :: ...	3	-	type cast
• , •	4	R	tupling
FORALL ... •	5	-	universal quantification
EXISTS ... •	5	-	existential quantification
SOME ... •	5	-	random selection
THAT ... •	5	-	unique selection
MOD •	5	-	modify
FLUSH •	5	-	flush
ISNEW •	5	-	is new
• !	6	-	definedness
• ^	6	-	undefinedness
• = •	7	-	equality
• /= •	7	-	inequality
• == •	7	-	identity
• =/= •	7	-	non-identity
• := •	7	-	binding
NOT •	8	-	negation
• AND •	9	R	conjunction
• OR •	10	R	disjunction
• XOR •	10	R	exclusive or
• => •	11	R	implication
• <=> •	12	R	equivalence
PREV •	13	-	previously
• ?	14	-	guard
• *	14	-	repetition
AFTER ... THEN •	15	-	after
FIN •	15	-	finish
• ; •	16	R	composition
• | •	17	R	choice

Table A.2: Operator priorities and associativities (continued).

Appendix B
Standard Library

In this appendix a number of components are given which constitute a "standard library". It is a subset of the Incremental Generic Library Of Objects (IGLOO), as developed within Philips from 1988 – 1991. They can be copied and reused in many typical formal specification tasks. Only a modest selection of components is presented here. The full IGLOO contains 25.000 lines of text (600 Kbyte), but 20% of this is comment, and moreover ± 20.000 of these lines are made by a generator to provide for the enumerations ENUM2, ENUM3, ... ENUM49, and similarly for items, records, unions and tuples.

The operator clause presented in Section 4.7 is used. In particular, the PREFIX operators are - and ', the high-priority INFIX LEFT operators are *, / and the low-priority INFIX LEFT operators are +, -. Finally there are INFIX relational operators <, >, <=, and >=.

B.1 Items

The component ITEM specifies a class with a single sort, without any restrictions imposed on the sort. The interpretation of Item is: the set of objects in the sort. When needed, we shall freely use variants of ITEM called ITEM1, ITEM2, etc., with sorts Item1, Item2.

```
LET ITEM :=
CLASS
  SORT Item    VAR
END
```

B.2 Ordered Items

The component WLO specifies a weak linear ordering. For i,j : Item, the intended interpretation is as follows: Item is the set of objects on which the linear order is defined; $i <= j$ is: the order relation holds between i and j.

The axioms WLO1 – WLO4 state that <= is reflexive, antisymmetric, linear, and transitive, respectively.

```
LET WLO :=
CLASS
  SORT Item    VAR
  PRED <= : Item # Item

  DECL i,j,k : Item

  AXIOM
  {WLO1} i <= i;
  {WLO2} i <= j AND j <= i => i = j;
  {WLO3} i <= j OR j <= i OR i = j;
  {WLO4} i <= j AND j <= k => i <= k

  THEOREM i <= j OR j <= i
END
```

B.3 Booleans

The component BOOL specifies the data type of Boolean values. For b, c is Bool the intended interpretation is as follows: Bool is the set of Boolean values; true is the Boolean value "true"; false is the Boolean value "false"; not(b) is the negation of b; and(b,c) is the conjunction of b and c; or(b,c) is the disjunction of b and c; imp(b,c) is the implication of b and c; eqv(b,c) is the equivalence of b and c; xor(b,c) is the "exclusive or" of b and c.

```
COMPONENT BOOL SPECIFICATION
EXPORT
  SORT Bool
  FUNC true  :              -> Bool,
       false :              -> Bool,
       not   : Bool         -> Bool,
       and   : Bool # Bool -> Bool,
       or    : Bool # Bool -> Bool,
       imp   : Bool # Bool -> Bool,
       eqv   : Bool # Bool -> Bool,
       xor   : Bool # Bool -> Bool
CLASS
  SORT Bool
  FUNC true  : -> Bool
  FUNC false : -> Bool

  DECL b,c : Bool

  PRED is_gen : Bool
  IND  is_gen(true);
       is_gen(false)
```

```
AXIOM
{BOOL1} true!;
{BOOL2} false!;
{BOOL3} true /= false;
{BOOL4} is_gen(b)

FUNC not : Bool -> Bool
IND  not(true ) = false;
     not(false) = true

FUNC and : Bool # Bool -> Bool
IND  and(false,false) = false;
     and(false,true ) = false;
     and(true ,false) = false;
     and(true ,true ) = true

FUNC or : Bool # Bool -> Bool
IND  or(false,false) = false;
     or(false,true ) = true;
     or(true ,false) = true;
     or(true ,true ) = true

FUNC imp : Bool # Bool -> Bool
IND  imp(false,false) = true;
     imp(false,true ) = true;
     imp(true ,false) = false;
     imp(true ,true ) = true

FUNC eqv : Bool # Bool -> Bool
IND  eqv(false,false) = true;
     eqv(false,true ) = false;
     eqv(true ,false) = false;
     eqv(true ,true ) = true

FUNC xor : Bool # Bool -> Bool
IND  xor(false,false) = false;
     xor(false,true ) = true;
     xor(true ,false) = true;
     xor(true ,true ) = false

% definedness
THEOREM not(b)!
        ; and(b,c)!
        ; or(b,c)!
        ; imp(b,c)!
        ; eqv(b,c)!
        ; xor(b,c)!
```

END

B.4   Natural Numbers

The component NAT uses the special number notation (NUMBER_NOTATION). It specifies the data type of natural numbers. For m, n : Nat the intended interpretation is as follows: Nat is the set of natural numbers; $succ(m)$ is the successor of m ($= m + 1$); $pred(m)$ is the predecessor of m ($= m - 1$); $m + n$ is the sum of m and n; $m - n$ is the difference of m and n; $m * n$ is the product of m and n; m / n is the integer quotient of m and n; $mod(m,n)$ is the rest of m when divided by n; $exp(m,n)$ is m to the power of n; $log(m,n)$ is the integer m-logarithm of n; $max(m,n)$ is the maximum of m and n; $min(m,n)$ is the minimum of m and n; $m < n$ is m is less than n; $m <= n$ is m is less than or equal to n; $m > n$ is m is greater than n; $m >= n$ is m is greater than or equal to n. The notations for constants are exported by NAT as well.

```
COMPONENT NAT SPECIFICATION
EXPORT
  SORT Nat
  FUNC succ : Nat         -> Nat,
       pred : Nat         -> Nat,
       +    : Nat # Nat -> Nat,
       -    : Nat # Nat -> Nat,
       *    : Nat # Nat -> Nat,
       /    : Nat # Nat -> Nat,
       mod  : Nat # Nat -> Nat,
       exp  : Nat # Nat -> Nat,
       log  : Nat # Nat -> Nat,
       max  : Nat # Nat -> Nat,
       min  : Nat # Nat -> Nat
  PRED <    : Nat # Nat,
       <=   : Nat # Nat,
       >    : Nat # Nat,
       >=   : Nat # Nat
  SIG NUMBER_NOTATION[Nat]
IMPORT
  NUMBER_NOTATION'[Nat]
CLASS
  SORT Nat
  FUNC zero :      -> Nat
  FUNC succ : Nat -> Nat

  DECL m,n,q,r : Nat

  PRED is_gen: Nat
  IND  is_gen(zero);
```

```
            is_gen(m) => is_gen(succ(m))

AXIOM
{NAT1} zero!;
{NAT2} succ(m)!;
{NAT3} succ(m) /= zero;
{NAT4} succ(m) = succ(n) => m = n;
{NAT5} is_gen(n)

FUNC pred : Nat -> Nat
IND  pred(succ(n)) = n

PRED < : Nat # Nat
IND  m < succ(m);
     m < n => m < succ(n)

PRED <= : Nat # Nat
IND  m <= m;
     m <= n => m <= succ(n)

PRED > : Nat # Nat
IND  succ(m) > m;
     m > n => succ(m) > n

PRED >= : Nat # Nat
IND  m >= m;
     m >= n => succ(m) >= n

FUNC + : Nat # Nat -> Nat
IND  m + zero = m;
     m + succ(n) = succ(m + n)

FUNC - : Nat # Nat -> Nat
IND  m - zero = m;
     m > n => m - succ(n) = pred(m - n)

FUNC * : Nat # Nat -> Nat
IND  m * zero = zero;
     m * succ(n) = m * n + m

FUNC / : Nat # Nat -> Nat
IND  m = n * q + r AND r < n => m / n = q

FUNC mod : Nat # Nat -> Nat
IND  m = n * q + r AND r < n => mod(m,n) = r

FUNC exp : Nat # Nat -> Nat
```

```
IND   exp(m,zero) = succ(zero);
      exp(m,succ(n)) = m * exp(m,n)

FUNC log : Nat # Nat -> Nat
IND   exp(m,q) <= n AND n < exp(m,succ(q)) => log(m,n) = q

FUNC max : Nat # Nat -> Nat
IND   m >= n => max(m,n) = m;
      m <= n => max(m,n) = n

FUNC min : Nat # Nat -> Nat
IND   m <= n => min(m,n) = m;
      m >= n => min(m,n) = n

AXIOM
{NAT6}   0 = zero;
{NAT7}   1 = succ(0);
{NAT8}   2 = succ(1);
{NAT9}   3 = succ(2);
{NAT10}  4 = succ(3);
{NAT11}  5 = succ(4);
{NAT12}  6 = succ(5);
{NAT13}  7 = succ(6);
{NAT14}  8 = succ(7);
{NAT15}  9 = succ(8);
{NAT16} 10 = succ(9);
{NAT17} FORALL n ( n=10 * tl(n) + hd(n) )

% definedness
THEOREM succ(n)!
        ; (m + n)!
        ; (m - n)!   <=> m >= n
        ; (m * n)!
        ; (m / n)!   <=> n /= 0
        ; mod(m,n)!  <=> n /= 0
        ; exp(m,n)!
        ; log(m,n)!  <=> m >= 2 AND n /= 0
        ; max(m,n)!
        ; min(m,n)!
END
```

B.5   Integer Numbers

The component INT uses NAT and the number notation. It specifies the data type of integers. For m ,n : Nat, p, q : Int, the intended interpretation is as follows: Int is the set of integers; int(m,n) is the integer corresponding to

$m - n$; int(m) is the integer corresponding to m; succ(p) is the successor
of p ($= p + 1$); pred(p) is the predecessor of p ($= p - 1$); $-p$ is the negative
value of p ($= -p$); $p + q$ is the sum of p and q; $p - q$ is the difference of p and
q; $p * q$ is the product of p and q; p / q is the integer quotient of p and q;
mod(p,q) is the rest of p when divided by q; max(p,q) is the maximum of p
and q; min(p,q) is the minimum of p and q; abs(p) is the absolute value of p
(of type integer); abs(p) is the absolute value of p (of type natural number); p
$< q$ is p is less than q; $p <= q$ is p is less than or equal to q; $p > q$ is p is greater
than q; $p >= q$ is p is greater than or equal to q. The notations for constants
are exported by INT as well.

```
COMPONENT INT SPECIFICATION
EXPORT
  SORT Int
  FUNC int  : Nat # Nat -> Int,
       int  : Nat        -> Int,
       succ : Int        -> Int,
       pred : Int        -> Int,
       -    : Int        -> Int,
       +    : Int # Int -> Int,
       -    : Int # Int -> Int,
       *    : Int # Int -> Int,
       /    : Int # Int -> Int,
       mod  : Int # Int -> Int,
       max  : Int # Int -> Int,
       min  : Int # Int -> Int,
       abs  : Int        -> Int,
       abs  : Int        -> Nat
  PRED <    : Int # Int,
       <=   : Int # Int,
       >    : Int # Int,
       >=   : Int # Int
  SIG NUMBER_NOTATION[Int]
IMPORT
  NAT,
  NUMBER_NOTATION'[Int]
CLASS
  SORT Int
  FUNC int : Nat # Nat -> Int

  DECL m,n,p,q : Nat,
       h,i,j,k : Int

  PRED is_gen : Int
  IND  is_gen(int(m,n))

  AXIOM
```

```
{INT1} int(m,n)!;
{INT2} int(m,n) = int(p,q) <=> m + q = p + n;
{INT3} is_gen(i)

FUNC int : Nat -> Int
IND  int(n) = int(n,0)

FUNC succ : Int -> Int
IND  succ(int(m,n)) = int(succ(m),n)

FUNC pred : Int -> Int
IND  pred(int(m,n)) = int(m,succ(n))

PRED < : Int # Int
IND  m + q < p + n => int(m,n) < int(p,q)

PRED <= : Int # Int
IND  m + q <= p + n => int(m,n) <= int(p,q)

PRED > : Int # Int
IND  m + q > p + n => int(m,n) > int(p,q)

PRED >= : Int # Int
IND  m + q >= p + n => int(m,n) >= int(p,q)

FUNC - : Int -> Int
IND  - int(m,n) = int(n,m)

FUNC + : Int # Int -> Int
IND  int(m,n) + int(p,q) = int(m + p , n + q)

FUNC - : Int # Int -> Int
IND  int(m,n) - int(p,q) = int(m + q, n + p)

FUNC * : Int # Int -> Int
IND  int(m,n) * int(p,q) =
     int(m * p + n * q , m * q + n * p)

FUNC / : Int # Int -> Int
IND  h = i * j + k AND 0 <= k AND k < abs(i) =>
     h / i = j

FUNC mod : Int # Int -> Int
IND  h = i * j + k AND 0 <= k AND k < abs(i) =>
     mod(h,i) = k

FUNC max : Int # Int -> Int
```

```
IND  i >= j => max(i,j) = i;
     i <= j => max(i,j) = j

FUNC min : Int # Int -> Int
IND  i <= j => min(i,j) = i;
     i >= j => min(i,j) = j

FUNC abs : Int -> Int
IND  abs(int(m,0)) = int(m,0);
     abs(int(0,m)) = int(m,0)

FUNC abs : Int -> Nat
IND  abs(int(m,0)) = m;
     abs(int(0,m)) = m

AXIOM
{INT4}   0::Int = int(0);
{INT5}   1::Int = int(1);
{INT6}   2::Int = int(2);
{INT7}   3::Int = int(3);
{INT8}   4::Int = int(4);
{INT9}   5::Int = int(5);
{INT10}  6::Int = int(6);
{INT11}  7::Int = int(7);
{INT12}  8::Int = int(8);
{INT13}  9::Int = int(9);
{INT14} 10::Int = int(10);
{INT15} FORALL i ( i >= 0 => i=10 * tl(i) + hd(i) )

% definedness
THEOREM int(n)!
      ; succ(i)!
      ; pred(i)!
      ; (-i)!
      ; (i + j)!
      ; (i - j)!
      ; (i * j)!
      ; (i / j)!  <=> j /= 0
      ; mod(i,j)! <=> j /= 0
      ; max(i,j)!
      ; min(i,j)!
      ; (abs(i)::Int)!
      ; (abs(i)::Nat)!
END
```

B.6   Enumerations

The component ENUM2 uses NAT. It specifies the 2-element data type of enumerated values. For x : Enum2 the intended interpretation is as follows: Enum2
is the set of enumerated values; x0 is the first enumerated value; x1 is the
second enumerated value; $nat(x)$ is the number of x; 'n is the enumerated
value corresponding to n; $succ(x)$ is the successor of x (= value with next
higher number); $pred(x)$ is the predecessor of x (= value with next lower
number). This data type can be generalised in a straightforward way to the
case of enumerated types with n elements ($n > 0$).

```
COMPONENT ENUM2 SPECIFICATION
EXPORT
  SORT Enum2
  FUNC x0   : -> Enum2,
       x1   : -> Enum2,
       nat  : Enum2 -> Nat,
       '    : Nat    -> Enum2,
       succ : Enum2 -> Enum2,
       pred : Enum2 -> Enum2
IMPORT
  NAT
CLASS
  SORT Enum2
  FUNC x0 : -> Enum2
  FUNC x1 : -> Enum2

  DECL a,b : Enum2

  PRED is_gen : Enum2
  IND  is_gen(x0);
       is_gen(x1)

  AXIOM x0!;
        x1!;
        x0 /= x1;
        is_gen(a)

  FUNC nat : Enum2 -> Nat
  IND  nat(x0) = 0;
       nat(x1) = 1

  FUNC ' : Nat -> Enum2
  IND  '0 = x0;
       '1 = x1

  FUNC succ : Enum2 -> Enum2
```

```
      IND   succ(nat(a)) = nat(b) => succ(a) = b

      FUNC pred : Enum2 -> Enum2
      IND   pred(nat(a)) = nat(b) => pred(a) = b

      THEOREM % Definedness
              nat(a)!;
              succ(a)! <=> a /= x1;
              pred(a)! <=> a /= x0
      END
```

B.7   Characters

The component CHAR uses ENUM256. It specifies the data type of characters.

```
COMPONENT CHAR SPECIFICATION
IMPORT
 ENUM256'
  RENAMING
   SORT Enum256 TO Char
                          { oct dec hex char      description }
      FUNC x0    TO "\00", { 0    0   0   NUL  ^@ Null }
           x1    TO "\01", { 1    1   1   SOH  ^A Start of heading }
           x2    TO "\02", { 2    2   2   STX  ^B Start of text }
           x3    TO "\03", { 3    3   3   ETX  ^C End of text }
           x4    TO "\04", { 4    4   4   EQT  ^D End of x-mission }
           x5    TO "\05", { 5    5   5   ENQ  ^E Enquiry }
           x6    TO "\06", { 6    6   6   ACK  ^F Acknowledge }
           x7    TO "\07", { 7    7   7   BEL  ^G Bell }
           x8    TO "\08", { 10   8   8   BS   ^H Backspace }
           x9    TO "\09", { 11   9   9   TAB  ^I Horizontal tab }
           x10   TO "\0A", { 12   10  A   LF   ^J Linefeed }
           x11   TO "\0B", { 13   11  B   VT   ^K Vertical tab }
           x12   TO "\0C", { 14   12  C   FF   ^L Form feed }
           x13   TO "\0D", { 15   13  D   VR   ^M Carriage return }
           x14   TO "\0E", { 16   14  E   SO   ^N Shift out }
           x15   TO "\0F", { 17   15  F   SI   ^O Shift in }
           x16   TO "\10", { 20   16  10  DLE  ^P Data link escape }
           x17   TO "\11", { 21   17  11  DC1  ^Q Device control 1 }
           x18   TO "\12", { 22   18  12  DC2  ^R Device control 2 }
           x19   TO "\13", { 23   19  13  DC3  ^S Device control 3 }
           x20   TO "\14", { 24   20  14  DC4  ^T Device control 4 }
           x21   TO "\15", { 25   21  15  NAK  ^U Negative ack.}
           x22   TO "\16", { 26   22  16  SYN  ^V Synchronous idle }
           x23   TO "\17", { 27   23  17  ETB  ^W End of x-mission bl.}
           x24   TO "\18", { 30   24  18  CAN  ^X Cancel }
           x25   TO "\19", { 31   25  19  EM   ^Y End of medium }
```

```
x26    TO "\1A",  { 32  26  1A  SUB  ^Z  Substitute }
x27    TO "\1B",  { 33  27  1B  ESC  ^[  Escape }
x28    TO "\1C",  { 34  28  1C  FS   ^|  File separator }
x29    TO "\1D",  { 35  29  1D  GS   ^]  Group separator }
x30    TO "\1E",  { 36  30  1E  RS   ^^  Record separator }
x31    TO "\1F",  { 37  31  1F  US   ^_  Unit separator }
x32    TO " ",    { 40  32  20  SPACE    Space}

x33    TO "!",
x34    TO "\"",    x35   TO "#",
x36    TO "$",     x37   TO "%",
x38    TO "&",     x39   TO "'",
x40    TO "(",     x41   TO ")",
x42    TO "*",     x43   TO "+",
x44    TO ",",     x45   TO "-",
x46    TO ".",     x47   TO "/",
x48    TO "0",     x49   TO "1",
x50    TO "2",     x51   TO "3",
x52    TO "4",     x53   TO "5",
x54    TO "6",     x55   TO "7",
x56    TO "8",     x57   TO "9",
x58    TO ":",     x59   TO ";",
x60    TO "<",     x61   TO "=",
x62    TO ">",     x63   TO "?",
x64    TO "@",     x65   TO "A",
x66    TO "B",     x67   TO "C",
x68    TO "D",     x69   TO "E",
x70    TO "F",     x71   TO "G",
x72    TO "H",     x73   TO "I",
x74    TO "J",     x75   TO "K",
x76    TO "L",     x77   TO "M",
x78    TO "N",     x79   TO "O",
x80    TO "P",     x81   TO "Q",
x82    TO "R",     x83   TO "S",
x84    TO "T",     x85   TO "U",
x86    TO "V",     x87   TO "W",
x88    TO "X",     x89   TO "Y",
x90    TO "Z",     x91   TO "[",
x92    TO "\\",    x93   TO "]",
x94    TO "^",     x95   TO "_",
x96    TO "`",     x97   TO "a",
x98    TO "b",     x99   TO "c",
x100   TO "d",     x101  TO "e",
x102   TO "f",     x103  TO "g",
x104   TO "h",     x105  TO "i",
x106   TO "j",     x107  TO "k",
x108   TO "l",     x109  TO "m",
```

```
              x110  TO "n",    x111  TO "o",
              x112  TO "p",    x113  TO "q",
              x114  TO "r",    x115  TO "s",
              x116  TO "t",    x117  TO "u",
              x118  TO "v",    x119  TO "w",
              x120  TO "x",    x121  TO "y",
              x122  TO "z",    x123  TO "{",
              x124  TO "|",    x125  TO "}",
              x126  TO "~",

              x127  TO "\7F",  { 177 127 7F  DEL      Delete}
              x128  TO "\80",  x129  TO "\81",
              x130  TO "\82",  x131  TO "\83",
              x132  TO "\84",  x133  TO "\85",
                         % etc.
              x254  TO "\FE",  x255  TO "\FF"
      END,
    NAT
  CLASS
    DECL c : Char

    PRED is_uppercase_letter : Char
    IND  nat("A") <= nat(c) AND nat(c) <= nat("Z")
         => is_uppercase_letter(c)

    PRED is_lowercase_letter : Char
    IND  nat("a") <= nat(c) AND nat(c) <= nat("z")
         => is_lowercase_letter(c)

    PRED is_letter : Char
    IND  is_lowercase_letter(c) OR is_uppercase_letter(c)
         => is_letter(c)

    PRED is_digit : Char
    IND  nat("0") <= nat(c) AND nat(c) <= nat("9")
         => is_digit(c)
  END
```

B.8   Tuples

The component TUP2 uses ITEM1, and ITEM2 (straightforwards variations of ITEM). It specifies the parametrized data type of 2-tuples. For i_1 : Item1, i_2 : Item2, t : Tup2, the intended interpretation is as follows: Item1 is the set of objects acting as the first elements of tuples; Item2 is the set of objects acting as the second elements of tuples; Tup2 is the set of tuples of objects of types Item1 and Item2; $\text{tup}(i_1, i_2)$ is the tuple consisting of i_1 and i_2; $\text{proj1}(t)$ is the first element of tuple t; $\mathtt{proj2}(t)$ is the second element of tuple t. This data type can be generalised in a straightforward way to the case of n-tuples $(n > 0)$.

```
COMPONENT TUP2[Item1,Item2] SPECIFICATION
ABSTRACT
  ITEM1,
  ITEM2
EXPORT
  SORT Tup2
  FUNC tup : Item1 # Item2 -> Tup2,
       proj1 : Tup2 -> Item1,
       proj2 : Tup2 -> Item2
CLASS
  SORT Tup2  DEP Item1,Item2
  FUNC tup : Item1 # Item2 -> Tup2

  DECL t    : Tup2,
       i1,j1 : Item1,
       i2,j2 : Item2

  PRED is_gen : Tup2
  IND  is_gen(tup(i1,i2))

  AXIOM
  {TUP1} tup(i1,i2)!;
  {TUP2} tup(i1,i2) = tup(j1,j2) => i1 = j1 AND i2 = j2;
  {TUP3} is_gen(t)

  FUNC proj1 : Tup2 -> Item1
  IND  proj1(tup(i1,i2)) = i1

  FUNC proj2 : Tup2 -> Item2
  IND  proj2(tup(i1,i2)) = i2
END
```

B.9 Unions

The component UNION2 uses ITEM1, ITEM2, and NAT. It specifies the parametrized data type of 2-unions. A warning is in order: instantiation of UNION2 must be done with *different* sorts for different Items! For i_1 : Item1, i_2 : Item2, u : Union2 the intended interpretation is as follows: Item1 is the first set of objects of the union; Item2 is the second set of objects of the union; Union2 is the union of Item1 and Item2; $\mathtt{union2}(i_1)$ is the object i_1 embedded in Union2; $\mathtt{union2}(i_2)$ is the object i_2 embedded in Union2; $\mathtt{cast1}(u)$ is u interpreted as an object of type Item1; $\mathtt{cast2}(u)$ is u interpreted as an object

of type Item2; is1(u) is: u is interpreted as an object of type Item1; is2(u)
is: u is interpreted as an object of type Item2.

```
COMPONENT UNION2[Item1,Item2] SPECIFICATION
ABSTRACT
  ITEM1,
  ITEM2
EXPORT
  SORT Union2
  FUNC union2 : Item1 -> Union2,
       union2 : Item2 -> Union2,
       cast1 : Union2 -> Item1,
       cast2 : Union2 -> Item2
  PRED is1 : Union2,
       is2 : Union2
IMPORT
  NAT
CLASS
  SORT Union2  DEP Item1,Item2

  DECL u     : Union2,
       i1,j1 : Item1,
       i2,j2 : Item2

  FUNC union2 : Item1 -> Union2
  FUNC union2 : Item2 -> Union2

  PRED is_gen : Union2
  IND  is_gen(union2(i1));
       is_gen(union2(i2))

  FUNC f : Union2 -> Nat

  AXIOM is_gen(u);
        union2(i1) = union2(j1) <=> i1 = j1;
        union2(i2) = union2(j2) <=> i2 = j2;
        f(union2(i1)) = 1;
        f(union2(i2)) = f(union2(i1)) + 1

  FUNC cast1 : Union2 -> Item1
  IND  cast1(union2(i1)) = i1

  FUNC cast2 : Union2 -> Item2
  IND  cast2(union2(i2)) = i2

  PRED is1 : Union2
  IND  is1(union2(i1))
```

```
   PRED is2 : Union2
   IND  is2(union2(i2))
END
```

B.10   Finite Sets

The component SET uses ITEM, and NAT. It specifies the parametrized data type of finite sets. For i : Item, s, t : Set the intended interpretation is as follows: Item is the set of objects contained in sets; Set is the set of finite sets of objects of type Item; is_in(i,s) holds if i is an element of s; empty is the empty set; ins(i,s) is the set s with i inserted; rem(i,s) is the set s with i removed; union(s,t) is the union of s and t; isect(s,t) is the intersection of s and t; diff(s,t) is the difference of s and t; subset(s,t) is s is a subset of t; card(s) is the cardinality of s; set(i) is the singleton set containing i; select(s) is an object contained in s (non-deterministic).

```
COMPONENT SET[Item] SPECIFICATION
ABSTRACT
  ITEM
EXPORT
  SORT Set
  FUNC empty  :                   -> Set,
       ins    : Item # Set -> Set,
       rem    : Item # Set -> Set,
       union  : Set  # Set -> Set,
       isect  : Set  # Set -> Set,
       diff   : Set  # Set -> Set,
       set    : Item        -> Set,
       card   : Set         -> Nat
  PRED subset : Set  # Set,
       is_in  : Item # Set
  PROC select : Set         -> Item
IMPORT
  NAT
CLASS
  SORT Set    DEP Item
  PRED is_in : Item # Set
  FUNC empty :              -> Set
  FUNC ins   : Item # Set -> Set

  DECL s,t : Set,
       i,j : Item

  PRED is_gen : Set
  IND  is_gen(empty);
       is_gen(s) => is_gen(ins(i,s))
```

```
AXIOM
{SET1} empty!;
{SET2} ins(i,s)!;
{SET3} NOT is_in(i,empty);
{SET4} is_in(i,ins(j,s)) <=> i = j OR is_in(i,s);
{SET5} ins(i,ins(j,s)) = ins(j,ins(i,s));
{SET6} ins(i,ins(i,s)) = ins(i,s);
{SET7} is_gen(s)

FUNC rem : Item # Set -> Set
IND  rem(i,empty) = empty;
     rem(i,ins(i,s)) = rem(i,s);
     i /= j => rem(i,ins(j,s)) = ins(j,rem(i,s))

FUNC union : Set # Set -> Set
IND  union(s,empty) = s;
     union(s,ins(i,t)) = ins(i,union(s,t))

FUNC isect : Set # Set -> Set
IND  isect(s,empty) = empty;
     isect(ins(i,s),ins(i,t)) = ins(i,isect(s,t));
     NOT is_in(i,s) => isect(s,ins(i,t)) = isect(s,t)

FUNC diff : Set # Set -> Set
IND  diff(s,empty) = s;
     diff(s,ins(i,t)) = rem(i,diff(s,t))

PRED subset : Set # Set
IND  subset(s,s);
     subset(s,t) => subset(s,ins(i,t))

FUNC set : Item -> Set
IND  set(i) = ins(i,empty)

FUNC card : Set -> Nat
IND  card(empty) = 0;
     NOT is_in(i,s) => card(ins(i,s)) = card(s) + 1

PROC select : Set -> Item
IN   s
OUT  i
PRE  s /= empty
POST is_in(i,s)

% definedness
THEOREM rem(i,s)!
```

```
              ; union(s,t)!
              ; isect(s,t)!
              ; diff(s,t)!
              ; set(i)!
              ; card(s)!
              ; select(s)! <=> NOT s = empty
      END
```

B.11   Finite Bags

The component BAG uses: ITEM, NAT, and SET. It specifies the parametrized data type of finite bags (= multisets). For i : Item, b,c : Bag the intended interpretation is as follows: Item is the set of objects contained in bags; Bag is the set of finite bags of objects of type Item; is_in(i,b) is i occurs at least once in b; empty is the empty bag; ins(i,b) is the bag b with one occurrence of i inserted; rem(i,b) is the bag b with one occurrence of i removed; union(b,c) is the union of b and c; isect(b,c) is the intersection of b and c; diff(b,c) is the difference of b and c; subbag(b,c) holds if b is a subbag of c; mult(i,b) is the number of occurrences (multiplicity) of i in b; bag(i) is the bag containing i only; set(b) is the set of all objects in b; select(b) is an object contained in b (non-deterministic).

```
      COMPONENT BAG[Item] SPECIFICATION
      ABSTRACT
        ITEM
      EXPORT
        SORT Bag
        PRED is_in  : Item # Bag,
             subbag : Bag  # Bag
        FUNC empty  :                 -> Bag,
             ins    : Item # Bag -> Bag,
             rem    : Item # Bag -> Bag,
             union  : Bag  # Bag -> Bag,
             isect  : Bag  # Bag -> Bag,
             diff   : Bag  # Bag -> Bag,
             mult   : Item # Bag -> Nat,
             bag    : Item        -> Bag,
             set    : Bag         -> Set
        PROC select : Bag         -> Item
      IMPORT
        NAT,
        SET[Item]
      CLASS
        SORT Bag    DEP Item
        PRED is_in : Item # Bag
        FUNC empty :              -> Bag
```

```
FUNC ins   : Item # Bag -> Bag

DECL i,j : Item,
     b,c : Bag

PRED is_gen : Bag
IND  is_gen(empty);
     is_gen(b) => is_gen(ins(i,b))

AXIOM
{BAG1} empty::Bag!;
{BAG2} ins(i,b)!;
{BAG3} NOT is_in(i,empty::Bag);
{BAG4} is_in(i,ins(j,b)) <=> i = j OR is_in(i,b);
{BAG5} ins(i,ins(j,b)) = ins(j,ins(i,b));
{BAG6} ins(i,b) = ins(i,c) => b = c;
{BAG7} is_gen(b)

FUNC rem : Item # Bag -> Bag
IND  rem(i,empty) = empty::Bag;
     rem(i,ins(i,b)) = b;
     i /= j => rem(i,ins(j,b)) = ins(j,rem(i,b))

FUNC union : Bag # Bag -> Bag
IND  union(b,empty) = b;
     union(b,ins(i,c)) = ins(i,union(b,c))

FUNC isect : Bag # Bag -> Bag
IND  isect(b,empty) = empty;
     isect(ins(i,b),ins(i,c)) = ins(i,isect(b,c));
     NOT is_in(i,b) => isect(b,ins(i,c)) = isect(b,c)

FUNC diff : Bag # Bag -> Bag
IND  diff(b,empty) = b;
     diff(b,ins(i,c)) = rem(i,diff(b,c))

PRED subbag : Bag # Bag
IND  subbag(b,b);
     subbag(b,c) => subbag(b,ins(i,c))

FUNC mult : Item # Bag -> Nat
IND  mult(i,empty) = 0;
     mult(i,ins(i,b)) = mult(i,b) + 1;
     i /= j => mult(i,ins(j,b)) = mult(i,b)

FUNC bag : Item -> Bag
IND  bag(i) = ins(i,empty)
```

```
FUNC set : Bag -> Set
IND  set(empty) = empty;
     set(ins(i,b)) = ins(i,set(b))

PROC select : Bag -> Item
IN   b
OUT  i
PRE  b /= empty
POST is_in(i,b)

% definedness
THEOREM rem(i,b)!
      ; union(b,c)!
      ; isect(b,c)!
      ; diff(b,c)!
      ; mult(i,b)!
      ; bag(i)!
      ; set(b)!
END
```

B.12 Finite Sequences

The component SEQ uses ITEM, NAT, SET, and BAG. It specifies the parametrized
data type of finite sequences. For i : Item, s,t : Seq, m : Nat the intended
interpretation is as follows: Item is the set of objects contained in sequences;
Seq is the set of finite sequences of objects of type Item; empty is the empty
sequence; cons(i,s) is the sequence s with i appended at the head of s; hd(s)
is the head of s (= element with index 0); tl(s) is the tail of s (= s with
its head removed); len(s) is the length of s (= number of elements of s);
sel(s,m) is the element of s with index m; cat(s,t) is the concatenation of
s and t; seq(i) is the sequence containing i only; rem(s,m) is the sequence s
with element with index m removed; rev(s) is the sequence s with its elements
in reverse order; bag(s) is the bag of all (occurrences of) objects in s; set(s)
is the set of all objects in s.

```
COMPONENT SEQ[Item] SPECIFICATION
ABSTRACT
  ITEM
EXPORT
  SORT Seq
  FUNC empty :                 -> Seq,
       cons  : Item # Seq -> Seq,
       hd    : Seq           -> Item,
       tl    : Seq           -> Seq,
       len   : Seq           -> Nat,
```

```
          sel    : Seq # Nat   -> Item,
          cat    : Seq # Seq   -> Seq,
          seq    : Item        -> Seq,
          rem    : Seq # Nat   -> Seq,
          rev    : Seq         -> Seq,
          bag    : Seq         -> Bag,
          set    : Seq         -> Set
   IMPORT
     NAT,
     BAG[Item],
     SET[Item]
   CLASS
     SORT Seq    DEP Item
     FUNC empty :              -> Seq
     FUNC cons  : Item # Seq -> Seq

     DECL i,j    : Item,
          s,t,u  : Seq,
          n      : Nat

     PRED is_gen : Seq
     IND  is_gen(empty);
          is_gen(s) => is_gen(cons(i,s))

     AXIOM
     {SEQ1} empty::Seq!;
     {SEQ2} cons(i,s)!;
     {SEQ3} cons(i,s) /= empty;
     {SEQ4} cons(i,s) = cons(j,t) => i = j AND s = t;
     {SEQ5} is_gen(s)

     FUNC hd : Seq -> Item
     IND  hd(cons(i,s)) = i

     FUNC tl : Seq -> Seq
     IND  tl(cons(i,s)) = s

     FUNC len : Seq -> Nat
     IND  len(empty) = 0;
          len(cons(i,s)) = len(s) + 1

     FUNC sel : Seq # Nat -> Item
     IND  sel(cons(i,s),0) = i;
          sel(s,n) = j => sel(cons(i,s),n + 1) = j

     FUNC cat : Seq # Seq -> Seq
     IND  cat(empty,s) = s;
```

```
            cat(cons(i,s),t) = cons(i,cat(s,t))

FUNC seq : Item -> Seq
IND  seq(i) = cons(i,empty)

FUNC rem : Seq # Nat -> Seq
IND  rem(cons(i,s),0) = s;
     rem(s,n) = t => rem(cons(i,s),n + 1) = cons(i,t)

FUNC rev : Seq -> Seq
IND  rev(empty) = empty;
     rev(cons(i,s)) = cat(rev(s),seq(i))

FUNC bag : Seq -> Bag
IND  bag(empty) = empty;
     bag(cons(i,s)) = ins(i,bag(s))

FUNC set : Seq -> Set
IND  set(empty::Seq) = empty;
     set(cons(i,s)) = ins(i,set(s))

% definedness
THEOREM hd(s)! <=> NOT s = empty
      ; tl(s)! <=> NOT s = empty
      ; len(s)!
      ; sel(s,n)! <=> n < len(s)
      ; cat(s,t)!
      ; seq(i)!
      ; rem(s,n)! <=> n < len(s)
      ; rev(s)!
      ; bag(s)!
      ; set(s)!
END
```

B.13   Finite Maps

The component MAP uses: ITEM1, ITEM2, and SET. It specifies the parametrized data type of finite maps.

For m, n : Map, x : Item1, v : Item2, s : Set[Item1] the intended interpretation is as follows: Item1 is the set of objects acting as arguments of maps; Item2 is the set of objects acting as values of maps; Set[Item1] is the set of finite sets of objects of type Item1; Set[Item2] is the set of finite sets of objects of type Item2; Map is the set of finite maps; empty is the empty map (= map with empty domain); add(m,x,v) is the map m with the value of argument x replaced by v; rem(m,x) is the map m with x removed from the domain; rem(m,s) is the map m with s removed from the domain; app(m,x)

is the value of map m applied to argument x; $\text{dom}(m)$ is the domain of the map m; $\text{ran}(m)$ is the range of the map m; $\text{restr}(m,s)$ is the map m restricted to the domain s; $\text{submap}(m,n)$ holds if the map m is a submap of the map n.

```
COMPONENT MAP[Item1,Item2] SPECIFICATION
ABSTRACT
  ITEM1,ITEM2
EXPORT
  SORT Map
  FUNC empty :                          -> Map,
       add   : Map # Item1 # Item2 -> Map,
       rem   : Map # Item1         -> Map,
       rem   : Map # Set[Item1]    -> Map,
       app   : Map # Item1         -> Item2,
       dom   : Map                 -> Set[Item1],
       ran   : Map                 -> Set[Item2],
       restr : Map # Set[Item1]    -> Map
  PRED submap : Map # Map
IMPORT
  SET[Item1],SET[Item2]
CLASS
  SORT Map    DEP Item1,Item2
  FUNC empty :                     -> Map
  FUNC add   : Map # Item1 # Item2 -> Map
  FUNC app   : Map # Item1         -> Item2

  DECL m,n : Map,
       i,j : Item1,
       v,w : Item2,
       s   : Set[Item1]

  PRED is_gen : Map
  IND  is_gen(empty);
       is_gen(m) => is_gen(add(m,i,v))

  AXIOM
  {MAP1} empty::Map!;
  {MAP2} add(m,i,v)!;
  {MAP3} NOT app(empty,i)!;
  {MAP4} app(add(m,i,v),j) = w <=>
         ( (i = j AND v = w) OR (i /= j AND app(m,j) = w) );
  {MAP5} i /= j => add(add(m,i,v),j,w) = add(add(m,j,w),i,v);
  {MAP6} add(add(m,i,v),i,w) = add(m,i,w);
  {MAP7} is_gen(m)

  FUNC rem : Map # Item1 -> Map
  IND  rem(empty,i) = empty;
       rem(add(m,i,v),i) = rem(m,i);
```

```
              i /= j => rem(add(m,i,v),j) = add(rem(m,j),i,v)

     FUNC rem : Map # Set[Item1] -> Map
     IND  rem(m,empty) = m;
          rem(m,ins(i,s)) = rem(rem(m,i),s)

     FUNC dom : Map -> Set[Item1]
     IND  dom(empty) = empty;
          dom(add(m,i,v)) = ins(i,dom(m))

     FUNC ran : Map -> Set[Item2]
     IND  ran(empty) = empty;
          ran(add(m,i,v)) = ins(v,ran(rem(m,i)))

     FUNC restr : Map # Set[Item1] -> Map
     IND  restr(m,empty) = empty;
          is_in(i,dom(m))
            => restr(m,ins(i,s)) = add(restr(m,s),i,app(m,i));
          NOT is_in(i,dom(m))
            => restr(m,ins(i,s)) = restr(m,s)

     PRED submap : Map # Map
     IND  submap(empty,m);
          submap(m,n) => submap(add(m,i,v),add(n,i,v))

     % definedness
     THEOREM rem(m,i)!
           ; rem(m,s)!
           ; dom(m)!
           ; ran(m)!
           ; restr(m,s)!
     END
```

Appendix C
Glossary of Terms

abstraction The process of consciously omitting certain details from a system's description.

abstraction function A function relating abstract objects to concrete representations for them by mapping the latter to the former. Abstraction functions need not be computed; they are meant for reasoning purposes.

algebraic specification A property-oriented specification of a data type by means of equations.

assertion A precise claim used to characterize sorts and operations. In the case of COLD-1, assertions are mainly formulae as used in first-order logic and dynamic logic.

axiom An assertion that is assumed to hold without proof. Like in Euclid's foundation of geometry, axioms provide a basis for further reasoning.

axiomatic specification A specification by means of axioms and/or pre- and post-conditions. Roughly, this amounts to algebraic specification (using equations as axioms) for data types and to specification in pre- and post-condition style for state-based systems.

component A unit of specification or implementation. A component is a module containing definitions, axioms and theorems, importing other components and possibly hiding the names imported and defined in part.

data type A set of objects together with operations to manipulate them.

domain The set of argument lists to which an operation can be applied.

dynamic logic A logic to reason about programs. The AFTER and FIN assertions of COLD-1 are taken from dynamic logic.

equation An assertion which claims that particular objects are equal.

first-order logic A logic with formulae built up from terms, predicates and connectives such as NOT, AND, OR, =>, etc., where the terms may contain logical variables, called object names in COLD-1, which are bound by enclosing quantifiers such as FORALL and EXISTS.

formal proof A proof in which all steps are justified precisely and completely by definitions, axioms and given rules of reasoning.

function A mapping between two sets, the domain and the range of the function. A function can only be applied to the elements of its domain and the results yielded by function application are elements of its range.

instantiation An instantiation of a parametrized component is a choice of actual parameters for it.

invariant A property that is preserved by an operation, a collection of operations, or whatsoever. Well-known from programming is the notion of a loop invariant, i.e. a property preserved by a loop-body.

model-oriented specification A specification style where the approach is to specify a system by defining a model of it. The model should have the desired properties of the system.

non-determinism An expression is non-deterministic if it permits more than one result in a particular state.

operation A general name for a function, predicate or procedure.

partial function A function that does not yield a result for all argument lists to which it can be applied.

post-condition An assertion used to delimit the possible effects of applying a function or procedure to an argument list, i.e. the possible results and, in case of a procedure, the possible state transformations.

pre-condition An assertion used to bound the circumstances under which a function yields a result or a procedure terminates successfully, i.e. the argument list and, in case of a procedure, the starting states. It is often defined as a sufficient condition, but in COLD-1 it is also a necessary condition.

predicate A mapping from a set, the domain of the predicate, to the truth values. A predicate can only be applied to an element of its domain and predicate application yields either true or false.

procedure An operation which is affected by and affects a state. A procedure is a state transformer; it transforms a state to another state by modifying state components. Like for functions, a procedure can only be applied to the elements of its domain and the results yielded by procedure application are elements of its range.

proof obligation An assertion that is claimed to follow from certain definitions and axioms. A proof obligation is discharged by proving that it holds.

property-oriented specification A specification style where the approach is to specify a system in terms of its desired properties. The desired properties determine models of the system.

range The set of results that may be yielded by application of a function or procedure.

side-effect An expression has side-effects if it permits a state transformation.

signature A set of names of sorts, functions, predicates and procedures.

sort A set of objects. Usually, a sort comes together with operations to manipulate them.

specification A precise description of all relevant details of a system.

state-based system A state-based system has a collection of states, one initial state and a number of state transformers, called procedures in COLD-1. The states of a system have a number of components. In COLD-1, these components are sorts, functions and predicates.

state transformation A modification of state components. In COLD-1, modification of a sort amounts to the creation of new objects and modification of a function or predicate amounts to modifying its result for certain or all argument lists.

strictness The principle that an expression that yields a result, or an assertion that yields true, has only immediate subexpressions – possibly none – that yield results.

term An expression that is not non-deterministic and has no side-effects.

theorem An assertion that is known to hold because it can be derived from axioms and definitions by given rules of reasoning.

Index

ABSTRACT, 71, 72
abstract hardware diagram, 139, 273,
    280, 301
abstract representation, 330
abstraction, 417
abstraction function, 240, 245, 322,
    417
Ada, 56
AFTER, 60
aggregation, 349
algebraic specification, 417
algorithmic definition, 46, 56, 61
algorithmic expression, 63
anagram program, 268
AND, 58
animation system, 339
applied occurrence, 106
architecture, 150
array, 41, 88, 89, 178, 269
assertion, 58, 388, 417
associativity, 383, 385
attribute, 345
auto-bisimulation, 250
automatic railway, 125, 341
AXIOM, 56
axiom, 43, 44, 56, 58, 417
axiomatic specification, 417

bag, 410
BEGIN, 68
binomial coefficient, 371
bit, 273, 356
black and white counter, 245
black box correctness, 356
BNF notation, 383, 385
body
    function body, 42, 261, 387

predicate body, 48, 387
procedure body, 53, 388
sort body, 51, 387
Boolean, 394
box diagram, 139, 289, 301
byte, 115, 278, 327, 349
byte adder, 276

C, 5, 13, 34, 40, 56, 190, 255, 266–
    268, 374
C++, 13, 345
call graph, 203, 255, 256
casting, 70, 109
CCITT, 18, 298, 316
character, 403
CLASS, 71, 72
class, 345
colour, 78
comment, 385
communication channel, 299
communication manager, 237
complete name, 104
COMPONENT, 71, 72
component, 1, 4, 71, 76, 89, 139,
    386, 417
component definition, 71, 87, 123,
    353
component name, 72, 76, 79, 112,
    386
concentrator switch, 280
conditional access unit, 76
configuration management system,
    248
conservative extension, 350
copy operator, 95, 99, 118, 120, 122
counter, 95, 96
cyclic redundancy check, 45

data flow diagram, 6, 10, 16, 18, 25, 186, 260
database management system, 51, 118, 334, 337
datatype, 417
DECL, 114
declaration, 114
DEF, 46, 50, 55
definedness, 59, 263
defining occurrence, 106
definition, 39, 106
   function definition, 41
   predicate definition, 47
   procedure definition, 52
   sort definition, 51
DEP, 44, 49, 52
description, 62, 88, 90–92, 123, 234, 353, 355, 385
detector, 159
DFD, 260
differentiated call graph, 256
direction, 128
division, 4
domain, 417
domain type, 42, 47, 53, 104
driver licenses, 206
dynamic behaviour, 60
dynamic logic, 417

Eiffel, 345
encapsulation, 336
END, 68, 71, 76
entity, 44, 388
enumeration, 402
equation, 56, 417
Estelle, 13
EXISTS, 58
EXPORT, 71, 72, 80
export, 72, 74, 76, 80
EXPORTING, 76, 77, 80
expression, 388
extendibility, 326, 339

FALSE, 58
feature, 346

few connections, 336
file system, 44, 48, 50, 52, 54, 353, 355
FIN, 60
finite bag, 410
finite map, 414
finite sequence, 412
finite set, 213, 408
firing, 291
first-order logic, 418
FLUSH, 17, 67
FORALL, 58
formal proof, 418
FORTRAN, 266
forward declaration, 47
FREE, 47, 50, 52, 56
free definition, 47, 280
FROM, 113
FUNC, 42
function, 40, 42, 418
   constant function, 43
   variable function, 44
function body, 387
function graph, 11, 28, 169, 243
functional programming, 46, 63, 371
functionality, 104

generalization, 349
generalized call graph, 256
glass box correctness, 358
graph diagram, 243
graphical language, 228
guard, 66

hardware diagram, 139, 273, 280, 301
hash map, 25, 30
Haskell, 46
Hasse diagram, 11, 28, 213
hidden name, 74, 251, 326
history variable, 72, 73, 101
HOOD, 33, 229
Horn clause, 49

identifier, 385

if-then-else, 226, 228, 263
IGLOO, 111, 123, 330, 393
imperative programming, 40, 56
IMPLEMENTATION, 89
implementation context, 355
implementation relation, 91
implicit universal quantification, 114
IMPORT, 71, 72
import, 71–74, 77, 99
import graph, 256
IN, 42, 47, 53
IND, 45, 49
inductive definition, 45, 58, 220
inductive proof, 370
INFIX, 19, 93
inheritance, 339, 346
INIT, 60
initial state, 40, 359
instantiation, 104, 111, 418
integer number, 398
interface, 230, 234
invariant, 16, 125, 182, 191, 198, 241, 294, 296, 314, 359, 364, 418
invoice system, 260
ISNEW, 60
item, 27, 91, 393
ITU, 298, 316, 318

keyword, 7, 16, 383, 384

LEFT, 19, 93
LET, 67, 91, 93
lexical unit, 383
line editor, 332
logic
    dynamic logic, 58, 60
    first-order logic, 58, 62
    temporal logic, 60, 62
logic programming, 49, 375
loop invariant, 191, 241, 365, 367
loop variant, 368, 370

many-sorted algebra, 40
map, 414

marking, 291
Mascot, 273
maximum value function, 228
memoization, 370
metric properties, 134, 137
mirroring, 341
ML, 46
MOD, 5, 14, 64
model-oriented specification, 418
modification right, 54, 65
modular structuring, 325
module
    non-parametrized module, 326
    parametrized module, 327
Mondrian, 259, 273
MSC, 18, 316, 318
multiple inheritance, 348
multistage switching, 284

name clash, 117, 119
Nassi-Shneidermann diagram, 226
nattup, 86
natural number, 396
network diagram, 259
NEW, 64
nibble adder, 274
non-determinism, 54, 58, 61, 64, 364, 418
non-deterministic choice, 66
NOT, 58

object creation, 65
object name, 67, 68, 114, 116
object-oriented design, 341, 345
object-oriented programming, 345
operator clause, 123
OPERATORS, 19, 93
OR, 58
ordered item, 91, 92, 393
ordering properties, 133, 136
origin, 95, 280
OUT, 42, 53
overloading resolution, 107

packet-oriented radio receiver, 292

paper supply, 308, 314
partial function, 42, 418
Pascal, 12, 40, 56, 190, 196, 300
path, 353
personnel database, 96
Petri net, 291
pinball machine, 121
place invariant, 294
pointer, 41
position, 132
POST, 42, 53
post-condition, 5, 16, 27, 42, 53, 58,
    61, 255, 264, 418
power supply, 140
PRE, 42, 53
pre-condition, 16, 27, 42, 53, 58, 61,
    72, 257, 263, 265, 418
PRED, 47
predicate, 40, 47, 418
    constant predicate, 48
    variable predicate, 48, 49
predicate body, 387
PREFIX, 19, 93
PREV, 60, 62
printing system, 301, 310
priority, 93, 263, 383
priority level, 385
PROC, 53
procedure, 40, 53, 418
procedure body, 388
procedure call, 65
programming variable, 41
Prolog, 50, 255, 299, 375
proof obligation, 91, 193, 240, 359,
    361, 363, 369, 419
property-oriented specification, 419
PROTOCOLD, 56, 288

qualifier, 104
QUALIFYING, 76, 77
qualifying, 77, 101, 139

random assignment, 65
range, 419
range type, 42, 53, 104

real-time aspects, 195
reliability, 326
RENAMING, 76, 77, 85, 87
renaming, 34, 76, 85, 97, 101, 109,
    153, 157, 196, 276
repetition, 66
reusability, 326, 339

safety, 176
SAT, 5, 14, 54
scope extension, 68
SDL, 18, 298, 301, 303, 309
seat reservation system, 350
section, 168
selective import, 328
selector, 156
sequence, 412
sequence chart, 18, 316, 318
sequential composition, 66
set, 408
side-effect, 58, 61, 419
SIG, 85
signature, 72, 80, 109, 230, 257, 419
SKIP, 64
Smalltalk, 345
SOME, 63
SORT, 51
sort, 10, 16, 40, 51, 279, 419
    constant sort, 51
    variable sort, 52
sort body, 387
SPECIFICATION, 71, 72, 89
specification, 419
specification context, 355
speed, 138
spooler, 303
SPRINT, 7, 289, 290, 299, 301
stack, 231
standard library, 16, 19, 71, 93, 110,
    111, 240, 393
state, 40, 359
state component, 40
    constant state component, 40
    dependent variable state com-
      ponent, 44

variable state component, 40
state signature, 40
state space sharing, 333
state transformation, 359, 419
state transformer, 40
state transition diagram, 6, 16, 24, 244, 298, 316
state-based system, 419
statechart, 221, 226, 244
STATEMATE, 226
statement, 64
STOP, 64
stopper, 154
strictness, 263, 419
strong typing, 103
student enrolment, 359
svar, 23, 29, 76, 77, 101
switch, 356
switching network, 284
symbol, 104, 385
SYSTEM, 92
system description, 92, 123, 353, 386

task assignments, 217
term, 61, 419
THAT, 62
THEN, 60
THEOREM, 56, 193
theorem, 56, 58, 193, 359, 419
time, 137

TO, 85, 87
toggle, 121
token, 385
token game, 294, 315
traction level, 129
train, 145
TRUE, 58
tuple, 82, 405
type, 386
typing, 107

undefined, 59, 263
union, 406

VAR, 44, 48, 52
variable, 330
VDM, 7, 365
vending machine, 9
Venn diagram, 169, 203
visibility consistency, 352
visible name, 326
voltage, 130

watch, 221
weak coupling, 328, 336
windowing system, 346

xmap, 20, 27
XOR, 58

Z, 7